Davidson
2013

THE CHESTER CYCLE IN CONTEXT, 1555–1575

Studies in Performance and Early Modern Drama

General Editor's Preface

Helen Ostovich, McMaster University

Performance assumes a string of creative, analytical, and collaborative acts that, in defiance of theatrical ephemerality, live on through records, manuscripts, and printed books. The monographs and essay collections in this series offer original research which addresses theatre histories and performance histories in the context of the sixteenth and seventeenth century life. Of especial interest are studies in which women's activities are a central feature of discussion as financial or technical supporters (patrons, musicians, dancers, seamstresses, wigmakers, or 'gatherers'), if not authors or performers per se. Welcome too are critiques of early modern drama that not only take into account the production values of the plays, but also speculate on how intellectual advances or popular culture affect the theatre.

The series logo, selected by my colleague Mary V. Silcox, derives from Thomas Combe's duodecimo volume, *The Theater of Fine Devices* (London, 1592), Emblem VI, sig. B. The emblem of four masks has a verse which makes claims for the increasing complexity of early modern experience, a complexity that makes interpretation difficult. Hence the corresponding perhaps uneasy rise in sophistication:

> Masks will be more hereafter in request,
> And grow more deare than they did heretofore.

No longer simply signs of performance 'in play and jest', the mask has become the 'double face' worn 'in earnest' even by 'the best' of people, in order to manipulate or profit from the world around them. The books stamped with this design attempt to understand the complications of performance produced on stage and interpreted by the audience, whose experiences outside the theatre may reflect the emblem's argument:

> Most men do use some colour'd shift
> For to conceal their craftie drift.

Centuries after their first presentations, the possible performance choices and meanings they engender still stir the imaginations of actors, audiences, and readers of early plays. The products of scholarly creativity in this series, I hope, will also stir imaginations to new ways of thinking about performance.

The Chester Cycle in Context, 1555–1575

Religion, Drama, and the Impact of Change

Edited by
JESSICA DELL,
DAVID KLAUSNER,
and HELEN OSTOVICH

ASHGATE

Published by

Ashgate Publishing Limited
Wey Court East
Union Road
Farnham
Surrey, GU9 7PT
England

Ashgate Publishing Company
Suite 420
101 Cherry Street
Burlington
VT 05401-4405
USA

Ashgate Website: http://www.ashgate.com

British Library Cataloguing in Publication Data
Dell, Jessica.
The Chester Cycle in context, 1555–1575: religion, drama, and the impact of change. – (Studies in performance and early modern drama)
    1. Chester plays. 2. Mysteries and miracle-plays, English – England – Chester – History and criticism. 3. English drama – Early modern and Elizabethan, 1500–1600 – History and criticism. 4. Cycles (Literature)
    I. Title II. Series III. Klausner, David N. IV. Ostovich, Helen.
    822'.051609–dc23

Library of Congress Cataloging-in-Publication Data
The Chester Cycle in context, 1555–1575: religion, drama, and the impact of change / edited by Jessica Dell, David Klausner and Helen Ostovich.
    p. cm.—(Studies in performance and early modern drama)
    Includes bibliographical references and index.
    1. Chester plays. 2. Mysteries and miracle-plays, English—England—Chester—History and criticism. 3. English drama—Early modern and Elizabethan, 1500–1600—History and criticism. 4. Cycles (Literature) I. Dell, Jessica. II. Klausner, David. III. Ostovich, Helen.

PR644.C4C44 2012
822'.051609—dc23
                                                                                            2012011244
ISBN 9781409441366 (hbk)
ISBN 9781409441373 (ebk)

Printed and bound in Great Britain by the
MPG Books Group, UK

Contents

List of Figures   *vii*
Notes on Contributors   *ix*
Acknowledgements   *xiii*

Introduction: The Chester Cycle in Context   1
    David Klausner, Helen Ostovich, and Jessica Dell

Part 1   The Chester Script

1   The Text of the Chester Plays in 1572: A Conjectural
     Re-Construction   19
     Alexandra F. Johnston

2   In the Beginning! A New Look at Chester Play One,
     Lines 1–51   37
     David Mills in conjunction with his wife, Joy

Part 2   Faith and Doubt

3   Doubt and Religious Drama Across Sixteenth-Century
     England, or Did the Middle Ages Believe in Their Plays?   47
     Erin E. Kelly

4   Dice at Chester's *Passion*   65
     Matthew Sergi

5   'Whye ys thy cloathinge nowe so reedd?': Salvific Blood
     in the Chester Ascension   79
     John T. Sebastian

6   Affective Piety: A 'Method' for Medieval Actors in the
     Chester Cycle   93
     Margaret Rogerson

Part 3   Elizabethan Religion(s)

7   The Chester Cycle and Early Elizabethan Religion   111
     Paul Whitfield White

8   'Erazed in the booke'?: Periodization and the Material Text
     of the Chester Banns   133
     Kurt A. Schreyer

Part 4   Space and Place in Chester

9   When in Rome: Shifting Conceptions of the Chester Cycle's
       Roman References in Pre- and Post-Reformation England   149
       Sheila Christie

10   Exegesis in the City: The Chester Plays and Earlier
       Chester Writing   161
       Mark Faulkner

11   Maintaining the Realm: City, Commonwealth, and
       Crown in Chester's Midsummer Plays   179
       Heather S. Mitchell-Buck

Afterword: Origins and Continuities: F.M. Salter and the Chester Plays   193
       JoAnna Dutka

Bibliography   *201*
Index   *219*

List of Figures

Pt. 1   The Expositor preaches the word of God to audiences in
the University of Toledo's production of *The Temptation*.
Courtesy of Heather S. Mitchell-Buck.   17

Pt. 2   Satan confronts Jesus in the University of Toledo's production
of *The Temptation*. Courtesy of Heather S. Mitchell-Buck.   45

Pt. 3   Christ separates the faithful from the damned in McMaster
University's production of *The Last Judgment*. Courtesy of
Heather S. Mitchell-Buck.   109

8.1   British Library MS Harley 2150, fol. 88^r detail. © British
Library Board.   137

Pt. 4   A troupe of Purdue University actors attempt to squeeze their
wagon through an archway at the University of Toronto campus
for their production of *The Fall of Man*. Courtesy of Heather
S. Mitchell-Buck.   147

A.1   A photograph of Professor F.M. Salter. Courtesy of his daughter,
Dr Elizabeth Salter.   194

Notes on Contributors

Sheila Christie graduated from the University of Alberta in 2007, where she completed a dissertation on cycle drama under the supervision of Garrett Epp. She went on to a SSHRC Post-Doctoral Fellowship in 2008, working with Pamela King at the University of Bristol, and took up a tenure-track appointment at Cape Breton University the following year. She teaches both dramatic literature and practical theatre, while her research focuses on aspects of popular culture ranging from cycle drama to fan fiction. She is currently working on a book called *The City's Stories: The Chester Play as Civic Transformation*. Recent publications include 'Bridging the Jurisdictional Divide: The Masons and the York Corpus Christi Play' in Margaret Rogerson's *The York Mystery Plays: Performance in the City*, and an article on Tudor Chester forthcoming in Greg Walker's and Tom Betteridge's *Oxford Handbook of Tudor Drama*.

Jessica Dell expects to defend her doctoral dissertation, entitled *Vanishing Acts: Absence and Magic in Early Modern Drama, 1550–1650*, in 2013. Her research examines how early modern playwrights employ absence as a theatrical device to enrich their representations of witchcraft and the supernatural. Recent publications include a co-authored review essay with Erin Julian and Chantelle Thauvette entitled 'Seduction and Salvation: Chester 2010 in Review' in *ROMARD* (2010) and a critical essay entitled 'Divided They Fall: (De)constructing the Triple Hecate in Spenser's *Cantos of Mutabilitie*' in *EMLS* (forthcoming). Currently, she is also in the process of co-editing an online edition of *The Three Ladies of London* with Dr Sarah Johnson for *Queen's Men Editions* online. From 2009 to 2011 she worked as an Internet Editorial Assistant for *Early Theatre*.

JoAnna Dutka is an emeritus professor of English at the University of Toronto and research associate at Trinity College, U of T. One of the founding members of the REED project, she edited the *REED Newsletter* from its inception until 1994 and now is on the editorial board of its successor, *Early Theatre*. She organized the first REED Colloquium and currently is a senior advisor to the project. Ongoing work is focused on the publication of the dramatic records of pre-Reformation Norwich along with the out-of-print post-Reformation REED volume edited by David Galloway. Research and teaching interests include early English music and drama (*Music in the English Mystery Plays*, 1980/2003); the N-Town plays; the history of children's literature; ethics and imaginative literature.

Mark Faulkner is lecturer in Old English at University College Cork. His doctoral research investigated various types of marks eleventh- and twelfth-century readers left in manuscripts which had been produced in Anglo-Saxon England.

Employment as the postdoctoral researcher on the Mapping Medieval Chester project, based at Swansea University subsequently introduced him to Lucian's *De laude Cestrie*, a late twelfth-century Latin encomium to Chester by Lucian, a local monk. Though gradually editing this text, most of his efforts are directed towards a monograph, *Ignota lingua: English literatures in the long twelfth century*, due out in 2013.

Alexandra F. Johnston is professor emerita of English, University of Toronto; fellow of the Royal Society of Canada; co-founder and director of Records of Early English Drama since its inception in 1975; chair of the PLS board almost constantly since 1975 and founding director of the Centre for Performance Studies in Early Drama; has been producer, director, dramaturge, actor and singer in many productions; principal of Victoria College, University of Toronto 1981–91 and acting principal 2003–04; editor or co-editor of six books and monographs, including *REED: York* (1979) and *REED: Oxford University and City* (2004). Among other print and web publications, she is the author of 64 book chapters and journal articles on medieval and early modern drama.

Erin E. Kelly is an assistant professor of English at University of Victoria specializing in sixteenth-century drama and Reformation religious discourse. Her publications include essays and articles on works by Thomas Lodge, John Foxe, Elizabeth Cary, and Anthony Munday. She is currently an associate editor for *Early Theatre*. Other projects in progress include a new edition of Shakespeare's *Taming of the Shrew* for the *Internet Shakespeare Editions* and a book manuscript on representations of religious conversion in early modern English drama.

David Klausner is professor of English and Medieval Studies at the University of Toronto, and director of the Centre for Performance Studies in Early Theatre. He has edited the REED collections for Herefordshire, Worcestershire, and Wales, and is presently editing the documents of the North Riding of Yorkshire. His editions of *Wisdom*, *The Pride of Life*, and *The Castle of Perseverance* have been published in the TEAMS Middle English Text Series. He has been closely involved in research through production since his first appearance as the Towneley Mactacio Abel's Garcio in 1967.

David Mills is a professor emeritus and formerly head of department in the School of English at the University of Liverpool. His career, as the bibliography of this volume attests, has produced studies of Chester that are virtual bibles for later generations of scholars. His works include edited collections with R.M. Lumiansky, *The Chester Mystery Cycle* (1974), and *The Chester Mystery Cycle: Essays and Documents* (1983) as well as several facsimile editions of Chester manuscripts; with Elizabeth Baldwin and Lawrence M. Clopper (eds), *Records of Early English Drama: Cheshire including Chester* (2007); as sole editor, *The Chester Mystery Cycle: A New Edition With Modernised Spelling* (1992); and a monograph, *Recycling the Cycle: The City Of Chester And Its Whitsun Plays* (1998), as well as many journal articles and chapters in books.

Heather Mitchell-Buck is an assistant professor in the English department at Hood College in Frederick, MD, where she teaches courses on medieval literature and culture. She received her Ph.D. in English from Duke University in December 2009. Her dissertation chronicled the prevalence of tyrants on the early English stage and explored what their continued popularity throughout the sixteenth century suggests about the power of 'medieval' Catholic resistance to the 'modern' Tudor Reformation. Her current research focuses on the changing conceptions of kingship in the city of Chester and its cycle of biblical plays throughout the sixteenth century.

Helen Ostovich is professor of English at McMaster University, where she teaches early drama and contemporary Canadian drama. She is the founding editor of *Early Theatre: a Journal associated with REED*; a senior editor for the Revels Plays; general editor of *Queen's Men's Editions*; and play-editor of six plays by Jonson (*Ben Jonson: Four Comedies* for Longman Annotated Texts, *Every Man Out of his Humour* for the Revels Plays, and *The Magnetic Lady* for the *Cambridge Works of Ben Jonson*), two plays for *Richard Brome Online*, and one for *Internet Shakespeare Editions*. She is currently editing *The Ball* for the Oxford Works of James Shirley, and *The Merry Wives of Windsor*, Q and F, for Norton Shakespeare 3. She co-edited, with Elizabeth Sauer, *Reading Early Modern Women: An Anthology in Manuscript and Print, 1550–1700* (Routledge), the winner of the Society for Early Modern Women's Best Collaborative Book of 2004 on the topic of early modern woman; and with Holger Syme and Andrew Griffin, co-edited *Locating the Queen's Men, 1583–1603: Material Practices and Conditions* (2009).

Margaret Rogerson is an associate professor in the department of English at the University of Sydney. Her research covers medieval theatre, Chaucer, and Margaret Atwood. She is the author of a recent study of the modern revivals of the York Corpus Christi Plays, *Playing a Part in History: the York Mysteries 1951–2006* (Toronto, 2009) and has edited a collection of essays on the York Plays, medieval and modern, *The York Mystery Plays: Performance in the City* (Woodbridge, 2011).

Kurt A. Schreyer teaches courses on Shakespeare and early English drama at the University of Missouri – St. Louis. His interests extend to a wide variety of genres and texts across the traditional medieval/Renaissance disciplinary divide, from Chaucer to Milton, and from epic and romance to devotional lyric. He is currently at work on a book entitled *Banning Shakespeare: Sixteenth-century Histories of the Early English Stage* in which he proposes that the Chester Banns may serve as a model for how the Shakespearean stage might have reflected upon its relationship to pre-Reformation mystery drama.

John T. Sebastian is associate professor of medieval literature at Loyola University New Orleans and earned his Ph.D. in Medieval Studies from Cornell University. He is the editor of the forthcoming TEAMS edition of the Croxton *Play of the Sacrament*, a play that he has also edited, along with the N-Town Mary Play and the mummings of John Lydgate, for the Broadview anthologies of British literature and medieval drama. He is currently preparing an essay on devotional images and the poetry of Lydgate for a volume on poetics and social practice. In a previous life, he could be spotted treading the boards in amateur productions of the *The Alchemist*, *The Revenger's Tragedy*, and *The Woman Hater*.

Matthew Sergi is an assistant professor of English at Wellesley College. He earned his Ph.D. in English and Medieval Studies from the University of California, Berkeley, where he recently completed his dissertation, *Play Texts and Public Practice in the Chester Cycle, 1422–1607*, a project which received the Medieval Academy's 2008 Schallek Award and UC Berkeley's 2010 Anglo-California Foundation Dissertation Grant. Matthew also has a BFA in Drama and English from NYU; he often works in both scholarly and creative capacities with independent theatre companies and performers.

Paul Whitfield White is director of Purdue's Medieval and Renaissance Studies program, as well as a professor of English. He specializes in Shakespeare, medieval drama, and early modern drama and literature. He has recently published *Drama and Religion in English Provincial Society, 1485–1660* (Cambridge UP, 2008). His other books include *Theatre and Reformation: Protestantism, Patronage, and Playing in Tudor England* (Cambridge UP, 1993); *Marlowe, History, and Sexuality: New Critical Essays on Christopher Marlowe* (AMS, 1998), which he edited for the Marlowe Society of America; and *Shakespeare and Theatrical Patronage in Early Modern England* (Cambridge UP, 2002), co-edited with Suzanne R. Westfall. Winner of the Department of English Award for Excellence in Graduate Teaching, he also served as director of Graduate Studies from 2000 to 2003.

Acknowledgements

The editors wish to thank the Social Sciences and Humanities Research Council of Canada particularly for their support in disseminating a new understanding of the Chester cycle's early modern performance of religion. We also express our gratitude to the University of Toronto's Graduate Centre for Study of Drama, the Centre for Medieval Studies, Victoria College, and St. Michael's College; and to McMaster University, especially the English and Cultural Studies department.

Introduction
The Chester Cycle in Context

David Klausner, Helen Ostovich, and Jessica Dell

The End of the Plays

In 1946, Harold Gardiner could write confidently that 'the popular religious stage of the Middle Ages owed its discontinuance to measures of repression by those in authority'.[1] Since Gardiner's time, records research has shown that the situation was considerably more complex than mere repression, and that the decline and eventual demise of civic biblical drama came about for a number of reasons, frequently local, rather than through a nation-wide policy of suppression. In some towns conscious efforts were made to adjust their plays to a protestant sensibility: Pamela King has shown that the revisions to the Coventry pageants made in 1534/35 by Robert Croo already showed the influence of protestant thinking in contrast to the 'confident sacramentalism' of the York plays.[2] These changes were made on a local basis, not as a matter of official policy, just as forty years later Robert Laneham complained of the local suppression of Coventry's Hock Tuesday pageant, which

> iz grounded on story, and for pastime woont too bee plaid in oour Citee yeerely: without ill exampl of mannerz, papistry, or ony superstition: and elz did so ocupy the heads of a number, that likely inoough woold haue had woorz tyll noow of late laid dooun, the knu no cauz why onless it wear by the zeal of certain theyre Preacherz: men very commendabl for their behauiour and learning, & sweet in their sermons, but sumwhat too sour in preaching awey theyr pastime.[3]

Even clearer evidence of local protestant revision can be found in the single surviving Norwich play, the Grocers' play of The Fall of Man, since we have

---

[1]   Harold Gardiner, *Mysteries' End: An Investigation of the Last Days of the Medieval Religious Stage*, Yale Studies in English 104 (New Haven, 1946), 113.

[2]   Only two of Coventry's plays survive, but these show a significant lack of Marian themes in contrast to the plays from York, N-Town, and Towneley. Pamela King, 'The York and Coventry Mystery Cycles', *REED Newsletter* 22 (1997), 25; Pamela King, '"Faith, Reason and the Prophets" dialogue in the Coventry Pageant of the Shearmen and Taylors', James Redmond (ed.), *Drama and Philosophy* (Cambridge, 1990), 37–46. See also Paul Whitfield White, *Drama and Religion in English Provincial Society, 1485–1660* (Cambridge, 2008), 68–76.

[3]   R.W. Ingram (ed.), *REED: Coventry* (Toronto, 1981), 273.

the play in two (partial) versions, a pre-Reformation text from 1533 and a post-Reformation text from 1565.[4] Norwich's 'protestantization' centres on the prelapsarian relationship between Adam and Eve as both loving and physical, in stark contrast to the celibacy indicated in Catholic versions of the story.

York's plays were performed in an atmosphere of strong civic control by the mayor and council, who saw the plays as 'one aspect of the prolonged struggle by the people of York and many others in the north against the advancement of the new religion'.[5] Local events, including the destruction of the Ouse Bridge by flooding in 1565, contributed far more to the decline of the plays than any widespread policy. The presence in York of Matthew Hutton as dean of York Minster (1567–89, and archbishop 1595–1605/06) had a profound influence on the plays. Hutton was a strong protestant and an adept administrator, his policies contrasting with the lax control of William Downham, bishop of Chester. Hutton disapproved of the plays, but his rejection of a 1568 performance of the Creed play implies that he was not guided by a national policy, 'ffor thoughe it was plausible 40 yeares agoe, & wold now also of the ignorant sort be well liked: yet now in this happie time of the gospell, I know the learned will mislike it and how the state will beare with it I know not'.[6] A sequence of mayors of differing religious persuasions complicated planning for performances; a request to perform the plays went to mayor Robert Criplyng in 1579, but the council of the North had in the meantime had enough of his Catholic sympathies and ousted him. A repeated request for performing the plays went to his successor, Robert Asquith who agreed that 'he and his brethren wold considre of their request'.[7] The request does not appear to have been acted upon, for there is no evidence of any further performances of the York plays after 1569.

Chester represents the most complex situation. The Late Banns, not explicitly dated but clearly post-Reformation, give frequent indications of a protestant revision of the plays, but on the evidence of the five surviving play manuscripts, some of the revisions implied by the Banns were not carried out. Some changes clearly did occur: *The Assumption of the Virgin*, produced by the 'wurshipffull Wyffys of this towne', was dropped soon after the composition of the Early Banns, for it appears in no other source, and the Bakers' *Last Supper* was dropped, perhaps, as Paul Whitfield White suggests, because of references to transubstantiation.[8]

---

[4]   JoAnna Dutka, 'The Lost Dramatic Cycle of Norwich and the Grocers' Play of the Fall of Man', *Review of English Studies* 35.137 (1984), 1–13. The Norwich Grocers' play only survives in an eighteenth-century transcription; see Norman Davis (ed.), *Non-cycle Plays and Fragments*, EETS SS 1 (London, 1970), xxii–xl.

[5]   Alexandra F. Johnston, 'The City as Patron: York', in Suzanne Westfall and Paul Whitfield White (eds), *Shakespeare and Theatrical Patronage in Early Modern England* (Cambridge, 2002), 163. Johnston outlines in full the complex story of the York plays under Elizabeth.

[6]   Alexandra F. Johnston and Margaret Rogerson (eds), *REED: York* (Toronto, 1979), 353.

[7]   Johnston, 'City as Patron', 172–3; Johnston and Rogerson, *York*, 393.

[8]   R.M. Lumiansky and David Mills, *The Chester Mystery Cycle: Essays and Documents* (Chapel Hill, 1983), 282; White, *Drama and Religion*, 90.

The play was revived in the 1550s with a substantially protestant view of the eucharist. The suppression of the feast of Corpus Christi in 1548 likely prompted the annotation on the BL Harleian 2150 text of the Early Banns that the play and procession 'in honor of the fest' which had been 'sett forth by the clergye' was now 'erazed in the booke'.[9] The Smiths' play also shows signs of protestant revision. In the Early Banns the Smiths perform 'Candilmas-day' and in early play-lists they produce *The Purification*. In the surviving play-texts, however, their play is primarily concerned with the Presentation in the Temple and Christ among the doctors (despite being labelled 'De Purificatione Beatae Virginis' in all manuscripts).[10]

David Mills's discovery of Christopher Goodman's 1572 letter to Archbishop Edmund Grindal expands our understanding of the process of revision by which Chester's plays continued to be performed until 1575. Goodman's list of popish 'absurdities' constitutes, in effect, a protestant wish-list for revision. Some, but hardly all, of Goodman's criticisms appear to have been acted upon, though it is not of course possible to attribute such revisions directly to Goodman's complaints. References in *The Resurrection* to transubstantiation were converted to a protestant view of the eucharist, and Simon the Apostle's speech in *Pentecost* is changed to replace penance with 'Christes blood and Passion' as the primary vehicle for the remission of sins.[11] Paul Whitfield White suggests that some of the phrasing of the Late Banns may involve a response to Goodman's criticisms. Goodman lists, for example, the episode of the two midwives in *The Nativity* among his absurdities; the author of the Late Banns appears to modify the spiritual significance of the apocryphal story, noting that the event appears in the play 'in sport'.[12] Goodman complains that the shepherds' attempt to sing 'Gloria in excelsis' is 'foolish descanting'; the Banns counter:

> The appearinge angell and starr upon Cristes birthe,
> the shepperde poore of base and lowe degree,
> you Paynters and Glaseers decke out with all myrthe
> and see that 'Gloria in Excelsus' be songe merelye.
> Fewe wordes in the pagiante make merthe trulye,
> for all that the author had to stande uppon
> was 'glorye to God on highe and peace on earthe to man'.[13]

---

[9] Lumiansky and Mills, *Essays and Documents*, 283 (ll. 162–3), 300.

[10] Ibid, 190–91; Sally-Beth MacLean, 'Marian Devotion in Post-Reformation Chester: Implications of the Smiths' "Purification" Play', Tom Scott and Pat Starkey (eds), *The Middle Ages in the North-West* (Oxford, 1995), 237–55.

[11] R.M. Lumiansky and David Mills (eds), *The Chester Mystery Cycle*, EETS SS 3 (London, 1974), 18.170–77, 21.347–50.

[12] Lumiansky and Mills, *Essays and Documents*, 289 (l. 95).

[13] Ibid, ll. 96–102. For the text of Goodman's letter, see Elizabeth Baldwin, David Mills, and Lawrence Clopper (eds), *REED: Cheshire, including Chester*, 2 vols (Toronto, 2007), 146–8.

As in Coventry, dissension over the plays in Chester was local, not a reflection of national policy. When Archbishop Grindal wrote to the civic authorities in 1572 (perhaps guided by Goodman's letter) to stay the performance of the plays in that year, his letter 'Came too late' and the plays were performed 'to the dislike of many'.[14] Goodman emphasizes the local nature of these disagreements when he notes that the lord president of the council of the North 'perceived Master Mayor so bent as he would not be stayed from his determination in setting forth the plays by any persuasions or letters'.[15]

Recusancy in Chester

Catholicism remained a vital force in the north of England through the whole of Elizabeth's reign. The repeated concerns of the council of the North led to archiepiscopal visitations of both the dioceses of York and Chester, but the very underground nature of much recusancy leads to difficulties in describing its extent. Hugh Aveling, the principal historian of Yorkshire's Catholic communities, regularly voices his frustration with the relatively small numbers of persons presented to the visitations. The numbers of the recusancy rolls do not, however, tell the whole story.[16]

Recusants were frequently protected by their friends and neighbours. William Chadderton, bishop of Chester, wrote to the privy council in 1584 reporting on the ecclesiastical commission's dealings with a number of prominent recusants. He also noted that 'there were also many recusantes of dyvers counties within the diocesse of Chester presented at the Lord Byshop of Chester his visitacion this last Sommer, but they cold not be indicted by reason the churchwardens and swornemen did not set down any certayne tyme of their absence'.[17] Beyond the limited numbers of the recusancy rolls, there is strong evidence of Catholic strength in Chester. The case of John Murren is exemplary. Murren had been chaplain to the Catholic bishop Edmund Bonner prior to his deprivation in 1559; in 1562 he was found to be distributing an anti-protestant pamphlet and preaching traditional religion in the city of Chester, but he was not arrested until 1583, more than twenty years later. The situation was exacerbated by the appointment of Bishop William Downham (1561–77), whose conservatism made him unwilling to invoke strong measures in the suppression of Catholicism. In 1567 the privy

---

[14]   Baldwin, Clopper, and Mills, *REED: Cheshire*, 136.

[15]   Ibid, 145. See also Lawrence M. Clopper, *Drama, Play, and Game: English Festive Culture in the Medieval and Early Modern Period* (Chicago, 2001), 286–93.

[16]   J.C.H. Aveling, *Post-Reformation Catholicism in East Yorkshire, 1558–1790* (York, 1960); *The Catholic Recusants of the West Riding, 1558–1790* (Leeds, 1963); *Northern Catholics: The Catholic Recusants of the North Riding of Yorkshire, 1558–1790* (London, 1966); *Catholic Recusancy in the City of York, 1558–1791* (London, 1971).

[17]   TNA, SP 12/167/40 cited by K.R. Wark, *Elizabethan Recusancy in Cheshire* (Manchester, 1971), 57.

council ordered him to undertake an investigation of recusancy in the diocese; the following year he had done nothing and was ordered to make a full visitation. He complied with this order, concluding that the people of the diocese of Chester were 'very tractable and obedient'.[18] With Downham as bishop and a strongly conservative civic administration, the privy council described Chester in 1574 as 'very sink of popery'.[19]

Of recusant drama there is barely a trace outside of Catholic participation in civic efforts in Chester, York, and Coventry to keep their biblical plays alive and local moves (largely undocumented) towards preserving parish plays and other traditional observances. The play of *Respublica*, though Catholic in intent (it seems to have been played before Mary at Christmas, 1553), is so bland that it could just as well have been played without offense before Edward or Elizabeth. The compilation of the Towneley plays under the patronage of the recusant Towneley family, however, should count as one of the most important events in recusant drama history, even though the compilation led to no performances.[20] *[certain?]* No hint of polemic Catholic drama appears until early in the seventeenth century, when records begin tracking several companies of travelling recusant players in the North Riding of Yorkshire.[21]

Sectarian Drama in Context, c. 1555–75

Although the conventional view of post-Edwardian religion is that violent sectarian squabbles marred the reigns of Mary I and the early years of Elizabeth, in fact this description, despite Foxe's *Acts and Monuments*, is overwrought. From the standpoint of drama, John Bale, formerly a Carmelite monk who converted to the protestant faith, was the first protestant propagandist for the stage, especially in his *King Johan* (late 1530s), a play that re-reads early English history by transforming John into a protestant hero defying the Roman Catholic church, only to be murdered by its adherents. Bale's basic argument, expounded

---

[18]   Christopher Haigh, *English Reformations: Religion, Politics, and Society under the Tudors* (Oxford, 1993), 255; R.K. Emmerson, 'Contextualizing Performance: the Reception of the Chester *Antichrist*', *Journal of Medieval and Early Modern Studies* 29.1 (1999), 108; S.J. Lander, 'The Diocese of Chester' in B.E. Harris (ed.), *A History of the County of Cheshire*, vol. 3 (Oxford, 1980), 20.

[19]   TNA, SP 12/48, ff. 73–4; cited by Christopher Haigh, *Reformation and Resistance in Tudor Lancashire* (Cambridge, 1975), 223.

[20]   Barbara D. Palmer, 'Recycling "The Wakefield Cycle": The Records', *Research Opportunities in Renaissance Drama* 41 (2002), 88–130.

[21]   Most prominently, the Simpsons' company, based in Egton, North Riding, whose existence is known from the legal records generated by protestant authorities' attempts to stop their touring performances. See G.W. Boddy, 'Players of Interludes in North Yorkshire in the Early Seventeenth Century', *North Yorkshire Record Office Review* 4 (December, 1976), 95–130.

at vitriolic length, is that the Church of Rome is 'antichristian', a theory that later protestant polemicists and playwrights continued. Bale's template for later pro-protestant plays transformed the Catholic instructional tool, the morality play, into a 'medium for advancing the Protestant viewpoint' by creating 'good' characters as protestants, 'and denigrating the Church of Rome' as devils. *King Johan* demonstrates with burning clarity Bale's sectarian case study, supported by the trial setting in which Widow England accuses the clergy of exploitation and subversion, and King John declares his support for protestantism and Tudor-style kingship.[22] But Catholic response to such theatrical condemnation was not on the same level, instead mostly moderating or muddling sectarian divisions in order to focus on what was the same in both religious views. Recently Alice Hunt has argued that the coronations of Mary and Elizabeth demonstrate the difficulty of pinning down sectarian drama quite so easily as Bale did: if recusant drama was a common form of expression that might have derived from Mary's reign, the plays themselves cannot establish that Mary represented purely a 'Catholic' party-line, or that subsequently Elizabeth represented a purely 'protestant' party-line dividing one kind of England from another in the black/white scheme that Bale suggests.[23]

Mary's own coronation rested on what Hunt contends is a triangulated structure: legitimacy of descent (as the child of Henry's first marriage); legitimacy of female rule (Mary was the first queen of England in her own right as first child and first daughter); and legitimacy of the parliamentary proclamation of her monarchical right. In that sense, barring issue of her body, she also established the right of Elizabeth as her legitimate heir. Both queens situated themselves as substitutes for the Virgin Mary, mothers of England, with Mary's marriage to Philip intending to produce world peace, and Elizabeth's virginity having a similar superhuman goal. Both associated themselves with biblical and classical figures of justice and truth. Both queens used the same motto, that truth is the daughter of time.[24] Both, in making these similar choices, sustaining a family tradition, blurred the borders between Roman Catholic ceremony and English Catholic adaptation or translation of ritual.

Nicholas Udall, whose play *Respublica* was presented at court celebrating Mary's coronation, managed to stay in Mary's good graces[25] without pushing a

---

[22]   See Rainer Pineas, *Tudor and Early Stuart Anti-Catholic Drama* (Nieuwkoop, 1972), 5–6; Paul Whitfield White also comments in *Theatre and Reformation: Protestantism, Patronage, and Playing in Tudor England* (Cambridge, 1993), chapter 2, on the pro-protestant anti-Catholic character of Edwardian court productions.

[23]   Alice Hunt, *The Drama of Coronation: Medieval Ceremony in Early Modern England* (Cambridge, 2008), chapters 4 and 5.

[24]   Ibid, 170: 'Veritas temporis filia'.

[25]   See Edward Arber's timeline for Udall, printed in his 1869 edition of *Ralph Roister Doister*, 4:

> 1554. Dec. 3. Date of a warrant dormer from the Queen to the Master of her Revels. [Reprinted in *The Loseley MSS*. Ed. by A.J. Kempe, F.S.A. London. 1836.] The warrant runs thus — 'Whereas our wellbeloued Nicholas Udall hath at soondrie seasons convenient heretofore shewed and myndeth hereafter to

particularly sectarian agenda either in protestant polemics or Catholic apology. In the play, Mary's supporters are the daughters of God: Truth, Justice, Compassion, and Peace; and Mary herself appears twinned as both Respublica, the widowed state (but not identical to Bale's Widow England), and Nemesis, the final figure of justice, confronting and punishing the vices despoiling the realm. As Greg Walker points out, the surprising aspect of *Respublica* is its silence on religious practices: although questions do arise on the role of priesthood and the nature of clerical office, the exploitation of church wealth, and the hiring of uneducated clergy for small parishes, the play argues fairly modestly for the restoration of church property, but Udall intended that restoration to go to the Edwardian protestant church, not the Roman Catholic church.[26] Walker sees the serious problem of the play residing in the female sovereign with absolute power, even though the larger female role of Respublica allows for a less authoritative woman with a different, perhaps less threatening, conception of female involvement in politics. On stage, nevertheless, that representation of the queen is 'frail, sensual, and manifestly carnal', blurring distinctions between state and sovereign as she seeks advice and listens to the complaints of her subjects. Visually and verbally, her physical reliance on the service of men, especially Avarice, is suggestively sexual, marked by bawdy references and suspicions cast on her even by the daughters of God.[27] David Bevington, on the other hand, sees a lighter touch in Udall's court comedies: *Ralph Roister Doister* (c. 1553–56) gives us Christian Custance as a heroine in line with Mary Magdalene, Susanna, and Hester in plays written for Mary's mother Katherine with their 'feminine values of concord, domesticity, and forbearance', values also pertinent to the representation of female figures in *Respublica*; and the lighthearted *Jack Juggler* (c. 1553–56) offers a 'defence of pleasure to a court weary of protestant sobriety'.[28] This latter Catholic entertainment became a protestant polemic only in the epilogue added to the print version in 1561, excoriating the magic of transubstantiation.

---

shewe his diligence in setting foorth of Dialogues and Enterludes before us for our regell disporte and recreacion.' ... And then goes on to authorize the loan of apparel for those purposes. Did the popularity of the dramatist, and her personal acquaintance with him, since they had worked together on Erasmus's *Paraphrase*, lead the Queen to condone the intense protestantism of the Preacher, even to the continuing of him in favour? Udall and Ascham, two noted protestants, are both favoured by Mary.

[26] Greg Walker, *The Politics of Performance in Early Renaissance Drama* (Cambridge, 1998), 185–9.

[27] Ibid, 192. See also Hunt, *The Drama of Coronation*, 134, who later describes the play as an 'invaluable response to the circumstances of Mary's accession' because it demonstrates the 'anomalous situation of female rule' and 'the ambiguity and instability of truth and meaning' (145).

[28] David Bevington, *Tudor Drama and Politics* (Cambridge MA, 1968), 123, 126. See also Greg Walker, *Plays of Persuasion: Drama and Politics at the Court of Henry VIII* (Cambridge, 1991), 130.

Each sovereign, that is, attempted to mediate sectarian views, despite or perhaps overriding the protestant assaults in print. In fact, each queen was crowned by the 'wrong' church, with little open hostility. Mary changed her oath of office to include obedience only to 'just and licit laws' and silently ordered oils from Brussels to anoint her, rather than allow protestant oils; and Elizabeth withdrew during her Roman Catholic ceremony into a curtained-off retreat so that no one saw her response to the mass, a move that also protected 'the varied beliefs of the observing clergy, councillors, noblemen and ambassadors in the Abbey'.[29] This balancing act for both queens was essential for maintaining the authority of court and church, even though the connection between church and state made the Elizabethan settlement of 1559 urgent policy for calming the conservative faction with some Catholic continuity, as well as stressing the difference between the Church of England and the Church of Rome. This balancing act is clear in the Elizabethan performances of the Chester cycle up to 1572 when Goodman began voicing his protests. Much other drama of the period – interludes, early histories, comedies – was not particularly bold in expressing sectarian divisions, with some notable exceptions. Most preferred to find other targets – or to seem to displace the real targets with attacks on education (as in Wager and Fulwell) and the marketplace, as we see in *New Custom* and in Wilson's *The Three Ladies of London*.

William Wager's *The Longer Thou Livest, The More Fool Thou Art* (c. 1568) emphasizes the importance of a good education by showing us its opposite. In terms of protestant theories of redemption, the play is pessimistic and unforgiving: Moros gets what he deserved – an afterlife in hell. Although Moros seems to have some interests that might seem redeemable to a modern audience – ecology or ethology (he knows where to find a red-shank's nest) and folklore (he loves traditional games, dances, and songs) – those are balanced unfavourably by his idleness, violent bullying, and name-calling. The play's hard line on education (Discipline is a tough teacher) labels Moros a 'wicked heart' and punishment only makes the boy defiant and surly. Theatrically, the situation allows Discipline to indulge in a lot of direct address to the audience, admonishing them to abhor Moros's errors. In fact, the play is very clear about Moros's gradual descent into damnation by refusing to learn responsible adult values, choosing the wrong friends, and settling disreputably into viciousness and folly. Despite the protestant argument that spectacle draws us away from contemplation of spiritual values, the audience sees and presumably processes the repeated visual motifs that accompany the tag-line title: beating a character who remains unrepentant and incorrigible, changing costumes and adding beards to show the downward spiral of the unregenerate boy to vicious adult and finally to mad old fool; and signs of the sinful soul in physical pratfalls, running away, and eavesdropping, corresponding to moral falls and betrayals.

Ulpian Fulwell's *Like Will to Like* (c. 1568) is just as pessimistic about humankind's state of sin, even though the playwright presents his ideas

---

[29]   Hunt, *The Drama of Coronation*, 128–9; and 153.

entertainingly through his Vice, Nichol Newfangle, whose 'master of ceremonies' role gives the audience continuous sneering commentary on their inescapable fates, punctuated by songs, dances, and hucksterism. Most of the moral instruction of the play is inverted: father-Lucifer gives a mock-blessing to his apprentice-son, quite overshadowing Virtuous Living's modest prayer to God, his father in heaven. Nichol as judge approves the boasts of criminals, instead of enacting punishments like the true judge Severity, who sends the guilty to the hangman. The chair that starts out as the seat of evil becomes the throne of Virtuous Living, crowned by Honour. But repentance is not an issue in the play: characters have already been divided into good and evil from the start, and although there seems to be reward for good, in fact the reward is preordained, not earned. For that matter, evil is punished, as might be expected, but the devil rides off with the Vice on his back, rescued from this plot to serve again in another. The lesson seems to be that humanity is corrupt and unregenerate, that even punishment serves no purpose, since evil will always resurrect when the opportunity is ripe. Nichol's survival is just another sign of society's enduring iniquity. The satirical edge of this play is very unlike the straightforward motifs of the Chester cycle's pious retracing of Jesus' life, in which Christ is king and the Antichrist defeated.

Like Nichol Newfangle, Ambidexter in Thomas Preston's *Cambises* (1569, but probably performed several years earlier) dominates the play by providing snappy commentary and slapstick puncturing any solemn piety, but his voice is not strident. He may seduce, regale, and cajole but his job seems to be to encourage Cambises to fall along the path of his royally misguided choices. Cambises begins as a young king trying to find the correct path to judicious rule. But he performs his only just action at the start of the play, punishing the corrupt viceroy Sisamnes, who is a kind of preview of the vicious tyrant Cambises becomes. As a mock-Herod, Cambises stages his own slaughter of the child in a drunken archery contest; a mock-Cain, he kills his only brother, and then orders the death of his queen when she protests the fratricide. In a final spectacle, his own sword, divinely inspired, stabs him fatally, and he expires mocked by Ambidexter's quaking imitation of death throes. As an expositor-figure, Ambidexter plays both sides, weeping at events – but then revealing crude laughter instead, snorting and farting in pleasure. As the play progresses, he is the inching corruption that worms its way into the centre of power to enjoy the final implosion. *Cambises*, in other words, is not that far off from *Everyman* in demonstrating that the good, despite steadfast faith, are powerless on earth and the sinful earn their way to hell through persistent evil deeds. This issue of faith versus works is a significant factor in the struggle for ecclesiastical reform, especially in the opposition between protestant insistence on faith or personal inspiration as the saving grace and Catholic insistence on deeds.[30]

New Custom (1573), unlike the plays of Wager and Fulwell, sallies forth in a much more particular and direct attack on church abuses, an excellent example of the growing political concern to infiltrate the conservative thinking of the

---

[30]   For further discussion of faith and works, see Alexandra Johnston's essay in Chapter 1.

provinces with proselytizing plays that put the case for continued ecclesiastical reform squarely.[31] As the Prologue states, 'All things be not soe as in sight they doe seeme'. The vice Cruelty revels in his atrocities against protestants; and from the start old-fashioned church leaders like Perverse Doctrine complain about youngsters reading the bible for themselves and preaching against church images, as they 'reuile at the holie sacrament, and transubstanciation' but know nothing of church policy: 'No booke now in their hands, but all scripture, scripture, / Eyther the whole Bible, or the new Testament', says the prelate contemptuously, likening their boyish 'audacitie bolde' in religious learning to 'cast[ing] perles to an hogge'. New Custom opposes the idea of purgatory, the mass, and other rites and ceremonies of the old church, which nullified sinfulness by finding ways (primarily through confession and absolution) of making 'Sinne now, no sinne': all the seven deadly sins can be entertained and all the ten commandments broken with impunity. Hypocrisy rules the day, flinging pardons and incense to cover up error. The Calvinist New Custom argues he represents the original Christian teaching, because he follows the Light of the Gospel in proclaiming faith as the way to God, whereas all the 'deeds' manufactured by a hypocritical church cannot save a soul. And by the end of the play, New Custom and Light of the Gospel have converted Perverse Doctrine to Sincere Doctrine, and restored the 'Primitive Constitution' of the church with faith and repentance the only tools ('For faith commeth by the woorde, when wee reade, or heare'), not vestments, or purchased pardons:

> But hee who puttes his religion in wearing the thing,
> Or thinks himself more holly for the contrarie doing,
> Shall proue but a foole of what euer condition
> Hee bee, for sure that is but mere superstition.

That is, as Bevington has pointed out, *New Custom* shows Elizabeth's 'policy of ... recovery of wayward Catholics' in its acceptance of converts and its focus on defining and justifying the new era: true protestantism is not so much 'revolutionary' but rather 'restored' to the ideas expressed by Jesus and the first apostles.[32] Christopher Goodman's contemporaneous objections to the remnants of Roman Catholicism in the Chester cycle clearly locate abuses as residing in the same theatrical images (costumes, props) in the church, as opposed to the sincere word of the bible. In that regard, Elizabeth Williamson points out the 'double lives' of stage properties taken from disestablished or stripped churches: they have their own histories and, within the world of the play, 'serve as highly charged reference points to the culture in which the plays were first produced', whether inciting tolerant nostalgia for the past or vituperation in the present.[33]

---

[31]   White, *Drama and Religion in English Provincial Society*, 173–4.

[32]   Bevington, *Tudor Drama and Politics*, 130–31.

[33]   Elizabeth Williamson, *The Materiality of Religion in Early Modern English Drama* (Farnham, 2009), 31. See also Eamon Duffy's discussion of indignant response in *The Stripping of the Altars* (New Haven, 2005).

Drama written post-1575 gradually withdrew from sectarian argument of the kind *New Custom* and its ilk produced. Partly from Leicester's Men, in the forefront of protestant drama,[34] came perhaps the last of such companies, the Queen's Men, who in 1583 included Robert Wilson, his *The Three Ladies of London* (written c. 1581), and its sequel *The Three Lords and Three Ladies of London* (1590). In *The Three Ladies of London*, antagonism to the Catholic church disguises itself as nationalism under siege by European invaders who come to enjoy English freedoms and jobs while contaminating their new environment. Most of the villains are Italian: Lady Lucre has a Venetian grandmother; Usury was trained in Venice; Simony in Rome; Dissimulation (half-Italian, half-Dutch) and Fraud (half-French, half-Scottish) are mongrels. The crudest villain is Mercatore, the Italian merchant who imports shoddy goods into England in order to destroy the native economy through wasteful expenditure that perverts English virtues. The cheap imports push English workers out of jobs, and Usury in particular introduces rack-renting, squeezing them out of housing and raising the cost of food as well, and finally killing Hospitality. Although in *Godly Queen Hester* (1527) the queen speaks out on the value of monastic hospitality, especially in feeding the poor and offering lodging to travellers,[35] this play shows us Hospitality as the spirit of the (protestant) English, not a religious duty so much as a natural recognition of human dignity. The English identity, that is, suffers confusion at the hands of the evil foreign perverters of social action, perhaps most clearly expressed by Sincerity, the protestant cleric who cannot find a living. The good deeds of Gerontus (the Jewish merchant) in forgiving debts and of the Muslim judge in following the spirit of the law are acceptable standards of decent behaviour because they stay where they belong (in Turkey) and they follow principles with which a good protestant could agree: they believe that true faith and an upright soul are more important than money.

The Chester Script

But what *were* true faith and an upright soul in Chester 1572? The recent discovery of the Goodman letters has fundamentally changed how we view Chester's last two large-scale productions of biblical drama. Goodman's detailed record of the cycle's heretical and dogmatically Roman Catholic elements in 1572 reveals a larger underlying social rift within the city of Chester itself. Under the reign of Elizabeth I, native Cestrians inevitably faced a conflict of loyalty between their Roman-founded heritage and their English-governed monarchy, a conflict that was heightened by opposing religious tensions. The essays in this volume address some of the key textual, historical, religious, and geopolitical issues that were

---

[34] White, *Theatre and Reformation*, 64.
[35] Walker, *Plays of Persuasion*, 108–10.

sparked by the city of Chester's unexpected (and potentially seditious) decision to once again mount their plays.

Opening this volume, Alexandra Johnston analyzes her experiences reconstructing the script of the Chester plays as they were performed in 1572, using only Goodman's eye-witness account and the 1591 Chester manuscript (the earliest surviving complete copy we have) as her baseline texts. Using these archival sources meticulously to authenticate and justify her editorial decisions, Johnston explains how she was able to recreate a modernized version of the Chester script for the Toronto production that reflects how the plays were organized and performed in 1572. She uses her intimate knowledge of the Chester manuscripts to advocate the need for a more holistic approach to the study of the Chester plays, and persuasively argues that (if we truly wish to understand the Chester cycle) we need to overcome the limitations of the manuscripts themselves by actively considering as many of the plays' production circumstances as possible.

Following this introduction to the Chester script, David Mills's essay demonstrates how feasible Johnston's holistic 'call-to-arms' is when put into practice. Although Mills begins his essay, as Johnston does, by commenting on the vital necessity of reading between the lines when studying the Chester scripts, his essay quickly moves into a nuanced, performance-based examination of the opening 51 lines of cycle's first play, *The Fall of Lucifer*. Noting key differences between these lines and the corresponding ones found in earlier extant cycle pageants, Mills argues that the Chester plays more clearly indicate a local resistance to changing royal policies than do any other surviving cycles or fragments. By focusing on the staging of God in play one, Mills explores how theology and performance come into conflict with one another throughout this opening segment of the Chester cycle.

Faith and Doubt

While Mills's essay primarily discusses how the Chester script readily lends itself to academic 'inference', his discussion of God also introduces the ongoing problem of exactly *how* Cestrians dramatized their faith. The authors in this second section of *The Chester Cycle in Context* consider how discourses of faith and doubt, conviction and uncertainty, intersect with one another in performance. Opening this discussion, Erin Kelly's essay argues that the cycle plays functioned as a type of exegetical experiment that helped audiences first confront and then purge everyday religious uncertainties. By analyzing the plays' metatheatrical elements, specifically those that actively cultivated disbelief among spectators, Kelly suggests that the plays walked audiences through a carefully scripted didactic exercise in order to help reinforce their spiritual convictions. After bombarding spectators with recurring episodes of doubt, the pageant plays eventually reward their audience by re-affirming Christian principles. These oscillating episodes of faith and doubt, however, make the Chester cycle especially vulnerable to the misinterpretation, criticism, and disapproval of hardcore religious fanatics like Christopher Goodman.

While Matthew Sergi's approach to faith and doubt in the Chester cycle differs vastly from Kelly's, his conclusion ends up speaking to hers in a profound way. Whereas Kelly explores alternating episodes of faith and doubt throughout the cycle as a whole, Sergi instead chooses to focus on a single dramatic event: the dice game played by Jesus' three torturers at his crucifixion. Sergi demonstrates how apparent chance in performance, as the torturers *gamble* for sole ownership of Jesus' clothes, actually reaffirms the 'fatal' inevitability of biblical events. Although (on the page) the dice game introduces the idea of the unforeseen into the play's otherwise linear account of biblical events, in performance both the dice game's unrealistic pace and improbable climax suggest that the play is in fact resistant to such wild unpredictability. Like Kelly, therefore, Sergi examines an aspect of the Chester cycle that potentially questions God's all-controlling influence over events only to demonstrate how the dramatic presentation of this same moment potentially opens the play up to a variety of new (and sometimes completely unexpected) meanings. Instead of stressing unpredictability, Sergi suggests that the dice game conspicuously emphasizes and reinforces orthodox notions of religious predestination.

Also commenting on the unique difficulties medieval and early modern actors faced when presented with the daunting task of dramatizing their faith, John T. Sebastian focuses on a specific moment of doubt in the Chester cycle; namely, the confusion Jesus' bloody but triumphant return to heaven causes in *The Ascension*. With his crucifixion wounds once again freshly visible for audiences and actors alike, God's angels ask Jesus a question that undoubtedly resonated with audiences: 'Whye ys thy cloathing nowe so reed?' From this position of uncertainty, however, Sebastian's essay uses Caroline Walker Bynum's theories[36] concerning blood imagery to argue that the ascension pageant provides spectators with a soteriological, albeit distinctly Catholic, explanation of the redemptive power of Christ. By making such a direct statement in a time of constant upheaval and religious change, Sebastian suggests that *The Ascension* offers its conflicted audience an image of religious stability that would have been as outwardly reassuring as it was inwardly appealing.

Taking this notion of inward seduction to its fullest extreme, Margaret Rogerson theorizes on the processes whereby actors and audiences would have connected with and potentially internalized the events of the Chester plays. In her essay, Rogerson argues that, through such dramatic techniques as 'affective piety', actors would have formed intense emotional connections with the parts they were meant to portray. Drawing on the remarkable real-life devotional methods of Margery Kempe, who (as a form of meditation) frequently imagined herself as being present at important biblical events, Rogerson suggests that Cestrian actors

---

[36] See Caroline Walker Bynum, *Wonderful Blood: Theology and Practice in Late Medieval Northern Germany and Beyond* (Philadelphia, 2007).

would have employed a similar technique when preparing to perform their biblical roles. This process of affective piety, however, exposed Cestrian actors to all the emotional uncertainties expressed by figures like Salome, the doubting midwife. Yet Rogerson also argues that such doubts and reservations are eventually exorcised, as doubt gives way to faith and disbelief melts into a renewed spiritual certainty within the cycle's overall narrative arc.

Elizabethan Religion(s)

The protracted issue of organized religion inevitably intrudes upon the discussion of faith and doubt in the Chester cycle. *Whose* faith and *whose* doubt did the plays primarily address? Goodman certainly believed that the pageants were too liberal (and vocal) in their dissemination of Catholic dogma, but was this in fact the case and how much local support did his opinions garner? It seems more logical to assume that the diversity of the people involved in the writing, production, and reception of the cycle would bring different (and at times conflicting) spiritual beliefs to the plays themselves, making it difficult (if not impossible) to definitively categorize them as 'belonging' to any one, singular religion. Paul Whitfield White's essay addresses precisely these issues. After defining some of the more prominent religious ideologies found in Chester during the latter half of the sixteenth century, White contemplates the extent to which categories such as 'Catholic', 'protestant', and 'recusant' actually apply to the Cestrian community that performed and watched the Chester cycle in the 1570s.

Whether warranted or not, however, Goodman's objections to the Chester cycle's Catholic elements did impinge upon how Cestrian organizers marketed and justified the production of their plays. Written, revised, and ultimately re-transcribed and glossed, the Chester Banns, Kurt Schreyer argues, provide valuable insight into the religious controversy that tainted and destabilized Chester's long-standing theatrical traditions. In the seventeenth century, years after the plays were successfully suppressed, Randle Holme transcribed a copy of the Late Banns into which he carefully reinserts all of its previously censored 'Catholic' material. Although Holme carefully 'cordons' (Schreyer's term) this material off from the main text, his treatment of the Banns introduces the possibility of reading the plays themselves as a type of palimpsest. Schreyer's essay examines the various surviving versions of the Chester script in order to comment upon how religious tensions shaped and irreversibly changed the Chester plays themselves.

Space and Place in Chester

Chester's civic identity had more at stake than investment in the mere production of its plays. It was fundamentally entrenched in both the script and celebratory significance of the performance event itself. As the plays were successively disputed, revised, censored, and eventually abridged, the Chester community also had to internalize change, as they were forced to re-evaluate their communal image and traditions. Sheila Christie's essay explores precisely this phenomenon. References to Romans abound in the pageant plays, but unlike other extant cycles, Christie argues, Chester's treatment of Roman characters is largely positive or (at the very least) sympathetic. Examining the roles of figures like Octavian and Pilate, Christie demonstrates how these potentially flattering depictions coincide with an older tradition of celebrating Chester's Roman origins. Christie convincingly establishes that in the earlier writings of Lucian, Ranulph Higden, and Henry Bradshaw, Rome was upheld as the quintessential model of earthly power. For a post-Reformation audience, however, Rome's Catholic allegiances inevitably clouded and dramatically impacted how Cestrians were permitted to identify with their own origin stories.

Mark Faulkner's essay examines the writings of Lucian, a Benedictine monk who lived in Chester during the late twelfth century, to determine how Goodman's objections affected the older traditions that initially helped imbue the Chester cycle with meaning. Using early maps symbolically and topographically to decode Lucian's *De Laude Cestrie*, Faulkner considers how the architecture and schematic layout of the city of Chester helped to reinforce thematically the spiritual journey encapsulated by the play's performance route, as well as the ways in which city and cycle collided to influence how everyday Cestrians spiritually viewed their own city.

Heather Mitchell-Buck's essay also examines the ways in which the Chester plays destabilized the theatrical boundary that separated the wagon-stage from the city proper in order to comment on the pressing contemporary issues faced by their Cestrian audiences. Firmly convinced that the Chester plays actively resisted post-Reformation policies, Mitchell-Buck examines how the cycle more specifically challenged a royal understanding of 'the greater good' in a desperate attempt to preserve its own local customs. Herod, Mitchell-Buck suggests, is a tyrannical imitator who convincingly 'feigns' the role of a good king. Herod's ability to adopt a persuasive and at times an unnerving and transparently efficient demeanour and rhetoric would have unsettled local audiences who were equally unsure of their own government.

Afterword

As JoAnna Dutka herself writes in her final comment, it seems somehow appropriate that this collection of new and ground-breaking essays concludes with a tribute to Professor Frederick Millet Salter (1895–1962), who helped to establish Chester studies as a legitimate academic field. In a poignant afterword, Dutka surveys Professor Salter's long and distinguished academic career. Balancing Professor Salter's scholastic contributions with a number of more personal anecdotes, Dutka respectfully reminds Chester scholars of the pioneers like Professor Salter, whose unstoppable vision and unflagging spirit have made this collection of essays possible.

PART 1
The Chester Script

Fig. Pt. 1   The Expositor preaches the word of God to audiences in the University
of Toledo's production of *The Temptation*.

Chapter 1
The Text of the Chester Plays in 1572: A Conjectural Re-Construction

Alexandra F. Johnston

One of the great challenges in the study of English medieval drama is the instability of the texts. Scholarship over the last fifty years has challenged our understanding of the manuscripts that have come down to us by revealing complex differences among the written artefacts that survived the iconoclasm of the mid-sixteenth century. The texts of the religious plays of England suffered from the same wilful destruction that so many of the other Catholic artefacts experienced, as they were destroyed by people driven by complex series of emotions ranging from sincere protestant piety to naked fear of imprisonment or worse if they were found with such 'seditious' material. Only three fragments of biblical drama survived the seventeenth century in the hands of their original owners. These are the guild copies of the Chester *The Trial and Flagellation of Christ and The Crucifixion*, the York *Doubting Thomas* and Robert Crow's copy of the Weavers' pageant of *The Purification and Christ and the Doctors* in Coventry. All the others were preserved, not by people interested in drama and its place in a proud medieval past, but by individual scholars and antiquarians anxious to preserve what they could from the wreckage of the dissolution of the monastic and other pre-reformation libraries. This group of men included the scholar Thomas Allen[1] of Gloucester Hall, Oxford – a hall established to accommodate notionally conforming church papists. Allen had begun acquiring manuscripts as early as 1563 and gradually built up the largest private collection of manuscripts in Oxford. In 1598, he was appointed to the committee to assist Thomas Bodley in the establishment of his library. Among Allen's protégés were Robert Hegge,[2] the original owner of the N-Town plays, and Sir Kenelm Digby,[3] whose name is still associated with one of the manuscripts containing several of the few surviving morality plays. In Ireland, Henry Ussher,[4] archbishop of Armagh, a contemporary of Allen, was also collecting manuscripts of religious material, including plays, that eventually found their way to Trinity

---

[1]   *The Oxford Dictionary of National Biography Online* <http://www.oxforddnb.com>.

[2]   Ibid.

[3]   Ibid.

[4]   Ibid.

College, Dublin. In the early seventeenth century, Robert Bruce Cotton,[5] who acquired the N-Town plays after Hegge's death, was an early member of the Society of Antiquaries and a major figure preserving this material along with John Selden.[6] These men, often Roman Catholics or with strong Catholic sympathies, sought to preserve these few written examples of a rich cultural heritage that had been rooted up and destroyed during a century and a half of religious dissension and civil war. Eighteenth-century book-collectors kept them safe and then began to sell them to public research libraries. Nineteenth-century scholars rediscovered these plays and began the process (that still continues) of seeking to understand the nature of these few texts in their own context.

The story of the Chester manuscripts is of a different order.[7] Only one manuscript witness to the Chester plays survives from before the suppression of the cycle. This witness is the Peniarth manuscript in the National Library of Wales of *The Coming of Antichrist* whose preservation history seems to be similar to that of the other play manuscripts. No complete manuscript of the Chester plays, however, survives before 1591, sixteen years after the final performance of the plays in 1575. Between 1591 and 1607 five copies of the plays were made. None is an exact copy of another and there are major variants especially between the last one written down in 1607 (H)[8] from the collection of Robert Harley, earl of Oxford,[9] now in the British Library, and the four others – the earliest (1591) now in the Huntington Library (Hm), two other British Library manuscripts, one Additional MS dated 1592 (A) and another in the Harleian collection dated 1600 (R), and one now in the Bodleian Library, Oxford dated 1604 (B).

The 1591 manuscript was signed by 'me Edward Gregorie scholler at Bunburye' – a town eleven miles southwest of Chester. Nothing is known of Gregorie and the early history of the manuscript is uncertain but, at some point, it was in the possession of the Egertons, an important Cheshire family, since the name 'John Egerton esq.' appears on folio 41.[10] The first three earls of Bridgwater (1579–1649, 1622–86, and 1646–1701) were all named John Egerton.[11] The duke of

---

[5]   Ibid.

[6]   Ibid.

[7]   Robert Lumiansky and David Mills, the editors of the EETS edition, provide a full discussion of the manuscripts in their introduction to Robert M. Lumiansky and David Mills (eds), *The Chester Mystery Cycle*, 2 vols, EETS SS 3 (1974) and 9 (1986); and also in their companion volume, published between the issuing of the two volumes of the edition by EETS: Robert Lumiansky and David Mills, *The Chester Mystery Cycle: Essays and Documents* (Chapel Hill, 1983). The following discussion is based on their work.

[8]   The letter designation for each manuscript is taken from Lumiansky and Mills, EETS, ix.

[9]   *ODNB Online.*

[10]   The details of the manuscripts and the scribes and owners who do not appear in the *Oxford Dictionary of National Biography* are taken from Lumiansky and Mills, *Chester Mystery Cycle*, 1.ix–xxvii.

[11]   *ODNB Online.*

Devonshire acquired the manuscript in 1821 from John Kemble and subsequently sold it to Henry Huntington for his new library in Pasadena, California. Huntington had already acquired the manuscript of the Towneley plays and these two important play texts are numbered Huntington Library MS 1 and 2.

The next two Chester manuscripts, the 1592 and 1600 British Library copies, were written down by George Bellin, the scribe of the Coopers' guild who also copied the other single play copy, *The Trial and Flagellation of Christ and The Crucifixion*, as an elegant copy for the archives of his guild in 1599. The 1592 and 1600 versions of the full text are not exact copies. He seems to have had access to other sources when he prepared the second version. The 1592 copy is lacking the banns and the proclamation and was probably written as a reading text. Its eighteenth-century owners were probably a prominent Cheshire family called Cowper. The British Library acquired it from a sale of Richard Herber's Library in 1836. The 1600 copy has both the banns and the proclamation and was part of the family collection of the four generations of Cheshire antiquarians all named Randle Holme (1571–1707). The manuscript was bought by Robert Harley, through the good offices of the bishop of Chester, in 1707 and was part of his collection deposited in the British Library in 1753. The 1607 manuscript was also part of the Randle Holme collection and also found its way to the British Library through the Harleian collection. It has the most variant readings of all the versions. Three scribes had a hand in its compiling including James Miller, a minor canon at Chester Cathedral. The 1604 manuscript, now in the Bodleian, is hurriedly written. A late seventeenth-century hand attributes the play to one William Bedford. Bedford became clerk of the Chester Brewers' guild in 1606. The manuscript was given to the Bodleian in 1710 by Richard Middleton Massey, one-time keeper of the Ashmolean Museum in Oxford.

All the identified scribes of the Chester manuscripts had close ties with the city and two have guild association. Their motives seem to have been to preserve a part of their city's past before it was irreparably lost. Four were preserved by prominent Cheshire families – the Egertons, the Cowpers, and the Holmes – all with antiquarian interests. One came early into the hands of an Oxford antiquarian. Two passed through the hands of noble book collectors. All of them eventually found their way to major libraries. For their creators and owners, these manuscripts seem to have been more artefacts than living theatre – monuments of the past to be preserved rather than guides for performance.

After an exhaustive analysis of the surviving manuscripts in order to choose a base text, the editors of the most recent Early English Test Society edition, Robert Lumiansky and David Mills, concluded

> that we could present the *whole* of the Cycle, as it has come down to us, most conveniently for the reader by using Hm as the base text with Play I in full from R, and with H's large differences – as well as the variants in the ending of XVIII

> in R – included as an Appendix. In addition, the three non-cyclic manuscripts
> could be presented in full in a second Appendix.[12]

They call the text contained in various forms in the manuscripts that have come down to us a 'cycle of cycles'.[13] None of the versions conforms to the description of the plays in the Early Banns of 1539–40 or the Late Banns of 1608–09, nor does any correspond to the description of the play that Christopher Goodman provides for us in the list of 'absurdities' he perceived in the play as it was performed in 1572 (see below). But this situation is not unique. The so-called 'banns' for the N-Town plays bristle with unresolved problems particularly in a manuscript that has been shown to be a compilation of several different plays cobbled together to make a meditation text.

Peter Meredith's pioneering work on the N-Town manuscript that revealed the hidden *Mary Play*[14] as well as the two-day Passion Play[15] shook the foundations of the literary analyses of the English biblical plays.[16] Up to that time the genre had been understood to be represented by four similar witnesses – the York plays, the Chester plays, the N-Town plays, and the Towneley plays. But with the N-Town plays revealed as an anthology, scholars began questioning the oddities in the Towneley plays such as the presence of two plays about the shepherds by the same playwright but no nativity play. Recent scholarship has suggested that the Towneley manuscript also represents an anthology of plays collected and handsomely written out to be a meditation text.[17] Then came the evidence from scholars associated with Records of Early English Drama who have been finding references to plays all over the country with no surviving texts (such as the Passion play at New Romney in Kent[18] and the Creation play in the parish of St Laurence, Reading[19]) but enough production evidence to make clear that the manuscripts

---

[12]   Lumiansky and Mills, *The Chester Mystery Cycle*, 1.xxxii–iii. The three non-cyclic mss are the Peniarth *Antichrist*, the Coopers' *Trial and Crucifixion*, and the Manchester Fragment – a portion of *The Resurrection*.

[13]   Lumiansky and Mills, *Essays and Documents*, 40.

[14]   Peter Meredith (ed.), *The Mary Play from the N-Town Manuscript* (London, 1987).

[15]   Peter Meredith (ed.), *The Passion Play from the N-Town Manuscript* (London, 1990).

[16]   For a recent update on the state of scholarship concerning medieval English drama see Richard Beadle and Alan Fletcher (eds), *Cambridge Companion to Medieval English Theatre*, 2nd edn (Cambridge, 2008).

[17]   Barbara Palmer, '"Towneley Plays" or "Wakefield Cycle" Revisited', *Comparative Drama* 22 (1988): 318–48 and 'Recycling "The Wakefield Cycle": The Records', *Research Opportunities in Renaissance Drama* 41 (2002): 88–130.

[18]   James Gibson, '"Interludum Passionis Domini": Parish Drama in Medieval New Romney', in Alexandra F. Johnston and Wim Hüsken (eds), *English Parish Drama* (Amsterdam, 1996), 137–48.

[19]   Alexandra F. Johnston, 'Parish Playmaking before the Reformation', in Clive Burgess and Eamon Duffy (eds), *The Late Medieval Parish*, Harlaxton Medieval Studies XIV (Donington, 2006), 325–41.

that have survived do not represent the whole tradition. Whereas, half a century ago, Hardin Craig could confidently write about English cycle plays as if all was known about them[20] and Rosemary Woolf could bring her considerable skill at close reading to a comparative study of the individual episodes,[21] today we stand on uncertain ground. Only the episodes in the York plays have any real claim to be acting texts and they are frozen in time – written down midway through the life of the plays in the 1470s to be used by the Common Clerk of the city who sat with the manuscript at the first station and noted down when changes had been made by a guild in performance. Because many notations appear in the margins, we know that the text, as it is preserved, does not represent the play as it was suppressed in 1569.[22] Individual episodes from N-Town and Towneley were undoubtedly copied from texts that had been used for acting but they have been moulded to fit their new context.

To further complicate our efforts to understand what we are dealing with, there have been compelling suggestions made about two of the morality plays. What has been preserved for us in the manuscripts of *Wisdom* and *Mankind* may indeed be acting texts but texts that represent particular performances. David Klausner has argued for a modular structure for *Wisdom* suggesting the possibility that one of its discrete modules, the 'masque of sin' – a satire 'in which the three Mights demonstrate their new characters in a series of three set dances ... centred around the legal profession' – reflects the interests of the audience and could have been replaced by a satire on the world of commerce for another audience.[23] More recently, John Geck has identified the named individuals from the audience in *Mankind* placing them in a very specific place at a very specific time.[24] *Mankind* otherwise shows all the marks of being a travelling play. The naming of those individuals would have no resonance in a different place at a different time but it would be easy to substitute other names and circumstances for another audience.

With the exception of *Everyman*, an import from the Netherlands, none of the English religious plays were printed and any could be and, in all probability, were altered to suit new playing situations. Shakespeare understood this tradition and uses it as a central plot device in *Hamlet*. After the prince has indulged himself with the players who have come to Elsinore, reciting long passages of poetry to their mutual delight, Hamlet, as almost an after-thought as he is sending them out with Polonius, converses briefly with the first player:

---

[20]   Hardin Craig, *English Religious Drama* (Oxford, 1955).

[21]   Rosemary Woolf, *The English Mystery Plays* (London, 1972).

[22]   Richard Beadle, *The York Plays*, EETS, SS 23 (2009), xix–xxii.

[23]   David N. Klausner, 'The Modular Structure of *Wisdom*' in David N. Klausner and Karen Marsalek (eds), *'Bring furth the pagants'*: *Essays in Early English Drama presented to Alexandra F. Johnston* (Toronto, 2007), 192–4.

[24]   John Geck, '"On yestern day, in Feverere, the yere passeth fully": On the Dating and Prosopography of *Mankind*', *Early Theatre* 12.2 (2009): 33–56.

> *Hamlet.* ... We'll hear a play tomorrow. Dost thou hear me, old friend; can you play the murder of Gonzago?
> *First Player.* Ay, my lord
> *Hamlet.* We'll ha't tomorrow night. You could for a need study a speech of some dozen or sixteen lines which I would set down and insert in't could you not?
> *First Player.* Ay, my lord
> *Hamlet.* Very well. Follow that lord. (2.2.514–20)[25]

Here Hamlet asks the players to alter their text, to speak lines of his devising so that he can 'catch the conscience of the king' (582). Similarly, a patron paying for a performance of *Wisdom* could ask for a satiric insertion to please (or embarrass) his invited audience. Other plays could be altered to suit changing playing conditions – the loss or addition of players or the availability of musicians, for example. And, as David Mills suggests in this collection,[26] we have no real sense of the non-verbal effects that were part of each performance.

The traditions of playing the Chester plays add further complications. Scholars have thought that the two northern cycles, Chester and York, were conceived and controlled in a similar way. Evidence from the records indicates that this is not so. In York, each guild owned the texts of its own play. We know this because the Mercers in the mid-fifteenth century made an arrangement with a group of men including 'Robert Hewyk of Leeds' over the performance of the Mercers' *Judgment*.[27] When the plays in York were to be performed, each guild performed the text that they had performed before unless a special arrangement made between or among the guilds allowed for changes in ownership – frequently recorded in the city records as a formal agreement. The biblical narrative in York is told in forty-eight (or so) self-contained plays. In Chester, the situation seems to have been quite different. The narrative existed, not in self-contained units, but in clusters of episodes that seem to have been divided into twenty-four 'pageants' to be played over three days. But the division of the episodes was determined by the city council every year the play was to 'go' and the guilds were called in to make a new copy of that year's assignment from the master copy of the text (which has not survived).[28] The recently published detailed records of the New Romney *Passion*

---

[25] Stephen Greenblatt et al. (eds), *The Norton Shakespeare*, 1st edn (New York, 1997), 1702.

[26] See Chapter 2.

[27] Alexandra F. Johnston and Margaret Rogerson (eds), *REED: York*, 2 vols (Toronto, 1979), 87. I have argued elsewhere that this marks the transferral of the play to the West Riding. It forms the basis of *Judgment* in the Towneley ms. See 'Fifteenth Century Yorkshire Drama: an Hypothesis', in John Haines and Randal Rosenfeld (eds), *Music and Medieval Manuscripts* (Aldershot, 2004), 263–79.

[28] See Alexandra F. Johnston, 'The *York Cycle* and the *Chester Cycle*: What do the Records Tell Us?' in A.F. Johnston (ed.), *Proceedings of the Nineteenth Conference on Editorial Problems: Editing Medieval Drama: Special Problems New Directions, Toronto, 1983* (New York, 1987).

Play seem to indicate that the same fluidity in the division of episodes existed there with a stationary performance 'in the round'.[29] There is also some evidence that the pageants at Coventry had a similar pattern of bringing together 'episodes' for a guild in any given year.[30] One way to describe the difference between the York plays and the Chester plays is to think of York as narrative beads in a chain, connected but each self-contained. Chester seems to have been conceived as a continuous rope of a finite length but cut into different portions every time it was played to suit the existing conditions. No one actual performance of the sequence, then, was like any other. The juxtaposition of one episode with another can influence how a modern critic interprets the episodes – where resonances or tensions are perceived, for example, or how the iconography of one story reflects on another. What then is the relationship between the analysis of a play on the page and the reception of that same play on the stage when the divisions are not the same?

This ambiguous relationship was the impetus behind the production of the Chester plays in Toronto in 2010. In the 1990s, a chance discovery by David Mills of a letter-book of the protestant divine, Christopher Goodman, in a small record office in North Wales changed forever the scholarly understanding of the nature of the Chester plays.[31] This discovery prompted our production. The book contains copies of the correspondence between Goodman and senior officials in church and state in northern England concerning the performance of the Chester plays in 1572.

On 10 May 1572, Christopher Goodman, along with two other Chester clerics, wrote to the newly appointed president of the North, Henry Hastings, earl of Huntingdon. Goodman had been born in Chester; he was not a 'foreigner' but had deep roots in the city. As he says in his 1575 letter to Mayor John Savage, he had a 'naturall loue to this Citie where I & my parent*es* were borne & broght vp for the most part'.[32] He was a fervent protestant who had spent time as a Marian exile among the reformers on the continent, including John Knox, and in parishes in Scotland and Ireland before returning to his native Chester in 1568.[33] He was alarmed by the preparations for the performance of the Chester plays in 1572, seeing in them a papist interpretation of the biblical story.[34] His letter of 10 May is full of anti-papal rhetoric beginning with the traditional explanation of the origin of the plays stating that the 'plays were devised by a monk about 200 years past

[29]   James Gibson (ed.), *REED: Kent*, 3 vols (Toronto, 2002), 748, 745 ff.

[30]   R.W. Ingram (ed.), *REED: Coventry* (Toronto, 1981), xvii–xviii.

[31]   David Mills discusses the letter-book in Elizabeth Baldwin, Lawrence Clopper, and David Mills (eds), *REED: Cheshire including Chester* (Toronto, 2007) 1.cxxxvii and 2.895–6.

[32]   Ibid, 169.

[33]   Ibid, cxxxvi.

[34]   For a more detailed analysis of the events that led to the suppression of the *Chester Plays* in 1575 see Alexandra F. Johnston, 'And how the state will beare with it I knowe not', *Medieval English Theatre* 29.2 (2008): 3–25.

& in the depth of ignorance, & by the Pope then authorized to be set forth'. He claims the plays were motivated 'in assured ignorance & superstition according to the Papist policy', clearly setting up an opposition between the city council full of Catholic sympathizers and 'all preachers & godly men' who oppose the plays and 'since the time of the blessed light of the gospell have inveyed & impugned as well in Sermons as otherwise, when occasion hath served'. Despite the efforts of the godly, the council prepared to perform the plays even though 'the same have neither been perused nor allowed according as by her Majesty in those cases it is provided'. Referring to a letter to the mayor sent 'by our Preachers' that fell on deaf ears, he appeals to Huntingdon to forbid the production 'in respect of your Zeal to godliness'.[35] For Goodman, the production is clearly associated with sedition claiming that the plays give 'great comfort to the rebellious papists, & some greater occasions of assembling & conference than their intentions well considered is at this present meet to be allowed'.[36] He concludes urging Huntingdon to 'leave nothing undone which shall be found convenient for the repressing of Papacy, & advancing of godliness, & avoiding of all occasions whereby either perill or danger to her Majesty or to the common weal might begin or grow'.[37]

Huntingdon turned the letter over to the president of the Ecclesiastical Commission of the North, Edmund Grindal, archbishop of York. Despite Grindal's efforts, the Chester Council defied his authority and carried on with their planned production. Goodman both attended and carefully wrote down a list of what seemed to his evangelical sensibilities to be the 'absurdities' the plays contained.[38] It is unclear from the arrangement in the letter-book whether he actually sent the list to the archbishop with his letter lamenting the performance but he did enter the list in his book thus providing a unique eyewitness account of a performance of English religious drama. When we began to consider a new production of the Chester plays, we looked carefully at Goodman's list of 'absurdities'. From it, we tried to deduce both how the text had been divided that year and the relationship between the content of the play Goodman saw and the content of the post-production manuscripts that have survived. If this eye-witness was true, then we might be able to produce the Chester plays in something close to the 1572 version that would allow the exploration of the questions about the analysis of a play on the page and the reception on the stage of that same play altered to fit the demands of a specific production. In other words, we could face head on the endemic instability of the texts of medieval English drama.

But first a text had to be created for the experiment from the material in the surviving manuscripts that corresponded to the evidence from Goodman of what he saw and heard. I accepted the challenge and, with the help of David Mills, who was intrigued by the whole experiment, edited the text following the clues provided

---

[35]   Baldwin, Clopper, and Mills, *REED: Cheshire*, 1.143.

[36]   Ibid, 1.143–4.

[37]   Ibid, 1.144.

[38]   The list of 'absurdities' is found in ibid, 1.147–8.

by Goodman. In May 2010, participating groups performed this text. Although I modernized the acting text, I did not invent any lines that were not either in the extant manuscripts somewhere or in Goodman's memorial reconstruction.

Many of the 'absurdities' that bothered Goodman reflect the use of apocryphal material in the Chester plays, but these were tangential to his essential concern – the presentation of a version of the Christian story from the theological position of the Roman Catholic church, not the newly established Church of England. It was this blatant presentation of Catholic doctrine that particularly upset him and led him to write to the authorities that the production would bring 'great comfort to the rebellious papists'.[39] His first concern was over the presentation and interpretation of the sacrament of the Lord's supper. His dismissive comment on the enactment of the institution of the sacrament in the pageant containing the re-enactment of the Last Supper, 'The sacrament made a stage play', is followed by his quotation of a stanza spoken by Christ in the resurrection episode:

> And therto a full ryche messe,
> in bred myn one bodie,
> & that bred I you gyve,
> your wyked lyffe to amend
> becomen is my fleshe,
> through wordes 5 betwyxt the prestes handes.

Here we have three elements of Catholic doctrine and practice concerning the Eucharist – communion only in one kind, the bread, the changing of that bread into the actual flesh of Christ (the doctrine of transubstantiation), and the efficacious enunciation of the necessary formula by a priest. The corresponding lines in the extant manuscripts read,

> And that bread that I you give,
> your wicked life to amend,
> becomes my fleshe through your beleeffe
> and doth release your synfull band. (18.174–7)[40]

Here we have a protestant interpretation of the sacrament where the bread becomes efficacious only through the belief of the recipient and has itself the power to absolve without the intervention of a priest.

The issue of salvation by works or by faith (so central to Luther's understanding of the scriptures) is also a part of the doctrinal message of the play as Goodman saw it. He comments on the Ascension sermon, 'Christ promiseth blyss for good works' while the extant text uncompromisingly presents the protestant understanding of salvation by faith,

---

[39] Ibid, 1.143.

[40] All quotations from the extant text are from Lumiansky and Mills, *The Chester Mystery Cycle*.

All that steadfast beleeffe hasse,
and fullye, save shall [be]. (20.75–6)

The 1572 performance and the extant text present the two opposing views of this hotly debated doctrine.

Goodman also heard the apostle Simon invoke the salvific properties of the sacrament of penance in his part of the repetition of the creed in the *Pentecost* pageant and carefully noted it down:

And I beleve with devotion,
of syn to have remission
throgh penance & contrition,
& heven whan I am dead

Whereas the extant text has Simon say:

And I beleeve with devotyon,
of synne to have remission
through Christes blood and Passion,
& heaven when I am dead. (21.347–50)

These three points of doctrine were among the most contested in sixteenth-century England. By endorsing the Roman Catholic interpretation of each, the producers of the Chester plays in 1572 were signalling their theological biases, justifying the concern of evangelicals, such as Goodman, about the nature of the 1572 production. The doctrinal issues were central to my consideration of why the proposed production of the plays in 1572 was so offensive to Goodman, and wherever it was possible for me to choose between the parallel texts that appear uncomfortably beside each other in the EETS edition of the plays, I chose the Catholic interpretation.

The doctrinal issues, though central to Goodman's perception of the plays, were not the major problems presented to me in the creation of our acting text. The list of 'absurdities' provided a 'description' – sometimes extensive but at other times cryptic – of each of the pageants that Goodman saw. No doubt what he saw was essentially the biblical narrative with its late medieval embellishments that survived in the manuscripts, but the way the pageants were divided is unlike any other extant manuscript or list. The first striking difference is that he saw twenty-three pageants where the extant text has twenty-four plays,[41] and yet his notes clearly record that no single episode is entirely dropped with the possible exception of *The Three Kings* (the visit of the Magi to Herod, see below). The major changes come in the first eleven plays. It is clear from his comments on pageant eleven, *The Purification of the Virgin Mary, and Christ's Appearance Before the Doctors*, 'Simeon to doubt of a virgin's birth & to put out the name of a maid twice out of

---

[41]   For the purposes of the discussion that follows I will refer to the series of episodes as they appear in the edited text as 'plays' and the series of episodes as described by Goodman as 'pageants'.

his book writing in place thereof a good woman' (the action of the first episode in play eleven, stanzas 4–15 lines 25–117) and 'Ioseph offereth a taper of wax' (the action of play eleven, stanza 19), that what he saw corresponds to the play. What he saw as pageant nine, however, is actually play seven – the famous Chester play of *The Shepherds*. So my initial challenge was to work out how the narrative up to *The Shepherds* was divided into eight pageants instead of six. There are three clues – two in the Old Testament sequence and one in the New Testament sequence. Goodman comments on what he saw in pageant four, 'Abraham ex merito should receive a son'. This appears in the extant text in play four, *Abraham, Lot, and Melchysedek: Abraham and Isaac*, stanza 22 lines 169–72, at the end of the Melchisedek episode. He remarks about what he saw in pageant five, *Moses and the Law: Balaack and Balaam*, 'The Ark called a Shrine' (meaning the ark of the covenant). This appears in the Moses episode of play five, stanza 8. There seems to be no problem here. The second 'absurdity' Goodman records in pageant seven, however, 'Also he [Joseph] reprehendeth marriage betwixt a young person & an old', occurs in the second episode of play six, *The Annunciation and the Nativity*, stanzas 16–20 lines 123–60. Goodman's comments on pageant eight,

> Sybil is brought in so superstitious a manner as is not commendable.
> Joseph grudging against tribute paying
> Two midwives to Christ Tibill and Salome
> The miracle of drying up of Salomes hands & the restoryng of the same
> And feigned miracles of Frier Bartholomew, of the temple of necromancy.
> Of 3 Suns appearing.
> Of the ox & ass honouring of Christ
> Sybill & Octavian talking together
> Octavian saw a maid with a child in her arms in a starr with a bright X in his head
> Octavian honoured him with *(blank)* & sensed the starr

make clear that what he saw as pageant eight was the rest of play six – the Octavian and Sybil episode and the actual birth of Christ with the midwives. To divide the first two episodes of play six from the rest makes sense in the extant text as a Messenger – a *Nuntius* – was written in at some point in the history of the Chester plays after Joseph's prayer to start a new episode:

> *Joseph.* … Lord God, most of might,
>   with weale I worshipp thee.
> *Nuntius.* Make rowme, lordinges, and give us waye
>   and lett Octavian come and playe,
>   and Sybell the sage, that well fayre maye
>   to tell you of prophecye. (6.175–80)

The challenge then came to divide the five and a half (more or less) plays from *The Fall of Lucifer* to *The Annunciation and Nativity* into seven pageants. There is very little help in Goodman's two comments on the Old Testament sequence. What he saw in pageant four, *Abraham, Lot, and Melchysedek: Abraham and*

Isaac, is in play four and what he saw in pageant five, *Moses and the Law: Balaack and Balaam, is* in play five. Given the amount of material between the reference to the ark of the covenant in stanza 8 of play five and Joseph's comment about old husbands with young wives in play six, pageants four and five cannot possibly have corresponded exactly to plays four and five. The first seven plays in the extant text contain the following episodes from the biblical narrative:

1	Creation and the Fall of Lucifer
2	Creation and Fall of Man
	Cain and Abel
3	Noah
4	Abraham and Melchisedek
	The Promise of Isaac
	The Sacrifice of Isaac
5	Moses and the Law
	Balaam and Balaack (Prophets)
6	Annunciation
	Joseph's Troubles
	Octavian and Sybil
	Nativity
7	Shepherds

As I wrestled with this problem, I looked at the real oddity of putting the Cain and Abel episode together with that of the fall of man in play two and wondered what would happen if I divided these two episodes. I looked at the extant text and there is a rather awkward musical interlude written in at some point to cover the passage of at least twenty years between the episode of the expulsion from the garden and the beginning of Cain and Abel:

> *Fourth Angel. …*
>   Therfore departe the must eycheone
>   Our swordes of fyer shall bee there bonne
>   And myselfe there verye fonne,
>   to flame them in the face. (2.421–4)
> *Minstrelles play.*

Adam then enters and starts the Cain episode by talking about his sons. The division of play two into pageants two and three pushed everything forward and, if I did this, how could I account for Goodman having seen the 'Abraham ex merito should receive a son' in pageant four and the 'Ark called a shrine' in pageant five? Here the episodic nature of the text becomes a key. By moving the Abraham and Melchisedek episode that comes at the beginning of play four back to join it with Noah it remains in Goodman's pageant four. If the Moses and the law episode with the reference to the ark of the covenant is also moved back to be included with the

Isaac episode, it remains in Goodman's pageant five but neither pageants four nor five are anything like plays four and five. Now the sequence looks like this:

1	Creation and Fall of Lucifer
2	Creation and Fall of Man
3	Cain and Abel
4	Noah
	Abraham and Melchisedek
5	The Promise of Isaac
	The Sacrifice of Isaac
	Moses and the Law

The episode of Balaam and his Ass comes next – a crowd-pleaser that appears in two distinct versions. The first, printed by Lumiansky and Mills in the main body of their edition from the Huntington manuscript, has a very confused and strange ending, although it is shared by three other manuscripts. The second is unique to the 1607 Harley manuscript edited by Lumiansky and Mills as an appendix. It shares the beginning of the episode with Balaam and his interaction with Balaack and the ass with the other manuscripts but its second half functions as a prophet play. To Balaam's gentile prophecy of the coming of the gentile kings are added the standard messianic prophecies from the Hebrew prophets. The play is much more doctrinally sound and, indeed, doctrinally conservative than the one printed in the main extant edition. Peter Travis believes that it is much more Marian in its emphasis.[42] In my reconstruction, I chose to let the crowd-pleasing Balaam and Balaack stand on its own ending with the prophecy of the kings. I then detached the other prophets and added them to the first two episodes of the Nativity sequence. The result was a sequence of pageants up to the shepherd play that looked like this:

1	Creation and Fall of Lucifer
2	Creation and Fall of Man
3	Cain and Abel
4	Noah
	Abraham and Melchisedek
5	The Promise of Isaac
	The Sacrifice of Isaac
	Moses and the Law
6	Balaam and Balaack
7	Prophets
	Annunciation
	Joseph's Troubles
8	Octavian and Sybil
	Nativity
9	Shepherds

---

42   Peter Travis, *Dramatic Design in the Chester Cycle* (Chicago, 1982), 67.

This reconstruction allows the pageants to conform to Goodman's numbering in his list of 'absurdities'.

This conjectural division of episodes had its problems in performance. Pageants four and five did not seem to 'work' particularly well in production because each contained a well-known and much-beloved episode – the charming Noah and the moving sacrifice of Isaac. Both directors seemed uneasy with what is clearly material extraneous to those well-made dramatic pieces. But why is the inclusion of the Melchisedek episode with Noah any more disturbing than its inclusion with the Abraham and Isaac episode, as it is in the extant text? We have been too used to teaching and performing this drama as individual episodes without the extra material. We have expectations of dramatic decorum that centre on the comic impact of the Flood story and the tragic potential of the Isaac story. Providing doctrinal 'markers' that would foreshadow the New Testament fulfilment of salvation history seems to have been as important to the original devisers of the Chester plays as presenting well-made plays. Our modern approach to this drama – to isolate the episodes – has led us to have expectations that were not necessarily those of the devisers.

Once I had established a conjectural sequence for the first nine pageants of the 1572 production, I came to a major crux. As we have seen, there is no doubt that play eleven, *The Purification of the Virgin Mary, and Christ's Appearance Before the Doctors*, and Goodman's pageant eleven correspond. But the content of Goodman's pageant ten must in some way have covered three plays in the extant text – play eight, *The Three Kings*, play nine, *The Offering of the Three Kings*, and play ten, *The Massacre of the Innocents*, that come between *The Shepherds* and *The Purification of the Virgin Mary, and Christ's Appearance Before the Doctors*. Goodman's rather confused comments on this pageant ten are: 'The kings honour the virgin in place of Christ, & yet no mention of kings' describing action in play nine and 'The souldiers of Herod use terms of neighbour princes not not … [*sic*]' that refers to action in play ten. Perhaps the episode of *The Three Kings* (play eight) was simply not performed in 1572 but we cannot assume that what Goodman doesn't remark on wasn't performed (he says nothing about the passion sequence). Plays eight, nine, and ten are three of the most remarkable of the Chester plays with the magic camels, the bombastic Herod of the first play and the tragic death of Herod in grief for his son in the third play. In creating the 1572 acting text, I assumed that all the material was crammed into one pageant and edited the three plays into one pageant of three episodes cutting the total length from 1145 lines to 905 lines – just twenty lines longer than the other 'giant' pageant in the Chester plays – *The Trial and Flagellation of Christ and The Crucifixion* (play sixteen).

As I moved into the Ministry sequence, the next clear correspondence between play text and the description of pageant contents was in *The Harrowing of Hell*. Goodman's description of pageant sixteen corresponds to play seventeen in the extant text:

A fable of Seth begging oyl in paradise to anoint Adam when he was sick. The deliverance of Adam &c out of hell & bringing these words to affirm his purpose Atollite portas
Enoch & Elias living in paradise in the flesh & the abiding there for a time.
Michael bringing the fathers out of hell with the cross hanging upon the theef's back.

We can also be reasonably sure that his pageant fourteen corresponds, at least in part, to play fifteen, *The Last Supper, and the Betrayal of Christ* since his comment, as we have seen, is 'The sacrament made a stage play'. Although he makes no comment on pageant fifteen, it must have corresponded to play sixteen, the long *The Trial and Flagellation of Christ and The Crucifixion*. Goodman makes a very cryptic and unhelpful comment on what he saw in pageant twelve: 'Iews swear by Mahound'. This expletive is not in the extant text of either of the episodes in play twelve, *The Temptation of Christ, and the Woman Taken in Adultery*, although such oaths would be plausible 'ad libs' as the Pharisees see their sins written in the sand. An equally unhelpful comment appears on pageant thirteen, 'God made the Mass'. Nevertheless, it is clear that he saw only five pageants between the Purification episode and *The Harrowing of Hell* rather than the six in the extant text. The text gives the following division of the episodes:

11	Purification
	Christ and Doctors
12	Temptation
	Woman Taken in Adultery
13	Blind Man
	Lazarus
14	Simon the Leper
	Entry
	Judas to High Priests
15	Last Supper
	Betrayal
16	Trials
	Flagellation
	Crucifixion

With only five pageants to cover this material and little to go on from Goodman's comments, I divided it this way:

11	Purification
	Christ and Doctors
12	Temptation
	Woman Taken in Adultery
	Blind Man
13	Lazarus

	Simon the Leper
	Entry
14	Judas to High Priests
	Last Supper
	Betrayal
	Trial before Annas and Caiaphas
	Denial of Peter
15	Trials continued
	Flagellation
	Crucifixion

Once that change is made the last eight plays (*The Harrowing of Hell* to *The Last Judgment*) correspond to Goodman's last eight pageants.

Goodman gives us no clue about how the pageants were divided into the three days of the production in 1572. In the interest of the 2010 production, however, I tried to balance the episodes performed each day by the number of lines. The traditional assumption of how the extant text was performed is that day one ran from *The Fall of Lucifer* to *The Offerings of the three Kings* (4,380 lines), day two from *The Massacre of the Innocents* to *The Harrowing of Hell* (3,642 lines) and day three from *The Resurrection* to *The Last Judgment* (3,158 lines).[43] To balance the length of each day, the imagined 1572 production was divided into day one, the creation episode to *The Shepherds* (3,705 lines); day two, the conflated Magi sequence to the crucifixion (4,010 lines); and day three, *The Harrowing of Hell* to *The Last Judgment* (3,493 lines). This division inevitably shaped the interpretation of the days' events just as the re-division of the episodes within the pageants did. Day one in the '1572' scheme ended with the annunciation to the Jewish shepherds rather than the adoration of the gentile kings; day two '1572' ended with the death of Christ and the apparent defeat of God, while day two in the traditional division ends with the beginning of the victory with the harrowing of hell. It is arguable that the '1572' division is more medieval, more Catholic than the division we have been led to believe was traditional. But it must be remembered that the first evidence we have of that division is from 1539–40 during the first Henrician reformation.

The study of medieval English drama is more bedevilled by the nature of the surviving manuscript witnesses than any other medieval genre. There is a famous moment in Bodleian e Museo 160 when the scribe who wrote this heading as he began his work, 'The prologe of this treyte or meditatione off the buryalle of Criste & mowrnyng þerat', realized one folio into his task that what he was copying was a play, not a treatise or meditation, and wrote this in the margin: 'This is a play to be played, on part on Gud Friday afternone, and þe other part opon Ester day after the resurrection in the morowe'. He then continued copying his exemplar

---

43   Baldwin, Clopper, and Mills, *REED: Cheshire*, 1.78–9.

adding speech headings.[44] The opposite is true in the manuscript of the N-Town plays which preserves perhaps the best-made plays in the canon – both long and episodic like *The Mary Play*, and *The Passion Play*, and single well-crafted biblical episodes such as *The Woman Taken in Adultery* and *The Trial of Mary and Joseph*. Much of the manuscript has no speech headings, but brief narrative passages describe the action followed by 'then he saith' or some variant. But arguably this play compilation was copied down to be used as a meditation text. The various Chester scribes in the late sixteenth and early seventeenth centuries seem to have been inspired to make many copies of the Chester plays through a combination of antiquarian curiosity and civic pride. We will never know what led the stubbornly recusant Towneley family apparently to commission the sixteenth-century equivalent of a coffee-table book containing a widely diverse collection of plays. The plays have been preserved for us in manuscripts that, for the most part, were not commissioned or compiled by people primarily interested in them as drama. The scholarly editions of the plays with which we are familiar and which are often used exclusively by critics interpreting the plays, trap them in editorial conventions that privilege the manuscript witness. Yet the plays lived – and still live – in performance. The discovery of Christopher Goodman's letter-book demonstrated that a particular performance of the plays in 1572 did not follow the text of the Chester plays as it has come down to us. The text as I conjectured for the 1572 performance based on his list of 'absurdities', however, cannot be taken definitively as what Goodman saw. There is too much not said in his list of 'absurdities' for what I provided as an acting text to have any real claim to represent what was actually played. To leave the plays un-played is to banish them to obscurity but, when we play them, we must bring everything we *can* know about the circumstances of their creation, their auspices, their performance conditions, and the nature of the surviving witnesses to bear on our productions. We can never 're-create' this drama but, through performance, we can come closer to an understanding of its power to teach and to move an audience.

---

[44]   Donald C. Baker, John L. Murphy, and Louis B. Hall Jr (eds), *The Late Medieval Religious Plays of Bodleian MSS Digby 133 and e Museo 160*, EETS ES 283 (Oxford, 1982), 141–2.

Chapter 2
In the Beginning! A New Look at Chester Play One, Lines 1–51

David Mills
in conjunction with his wife, Joy

'What's so sacred about a bloody text?'[1] That remark was made at a conference in 1974 and marked the great change from the 1960s onwards in medieval drama. The drama had broken away from its purely literary context as the pre-Shakespearean precursor. How the Wycliffite preacher c. 1400 must have muttered 'I told you so' since he had warned us of the move to give greater precedence to the drama rather than to the word of God when he said:

> And so thes miraclis pleyeris and the fawtours of hem ben verre apostaas, bothe for they puttun God bihinde and ther owne lustis biforn, as they han minde of God onely for sake of ther pley and also for they deliten hem more in the pley than in the miraclis silf, as an apostata more delitith him in his bodily winning than in the trowthe of God and more preisith seemely thingis withouteforth than ony fairnesse withinneforth to Godward.[2]

Indeed, Christopher Goodman, some two hundred years later, in his complaint to the archbishop of York about the plays, points out that the text is not an agent of control since it is not only subject to change in its written form but to further change by the actors in performance: 'For albeit divers have gone about the correction of the same at sundry times & mended divers things, yet hath it not been done by such as are by authority allowed, nor the same their corrections viewed & approved according to order, nor yet so played for the most part as they have been corrected.'[3] Clearly, there was, and is, a need to understand more about possible staging and its effects.

---

[1]   *The Drama of Medieval Europe*. Proceedings of the Colloquium held at the University of Leeds 10–13 September 1974 (Leeds: University of Leeds Graduate Centre for Medieval Studies, 1975), 55, l. 7.

[2]   Clifford Davidson, *A Tretise of Miraclis Pleyinge* (Kalamazoo, 1993), 109–10, ll. 558–65.

[3]   Elizabeth Baldwin, Lawrence M. Clopper, and David Mills (eds), *REED: Cheshire* (Toronto, 2007), 1.146, ll. 1–5.

An obvious consequence of this concern is to recognize the need for an emphasis on the visual as well as the verbal. Thus, for example, play one of Chester,[4] at which we will be looking, *The Fall of Lucifer*, achieves a major dramatic effect by the creation of scenery and costumed angels and the filling of the original empty space with light and colour and people with obviously unquantifiable effects on playing time. And other aspects of performance are significant for both playing time and the impact of the performance, including the pace and style of delivery and movements of actors across the playing space. All of this detail concerns what may be read between the lines rather than what is actually written – matters of inference – but the text remains, nonetheless, the main provider of evidence. What it may not tell us directly, it may provide as grounds for inference.

So, I want to look at what is less obvious, in other words what happens between the words in a particular speech and, for this purpose, I have chosen to focus on the possible effects of the opening speech of play one and its possible implications for staging and movement.

A Voice in the Darkness

It is a curious fact that all four extant play cycles begin with the words 'Ego sum alpha et oo, primus et novissimus' ['I am alpha and omega, the first and the last'].[5] Despite this agreement, however, the status accorded to the quotation in each manuscript varies. In N-Town and York it stands above the first speech and there is no indication of its speaker, or even if it forms part of the spoken text. In Towneley it constitutes the first spoken line of the play, being line 1 of God's opening speech. Towneley then proceeds to translate it. In these three cycles God enters and the play begins with a direct address by God to the audience. In Chester, however, the situation is different. The Latin quotation acquires a different status since it appears as a stanza on its own and is repeated at the head of play two, where we move from the creation of the angels to the creation of man and the start of human time. And it appears again at the head of play twenty-four, *The Last Judgment*, where God brings that time to an end. Thus it seems in itself more important. The other half of the short quatrain: 'It is my will it shoulde be soe; / Hit is, yt was, it shalbe thus' is clear in its meaning. Everything that happens is under God's control and at his will. The quotation in Latin is never translated but the words have a useful dual meaning, as have the unclear references of 'it', 'so', and 'thus'. The ambiguity of the Latin is useful. God exists there before and beyond human time, but he is also

---

[4]   For editions of the cycles, see R.M. Lumiansky and David Mills (eds), *The Chester Mystery Cycle*, 2 vols, The Early English Text Society (Oxford, 1974); Richard Beadle (ed.), *The York Plays*, The Early English Text Society (Oxford, 2009); Stephen Spector (ed.), *The N-Town Play*, 2 vols, The Early English Text Society (Oxford, 1991); and Martin Stevens and A.C. Cawley (eds), *The Towneley Plays*, 2 vols, The Early English Text Society (Oxford, 1994).

[5]   Revelations 22:13.

here at the beginning and end of the plays. More important from the point of view of the producer is the isolation of this quatrain from the lines that follow. It has a different form, it lacks semantic continuity, and is very different in tone from what follows. Although it is attributed to God, the kind of opening speech you would expect from the other three cycles begins only at line 5 and it seems likely that in Chester it is at line 5 that God makes his entrance. The quatrain, therefore, could be played without his presence, a voice without visible actor, possibly contrary to the expectations of the waiting audience.

Seeing is not Believing

God's introduction of himself attempts to confront a major problem of drama, the conflict in the figure of God between theatrical performance, or performative event, and theology. God is, in a sense, a construct, an abstract, potentially blasphemous when represented in human form, but he also has attributes which are representations of omniscience and timelessness. Moreover, he represents three figures in one, father, son, and holy spirit. Drama, on the other hand, operates with a tangible and visible model with character and motivation and cannot escape from its own literalness except by the imagination of the audience. As the Chester Late Banns put it defensively:

> For then shoulde all those persones that as godes doe playe
> in clowdes come downe with voyce, and not be seene;
> for noe man can proportion that Godhead, I saye,
> to the shape of man – face, nose, and eyne.
> But sethence the face-gilte doth disfigure the man, that deme
> A clowdye coveringe of the man – a voice onlye to heare –
> And not God in shape or person to appeare. (196–202)[6]

Paradoxically, the literalism embodied in the Arian doctrine, by which the three figures of God are distinct, is reinforced necessarily in the plays by giving God visible form. The orthodox doctrine of the church expressed in the Athanasian Creed is, however, that these three characters are united in a single figure of the trinity and to believe otherwise is heresy. All that drama can do to meet these demands is to acknowledge them from the outset of the play, which is the first priority of the speech of God. So, all of the cycles begin with the quotation from Revelation and then move on to explore the attributes of the godhead. York differs from the others in that it gives no place, in its exploration, to the triune nature of the godhead. N-Town, for example, addresses the issue immediately and directly:

---

[6]   R.M. Lumiansky and David Mills (eds), *The Chester Mystery Cycle: Essays and Documents* (Chapel Hill and London, 1983), 294. All citations from the Late Banns are from this edition. Notwithstanding line 197, Chester does suggest that, occasionally, the cloud effect might be possible, e.g. play three, SD before l. 1 and play twenty-four, l. 356 and SD.

My name is knowyn, God and kynge.
...
I am oo God in personys thre,
Knyt in oo substawns.
I am þe trewe Trenyté
    Here walking in þis wone.
Thre personys myself I se
Lokyn in me, God alone. (1.12–17)

Towneley is equally succinct and simple in its statement:

Ego sum alpha et o,
I am the first, the last also,
Oone god in magesté;
Meruelus, of myght most,
Fader, and son, and holy goost,
On God in Trinyté. (1–6)

In this section of the speech Chester again differs from the other three cycles in a variety of ways.[7] Its beginning sounds conventional enough: 'I ame greate God gracious, / Which never had begyninge' (5–6). But underneath these lines lies an Anglo-Saxon alliterative verse structure. And as he goes on the problems start to arise: 'The wholl foode of parente is sett / in my essention' (7–8).What does this mean? It is easy enough to make a guess – that God created all of mankind. Perhaps, indeed, it is a paraphrase of John 1:3: 'All things were made by him; and without him was not anything made that was made.' But within that quotation the introduction of a Latin-based word 'essention' produces a more complicated expression. The scribes clearly could not understand Latin and so wrote 'essention' in place of 'essencia' with its technical meaning of 'divine essence or being'. Indeed George Bellin, the scribe of manuscripts A and R, would have been surprised to find both 'essention' and other Latinate terms included in the *Middle English Dictionary* as the sole example of their meaning when they are in fact errors. The speech continues:

I ame the tryall of the Trenitye
which never shalbe twyninge,
pearles patron ymperiall,
and Patris sapiencia. (9–12)

Again there is a problem of semantics since the meaning of 'tryall' is not at all clear. *MED* defines it as 'Theologically, a whole containing three parts; also, a unit within a tripartite whole, one part of the Trinity' but, again, the only examples given are this one and another later in the speech at line 28. The last three lines of this group of four are understandable but in some ways unnecessary.

---

7   See further Lumiansky and Mills, *The Chester Cycle*, 2.6–7, notes to ll. 5–51, 5–6, 7–8, 9, and 11–12.

Proceeding through the rest of stanzas 2 and 3, the text continues to throw out romance words, Latinate word-forms, and technical theological terms, making the subject unclear where the other cycles make it clear, and, incidentally, occupying more space than the other cycles do. If we view the problem from the point of view of the audience as it stood in a Chester street, what stands out are the sound and the impressiveness of the expressions used to present the trinity. So opaque is this presentation that the dramatist actually fails to name the three beings of the trinity at all. Overall, the sentences, despite being sonorous and attention-grabbing, are too complex and the lines provide insufficient breathing spaces for the actor, making understanding of the concepts difficult for the audience.

Chester may have had a play of the trinity at an earlier date. The feast of Holy Trinity was widely celebrated[8] and Chester had a church dedicated to it as well perhaps as a fraternity. Scholars have paid little attention to the latter because there is only one passing reference to it: 'perhaps a religious guild linked to the fraternity of the Blessed Trinity, the Assumption of Our Lady and St Anne established in 1361 and which may have replaced the earlier guild of St Mary'.[9] Since the sorority was probably responsible for the play in honour of the virgin,[10] could the former fraternity have been responsible for the equivalent play in honour of the trinity? In the present cycle such a play would obviously be *The Coming of Antichrist* with its direct reference to the power of the trinity:

> Three persons, as thou leeve may,
> In on godhead in feere –
> Father and Sonne, that ys noe naye,
> and the Holye Ghoost styrringe aye.
> That ys one God gerey;
> binne all three named here. (23.492–7)

This long, complex, and declamatory exposition of the trinity also has the effect of postponing the key moment when God creates the angels, which the other cycles seem to hasten towards. Moreover, there is a kind of hiatus after line 35: 'Nowe sithe I am soe soeleme / and set in my solatacion' (36–7).

The Creator and his Creations

The movement from God's self-definition to his role as creator seems, in the other three cycles, to happen abruptly; for example, N-Town:

---

[8]   W.K. Lowther Clarke and Charles Harris, *Liturgy and Worship: A Companion to the Prayer Books of the Anglican Communion* (London, 1932, rpt 1936), 209, 264, 398.

[9]   Jane Laughton, *Life in a Late Medieval City: Chester 1275–1520* (Oxford, 2008), 193.

[10]   Early Banns, 128–31; Lumiansky and Mills, *Chester: Essays and Documents*, 282.

> Myself begynnyng nevyr dyd take,
>   And endeles I am thorw myn owyn myth.
> Now wole I begynne my werke to make. (27–9)

And Towneley:

>   That I haue thoght I shall fulfil
> And manteyn with my myght.
> At the begynnyng of oure dede
> Make we heuen and erth on brede. (17–20)

The nearest we come to motivation is in York:

>   Sen I am maker vnmade and most es of mighte,
>   And ay sall be endeles and noghte es but I,
>   Vnto my dygnyté dere sall diewly be dyghte
>   A place full of plenté to my plesyng at ply. (9–12)

All run straight on from God's self-description to the act of creation. In Chester, however, the transition is slower and appears to be marked by the words 'Nowe' and 'sithe'. With them the direction changes. God begins his acts of creation but is it possible that the 'Nowe' and 'sithe' underlined a change of situation as well as tone? 'Nowe sithe I am soe soeleme / and set in my solatacion' (36–7). There are no stage directions, specifically no direct mention of that key item of stage furniture, God's throne, but these two lines surely make its presence clear and, indeed, suggest that he has just sat down 'in my soletacion', defined by *MED* as 'joy, happiness' in an entry that again gives this play as the only use of this erroneous form. Has God been, up to now, standing on a high level and now descends to his throne? There are several reasons to support such a possibility. This statement makes it clear that a change of position has taken place but there is also a change of tone. God's words, up to now, addressed the gathering crowd in declamatory style and required an imposing presence and a strong delivery. Had he been sitting throughout that part of his speech, the audience's sense of the godhead would have been diminished. A move from standing to sitting, together with the greater simplicity of both the words and sentence forms used to address the audience round the wagon directly –

>   a biglie blesse here will I builde,
>   a heaven without endinge,
>   and caste a comely compasse
>   by comely creation (38–41)

mean that the tone becomes more intimate. Later, when God says that he will leave to view this bliss in every tower – 'For I will wende and take my trace / and see this blesse in every tower' (110–11) – he must go somewhere else, probably the high place he originally occupied, which allows him to look down on the scene below. So, from his throne, God creates the endless heaven and the enclosed space and calls up the nine orders of angels. At this point his seat becomes not only his throne, a symbol of his majesty, but also, within the context of the play and cycle, a director's chair, as God creates his setting, calls up his actors, and sets them moving. This stage property establishes his will and his play.

God's speech is, it seems to me, in fact a paced movement from silence, through voice alone, to a boasting presence, to his filling of the originally empty space with colourful scenery and a throng of angels. The speech serves, therefore, a more structural purpose than the equivalent speeches in the other three cycles. It points to the truth of the Late Banns' description: 'Good speeche! Fine playes! With apparell comlye!' (69).

Having said this, I have two caveats to offer. First, Chester, in its present form, is the latest of our cycles and may therefore have been working consciously against a more hostile authority and also the other plays. Second, this is offered as one opinion about the problems and solutions that might face a director and should not be regarded as in any way definitive.

PART 2
Faith and Doubt

Fig. Pt. 2   Satan confronts Jesus in the University of Toledo's production of *The Temptation*.

Chapter 3

Doubt and Religious Drama Across Sixteenth-Century England, or Did the Middle Ages Believe in Their Plays?

Erin E. Kelly

In his 1572 catalogue of 'Notes of the absurdities ... in the Chester plays', Christopher Goodman lists a number of instances in which the plays present events not recorded in the bible.[1] Since the two midwives who attend Mary as she gives birth to Jesus derive from extra-scriptural texts like *The Golden Legend*, and the encounters of Enoch and Elias (Elijah) with Antichrist are based on Catholic exegetical traditions, it is not surprising that the reform-minded Goodman would deem them problematic (147.8–9, 148.21–2). Less easy to explain, this essay argues, is Goodman's criticism that the Chester performances featured in their last supper pageant 'The sacrament made a stage play' (147.31–2).[2] Consideration of what Goodman might have meant when he jotted the phrase 'stage play' suggests how English religious drama across the sixteenth century connected intimately and intricately with experiences of faith and doubt. Recognizing how plays generate doubt allows us to understand why dramatic performance, which was not only seen as conducive to strengthened faith by traditional Christians but also as in keeping with the goals of early evangelical authors, came to be perceived as irredeemably problematic by later reformers seeking a more perfect protestant church and state.[3]

---

[1]   Elizabeth Baldwin, David Mills, and Lawrence Clopper (eds), *REED: Cheshire including Chester* (Toronto, 2007), 1.147–8. Subsequently cited by page and line number in the text.

[2]   David Mills suggests that Goodman's 'absurdities' offer three types of criticisms, in that the plays emphasize 'Catholic doctrine ... apocryphal and legendary material ... and indecorous representations' ('The Chester Cycle', in *The Cambridge Companion to Medieval English Theatre*, Richard Beadle and Alan Fletcher [eds], 2nd edn [Cambridge, 2008], 130). The comment about 'The sacrament made a stage play', however, does not fit neatly into any of these categories and thus cannot be explained only as a complaint that the play strays from literal interpretation of scriptural sources. For discussion of the sort of biblical reading Goodman and like-minded reformers favoured, see James Simpson, *Burning to Read* (Cambridge MA, 2007), esp. 106–41.

[3]   Terminology used to describe those who remained faithful to the traditional church and those who broke from it cannot help but take sides in long-standing historiographic debates.

Goodman's comment might be seen as rejecting Chester's *The Last Supper* for disseminating papist superstition, such as belief in transubstantiation. If so, his complaint would be a typical example of a reform-minded protestant lambasting the Roman Catholic mass as a series of spiritually empty theatricalized mutterings and gestures.[4] Perhaps referring to the first section of *The Last Supper* in which Jesus associates himself with the 'pascall lambe' that 'eaten must be' or to a lost segment of the Corvisors' play, Goodman seemed outraged by the sense that the cycle of plays showed that 'God made the Mass' (147.31).[5] But if the sacrament as understood by Chester authors, performers, and patrons was the spectacular Catholic mass Goodman recognized as a mere stage play, then why would it be a problem to represent it onstage?

Such criticism does not apply to *The Last Supper* as it survives. Indeed, the play in its existing form could serve as support for Elizabethan reformers' complaints about papist elements persistent in English protestant church ritual. The climactic moment of the performance features the player portraying Jesus breaking and distributing bread in a way that more closely resembles what some radical reformers unsuccessfully argued should be regular practice in the Elizabethan church than any Catholic ritual. Christ and his apostles sit as they share bread and wine, enacting the physical position for receiving communion favoured by the authors of the 1572 treatise 'A View of Popish Abuses yet Remaining in the English Church' who explained that 'kneeling, which beside that it hath in it a show of papistry doth not so well express the mystery of this holy supper. For as in the old testament, eating the paschal lamb standing signified a readiness to pass, even so in receiving it now sitting, we signify rest, that is a full finishing through Christ of all the ceremonial law'.[6] The table around which the Chester apostles gathered might or might not have been covered with the 'fair white linen cloth' ordered by *The Book of Common Prayer*, but it surely was a

---

To distinguish the first wave of English protestants who took up the ideas of Luther and those who followed them with inspiration from Calvin's Geneva from each other, I follow MacCulloch in referring to the former as 'evangelical' reformers and the latter as reform-minded or later protestants; see Diarmaid MacCulloch, *Reformation* (London, 2003), xx. Following Duffy, I refer to those who were not aligned with protestants as following the 'traditional' faith, although I do label traditional church ritual as Catholic; see Eamon Duffy, *The Stripping of the Altars* (New Haven, 1992), esp. 1–9.

[4]   For examples, see Michael O'Connell, *The Idolatrous Eye* (New York, 2000), 14–15, 33. Numerous instances of this sort of rhetoric can be easily found in John Foxe, *Acts and Monuments* (London, 1563; STC 11222), esp. 1051 and 1066, which is readily available through *Acts and Monuments [...]. The Variorum Edition* [online] (hriOnline, Sheffield, 2004), <http://www.hrionline.shef.ac.uk/foxe/> (accessed 15 September 2010).

[5]   R.M. Lumiansky and David Mills (eds), *The Chester Mystery Cycle*, EETS SS 3 (London, 1974), 15.7, 14. Subsequent references to plays in this edition will be cited by play and line number in the text.

[6]   This document is appended to the end of *An Admonition to the Parliament* (Hemel Hempstead[?], 1572; STC 10847), B3r-D4r, C1r.

table, not an altar of the sort Archbishop Edmund Grindal ordered in 1571 to be 'utterly taken down and clear removed even to the foundation'.[7] If one takes these elements of *The Last Supper* seriously, then Goodman's comment must be seen to deride the performance as performance, the play as a play, because he thought it inherently sacrilegious to represent even a perfectly executed religious ritual in a theatricalized performance.[8]

Goodman's critique thus not only echoes anti-Catholic polemic but also resonates with English protestant anti-theatrical and iconoclastic discourse. Evangelical critics of Catholic ritual labelled the mass a play to denigrate its elevation of the host and other elements as ludicrous playacting, but such arguments necessarily hint that stage shows were seen as powerful. Starting with the *Treatise of Miraclis Pleyinge* and running through the works of William Prynne, reform-minded English authors rejected drama for making idols of stage players and props. Such treatises lament that spectators are liable to over-identify with what is presented onstage and to be led into immoral behaviour. At a minimum, their authors identify play-going as a tempting type of idleness and as an inherently sinful activity, part of a constellation of behaviours characterized by their opposition to active religious faith. To represent scriptural subject matter or religious ritual in such a form was thus an act of sacrilege, putting new wine in old flasks.[9] More worrisome, though, to anti-theatrical writers was that these forms could be so appealing; perhaps because of their emphasis on entertainment, plays render audiences too willing to believe in what they see onstage.[10]

---

[7]   *The booke of common praier, and administration of the Sacramentes* (London, 1559; STC 16292), M1r; *Injunctions Giuen by the most reuerende father in Christ, Edmonde ... in his Metropoliticall visitation of the Prouince of Yorke* (London, 1571; STC 10375), A2v.

[8]   Matthew Hutton, dean of York, offers precisely this sort of objection in a 1576 order forbidding performance of cycle plays at Wakefield: 'This daie vpon intelligence geven to the saide Commissioners that it is meant and purposed that in the towne of Wakefeld shalbe plaied this yere in Whitsonweke next or therabouts a plaie commonlie called Corpus Christi plaie which hath bene heretofore vsed there / Wherein thy are done tundrestand that there be many thinges vsed which tende to the Derogation of the Maiestie and glorie of god the prophanation of the Sacramentes and the maunteynaunce of superstition and idolatrie / The said Commissioners Decred a lettre to be written and sent to the Balyffe Burgesses and other the inhabitantes of the said towne of Wakefield that in the said playe no Pageant be vsed or set furthe wherein the Maiestye of god the father god the sonne or god the holie ghoste or the administration of either the Sacraments of Baptisme or of the lordes Supper be counterfayted or represented / or any thinge plaied which tende to the maintenaunce of superstition and idolatrie or which be contrarie to the lawes of god or of the Realme.' See A.C. Cawley (ed.), Appendix I, *The Wakefield Pageants in the Towneley Cycle* (Manchester, 1958), 125.

[9]   Extended discussions of these anti-theatrical tracts can be found in O'Connell, *Idolatrous*, esp. 14–35 and Jonas Barish, *The Antitheatrical Prejudice* (Berkeley, 1981), 66–190.

[10]   Arguably, literary critics have made related arguments about how theatrical performances affect audiences. Louis Montrose in *Purpose of Playing* (Chicago, 1996), 30–32 suggests that English people longed for the engagement with 'symbolic forms' once offered by Catholic religious ritual and the religious drama it inspired, shifting their

Anti-theatrical arguments stress how audiences might be corrupted by what they see, equating plays in performance with idolatry. Both medieval proponents and critics of religious drama seem to have considered the scenes presented a type of image, what the Wycliffite *Treatise of Miraclis Pleyinge* refers to as 'quike bookis'.[11] The assumption that a play is a form of idol-worship seems to explain why Genevan reformers such as William Farel denounced religious plays in Geneva as having the potential to corrupt audiences just as idols had the power to pollute a chapel or a city. Marian exile Michael Cop preached a sermon condemning a production depicting the acts of the apostles during the time Christopher Goodman was in the city.[12] Scholars discussing English anti-theatrical arguments by Stephen Gosson, Philip Stubbes, and William Prynne and events like the Puritan shuttering of London theatres in 1642 regularly describe condemnation of plays as an extension of the iconoclastic vehemence earlier protestants directed at statues and shrines.[13]

While Goodman's statement might be seen as part of this anti-theatrical, image-hating protestant tradition, it cannot be seen as one voice in a unified chorus. The prominent reformer Martin Bucer viewed plays as a means to provide moral and religious education, not to mention wholesome entertainment, to young people.[14]

---

attention to 'spectacles of royal and civic power' found in later plays as a substitute. Stephen Greenblatt in *Shakespearean Negotiations* (Berkeley, 1988), 125–7 points out ways early modern commercial plays appropriate but empty out the outward manifestations of traditional religious practice. More recent studies of how protestant or Catholic controversies resonate through later plays similarly stress that their representations of the most theatrical expressions of belief must be disguised, parodied, interrupted, or otherwise contained seemingly because of the assumption (by contemporary critics themselves or by early modern officials) that audience members would over-identify with what they saw onstage, believing it to be problematically real; see Jeffrey Knapp, *Shakespeare's Tribe* (Chicago, 2002), 8.

[11] Clifford Davidson (ed.), *A Treatise of Miraclis Pleyinge* (Kalamazoo, 1993), 104–379. For reconsideration of the goals of this argument, see Lawrence Clopper, 'Is the *Treatise of Miraclis Pleyinge* a Lollard Tract Against Devotional Drama', *Viator* 34 (2003): 229–71.

[12] For discussion of these episodes, see Paul Whitfield White, 'Calvinist and Puritan Attitudes towards the Stage in Renaissance England', *Explorations in Renaissance Culture* 14 (1988), 42–3.

[13] For arguments equating plays with images, see Clifford Davidson, 'The Anti-Visual Prejudice', in Clifford Davidson and Ann Eljenholm Nichols (eds), *Iconoclasm vs. Art and Drama* (Kalamazoo, 1989), 33–46, and Theodore K. Lerud, *Memory, Images, and The English Corpus Christi Drama* (New York, 2008), esp. 51–62. For discussion of attempts to ban plays as a form of iconoclasm, see Clifford Davidson, '"The Devil's Guts": Allegations of Superstition and Fraud in Religious Drama and Art during the Reformation', in *Iconoclasm vs. Art and Drama*, 92–144.

[14] A translation of the section of *De Honestis Ludis* (published 1551) in which Bucer commends well-regulated religious plays can be found in Glynne Wickham, *Early English Stages, 1300 to 1660* (London, 1963), 2.329–31.

Calvin permitted the performance of religious drama in Geneva, and his successor Theodore Beza wrote a play about Abraham and Isaac.[15] English protestants seem to have followed the model provided by such continental reformers since the 1560s and 1570s witnessed the staging and printing of numerous reform-minded protestant plays designed to disseminate protestant doctrine, twenty-five of which have survived.[16] Goodman's comment was therefore not a reflection of protestant, Calvinist, or even Puritan thought; rather, it marks a cultural shift taking place from the first generation of English reformers that employed drama to a second generation that despised it.

Goodman's complaints pivot on key differences emerging between both reformed and traditional (protestant and Catholic) as well as between evangelical and reformed (first-generation and second-generation protestant) understandings of the purposes of religious drama. Protestant theologians debated whether images and plays would convert or corrupt those who viewed them even as protestant authors turned their hands to playwriting. Considering sixteenth-century English drama in the context of these shifting conditions suggests how audience members might have experienced religious belief in relation to key plays of the Chester cycle differently from how protestant reformers encouraged spectators to encounter drama that reworked cycle play conventions for evangelical purposes. Analyzing the stated goals and likely effects of religious drama from the time when the Chester cycle first shifted to Whitsun to the time when it was recorded in surviving manuscripts suggests that it was not just anti-Catholicism, iconoclasm, iconophobia, or a shift in the material conditions under which drama was written and performed that made a reform-minded protestant like Goodman hostile to religious drama. More significantly, Goodman's comments reflect an emerging understanding of the kind of belief generated by religious plays. The close association between drama and doubt is what best explains why later reformers, including Goodman, came not only to perceive cycles as impossible to reform but also to identify theatricalized performances of religious subject matter as an inappropriate and ineffective means of promoting unified protestant belief.

Those who study mystery cycles have long abandoned the notion that such drama manifested and regenerated a communally coherent experience of religious faith. But even arguments that debate whether plays like those performed in Chester reinforced social distinctions between townspeople and outsiders, highlighted structural inequalities among members of the town, allowed different groups to compete within the confines of a contained project, or even made possible

---

15   White, 'Calvinist and Puritan', 42–4.

16   The existence of such plays has been documented and discussed by John King, *English Reformation Literature* (Princeton, 1982), esp. 271–318 and most insightfully by Paul Whitfield White, *Theatre and Reformation* (Cambridge, 1993). The count of protestant biblical plays derives from Paul Whitfield White, 'The Bible as Play in Reformation England', in Jane Milling and Peter Thomson (eds), *The Cambridge History of British Theatre, Vol. 1: Origins to 1660* (Cambridge, 2004), 87–115.

oppositional subject positions still assume that, if plays were designed to teach audiences about or to foster some kind of religious belief, we have a sense of what that belief was like.[17] Official church doctrine, particularly eucharistic theology, was communicated through representations of biblical episodes, particularly the life of Christ, to generate sound faith and pious actions amongst the laity.[18] Whether scholars should ascribe the origins of these didactic goals to lay spiritual energies or to a clerical agenda or to some combination thereof is still open to debate.[19] Nevertheless, such religious faith is often described as a ubiquitous feature of medieval society, as what Charles Taylor calls 'a fact of experience' more than what we would label a 'theory' or 'belief', a unified system within which one might be alienated but outside of which one could not imagine existence.[20] The massive play cycles that emerged in towns like Chester, because they required cooperation among and participation from almost all members of a community, might be understood as monuments to this sort of belief.

But Steven Justice's recent article 'Did the Middle Ages Believe in Their Miracles?' challenges this understanding of pre-modern faith. Focusing on medieval narratives about contemporary miracles, Justice points out that these texts do not assume an awed and devout response to incidents in which saintly individuals instantaneously heal the sick or mysteriously describe far-off or future events. Rather, these narratives demand scepticism and even inspire doubt about the truth of what seems to some eye-witnesses to have been a miracle. Such doubt inheres to the structure and content of these narratives since there is no need to tell miracle stories if everyone already believes in them. Indeed, to suggest that everyone experienced the same kind of belief all the time is to profoundly

---

[17]   Analyses of cycle plays that associate their performances with social and economic tensions include John C. Coldewey, 'Some Economic Aspects of the Late Medieval Drama', in John C. Coldewey and Marianne Briscoe (eds), *Contexts for Early English Drama* (Bloomington, 1989), 77–101; Sarah Beckwith, *Signifying God: Social Relation and Symbolic Act in the York Corpus Christi Plays* (Chicago, 2001), 42–55; and Clifford Davidson, 'York Guilds and the Corpus Christi Plays: Unwilling Participants?' *Early Theatre* 9.2 (2006): 11–33. Claire Sponsler suggests that cycle plays enabled audience members to imagine themselves in opposition to their communities in 'The Culture of the Spectator: Conformity and Resistance to Medieval Performances', *Theatre Journal* 44.1 (1992): 15–29; this essay also offers a helpful overview of earlier scholarship promoting the 'communal' theory of medieval drama (17–19).

[18]   This set of assumptions is often implicit in arguments about cycle plays but is clearly expressed in Alexandra Johnston, 'An introduction to medieval English theatre', in Richard Beadle and Alan Fletcher (eds), *The Cambridge Companion to Medieval English Theatre*, 2nd edn (Cambridge, 2008), 1–25; Johnston links changes in church ritual and theology to 'the rise of drama for the laity', suggesting that drama was a means of educating everyday Christians about the essentials of their faith (4–7).

[19]   See Lawrence Clopper, *Drama, Play, and Game* (Chicago, 2001), esp. 207.

[20]   Charles Taylor, *A Secular Age* (Cambridge, 2007), 39. This passage is quoted and analyzed by Steven Justice in the article referenced below.

misunderstand the nature of religious faith. Referring to Aquinas's maxim 'Fides est de non visis', faith is in what you do not and cannot see, Justice argues that medieval faith was always characterized by doubt, doubt that made lively faith possible and that made rituals, sacraments, and participation in cycle plays both appealing and necessary.[21]

Taking Justice's theorizing of medieval faith seriously raises the question 'Did the middle ages believe in their plays?' Seeing doubt as key to traditional experiences of faith helps explain why the cycle plays, within their orthodox narrative of events stretching from creation to last judgment, include theatrical and metatheatrical elements that would arouse religious doubt in their audiences. Not surprisingly, such moments can be found in Towneley's *Thomas of India*, a play that explicitly values faith on the part of those who believe without seeing while having its characters repeatedly express disbelief in terms related to theatrical performance.[22] The play opens with Mary Magdalene calling upon the apostles to believe her news that Christ is risen by imploring 'Trist ye it and knawe' (28.3) and demanding 'Putt away youre heresy, / Tryst it stedfast and cowth' (28.23–4). Peter's and Paul's explanations of why they give no credit to Mary's eye-witness account emphasizes that appearances can be deceiving, but Paul stresses that it is Mary herself who cannot be believed:

> [I]t is wretyn in oure law,
> Ther is no trust in womans saw,
> No trust faith to belefe;
> For with thare quayntyse and thare gyle
> Can they laghe and wepe somwhile,
> And yit nothyng them grefe. (28.29–34)

As Paul condemns women not just for being inherently sinful, but for being sinful while presenting to the world the outward signs of religious faith, he points out that Mary cannot be trusted because she is too skilful an actor. This declaration from Paul and similar lines set off ripples of metatheatrical ironies across the rest of the play. The audience knows that Mary's news is true, Paul's misogynist rejection of it mistaken, because they know scripture and because have just seen the staged appearances of the resurrected Jesus before Mary Magdalene in *Resurrection* (twenty-six) and before fishermen in *Pilgrims* (twenty-seven). Yet Paul's statement simultaneously reminds them that the player performing the role of Mary Magdalene is only feigning the affective response one would have to being the first to witness the risen Christ. Paul's slights against women might be incorrect, but his warning about those who 'laghe and wepe somwhile, / And yit

---

[21]   Steven Justice, 'Did the Middle Ages Believe in Their Miracles?' *Representations* 103 (2008), 12.

[22]   Martin Stevens and A.C. Cawley (eds), *The Towneley Plays*, EETS SS 13, 14 (Oxford, 1994). Subsequent references to plays in this edition will be cited by play and line number in the text.

nothing theym grefe' could apply to all the performers who appear in this and other cycle plays. As a result, the play's most metatheatrical elements simultaneously generate doubt and encourage lively faith in audience members.

How did the people of Chester believe in what their cycle plays presented to them? They would have witnessed doubt from characters who act out their scepticism about orthodox belief, such as Simeon who feels the need to correct the erroneous prophecy that a virgin will give birth to the messiah (11.33–40). The cycle's many expositor figures suggest that an audience would need to have its faith reshaped after witnessing miraculous events like the annunciation and the nativity (6.564–643, 699–722), but among the Chester plays, the clearest example of productive doubt being linked to theatricality appears in the Dyers' *The Coming of the Antichrist*.[23] Antichrist's first appearance onstage features him delivering an ornate oration in Latin. His later declarations that he is 'Your saviour … Messias, Christ, and most of might, / that in the lawe was you beheight' (23.11–14) could be greeted with some scepticism – after all, this play follows one in which an Expositor declares 'As mych as here wee and our playe, / of Antechristes signes you shall assaye. / Hee comes! Soone you shall see!' (22.338–40). At least for the duration of the Latin speech, however, it might be unclear to the audience whom the player before them was impersonating; another expositor, a prophet, an apostle, or Christ himself might make remarkably similar appearances. In a group of plays that features numerous actors representing Jesus, Antichrist is much like one more player, most dangerous at the moments when his performance is most persuasive.

When the Antichrist presents miracles similar to those performed by Jesus in earlier plays, all miracles seem open to being perceived as nothing more than theatrical performances. The Antichrist not only fools an onstage audience into believing he is divine by raising the dead and resurrecting himself (23.77–104, 120–33), but also reminds the Chester audience that all the miracles they have seen on pageant wagons are merely stage tricks. These self-consciously theatrical and false miracles might even suggest the possibility that marvels performed by the historical Jesus and his apostles were also magical illusions. The play's climax privileges the body of Christ over the power of the Antichrist and thus precludes such radical doubt; when Enoch and Elijah perform the rituals that bless bread (and perhaps transubstantiate it into Corpus Christi), they become associated with a physical object that can distinguish between true Christian and false demonic sanctity both for the kings who have been duped by Antichrist as well as for all individuals watching the play (23.565–76). Still, their blessed wafer remains a prop in a play, Elijah and Enoch only players. All is feigned: the question of how to tell when one is seeing a real miracle persists.

---

[23]   For a rich discussion of the many ways in which this play seems to have been understood across the sixteenth century, see Richard K. Emmerson, 'Contextualizing Performance: The Reception of the Chester *Antichrist*', *Journal of Medieval and Early Modern Studies* 29.1 (1999): 89–119.

As these examples suggest, not just the content but the very form of religious drama could remind audiences that performance simulates outward signs and rituals of faith and thus generates doubt about religious truth. It seems, however, that such doubt was not antithetical but rather central to medieval belief. Through the doubts they generated plays might foment active devotion, giving audience members the impetus to reinvigorate their faith by participating in church rituals or by reading scripture, activities suggested by the Chester plays' numerous references to scriptural authority and orthodox doctrine. It does not follow, however, that experiences of scepticism sparked by religious drama emerged (or were generated) only to be contained by well-regulated and hierarchical medieval religious institutions. The complexity and heterogeneity of the period that gave rise to cycle plays in England, characteristics that have led James Simpson to label it a time of true 'reform' in contrast to the 'revolutionary' simplifications and centralizations of evangelical culture, encouraged the polyphonous performances of cycle plays to thrive.[24] These qualities of the plays also help to explain why they could be adapted and performed well into the reign of Elizabeth so that committed protestants like Christopher Goodman could see them. As Theresa Coletti has argued, the same 'medieval foundations' that led the Chester plays to focus on signs, prophecies, and the nature of divine power might serve as 'common ground with early modern popular religious and academic theology'.[25] These medieval elements likely to generate doubt in audience members also made it possible for the plays to be revised, accreting reformed and early modern elements, across the sixteenth century until they reached the state in which they were transcribed in manuscripts that survive today.

Medieval cycle drama does not insist and rely on a single audience response, but religious authors had good reasons to imagine that it did starting as early as the 1530s. Attempts to delimit precisely what constitutes correct and incorrect reception are ubiquitous in plays by evangelical reformers who reworked the conventions of traditional drama to promote protestant doctrine. John Bale's *God's Promises*, *Johan the Baptystes Preachynge*, and *The Temptation of our Lord*, along with several works now lost, have been described as pieces of a reformed cycle performed for elite and popular audiences under the patronage of Thomas Cromwell in the reign of Henry VIII and during Bale's ultimately unsuccessful

---

[24]   James Simpson, *Reform and Cultural Revolution* (Oxford, 2002), 2. A helpful critique of Simpson's arguments about drama is offered by Richard K. Emmerson, 'Dramatic History: On the Diachronic and Synchronic in the Study of Early English Drama', *Journal of Medieval and Early Modern Studies* 35.1 (2005): 39–66.

[25]   Theresa Coletti, 'The Chester Cycle in Sixteenth-Century Religious Culture', *Journal of Medieval and Early Modern Studies* 37.3 (2007), 542. For a related argument, see also Paul Whitfield White, 'Reforming Mysteries' End: A New Look at Protestant Intervention in English Provincial Drama', *Journal of Medieval and Early Modern Studies* 29.1 (1999): 121–47.

stint as a bishop in Ireland under the auspices of Edward VI.[26] Bale's plays are likely but a few surviving examples of a larger body of reformed responses to cycle plays that includes works by other evangelical writers such as Thomas Becon. Best known for his popular devotional work *The Sick Man's Salve*, Becon also composed *A newe dialog betwene thangell of God, & the shepherds in the felde*, a text John King has argued is a protestant version of a nativity play.[27] As these plays rely on the form but implicitly reject the content of traditional cycle drama, they are revolutionary, imagining Catholic beliefs exemplified by the feast of Corpus Christi (and the plays once associated with it) as a monolithic superstition that true Christians should expose and then discard.[28]

Not surprisingly, first-generation protestant drama shares with its traditional cycle forbears a focus on biblical events, for example Moses receiving the ten commandments and the shepherds being informed of their saviour's birth. But perhaps because of a concern that visually representing scriptural events made it more likely that their subject matter might become or be perceived as corrupted, plays by Bale and Becon diverge from their models in mostly avoiding references to, much less onstage simulations of, miracles.[29] Pater Coelestis and Justus Noah in *God's Promises* talk about how a rainbow will signify that 'The sees and waters so farre nevermore shall rage' (260), but ark, animals, and rainbow never appear. Explaining to the audience the significance of God's pact with humanity never to destroy the earth again with water seems more important than showing a symbol of that pact. In *The Temptatcyon of our Lord*, Satan Tentator disguises himself as a desert hermit by donning monastic garb (75–81), thus causing Christ's refusal of his request to turn stones into bread to function as a dismissal of the necessity

---

[26]   All subsequent parenthetical references to these plays are to line numbers in Peter Happé (ed.), *The Complete Plays of John Bale*, vol. 2 (Cambridge, 1986). For discussions of Bale's life and works, see King, *English*, 56–75 and 271–7; White, *Theatre*, 12–41; and Simpson, *Reform*, 528–39.

[27]   King, *English*, 290–97. Parenthetical references for this play are signature numbers in Thomas Becon, *A newe dialog betwene thangell of God, & the shepherdes in the felde concernynge the natiuite and birthe of Jesus Christ our Lorde & Sauyoure* (London, 1547[?]; STC 1733.5).

[28]   See Simpson, *Reform*, 7–33, for a discussion of how the idea of modernity relies upon othering the medieval by defining it as coherently superstitious; Simpson introduces in his argument the idea that protestant 'reformers' should more properly be termed revolutionaries since they seek to make a radical break from past traditions.

[29]   For an overview of why reformers might think visual representation more likely to corrupt than verbal expression, see Davidson, 'The Devil's Guts', 130–32. There is not, however, a complete lack of visual elements in these plays. For instance, *Johan the Baptystes Preachynge* features a dove speaking with the voice of God that descends at the moment when John baptizes Jesus. In *The Temptation of Our Lord*, Jesus strides down a flight of stairs rather than throwing himself to the ground. Moreover, since several of these plays (especially Becon's) feature songs, these are plays with some entertainment value, not anti-theatrical theatre or barely staged dialogues, contrary to what Simpson suggests (*Reform*, 532–5).

of spectacular miracles and as a condemnation of papist superstitions about visual signs. Replacing stage effects that represent miracles are numerous quotations from the bible in English. Anyone who reads Bale's plays with a bible on hand will understand why Bale's title pages claim he has compiled, rather than authored, these works. Becon's text references paraphrases of and quotations from scripture in densely packed marginal glosses.[30]

More significant than a turn away from the visual to the verbal, however, what makes Bale's and Becon's plays distinct from the cycles they imitate is their relentless insistence that a necessary condition of faith is knowledge of Christian doctrine and scripture. For this reason Becon's play alters the relationship between the angel and shepherds one finds in related cycle plays. In the Towneley *Second Shepherd's Play*, we see shepherds engaged in the business of sheep-swindling and country justice before they hear 'Gloria in Excelsis' (13.1–919). In Chester's cycle, the shepherds feast and wrestle before being dazzled by a blazing star and the sound of the angel's call (7.1–357). Both plays utilize the angel as a catalyst that shifts the shepherds from worldly existence to contemplation of the Christ child and thus, instantaneously, from lax to active faith. In contrast, Becon's angel begins to teach and preach before the shepherds enter. Working his way through numerous theological points, the angel catechizes the shepherds about the spiritual nature of Christ's kingdom and about the mechanisms of salvation, emphasizing the importance of God's mercy rather than meritorious works. The shepherds acknowledge the purpose of the angel's long speeches in their few interjections, as when they declare '[W]e greatly desire in this case / To be taught of thee so bounteous' (B6r). The longest speech uttered by the shepherds paraphrases in twenty-one quatrains (C8v-D1v) the major points relayed by the angel, thus revealing how well these pupils have learned their lessons. By the end of the play, the key point is that humans can achieve faith only in so far as individuals can come to God through understanding his teachings. The play's goal is to offer the shepherds, and thus its audience, such proper and properly limited knowledge.

Emphasis on knowledge is also at the core of Bale's plays. *God's Promises* opens with Baleus Prolocutor arguing for the value of the play by stating,

> Advantage might spring by the search of causes heavenly,
> As those matters are that the Gospell specify,
> Without whose knowledge no man to the truth can fall
> Nor ever attaine to the lyfe perpetuall. (4–7)

Bale distinguishes his play from other religious drama by having his prologue warn the audience not to expect 'tryfleing sporte / In fantasye fayned, nor soche lyke gaudysh gere' (17–18) for knowledge, not entertainment, is what 'shall your inwarde stomake stere / To rejoice in God for your justyfycacyon, / And alone in Christ to hope for your salvaycon' (19–21). Similarly, the prologue informs the

---

[30]   King observes that these glosses make the printed dialogue resemble 'a Protestant tract' as much as a play (*English*, 291).

audience of *The Temptation of our Lord* that their task as they watch the play is to 'Lerne' (15) since at this performance 'wyll Christ teache you in our next comedye; / Ernestly prente it in your quycke intelligence' (31–2). In *Johan the Baptystes Preachynge*'s 492 lines of text, the word 'knowledge' and its close cognates appear twelve times (not counting closely related words like 'edify', 'trow', and 'learn'). The prologue prepares the audience for this emphasis by directing them

> To accepte these newes and heavenlye verytees,
> Which are for our synne most soverayne remedye,
> And for our sowles healthe so highly necessarye,
> That without knowledge of them, we can not have
> A true fayth in him which dyed our sowles to save. (17–21)

Bale's drama does not elide knowledge with faith as his and Becon's plays repeatedly define faith as a gift from God. Understanding of doctrine, however, is presented as a necessary condition of true faith. An individual is most likely to receive God's gift after achieving knowledge.

Yet even as Becon's and Bale's plays present to their audiences knowledge that could set them on the path to true belief, they include theatrical, often visually striking, elements that might stimulate doubt. When Satan comes to Christ in the guise of a hermit, his costume lays waste to a traditional association between monastic garb and religious piety.[31] But it also calls attention to the fact that the appearance of sanctity can be either a manifestation of true faith or, as John the Baptist says when condemning the Pharisees and Sadducees, 'An outward pretence ... of holiness' (225). The players portraying Jesus Christus, Johanes Baptista, and Pater Coelestis are open to the same accusation as they outwardly and convincingly represent divine sanctity they do not necessarily possess. Bale's and Becon's plays make numerous attempts to contain any uncertainty they might generate. They rely on scriptural references and allusions to both sermons and catechisms to link their plays to widely recognized textual expressions of religious truth. Simultaneously, they limit interpretative possibilities through extensive use of prologues, epilogues, and other moments in which speakers directly address the audience and tell them how to understand properly what they have just seen. Such obvious efforts to generate a unified and informed response from a crowd, however, raise questions about whether drama is an appropriate medium for such a message.

Anxiety about whether theatrical performance can communicate religious truth was being expressed as early as the 1560s, as evidenced by the prologue to Lewis Wager's *Life and Repentance of Mary Magdalene*.[32] Even though this speaker

---

31   White, *Theatre*, 34–41, reads as iconoclastic similar moments in which vices disguise themselves as Catholic clerical figures in *Three Laws* and *King Johan*.

32   Parenthetical references cite Lewis Wager, *Life and Repentance of Mary Magdalene*, in Paul Whitfield White (ed.), *Reformation Biblical Drama in England* (New York, 1992), 1–66. For discussions of this play, see White's introduction, xix–xxxiv, as well as White, *Theatre*, 80–88.

notes of those who have 'spitefully despised' his troupe's playing 'I think they can alleage no reason' (12, 13), he spends six stanzas defending the value of religious drama. The prologue confidently declares, 'I saie, there was neuer thing inuented / More worth, for mans solace to be frequented' (36–7), but the play seems less sure of its implicit answers to questions like

> Doth not our faculty learnedly extol vertue?
> Doth it not teache, God to be praised aboue al thing?
> …
> What godly sentences to the mynde doth it bring? (31–5)

Mary's conversion seems a model for the audience as she first encounters and hears a sermonizing speech from God's Law (1113–48) who leads her to Knowledge of Sinne (1189–308, esp. 1189 and 1296) who prepares her to encounter, receive forgiveness from, and be introduced to Faith and Repentance by Christ Jesus (1321–540). Yet the straightforward message of salvation through faith is repeated not only in Christ's scripturally based explanation of 'the truth' (1853) to Simon the Pharisee but also throughout long speeches by Justification and Love that gloss for Mary the theological significance of the play (2049–134). While the play's content insists that knowledge is a necessary step towards faith, its relentless repetition and refining of the same few points hints that such knowledge might be difficult to obtain from a play featuring such distractions as an actor portraying Mary Magdalene washing Christ's feet with 'her' false hair, even if the action is performed as the stage direction insists '*as it is specified in the Gospell*' (1828 SD).[33] This stage Magdalene might well appear to be 'a harlot' (1836), as Infideltie calls her, more than a saint for having performed bawdy songs before a paying audience, no matter how convincing the simulation of tearful piety that follows.

As examples from cycle plays and from evangelical reworkings of traditional dramatic forms make clear, religious drama always makes doubt available when it embodies doctrine with players who necessarily feign sanctity during the time they are onstage. Religious plays therefore seem more compatible with expressions of religious faith reliant upon doubt than those dependent upon knowledge. Understanding this basic principle helps to explain the subtle and complex intersections between drama and faith in England across the entire sixteenth century. Scholars of renaissance and medieval drama have systematically chipped away at assumptions that sixteenth-century religious drama can be called either early modern and reformed or medieval and Catholic.[34] What's more, protestant

---

[33] Since Wager's play never requires more than five players, it seems intended for a small, traveling company that could feature its boy in the role of Mary Magdalene. See White, 'Bible as Play', 100–101 for analysis of the implications of having boy actors portray women in reformation drama.

[34] Emmerson, 'Dramatic' as well as David Aers and Sarah Beckwith, 'Reform and Cultural Revolution: Introduction', *Journal of Medieval and Early Modern Studies* 35.1 (2005): 3–11 suggest that this statement is more true of medievalists than early modernists,

drama has been demonstrated not to have immediately yielded or given rise to a secular, professional, London-centred theatre scene. Drama with medieval origins, like the Chester plays, was performed well into the 1570s. Thus, reform-minded protestants like John Bale, Thomas Becon, and Lewis Wager wrote plays that were successfully performed and printed while Catholic cycle plays were still being staged and revised. Such explicitly religious drama in both popular and academic settings existed concurrently with the construction of the first permanent playhouses in London suburbs, playhouses that showcased numerous plays one cannot argue were entirely secular and unconcerned with religious controversy.[35] Studies of the Queen's Men, among other companies, show that plays continued to be used to promote protestant politics and religion well into the reign of Elizabeth.[36] The so-called 'turn to religion' in early modern studies has documented the many ways in which plays associated with London's private and public theatres represented and wrestled with religious experience.[37] There is, in short, a continuous, if multifaceted, tradition of religious drama in Tudor England that can be traced from 1485 to 1603.

While recent scholarly work helpfully explores the complexity and continuity of sixteenth-century religious drama there remain ruptures that require explanation. Despite having models to follow like Bale, English protestant ministers seem to stop writing religious plays around 1580. Jeffrey Knapp convincingly demonstrates that not all English protestant clergy exhibited an anti-theatrical prejudice by showing that some continued to write and perform in plays as part of their university education after this date. Yet most of what Knapp calls 'clerical plays' focus on 'almost exclusively secular subject matter'.[38] Reasons why evangelical ministers came to abandon drama as a medium for communicating godly ideas to general audiences remain under-theorized. The notion that they did so because the establishment of permanent playing spaces in London made it impossible to divorce popular drama from physical sites of lewd behaviour seems inadequate in light of REED research, especially Paul Whitfield White's synthesis of it demonstrating that provincial and parish drama thrived well into the reign of James.[39] Patrick Collinson's assertion that a shift from iconoclastic to iconophobic attitudes among second-generation reformers led such serious protestant thinkers

---

but recent studies like Beatrice Groves, *Texts and Traditions: Religion in Shakespeare* (Oxford, 2007) are beginning to correct this imbalance.

[35]   For discussions of the first permanent London-area playhouses, see Julian Bowsher and Pat Miller, *The Rose and the Globe – Playhouses of Shakespeare's Bankside, Southwark* (London, 2010), esp. 19.

[36]   See Scott McMillin and Sally-Beth MacLean, *The Queen's Men and Their Plays* (Cambridge, 1998), 18–36.

[37]   Ken Jackson and Arthur Marotti, 'The Turn to Religion in Early Modern English Studies', *Criticism* 46.1 (2004): 167–90.

[38]   Knapp, *Shakespeare's*, 3.

[39]   Paul Whitfield White, *Drama and Religion in English Provincial Society* (Cambridge, 2008).

to abandon images, ballads, and plays as polemical and devotional tools has been criticized and corrected by historians including Collinson himself.[40] Yet the stubborn fact remains that we have no examples of explicitly religious drama by a protestant minister that can be dated later than Nathaniel Woodes's 1581 *Conflict of Conscience*.[41]

The problem seems to be with the nature of dramatic performance. Not just the visual elements of theatre, but also the fact that individuals could so easily appear to be something they are not, made the form Bale used to expose religious hypocrisy likely to generate religious doubt. By the second half of Elizabeth's reign, a period in which a range of confessional identities might be taken up by a religious individual, the most precise protestants might well have seen drama as too unpredictable a medium for disseminating straightforward doctrinal points.[42] Hotter protestants still regularly presented religious doctrine and polemic in drama-like forms, including catechisms and dialogues, but such texts were rendered less problematic by circulating for private readers, not popular performance.[43] A minister might enhance his sermon with an entertaining declamatory style, but his performance was limited by the implication that the preacher acted transparently in the role of himself.[44] Some reform-minded authors turned their strictly defined notions of religious truth into attacks on drama as they witnessed (and were sometimes satirized by) popular plays that promoted an Erasmian ecumenical vision of the sort Knapp associates with the dramatic authors he calls 'Shakespeare's Tribe'. Only by comparing the plays of Chester and other cycles to works by Bale and Becon that offer a reformed and revised version of this sort of entertainment can we understand why the most pure protestants so quickly shifted from writing to condemning drama. Indeed, such analysis calls attention to what makes drama unique as a literary genre. If drama when fully realized in live performance always encourages doubt, then it is a form that is well suited to, and

---

[40]   See Patrick Collinson, *From Iconoclasm to Iconophobia* (Reading, 1986). That English protestants utilized many types of visual imagery has been demonstrated ably by John King, *Tudor Royal Iconography: Literature and Art in an Age of Religious Crisis* (Princeton, 1989) and Huston Diehl, *Staging Reform, Reforming The Stage* (Ithaca, 1997), among others.

[41]   Nathaniel Woodes, *Conflict of Conscience* (London, 1581; STC 25966 and 25966.5); the title page of this explicitly Calvinist play identifies its author as 'Minister at Norwich'.

[42]   For an introduction to the idea that the reformation shifted from a dichotomous relationship between traditional religion and an evangelical movement to a plethora of confessional identities, see Wolfgang Reinhard, 'Reformation, Counter-Reformation, and the Early Modern State: A Reassessment', *Catholic Historical Review* 75.3 (1989): 383–404.

[43]   See Ritchie Kendall, *The Drama of Dissent* (Chapel Hill, 1986) for helpful analysis of such texts.

[44]   Bryan Crockett, *The Play of Paradox: Stage and Sermon in Renaissance England* (Philadelphia, 1995) argues that the performative elements of theatre and pulpit were often too close for comfort, at least for reform-minded protestants; see esp. 31–49.

that reveals continuity between, the 'reforming' mindset of traditional Catholic devotion and Elizabethan prayer-book protestantism.[45] It would simultaneously be troubling to anyone who attempted to promote a simple, unified, revolutionary ideology.

A list of atheistic blasphemies recorded about twenty years after Goodman wrote his list of 'absurdities' to the archbishop of York suggests reform-minded protestants were right to worry about religious drama. The 'Baines Note' accusing Christopher Marlowe of 'damnable judgment of religion and scorn of God's word', usually dated to 1593, reports that the playwright 'affirmeth that Moses was but a juggler' and that 'angel Gabriel was bawd to the holy ghost because he brought the salutation to Mary'.[46] It seems unlikely that the young Marlowe could have attended cycle plays although he might have witnessed other religious drama and pageantry in his native Canterbury.[47] In any case, the Baines note more securely serves as a record of popular conceptions of what constituted outrageous misbelief than of Marlowe's personal faith.[48] But, as Goodman might have predicted, anyone who witnessed portrayals of scripture in Chester could reach erroneous conclusions similar to those the Baines note lists. When Chester's pageant shows Moses rewriting on tablets the commandments that had been previously scribed by God himself, an audience member could suspect, as Marlowe supposedly said, that Moses used his knowledge of 'the arts of the Egyptians to abuse the Jews being a rude and gross people'. Chester's Gabriel might not seem a pander, but the play in which he appears features Joseph sounding like a cuckolded husband when

---

[45] This helpful term for Elizabethan Christians who conformed to the rituals and practices demanded by the official church derives from Judith Maltby, *Prayer Book and People in Elizabethan and Early Stuart Culture* (Cambridge, 1998).

[46] 'The Baines Note' (BL MS Harley 6848, ff. 185–6) is reproduced in Frank Romany and Robert Lindsey (eds), *Christopher Marlowe: The Complete Plays* (London, 2003), xxxiv–xxxv. For a helpful discussion of this document, see the introduction in the same volume, xx.

[47] The scant surviving evidence of civic biblical drama and saint plays in Kent suggests that such performances ceased in the 1530s, except for a passion play at New Romney that was presented as late as 1568. Marlowe's baptism in 1564 makes it unlikely he could have seen such performances. His connection to the King's School, however, would likely have exposed him to performances and pageantry associated with the cathedral. Certainly, an older alumnus of the same school, the anti-theatrical writer Stephen Gosson, had experiences of religious plays being performed and of performances in churches about which he would later complain. For information about performances in Canterbury, see James M. Gibson (ed.), *REED: Diocese of Canterbury* (Toronto, 2002), esp. lvi–lxiv. For discussion of churches as playing spaces, see Paul Whitfield White, 'Drama in the Church: Church-Playing in Tudor England', *Medieval and Renaissance Drama in England* 6 (1993), 15–35 and Jeanne McCarthy, '"The Sanctuarie is become a Plaiers Stage": Chapel Stagings and Tudor "Secular" Drama', *Medieval and Renaissance Drama in England* 21 (2008): 56–86.

[48] Helpful discussion of theories for interpreting the Baines note can be found in David Riggs, 'Marlowe's Quarrel with God', in Paul Whitfield White (ed.), *Marlowe, History, and Sexuality* (New York, 1998), 15–37, esp. 29–33.

he queries, 'Whoe hasse made her with chyld?' (6.124). Arguably, one reason why Goodman found it worth recording that 'Joseph chargeth his wife with open words, contrary to the Scriptures' (147.4) is that such exclamations could spark uncertainty about the virgin birth.

For reformers like Bale, Becon, and Goodman, experiencing such doubts and confusions could only lead to ill-formed belief, if not to superstition and heresy of the sort expressed in the Baines note. For those who experienced Chester plays in the context of a traditional faith community, this sort of doubt could reinvigorate faith. Marlowe might at some point in his life have followed speculation about the truth of scripture past reformation precepts into the realm of heterodoxy, heresy, and atheism, ultimately coming to see all religion as mere performance. Other playwrights contemporary to Marlowe seem more commonly to have represented religious doubt in ways that encouraged conformity and toleration. Such open-mindedness seems less in keeping with the teachings of evangelical reformers than with the traditional belief system associated with the medieval church, especially the assumption that doubt of the sort generated by dramatic performances of religious subject matter might lead to revived and lively faith.

Chapter 4
Dice at Chester's *Passion*

Matthew Sergi

In the gospels, the Roman crucifiers' gambling for Jesus' seamless garment at the foot of the cross is an act of the utmost profanity. And yet, as Matthew observes in his gospel, the crucifiers' gesture of disrespect lifts Jesus up further as the Messiah, by fulfilling a prophecy from Psalm 21:19: 'diviserunt sibi vestimenta mea et super vestem meam miserunt sortem' ['They divided among themselves my garments / and upon my vestment they cast lots'].[1] To the crucifiers, casting lots leaves events to chance; to Matthew, casting lots affirms that events are preordained fulfillments of God's promises. Like the Towneley plays and other contemporary variations on the scene, the Chester *Passion* renders the scriptural 'miserunt sortem' as a dice game.[2] Below, I discuss the staging cues embedded in the dark humour of Chester's dice game, which render its comedy anti-naturalistic to the point of absurdity – though glosses of the *Passion* as far back as 1607 have obscured its meaning simply by trying to make sense of it.

While the details of early performance cannot always be determined reliably, it is often possible to extrapolate and reconstruct certain performance logistics by ascertaining the practical requirements of extant dialogue, in a way that can allow scholars to incorporate new performance data into close analysis of the dramatic text. The Chester dice game provides a useful example of the value of such a reconstruction, because it reveals discontinuities between the written scene and its implicit comic staging. If the actors perform the nonsensical text of the dice game as written, they will flatten the dramatic diegesis and, in doing so, draw attention to the artifice of its frame. At multiple levels, from written dialogue to live performance, the Chester dice game draws attention to the inability of any scripted

---

[1]   Aloisius Gramatica (ed.), *Bibliorum Sacrorum, Iuxta Vulgatam Clementinam, Nova Editio* (Vatican, 1913), 480, 955. Translation mine.

[2]   For the Towneley *Play of the Dice* see Martin Stevens and A.C. Cawley (eds), *The Towneley Plays*, 2 vols, EETS SS 13 and 14 (New York, 1994), 1.309–22. Other early English examples include Lydgate's *Testament* ('Beholde the knyghts / which by their frowarde. Sate for my clothes / at the dyce to pley chaunce'), and the anonymous translation of scripture in the Church of England's 1534 *A Prymer in Englyshe* ('and as for his knytte cote which was without seme / because it coulde not wel be cut, they casted dyce for it that the. xxii. psalme myghte be fulfylled'). Manuscript images from both texts are available at *Early English Books Online* <http://eebo.chadwyck.com>. See John Lydgate, *The testament of Iohn Lydgate monke of Berry* (British Library, 1520; STC: 1:21), image 11 of 13; see also *A Prymer in Englyshe* (Bodleian Library, 1534; STC: 111:04), image 64 of 176.

action to enact the true operation of chance. It locates Matthew's portentous sense of prophecy and fulfillment in the medium of drama itself, aligning the divinely preordained with the theatrically pre-scripted, and opposing both to the limited logic of worldly happenstance. I argue here that the cartoonishly flat comedy implicit in the Chester dice game is richly symbolic, especially in contrast to non-comic elements of the cycle, to the Towneley *Play of the Dice*, and to aggressive Henrician reforms of recreation.

In the four out of five full-cycle manuscripts known as the Group Manuscripts, which descend from a lost source not shared by James Miller's fastidiously edited British Library MS Harley 2124, Chester's four Jews – who stand in for Jesus' Roman crucifiers in the *Passion* – call out their scores in confusing terms. The First Jew does not announce his score, but the Second Jew's confidence that 'this coate shalbe myne' (128) is confirmed by what he calls a 'good araye' (130) of 'dubletts'.[3] The Third Jew's 'cator-traye' (i.e., 'quatre-trois', 133) beats the 'dubletts' decisively, enough that the Third Jew tells his opponent 'goe thou thy waye … and leave this [garment] with mee' (134–6). The Fourth Jew's 'synnce' (i.e., 'cinques' or 'cinq', 143, 147) beats all previous rolls, an undeniably winning roll, 'well wonne … that every man might see' (146–8).

R.M. Lumiansky and David Mills gloss 'dubletts', 'cator-traye', and 'synnce' as 'three twos', 'three fours', and 'three fives', respectively.[4] I have found no evidence, however, to support those glosses.[5] In other late medieval and early modern texts, the terms are most often used in games involving two dice, though the Jews' game certainly involves 'dyce three' (90). Then again, as in modern

---

³   All references to the Chester plays are from R.M. Lumiansky and David Mills (eds), *The Chester Mystery Cycle*, 2 vols, EETS SS 3 and 9 (New York, 1974 and 1986). For more information on James Miller ('the first editor of the Chester cycle') and his manuscript, see R.M. Lumiansky and David Mills (eds), *The Chester Mystery Cycle: Essays and Documents* (Chapel Hill, 1983), 76. Parenthetical citations are to the line numbers.

⁴   Lumiansky and Mills, *Chester Mystery Cycle*, 2.250.

⁵   Multiple instances of the words have been collected in the *Oxford English Dictionary* and the *Middle English Dictionary*. See *OED*, s.v. 'doublet' 3a, 'cater, *n.* 2' 2a and 2b, 'trey, *n.*' 3; *MED*, s.v. 'cater, *num.*', 'trei, *n.*' 3. None of those instances use the terms according to the meanings that Lumiansky and Mills attribute to them. I have also run searches on multiple possible variant spellings of the terms through *Early English Books Online*, but have found no evidence to support Lumiansky and Mills's glosses. In researching this essay I have looked closely through the following early English works, but still have not found support for the glosses: Gilbert Walker, *A Manifest Detection of the Moste Vyle and Detestable Vse of Diceplay*, in Arthur F. Kinney and John Lawrence (eds), *Rogues, Vagabonds, and Sturdy Beggars: A New Gallery of Tudor and Early Stuart Rogue Literature Exposing the Lives, Times, and Cozening Tricks of the Elizabethan Underworld* (Amherst, 1990), 59–84; W.L. Braekman, 'Fortune-telling by the Casting of Dice: A Middle English Poem and its Background', *Studia Neophilologica* 52.1 (1980), 3–29; Charles Cotton, *The compleat gamester* (Harvard University Library/Wing c6382 136:12, London, 1674); Lambert Daneau, *Discourse of Gaming*, in *True and Christian friendshippe*, trans. Thomas Newton (London, 1586; British Library, STC [2nd edn]: 6230).

poker, early English gamblers sometimes named only the important cards (or dice) in a hand (or throw) of more than two. In 1674, for example, Charles Cotton reports that the game 'In and In' is 'play'd with four Dice – Out is when you have thrown no Dubblets on the four Dice; Inn is when you have thrown Dubblets of any sort [on the four dice], as two Aces, two Deuces'.[6] Here and elsewhere, 'dubblets' clearly refers to any pair of dice that show the same number, regardless of what that number is. Two French or Latinate numbers together usually signified a particular pair of numbers (as in 'cator-traye'; compare to terms like 'Ace-Ten' in modern blackjack or poker). Gilbert Walker's 1538 *Manifest Detection of Diceplay* uses 'cator-traye' only to signify a roll of one four and one three; the fifteenth-century game-poem 'Fortune-Telling by the Casting of Dice' uses only 'catores traye' – with 'cator' consistently in the plural – for a roll of three fours.[7] As for Chester's final dice roll, the Group Manuscripts offer spellings of 'synnce', 'synnes', 'since', or 'synke'. Except in the final case, these spellings could signify 'cinq' in the singular or plural, while the final case looks decisively singular; there is no reason, then, to prefer Lumiansky and Mills's reading of 'fives' (i.e., all fives) over 'five' (that is, in total, or on one die).

In short, the Group Manuscripts' game-rules match no medieval or early modern gambling game that I have been able to find.[8] The Jews have rolled a pair, then a three and four, then a five (perhaps two or three fives), but each boastful dicer is convinced that his roll is good enough to win the garment – until he loses to the dicer who follows him. Since the second and third rolls are named according to the scores on only two out of three dice ('dubletts' and 'cator-traye'), winning the game cannot be a matter of scoring the highest total on all dice.[9] The Towneley *Play of the Dice* provides a helpful counter-example here. Its game, in which the highest total score wins, is simple and clear. Its dicers roll thirteen, then eight, then seven, then fifteen: an out-of-order series that realistically simulates the unpredictability of chance, especially when the unexpected fifteen suddenly beats Pilate's thirteen (351). Pilate's ability to claim the robe regardless of chance (369–71) – as a function of his earthly power – is a somewhat chilling comment on the absence of fair play under tyranny.

The Chester Group Manuscripts' dice rolls, as the Jews interpret them, seem to count purposefully upward – though they do so in a way that is disconnected

---

6   Cotton, *The compleat gamester*, 164 (image 91 of 125).

7   Walker, *A Manifest Detection*; Braekman, 'Fortune-telling by the Casting of Dice'; *MED* s.v. 'cater, *num.*'

8   'Novem-cinq' is the game used in all the examples in Walker, *A Manifest Detection*, and also described in Cotton, *The Compleat Gamester*; in it, a five is an especially bad roll.

9   Furthermore, if the game were won by the player who scored highest – which does not seem to be the case, since all three dice are never named, nor is the sum – then the Third Jew should beat the Fourth Jew. The most likely reading for the Fourth Jew's 'synnce' is as a total score of five, while the Third Jew's 'cator-traye' must total at least eight (playing with three dice, if one die shows four dots and another shows three).

from any attested usage of the terms. Each player is himself numbered, and rolls
in turn: the Second Jew's 'dubletts' (which sounds like 'deux'), the Third Jew's
'cator-traye' ('quatre', 'trois'), the Fourth Jew's 'synnce' ('cinq'). The fact that the
Jews boast of each successive score as a sure winner, and then watch each score
trump the one before it, has the opposite effect from Towneley's simulation of
unpredictability: the series suggests that chance has given way at Chester to fate,
to absurd humour, to cheating, or to all of these.[10] Indeed, the Jews' scores seem to
work better as puns than as quantities in any real game; they may only be a pastiche
of gambling terms nonsensically recited in a display of oblivious foolishness, like
the Chester shepherds' misreadings of the Latin *Gloria*. Just as sexual jokes find
their way into the shepherds' gibberish, there could easily be a Middle English
pun on the Jews' 'doublet' (Jesus' garment), and perhaps on 'synke' as 'a pit for
sewage, a cesspool' (creating a pun at the expense of the Fourth Jew when the
First Jew looks at him and announces, 'synke there was / that every man might
see', 147).[11] Any or all of these readings make clear that the Jews' score-calling
subsumes realistic chance under comic conceits. Arnold Williams has criticized
the Chester cycle because it lacks 'the naturalism which fifteenth-century revisers
introduced into the other cycles'; I contend that Chester's anti-naturalistic comedy,
as the dice game exemplifies, is symbolically rich *because* it is simple and flat.[12]
The senselessness of the game bears meaning – and the Chester *Passion*'s game of
dice evacuates itself of sense at multiple levels beyond score-calling.

While the Towneley stage directions tend to be sparser than those at Chester,
the Towneley Torturers' dialogue makes quite clear precisely when each dice roll
should occur and what score should be the result. I have inserted those rolls in
brackets:

> *Pilatus*. I assent to youre sayng; assay now I shall,
>   As I wold at a wap wyn al at ones. [Roll: 13]
> *2 Tortor*. Aha, how now! here ar a hepe.
> *Pilatus*. Haue mynde then emang you how many ther ar.
> *3 Tortor*. xiii ar on thre, thar ye not threpe.
> *Pilatus*. Then shall I wyn, or all men be war.
> *1 Tortor*. Truly, lord, right so ye shall;
>   Bot grefe you not greatly, the next shall be nar,
>   If I haue hap to my hand – haue here for all! [Roll: 8]

---

[10]   Lumiansky and Mills's glosses of 'three twos', 'three fours', and 'three fives' create
an even more comically improbable series – think of the cinematic poker games in which
obviously cheating players present four-of-a-kind, then a straight flush, then a royal flush.
Those glosses, which would suggest that chance has been compromised in the *Passion* –
both by the possibility of cheating and by the fatalism of prophecy – would strongly support
the arguments I put forward in this essay. Since I have thus far been unable to find support
for the glosses, however, I have not included a further discussion of them.

[11]   *OED*, s.v. 'doublet, *n*.' 1a; 'sink, *n*.' See also Lumiansky and Mills, *Chester Mystery
Cycle*, 2.117, on the puns in the shepherds' gibberish.

[12]   Arnold Williams, *The Drama of Medieval England* (East Lansing, 1961), 57.

> *Pilatus.* And I haue sene as greatt a freke of his forward falyd;
>   Here are bot viii turnyd vp all at ones.
> *1 Tortor.* Aght? a, his armes, that is yll! (327–38)

Pilate announces his upcoming roll as a future event ('assay now I shall', 327) when the results of the roll are as yet just the stuff of wish and desire ('I wold at a wap wyn', 328). The dice must land immediately before the Second Torturer exclaims 'Aha', after which the roll is spoken of as a present fact ('here ar a hepe', 329). The remaining rolls proceed in the same way: the verb tenses pivot from future to present after a phatic or imperative utterance cues the throw ('Aha' at 329, 'haue here' at 335, 'war you away / Here' at 344–5, 'I byd you go bet' at 350). The timing ensures that the characters' positive or negative reactions to the dice throws are synchronized with the vicissitudes of a seemingly random series of scores.

Like the Towneley plays, the Chester Group Manuscripts rely on verbal cues rather than stage directions in their representations of the dice game, but their cues are much less clear to modern readers. The Group Manuscripts' cues tend to divorce the action of the rolls from the players' reactions to them:

> *Secundus Judeus.* Take! [Roll 2] Here, I darre laye,
>   Are dubletts in good araye.
> *Tertius Judeus.* [Roll 3A?] Thou fayles, fellowe, by my faye,
>   to have this to thy fee,
>   for here is cator-traye.
>   Therefore, go thou thye waye
>   and as well thou maye,
>   and leave this with mee. [Roll 3B?]
> *Quartus Judeus.* Fellowes, verament,
>   I read we be at on assent. (129–38)

The Third Jew boasts of his win ('Thou fayles') as soon as he speaks. Nor is his boast idle: it is part of a sentence structured causally around the word 'for', with the effect preceding the cause (i.e., 'you fail, because I have rolled cator-traye'). At only two moments can the Third Jew roll the dice in order to preserve the logic of his lines, marked by 'Roll 3A' and 'Roll 3B', above. Roll 3A would require the Third Jew to roll silently before he speaks, so that the first thing he says is in response to his own roll of 'cator-traye'. Roll 3B would require that both 'dubletts' and 'cator-traye' refer back to Roll 2: in other words, the Third Jew argues that a pair would usually win, but not when a four and a three are also present in the same roll (i.e., a roll of 3-3-4 or 3-4-4). In that reading, the Third Jew must then throw Roll 3B after the fact without addressing his own score.

Either roll, 3A or 3B, would present a naturalistic interpretation of the dialogue. Both readings, however, require uncharacteristic pauses in the clownish banter, to leave enough time for the otherwise talkative Third Jew to pick up, shake, toss, and wait for his dice to land, without speaking. Roll 3B might allow the Third Jew to pick up the dice as early as 'Therefore, go thou thye waye', but it would force him to take his own turn without commenting on it or reacting to his score. A silent roll would be out of character for any torturer at Chester; rather, it would weaken the contrast of the Jews to the laconic Jesus in this scene.[13] Whether they are punching, spitting, hammering, or gambling, the four Jews elsewhere find it necessary to describe most of their actions as they execute them. The need for such narration is particularly high in outdoor theatre when engaging with small props that are difficult to see, like nails (or dice): 'I shall dryve one / this nayle to the end' (171–2); 'will yee see / howe sleight I shalbe / this fist, or I flee, / here to make fast?' (177–80); 'I dryve yn / this ilke iron pynne' (194–5); 'Fellowes, will you see / howe I have stretched his knee?' (209–10).

The Second Jew's Roll 2 is a good example of such narration. His imperative 'Take! Here', like the Towneley First Torturer's 'haue here', must cue a dice roll (probably 'Take!' when the dice are thrown and 'Here' when they land). There is little else that 'Take' could mean. One-syllable exclamations, particularly words that affirm immediacy and presence (like 'here'), signify the four Jews' percussive physical action in Chester's *Trial and Flagellation of Christ* buffeting episode, where they clearly represent individual punches:

> *Primus Judeus.* For his harming *here*
>   [nighe] will I near ... (70–71)
> *Primus Judeus.* Fye upon the, freyke!
>   *(dans alapam)* Stowpe *nowe, nowe,* and creake. (86–7)[14]

Based on stylistic precedent, the *Passion*'s Second Jew should cast the dice on 'Take! Here', and then the Third Jew should pick up the dice as he says 'Thou fayles' and cast them while speaking 'for *here* is cator-traye'. The distinction between that reading (Roll 3C, below) and the alternate readings containing Roll 3A or 3B (above) is clearest when performed aloud.

> *Secundus Judeus.* Take! [Roll 2: 'dubletts'] Here, I darre laye,
>   Are dubletts in good araye.
> *Tertius Judeus.* Thou fayles, fellowe, by my faye,
>   to have this to thy fee,
>   for here [Roll 3C: 'cator-traye'] is cator-traye.
>   Therefore, go thou thye waye
>   and as well thou maye,
>   and leave this with mee. (129–36)

---

[13] Sarah Beckwith has written on the contrast between the crucifiers' prolixity and Jesus' silence in the York *Crucifixion*; the same effect clearly occurs in the corresponding episode at Chester. See Sarah Beckwith, *Signifying God: Social Relation and Symbolic Act in the York Corpus Christi Plays* (Chicago, 2001), 65–70.

[14] The repetition of *nowe* in the second example only occurs in one of the five full-cycle manuscripts (Huntington Library MS 2, San Marino California). See Lumiansky and Mills, *Chester Mystery Cycle*, 1.xii–xiv and textual notes at 288.

The Third Jew claims his win, *then* casts the roll by which he claims his win. As soon as the Second Jew says 'I darre laye', 'cator-traye' is already predicted in the stanza's rhyme scheme – and the boast that the Third Jew makes, building toward the causal 'for', seems to play consciously with that prediction. A naturalistic actor, concerned with the illogic of hints that the Third Jew knows his score ahead of time, might read the lines as an overconfident boast that claims the winnings before they are won, with no foreknowledge. That actor would have to ignore, or creatively undermine, the causal construction built upon the word 'for' ('you fail, *because* here is "cator-traye"') – working against the text for his interpretation. He would also have to ignore the implicit prediction of his score in the rhyme scheme of the stanza initiated by his opponent, limiting the text's capacity for wordplay.

As written, the text most readily points toward a different (and less anachronistic) style of performance, more like the artifice typical of commedia dell'arte, in which actors do not pretend to be unaware of the conceits that govern their narrative. The timing of Chester's dice rolls, like the naming of the scores, thus prioritizes comedy over sense. It calls for actors not only to announce nonsensical scores, but also to time those announcements to suggest that all players know the scores before they see them, in lines whose rhyme scheme builds upon the predictability of those announcements. That comic progression of scores, each one beating the one before it, is repeated in the same order at each wagon station, every year that the players perform. In privileging comic artifice over diegetic logic, Chester's *Passion* underscores the fact that not only the players, but also the audience members, anticipate the scores and their sequence from station to station and from year to year. Fittingly, then, in contrast to the Towneley torturers' emphatic expressions of shock, fury, and elation at the results of their rolls, the Chester Jews never respond to their scores with anything resembling surprise.

Lumiansky and Mills have called James Miller, the scribe of Harley 2124 whose version often disagrees with the Group Manuscripts, 'the first editor of the Chester cycle'.[15] They suggest that Miller 'seems not to understand' the scoring terms, but a closer look at Miller's text reveals what may be an attempt to make more sense of the game – a possibility more in keeping with Miller's usual fastidiousness.[16] I include Miller's unique readings in italics, with Group Manuscript variants in brackets:

> *Secundus Judeus.* Take! Here, I darre laye,
>   *a rowndfull in good fay.*   – *Jacet et perdit.*
>   [are dubletts in good araye.]
> *Tertius Judeus.* Thou fayles, *fellowe,* by my faye,
>   to have this to thy fee,
>   for *it was* cator-traye.
>   [for here is cator-traye.]
>   Therefore, go thou thye waye   – *Jacet et perdit.*
>   and as well thou maye,
>   and leave this with mee. (129–36)

15   Lumiansky and Mills, *Essays and Documents*, 76.
16   Lumiansky and Mills, *Chester Mystery Cycle*, 2.250.

Miller, who may have been a witness to the final performances of the *Passion*, adds stage directions in the margins and places them within one line of where I have estimated Rolls 2 and 3C. The rolls' timing has not shifted from the Group Manuscripts; rather, the logic of the dialogue shifts to fit the timing. The Second Jew's 'dubletts' becomes 'a rowndfull', an unspecified roll. Miller's Third Jew names the Second Jew's roll in the past tense ('Thou fayles … for it was cator-traye'), announcing after the fact that the 'rowndfull' contained a three-four combination, and then rolling. Just as he often corrects the meter of his exemplar (by adding 'fellowe' above, for instance), Miller seems to have attempted to introduce order into the dice game.

The timing of Miller's stage direction for the Fourth Jew, however, still overtly assumes that the players and onlookers have implicit foreknowledge of the scores:

> *Tertius Judeus.* and as well thou maye,
>   and leave it with mee. [Roll 4A?]
> *Quartus Judeus.* Fellowes, verament,
>   I read you all on assent.
>   This gaye garment
>   that is withou seame,
>   you give by my judgment
>   to mee this vestement,   *– Jacet et vincit.* [Roll 4B]
>   for syyes God hath me sent,
>   thinke you never so sweene. (134–44)

Logically, the Fourth Jew should have to roll the winning 'syyes' (Miller's version of 'synnce') at Roll 4A, since his first line begins a sentence that claims the garment as his winnings by unanimous assent of his fellows.[17] In performance, Roll 4A would introduce a problem with pacing and character: the boastful Fourth Jew would have to roll in silence before speaking. Miller places the winning roll at 4B, six lines *after* the Fourth Jew starts claiming his winnings. That claim, like the Third Jew's, comes in a sentence structured causally around the word 'for' (i.e., 'I advise, by way of my judgment, that you give the gay garment to me, *for* [because] God has sent me "syyes"'). For a naturalistic actor to retain Miller's stage direction but to still disallow the Fourth Jew's foreknowledge of the roll, he must in some way resist the extant text so that the six lines do not lead up to the causal 'for'.

The modern actors for the Chester 2010 *Passion* in Toronto were not working within any assumed context of naturalism. In the base text for that production, Alexandra Johnston places the dice rolls on the same lines that Miller does:

> *3rd Soldier.* Thou fails, fellow, truly,
>   to have this to thy fee,
>   for here is quatre-trais.

---

[17]   'Syyes' is less likely a variant on 'cinq' than on 'six' (though Miller's First Jew still refers back to the same roll as 'synke' later on). Perhaps Miller saw it as illogical that the Fourth Jew should win with a five (see note 8), and so attempted (if only partially) to emend it.

He throws and loses.
Therefore go thou thy way,
and as well thou may,
and leave this with me.
4th Soldier. Fellows, verament,
I propose we be at one assent.
This gay garment
that is without seam,
you give by judgement
to me this vestment,
He throws and wins.
for cinques God hath me sent,
think you never so swem.[18]

In Johnston's version, the Third Soldier announces the defeat of his opponent, *then* explains that defeat to have been caused by 'quatre-trais', *then* rolls, and *then* claims the robe as his own. The Fourth Soldier begins his claim well before he wins. Johnston's comma after 'vestment' (mimicking Lumiansky and Mills's punctuation) makes clear that the sentence built around 'for' is continuous and causal, though its effect precedes its cause (*'He throws and wins'*). Johnston's and Miller's texts do not require stringent realism from their gamblers – only boastful and brash comedy.

In all five medieval manuscripts the First Jew graciously confirms the Fourth Jew's win (though perhaps with a subtle pun on 'synke', as I mention above):

[W]ell wonne yt thou hasse,
for synke ther was
that every man might see. (145–8)

For the absurd game of the Chester *Passion*, visual confirmation of the dice score is all that is needed to assure all players of fairness: 'every man might see' the 'synnce'. In contrast, the Towneley dice game is interrupted by Pilate's two accusations of cheating, which assume visual confirmation to be suspect.[19] But in the streets of Chester, outside the diegesis, such an affirmation of faith in visuality comically contrasts with what the players are actually doing: staring blankly at mimed dice (as at Chester 2010), or falsifying the scores on prop dice (which could not actually have come up 'dubletts', 'cator-traye', and 'synnce' at every performance) – evidence that *no* man might see. No medieval player or audience expected any suspension of disbelief in order to enjoy the play, but the dice game's comedy exploits the unreality and superficiality of the diegesis, which is most evident when the First Jew visually confirms the final score in his mock-game.[20]

---

18 Email with Alexandra Johnston, 18 May 2010.

19 Towneley *Play of the Dice*, ll. 351–62.

20 V.A. Kolve, *The Play Called Corpus Christi* (Stanford CA, 1966), 22–3.

The gamblers' flawed reliance on visuality is a reminder that Chester's version of the Passion re-imagines Jesus' crucifiers as four *Jews*. Sheila Christie points out elsewhere in this volume that the Chester cycle presents unusually positive characterizations of Octavian, Pilate, and other Roman characters; it makes sense that the cycle should reassign Rome's worst biblical sins to non-Roman characters. Meanwhile, V.A. Kolve has already argued convincingly that the presence of the crucifiers' unserious dice game is a symptom of their inability to see the human impact of their acts – supporting Jesus' judgment that they 'know not what they do'.[21] In addition, the live performance of the Chester dice game embeds the Jews' blindness in a specifically Christian interpretive context by implying a distinction between literal and figural hermeneutics. The First Jew sees and reads what he believes to be plain information in front of him, while the Christian witnesses around him can see that he is looking at nothing at all, or reporting false scores from prop dice. Within the conspicuously thin diegesis, none of the Jews sees anything unusual or portentous about the improbable progression of nonce-rolls, nor about his opponents' ability to predict those rolls before they are cast. Chester's Jews are clowns who wander into the most portentous moment in Christian history and who, unable to see its fatalism, try to play with chance. Chance fails in the Towneley version too, but it fails because Pilate's earthly power supersedes it; at Chester, the power that defeats chance exists outside of the Jews' world, where the Christian revellers sit, laughing – and where the visibly present bleeding God waits and watches knowingly. In the same way that they are oblivious to the Cestrian comic pattern that governs their actions, the Jews are unaware of the still greater divine pattern that contains them. They quite literally forget – and have to be reminded by an annoyed Caiaphas – that Jesus stands there before them, waiting for the prophecy to get underway: 'Men, for cockes face / how long shall pewee-ars / stand naked in that place? / Goe nayle him on the tree!' (149–52). 'For cockes face' reminds us of the presence of Jesus' body and gaze, while its use as a phatic oath emphasizes the Jews' lack of attention to that body and gaze. The conspicuous lack of realism and failure of visuality in the comic dice game provides a stark contrast to Jesus' physical, visible presence nearby, and to the tragic torture that Jesus undergoes. The Chester 2010 *Passion* mimed the dice, but it used unsettlingly realistic stage make-up for the wounds on Jesus' back. The body of Christ in the modern production was especially shocking, moving, and meaningful because it stood in contrast to the less realistic conceits that surrounded it. That powerful contrast was not an accident of modern staging; rather, it is implicit in the extant text of the Chester *Passion*.

At the end of the dice game, the Fourth Jew brags that his dicing win is divine: 'you give by judgment / to mee this vestement, / for synnce God hath me sent' (141–3). These lines introduce the notion that the Jews believe that their game of chance constitutes an appeal to divine right. In the context of performance, however, the fact that Jesus himself is standing unnoticed, naked, and awaiting

---

[21]   Ibid, 175–205.

his fate, asserts that the nature of that divine order is not what the Jews expect. Early English writing on gambling acknowledges that lots and dice can be a valid gauge of divine intention. Lambert Daneau's *Discourse of Gaming* (translated into English by Thomas Newton of Cheshire) distinguishes between good, serious reasons to cast lots and 'sporting toyes and friuolous causes', which 'tempt God', 'as though we would make God, seruaunt to our vanities and pastimes'.[22] In *Dives and Pauper*, Pauper condemns lot- and dice-casting 'withoutyn nede and only for vanyte', but accepts both for the 'ʒeuyng of þyng þat may nouʒt wel ben departyd, or whan men ben in doute what is to don'.[23]

Significantly, the Chester cycle is the only medieval biblical cycle to stage the Apostles' lot-casting at Pentecost. Peter's plea for a sign from God – 'lord, that knowest all thinge … shewe us here by some tokeninge / whom that we shall take' (50–52) – is, fundamentally, no different than the Fourth Jew's 'synnce God hath me sent'. By Daneau's and Pauper's standards, the four Jews' lot-casting is acceptable in that it doles out property that 'may nouʒt wel ben departyd'. It is only because the *Passion* sets up its dice-playing as hollow and simple, a false appeal to divinity that undeniably falls on the side of frivolity and vanity, that it can stand in contrast to the Apostles' proper lot-casting. Considered together, the *Passion* and the *Pentecost* map out the full range of human relationships to chance and to divine providence. The dice game illustrates the hazards of misinterpretation and self-deception; after the dice have already been cast, the Fourth Jew retroactively claims to understand God's intentions even as he prepares to crucify God's son. In contrast, Peter recognizes his own subjection to Providence, asking for a sign ('some tokeninge') to guide him before he casts the lots. The Chester plays thus provide their audiences with positive and negative examples of hermeneutics, demonstrating clearly how Christians should and should not respond to signs from God.

The symbolic power of the dice game, meanwhile, must have shifted considerably in performances after 1528. In that year, Henry VIII proclaimed a universal prohibition of 'Dyce Cardes and other vnlaufull games'.[24] Other monarchs had prohibited these practices before, but only for certain classes or groups (apprentices, servants, clergymen, labourers, or artisans); Henry not only commands all of England to stop gambling, but also authorizes his men to seize and burn the dice, cards, and other gaming equipment, especially if they find them in 'any Hosterye Inne or Alehouse'.[25] The inflammatory rhetoric of that proclamation found its way into the 1540 legislation of Cestrian mayor

---

[22]   Daneau, *Discourse of Gaming*, images 50–51 of 60.

[23]   Priscilla Heath Barnum (ed.), *Dives and Pauper* EETS 275 (Oxford, 1994), 1.part 1.166–7.

[24]   Henry VIII, *The proclamacion made and de[vised by the] kynges hyghnesse our soueraygne lorde and his honorable counsaile* (London, 1528; British Library, STC [2nd edn]: 7771), image 2 of 2.

[25]   Ibid.

Henry Gee, which proscribed 'vnlaufull games' locally.[26] Henry VIII presumably targeted hostelries, inns, and alehouses because, as spaces that were at once public and enclosed, they provided room for prohibited practices but hid them from the view of authorities. Walker and Daneau assume throughout their sixteenth-century treatises that dice gambling remains a common practice behind closed doors. The Chester *Harrowing*'s distinctly Cestrian Alewife is certainly guilty of 'Usynge cardes, dyce, and cuppes smale' in her establishment (33ƒ).

An indoor context sheds further light on the Chester *Passion* dice game. As the episode begins, the First Jew tells his fellows to lay Jesus' garment 'on boord or we blyn!' (88); ME *boord* is only attested for wooden surfaces.[27] The 'boord' can be explained with some strain as the floor of the wagon, though it is most probable that the dice game (as at Chester 2010) would have taken place in the *platea*, rather than on the wooden floor of the wagon, whose space would already have been crowded by three crosses. As Lumiansky and Mills point out, however, the First Jew's reference to a wooden surface remains confusing, since his scene is meant to take place outdoors.[28] Even more confusing is the Second Jew's reference to a 'halle': 'Iche man in this halle / wottes I doe not amysse' (111–12). The editors comment:

> [A 'halle'] seems inappropriate to the setting on Calvary and seems rather to be part of an appeal to the audience. It might be used as evidence of an indoor performance, in a hall. Alternatively, the noun may represent *hale* n (2), MED 'a temporary structure for housing, entertaining, eating meals, etc.; an open pavilion, a tent', of which *halle* is a recorded variant.[29]

The lines may suggest that the dice game represents a fragment of the cycle that dates back to fifteenth-century Corpus Christi stationary performances.[30] A pavilion or tent would be unnecessary (and difficult to build) around most of the sixteenth-century wagon stations, which were surrounded by Chester's elevated Rows. In the context of their sixteenth-century performance and inscription, 'boord' and 'halle' suggest instead that dicing is an activity which automatically brings with it some assumption of an indoor setting. These terms thus imply that, in the Chester *Passion*, the indoors is displayed outdoors.

In 1570, Elizabeth I tempered Henry's proclamation somewhat, legalizing previously 'unlawful games', prohibiting the dicer from playing 'for his ... gayne, lucre, or lyuyng' (unless he made £100 or more per year) and ordering local

---

[26]   In the dissertation chapter from which this essay is drawn, I discuss at more length the similarity between the two decrees. See Elizabeth Baldwin, Lawrence M. Clopper, and David Mills (eds), *REED: Cheshire including Chester* (Toronto, 2007), 1.75.

[27]   *MED*, s.v. 'boord, *n.*'

[28]   Lumiansky and Mills, *Chester Mystery Cycle*, 2.249–50.

[29]   Ibid.

[30]   For the stationary performances, see Lawrence M. Clopper, 'The History and Development of the Chester Cycle', *Modern Philology* 75.3 (1978), 220–21.

authorities to search for and seize (but not to burn) the gaming equipment.[31] Still, a 1591 'Report of the Council of the North on Abuses in Cheshire' suggests a disconnection between Tudor gaming laws and their local execution:

> In Churche townes and in divers other places of those Counties, Cockefightes and other exceeding unlawefull games are tolerated vpon Sondaies & holidays at the tyme of devyne Seruice, And oftentimes thereat are present divers of the Iustices of the peace of the same Counties, And also some of the eccliasticall Commisioners.[32]

This weak enforcement of English law in Cheshire might remind us of the many conflicts between sovereign and local power recently described by Robert Barrett and Tim Thornton, but it resonates especially with the final two performances of the Chester cycle itself, another *game* condoned by local authorities despite its 1572 prohibition by authorities outside Cheshire.[33] Sixteenth-century Cestrian players, whose participation in the plays was itself an act of resistance against Tudor reforms that were systematically destroying local traditions, might have delighted in the mock-up of an illegal form of recreation (dice gambling) *within* a questionably legal form of recreation (the cycle). The cartoonish artifice of that *pleie*-within-a-*pleie* (the early English term *pleie* encompasses sports, spectacles, theatrics, and gambling) at once ensures that its players are not actually engaging in any illicit activity and emphasizes the metadramatic impact of their flippant mock-up.[34] On a theological level, the mock-dice game affirms the blindness of the Jews to the portents of the crucifixion and to the inevitable progression of prophecy, creating a gap between the ignorance of the characters and the hermeneutic sophistication of the Christian actors and their audience of revellers. On a political level, the dice game functions at the moment of performance as a ludic practice specifically and fervently prohibited by the sovereign's earthly authority, though condoned by local authority; resistance is thus representationally acted out in the open air, long after actual dice-play had had to retreat indoors. In contrast to the triumph of Pilate's authority in the Towneley dice game, in which earthly tyranny subdues the workings of chance, victory in the Chester dice game belongs to God, to whom chance is utterly subject. The game staged by the performance of the Chester *Passion* is thus simultaneously a reassertion of divine order and a challenge to secular authority.

---

[31]   Elizabeth I, *The effect of certaine braunches of the statute made in anno xxxiii Hen. viii* (London, 1570; Queen's College Library, STC [2nd edn]: 8047.4), image 1 of 1.

[32]   Baldwin, Clopper, and Mills, *REED: Cheshire*, 844.

[33]   Ibid, xxxvii. See Robert W. Barrett, Jr, *Against All England: Regional Identity and Cheshire Writing, 1195–1656* (Notre Dame, 2009); Tim Thornton, *Cheshire and the Tudor State, 1480–1560* (New York, 2000).

[34]   On *pleie*, see Kolve, *The Play Called Corpus Christi*, 11–19. See also Lawrence M. Clopper, *Drama, Play, and Game: English Festive Culture in the Medieval and Early Modern Period* (Chicago, 2001), 11–19.

Chapter 5
'Whye ys thy cloathinge nowe so reedd?': Salvific Blood in the Chester *Ascension*

John T. Sebastian

In the early 1570s, Christopher Goodman, a puritan divine newly returned to his native Chester following a period of exile to the continent during the reign of Mary, undertook to bring a swift end to Chester's venerable tradition of staging biblical drama.[1] His objections to the endurance and enshrinement of 'Popish policy' in the city's plays survive in letters dating from 1572 and addressed to Henry Hastings, earl of Huntingdon (in his capacity as lord president of the council of the north) and to Edmund Grindal, archbishop of York.[2] In his correspondence with the latter – and at the archbishop's behest – Goodman appended a memorable play-by-play inventory of the 'absurdities' contained within the individual biblical pageants, brief notes that reduce the plays to a series of instances of disputed doctrine and scriptural anomalies.[3] Regarding the Chester Tailors' *Ascension*, Goodman

---

[1]   For Goodman's career, see Elizabeth Baldwin, Lawrence M. Clopper, and David Mills (eds), *REED: Cheshire including Chester*, 2 vols (Toronto, 2007), 1.cxxxvi, and Dan G. Danner, 'Christopher Goodman and the English Protestant Tradition of Civil Disobedience', *Sixteenth Century Journal* 8.3 (1997), 61–7. In 1558, while in exile in Geneva, Goodman penned a tract entitled *How Superior Powers Ought To Be Obeyd* [STC 12020], in which he advocated the overthrow of secular powers when they failed to uphold the law of God and defended tyrannicide as a sometimes necessary form of resistance. With Mary in mind, Goodman also vehemently denied the legitimacy of female monarchs, a position that rendered his return to England upon Mary's death and Elizabeth's accession all the more complicated. He officially recanted his opinion in 1571. See Danner, 'Christopher Goodman', 66.

[2]   The letters are contained in Ruthin, Denbighshire Record Office, DD/PP/839 and are printed in Baldwin, Clopper, and Mills, *REED: Cheshire*, 1.143–8.

[3]   Goodman's claim to have culled these 'absurdities' from out of the 'old originall' suggests that he derived his list from a text of the plays rather than from a performance, although none of the extant manuscript copies of the Chester cycle conform exactly to the contents of the plays as described by Goodman. See Baldwin, Clopper, and Mills, *REED: Cheshire*, 1.xxxvii and 145, and also Alexandra F. Johnston's essay in this volume. David Mills, 'The Chester Cycle', in Richard Beadle and Alan J. Fletcher (eds), *The Cambridge Companion to Medieval English Theatre*, 2nd edn (Cambridge, 2008), 130, characterizes Goodman's 'absurdities' as falling into three categories: doctrinal errors, unauthorized apocryphal accretions, and moments of indecorousness. His critique of the pageant on the ascension, the subject of this essay, belongs to the first of these categories.

remarks with characteristic terseness that in the play 'Christ promiseth blyss for good works'.[4] At issue for Goodman is an otherwise unremarkable passage in which Jesus vows

> that good men that on yearth be lent
> shall knowe appertlye
> howe gratiouslye that I them bought;
> and *for good workes* that I have wrought
> everlastinge blysse that they sought,
> to preeve the good worthye. (20.139–44, emphasis mine)[5]

For Goodman, who had made the acquaintance of John Knox and John Calvin during his exile, the notion that human beings could merit salvation as a reward for good works, or that justification might be achieved by any means other than faith alone, was a sure sign of the play's popish ignorance.[6] In an era of political and religious upheaval that had witnessed the martyrdom of both protestants and Catholics by successive regimes, few issues could have seemed more urgent than the means by which salvation itself was guaranteed. Indeed, as David Mills has

---

Elsewhere Mills observes that Goodman's objections did not derive from some rigid sense of puritan anti-theatricalism but from his belief that the plays celebrated the city's superstitious past. See David Mills, 'Some Theological Issues in Chester's Plays', in David N. Klausner and Karen Sawyer Marsalek (eds), *'Bring furth the pagants': Essays in Early English Drama Presented to Alexandra F. Johnston* (Toronto, 2007), 213–14.

⁴   Baldwin, Clopper, and Mills, *REED: Cheshire*, 1.148.

⁵   For the text of the Chester plays, see R.M. Lumiansky and David Mills (eds), *The Chester Mystery Cycle*, 2 vols, EETS SS 3 and 9 (London, 1974–86). All references are to pageant number followed by line number according to Lumiansky and Mills's numeration. Despite the fact that Goodman's 'old originall' seems not to have corresponded in all of its particulars to Huntington MS 2 (Hm), the base text for the EETS edition of the Chester cycle, I have chosen to cite Lumiansky and Mills's text for ease of access; however, I only cite lines from the play that also appear in Johnston's reconstruction of the text based on Goodman's notes that she prepared for the 2010 staging of the plays in Toronto.

⁶   As recently as 1547, the bishops at the sixth session of the council of Trent had decreed that 'to those who work well right to the end and keep their trust in God, eternal life should be held out ... as a grace to be faithfully bestowed, on the promise of God himself, for their good works and merits' and condemned anyone who 'says that the just ought not, in return for good works wrought in God, to expect and hope for an eternal reward from God through his mercy and the merit of Jesus Christ, if by acting rightly and keeping the divine commandments they persevere to the end'. Norman P. Tanner, S.J. (ed.), *Decrees of the Ecumenical Councils*, 2 vols (Washington, 1990), 2.677–8 and 680: 'Atque ideo bene operantibus usque in finem et in Deo sperantibus proponenda est vita aeterna, et tamquam gratia filiis Dei per Christum Iesum misericorditer promissa ... merces ex ipsius Dei promissione bonis ipsorum operibus et meritis fideliter reddenda'; 'dixerit, iustos non debere pro bonis operibus, quae in Deo fuerint facta, exspectare et sperare aeternam retributionem a Deo per eius misericordiam et Iesu Christi meritum, si bene agendo et divina mandata custodiendo usque in finem perseveraverint'. The translations are Tanner's.

observed, by the time that Goodman returned to the city of his birth 'Chester's plays had become a touchstone for wider political and religious controversies, indices of the conflict of local autonomy and Tudor centralism'.[7] Within such a climate, and for a radical like Goodman, the image of Jesus proclaiming the redemptive potential of 'good workes' before a public assembly could be nothing short of incendiary, a deliberate act of defiance on the part of recalcitrant Cestrians and a direct assault on secular and ecclesiastical authority in the wake of the Elizabethan settlement.[8]

Goodman's protest, in the case of *The Ascension*, was disproportionate to its cause, since the playwright actually places very little if any theological emphasis on the disputed lines. In fact, lines 142–4 of the script are so syntactically tortured that the scribe of MS Harley 2124 'corrected' the passage to read 'for good workes *that they* wrought', perhaps because he mistakenly understood the works to be wrongly or ambiguously attributed to Jesus and not to those being saved.[9] Yet Goodman, despite his fear-mongering rhetoric and almost boorishly reductive interpretation of the plays, nevertheless manages to recognize what is unique about the Tailors' particular depiction of the ascension: its attention to salvation. For while the faith-works debate never rises in the play to the level of theological importance that Goodman later ascribes to it, the playwright does emphasize *cruor Christi*, the blood of Christ outpoured, as the primary instrument of human salvation. Blood stands as the play's central symbol and, in the form of individual droplets, becomes the currency that redeems Christian souls.[10] In what follows I examine the play's relationship to its varied and various sources in order to draw attention to the complex theology concerning blood that underpins the playwright's understanding of the ascension less as an historical event from the life of Christ and more as part of the ongoing and unfinished work of salvation that

---

[7]   Mills, 'The Chester Cycle', 131.

[8]   For the North's resistance to religious and political change throughout the sixteenth century, see Michael Bush, *The Pilgrimage of Grace: A Study of the Rebel Armies of October 1536* (Manchester, 1996); R.W. Hoyle, *The Pilgrimage of Grace and the Politics of the 1530s* (Oxford, 2001); and K.J. Kesselring, *The Northern Rebellion of 1569: Faith, Politics, and Protest in Elizabethan England* (Basingstoke, 2007).

[9]   Lumiansky and Mills, *The Chester Mystery Cycle*, 1.375 and 2.304.

[10]   For the medieval theological distinction between blood as *sanguis* and as *cruor*, see Caroline Walker Bynum, *Wonderful Blood: Theology and Practice in Late Medieval Northern Germany and Beyond* (Philadelphia, 2007), 17–18. Bynum's remarkable book has inspired and influenced my thinking about blood in the ascension play, but she is by no means the only scholar to remark on the spiritual as well as the artistic privileging of blood in the medieval and early modern periods. In addition to studies by Mills, Davidson, and Covington cited below, see also Leah Sinanoglou, 'The Christ Child as Sacrifice: A Medieval Tradition and the Corpus Christi Plays,' *Speculum* 48.3 (1973): 491–509; John Spalding Gatton, '"There must be blood": Mutilation and Martyrdom on the Medieval Stage', in James Redmond (ed.), *Violence in Drama*, Themes in Drama 13 (Cambridge, 1991), 79–91; and Bettina Bildhauer, *Medieval Blood* (Cardiff, 2006).

reaches its culmination only in the last judgment. Shifting our perspective from history to eschatology enables us to appreciate blood as the narrative lynchpin linking the plays of the second day of Chester's Whitsuntide performance, with its emphasis on Jesus' humanity and its climax in the passion and crucifixion, to the plays of the third and final day, in which salvation is finally achieved and Christ's dual nature as God and man is fully revealed. Ultimately I wish to suggest that this foregrounding of blood may justify our thinking of the Chester cycle as, if not a *corpus Christi* play, then perhaps as a *cruor Christi* play.[11]

Although patristic and early medieval theologians subsequently ascribed tremendous importance to the ascension, the two Lucan accounts that are the primary biblical sources for this episode are narrated with great economy. In his gospel, Luke reports that Jesus 'led them out as far as Bethania: and lifting

---

[11]   The importance of blood in the Chester *Ascension*, and its place in sixteenth-century religious polemic, has not gone unremarked. Mills, 'Some Theological Issues in Chester's Plays', 225–6, very briefly considers the special attention paid to blood in the latter pageants of the cycle as evidence of revisions made to the text in response to the spread of protestant theology. Given that the playwright shares an interest in the saving power of blood with several of his Catholic predecessors, including John Mirk and the author of the *Stanzaic Life of Christ* (discussed below), the pronounced role of blood in the Chester cycle strikes me less as a concession to new spiritual authority than the relic of traditional religion. It is, however, important to avoid drawing too sharp a distinction here, for while reformist iconoclasm in England certainly stood in contrast to the kinds of stylized representations of Christ's blood depicted in the plays and in visual art, a similar emphasis on blood as the vehicle of salvation is to be found in protestant theologies of the sixteenth century and beyond. In his commentary on Hebrews 10:19, for instance, Calvin echoes Chester's play of last judgment, which I discuss below, in remarking on the eternality of Christ's sacrifice:

> He [i.e., Paul] says *by the blood of Jesus* [in Hebrews 10:19] because the door of the sanctuary was not opened for the solemn entrance of the high priest except by the intervention of blood. He goes on to note a difference between this blood and that of beasts. The blood of beasts did not long retain its power because it immediately began to decay, whereas, since the blood of Christ is not corrupted by any decay but flows continually in unadulterated purity, it will suffice for us to the end of the world. ... This is the continual consecration of His life that the blood of Christ is continually being shed before the face of the Father to spread over heaven and earth.

William B. Johnston (trans.), *Calvin's Commentaries: The Epistle of Paul the Apostle to the Hebrews and The First and Second Epistles of St. Peter* (Grand Rapids, 1963), 140–41. For Calvin's Latin text, see Ioannis Calvini, *Comentarii in omnes epistolas S. Pauli, atque etiam in epistolam ad Hebraeos* (Amsterdam, 1671). The beginnings of a soteriology founded upon an offering of blood can be traced in Christian thought back to Hebrews 9:11–10:18, in which the author reflects on the nature of Jesus' sacrifice. See also Calvin's commentary on Romans 3:24, in which he describes the righteousness of God's justification of humankind through mercy by means of an Aristotelian/scholastic schema in which Christ's blood becomes the material cause of justification. See *Calvin's Commentaries: The Epistles of Paul the Apostle to the Romans and to the Thessalonians*, trans. Ross Mackenzie (Grand Rapids, 1961), 74–5.

up his hands, he blessed them. And it came to pass, whilst he blessed them, he departed from them, and was carried up to heaven. And they adoring went back into Jerusalem with great joy'.[12] The opening chapter of Acts adds only a few details to the gospel account, among them the presence of the iconic cloud:

> And when he had said these things, while they looked on, he was raised up: and a cloud received him out of their sight. And while they were beholding him going up to heaven, behold two men stood by them in white garments. Who also said: 'Ye men of Galilee, why stand you looking up to heaven? This Jesus who is taken up from you into heaven, shall so come, as you have seen him going into heaven.'[13]

These six verses only hint at the spectacle that would eventually attend narrative and visual representations of the ascension and do not mark the exceptionality invested in it by subsequent interpreters, who observed that never before had human flesh entered heaven.[14]

In its broad outline, the Chester *Ascension* mirrors these New Testament accounts. The pageant opens with Jesus among his gathered apostles that 'sytten in companye' (20.1). Much of the immediately ensuing dialogue follows Luke 24 with occasional interpolations and amplifications. Jesus bestows his greeting upon his faithful disciples, who in turn entreat their master to reveal to them the time of the eschaton. Jesus declines but announces the coming of the holy spirit to the apostles and commissions them to spread his teachings throughout the world. Jesus then, according to a stage direction in the surviving manuscripts, 'shall lead the disciples into Bethany; and when he shall have reached the place, Jesus shall speak as he ascends, standing in the place where he ascends' (20.96+ SD).[15]

In the play's most pronounced departure from the Lucan narratives, the ascension itself is accompanied by dialogue sung by Jesus and the attendant angels using text adapted not from Luke or Acts but from the 63rd chapter of Isaias, wherein the prophet foretells the messiah's triumph over his enemies. As Jesus begins his movement heavenward, he is hailed by Primus Angelus, who wonders in song, 'Quis est iste qui venit de Edom, tinctis vestibus de Bosra [Who is this that cometh from Edom, with dyed garments from Bosra]?', to which Jesus replies, 'Ego qui loquor justitiam et propugnator sum ad salvandum [I, that speak justice,

---

[12]   Luke 24:50–52 (Douay-Rheims translation).

[13]   Acts of the Apostles 1:9–11. The two Lucan accounts of the ascension are analyzed in J.G. Davies, *He Ascended into Heaven: A Study in the History of Doctrine* (New York, 1958), 39–43 and 47–68. I wish to extend my thanks to Johanna Kramer for first putting me in touch with Davies's still unsurpassed study. Other New Testament allusions to the ascension add little to Luke's narratives.

[14]   Davies, *He Ascended into Heaven*, 87.

[15]   'Tunc adducet discipulos in Bethaniam; et cum pervenerit ad locum, ascendens dicat Jesus, stans in loco ubi ascendit.'

and am a defender to save]' (20.104+ [c] and [e]).[16] The angels, nonplussed, respond in chorus: 'Et vestimenta tua sicut calcantium in torculari [And thy garments like theirs that tread in the winepress]?' (20.104+ [f]).[17] Jesus concludes their exchange by declaring 'Torcular calcavi solus, et de gentibus non est vir mecum [I have trodden the winepress alone, and of the gentiles there is not a man with me]' (20.104+ [g]).[18] Richard Rastall has identified a possible musical source for this Isaian dialogue in the vespers antiphons for the feast of the blood of Jesus, although he notes that these are found only in the Roman rite and have yet to be located in any Sarum sources (and in any case were not part of the liturgy for the feast of the ascension).[19] As Lumiansky and Mills have shown in their analysis of the cycle's sources and analogues, the Chester playwright sought textual inspiration beyond the usual authorities in recasting his biblical narratives, and his treatment of the ascension in particular is certainly no exception.[20] The introduction of this material from Isaias into the narrative here abruptly and dramatically shifts our attention away from the ascension as Christ's final appearance to his disciples and onto blood and its salvific instrumentality.

This dialogue, first sung in Latin antiphonally between an ascending Jesus and the attendant angels, is then repeated and greatly elaborated in spoken English for the benefit of the Cestrian audience, and at this moment in the play Jesus speaks the line that so troubled Christopher Goodman. Tertius Angelus, astonished by Jesus' bedraggled appearance upon entering the heavens, inquires:

> Whye ys thy cloathinge nowe so reedd,
> thy bodye bloodye and also head,
> thy clothes also, all that binne ledd,
> like to pressars of wyne? (20.121–4)

Still under the influence of Isaias, the playwright has Jesus gesture repeatedly not merely toward his gore-stained garments but to the persistent freshness of the blood he has shed in this, the dramatic and the theological climax of *The Ascension*:

> For the devill and his powere
> that mankynd brought in great dangere.
> Through death one crosse and blood so clere
> I have made them all myne.
>
> These bloodye droppes that yee nowe see
> all the fresh shall reserved bee
> tyll I come in my majestie

---

16   See Isaias, 63:1.

17   Ibid, 63:2

18   Ibid, 63:3.

19   Richard Rastall, 'Music in the Cycle', in R.M. Lumiansky and David Mills (eds), *The Chester Mystery Cycle: Essays and Documents* (Chapel Hill, 1983), 150.

20   Lumiansky and Mills, *The Chester Mystery Cycle: Essays and Documents*, 87–110.

to deame the laste daye.
This blood I shedd, wytnes bere to mee,
and dyed for man on roode-tree,
and rose agayne within dayes three –
such love I love thee aaye.

Theise droppes nowe with good intent
to my Father I will present
that good men that on yearth be lent
shall knowe appertlye
howe gratiouslye that I them bought;
and for good workes that I have wrought
everlastinge blysse that they sought,
to preeve the good worthye;

and that the wycked may eychone
knowe and see all one
howe wortheleye they [forgone]
that blysse that lasteth aye.
For theise causes, leeve yee mee,
the droppes I shedd on roode-tree.
All fleshe[21] shall reserved bee
ever, tyll the laste day. (20.125–52)

In offering some explanation for his shocking demeanour, Jesus speaks on behalf
of a theology of salvation that understands the bloody droplets as a kind of
currency by means of which Jesus can purchase human redemption.[22] By looking
simultaneously backward to the passion and forward to the last judgment, Jesus
emphasizes a perpetually unfolding present in which the work of salvation is always
begun yet never finished and in which the blood of his sacrifice is maintained in
a state of eternal freshness. In her recent study of blood and blood theology in the
late middle ages, Caroline Walker Bynum has shown that 'In contrast to many
sixteenth-century images, and many southern European ones, that show a body
[i.e., of Christ] with drying, or healed, or even luminescent scars, fourteenth- and
fifteenth-century northern representations often depict the risen Christ with blood
running from feet and hands to pool in fresh, red circles below' and further notes
that a number of surviving visual depictions of the judgment accentuate the blood
freely flowing from Christ's wounds.[23] Like the images discussed by Bynum,

---

[21]   Four of the extant manuscripts read *freshe* for *fleshe* here. Cf. line 130.

[22]   For the late-medieval emphasis on the individuated drops of blood in art and
theology, see Bynum, *Wonderful Blood*, 173–92.

[23]   Ibid, 154. Clifford Davidson, 'Sacred Blood and the Late Medieval Stage', in
History, Religion, and Violence: Cultural Contexts for Medieval and Renaissance Drama
(Aldershot, 2002), 185, remarks that one of the effects of protestant iconoclasm of the
sixteenth and seventeenth centuries was a general depreciation of the sacred status of Christ's
blood, which lost its imaginative and theological hold as depictions of the crucifixion faded

Chester's Jesus proffers bloody drops as a symbolic reminder not of the passion as an historical event but of the Anselmian necessity of Christ's suffering for the sake of humanity; blood is, in other words, not merely an effect of human cruelty but more importantly the cause of, and price for, human bliss.[24]

Yet neither Luke nor Acts says anything about blood or much about Jesus at all. The latter focuses our attention instead on the contrasting dispositions of the angels who escort Christ heavenward and on the apostles whose apparent confusion prompts the angels to ask them why they are staring toward heaven. The author of Acts gives no thought to the condition of Christ's human body at the moment of the ascension, a favourite preoccupation of later interpreters, and mentions none of the blood that seems to have so fascinated the Chester playwright. The corresponding moment in Luke's Gospel is even more barren of detail. In the Chester episode, however, a peculiar and pronounced bafflement on the part of the angels quickly displaces the uncertainty of the apostles as a focal point of the narrative. The apostles seem to fade from view at least temporarily – they re-enter the scene following the ascension to conclude the pageant – so that the angels may interrogate Jesus, whose unexpected appearance among them has caught them unawares. This point is underscored by a bilingual stage direction surviving in several of the extant manuscripts that indicates: 'Tunc Jesus ascendet, et in ascendendo cantet (God singeth alonne)' (20.104+ SD). One is struck by the conspicuous absence of what the N-Town manuscript so frequently identifies as the 'Heavens singing' in the English postscript, 'God singeth alonne'. Rather than with triumphant song Jesus is greeted with suspicion. Who are you? Why are your clothes so red? And why do you look like you've just climbed out of a wine vat? It falls to Jesus to explain to everyone – angels, apostles, and audience alike – what has just played out before them.

In contrasting the Chester *Ascension* with its counterpart in the Towneley anthology, Peter Travis has described the Chester play as intentionally ritualized, a rite of passage with roots in the liturgy that avoids the emotionality inherent in what Travis calls a '"tragic" interpretation' of the play; that is, one that inadvertently emphasizes the grief of the apostles upon the departure of Jesus.[25] And, in fact, comparing the Chester *Ascension* to other surviving dramatizations of Christ's final moments on earth serves only to highlight further the Chester playwright's

---

from view. Davidson's emphasis on the blood of the crucifixion as a means for medieval audiences to identify with Christ through a communal and commemorative act of atonement differs from my own understanding of the blood of the ascension as the currency that makes redemption possible.

[24]   For a different reading, see Kathleen M. Ashley, 'Divine Power in Chester Cycle and Late Medieval Thought', *Journal of the History of Ideas* 39.3 (1978), 388, who argues that the Chester cycle's emphasis on the divinity of Christ over and against his humanity is consistent with the treatment of divine power in philosophical nominalism. But the passion as a requisite for salvation in the Chester cycle is more reminiscent of Anselmian theology than Ockhamist philosophy.

[25]   Peter W. Travis, *Dramatic Design in the Chester Cycle* (Chicago, 1982), 198.

eclectic approach to his material. The ascension is portrayed in all four of the more or less complete English biblical cycles. York, Towneley, and N-Town are similar to one another in preserving the contrast between apostolic puzzlement and angelic certitude that concludes the account in Acts. All three compilations also elaborate the biblical narrative by extending the role granted to the angels, who immediately interpret the historical and soteriological significance of the ascension for the benefit and instruction of the rest of the characters as well as the audience.[26] Chester, however, very noticeably parts company with the relatively conservative treatments of the ascension in the other three cycles. The Chester playwright is far less interested in interpretations of the play that linger too long on the meaning of the historical event or on human responses to it than he is in the meaning of blood. The ascension furnishes the playwright with an opportunity to adumbrate God's universal plan for humankind and to advance a soteriology that distinctively locates salvation in the *cruor Christi*, the blood of Christ outpoured.

Neither the dramatist's heightened attention to Christ's blood at the moment of the ascension nor the subsequent confusion of the angels is without precedent, however. As Frances A. Foster and Robert H. Wilson demonstrated over seventy-five years ago, the immediate source for these elaborations in the Chester *Ascension* is the mid to late fifteenth-century *Stanzaic Life of Christ*, itself the work of an anonymous Cheshire writer. The author of that poem incorporates Isaias' prophecy about the conqueror from Edom into the narrative of the ascension as well, noting that some of the angels in heaven were ignorant of Christ's redemption of humanity or even of his having assumed human form. 'Therefore', the poet writes, 'they wondered on that sight / ... / And Christ all bloody and so dight' (8958, 8960).[27] The lesser angels ask for clarification from the greater angels using language borrowed from Isaias: '*quis est iste qui venit de Edom*'? The poet elaborates in English:

> Who was he that came there so
> out of the bloody world of sin
> and from hell so stoutly there? (8978–80)

The dialogue continues in much the order that the Chester playwright later reproduced it, and to the question 'Why is thy clothing now so red?' (8993) the narrator of the *Stanzaic Life of Christ* replies in his own voice:

> This very question asked they
> for his body was bloody,
> which blood he kept well alway
> that from his body went none by,

---

[26] Here as elsewhere Towneley follows York closely and extends even further York's elaboration of Acts 1:11 in its presentation of the angels. The N-Town playwright handles the ascension and the election of Matthias in a mere 90 lines and thus offers at best a perfunctory treatment of Christ's return to heaven.

[27] Frances A. Foster (ed.), *A Stanzaic Life of Christ*, EETS 166 (Oxford, 1926).

and bloody streams he preserved ay,
as Bede says, I shall tell why,
five causes in good fay
him needed to keep it skillfully. (8997–9004)

The narrator then proceeds to enumerate the five causes of Jesus' persistent
bleeding, namely, to continue to nourish belief in his own resurrection; to be able
to offer the blood to the father on behalf of humankind; to demonstrate his mercy
toward those who would be redeemed; to confirm his victory over the devil; and to
remind the damned of the justness of their own reward. Approximations of these
same causes can be found in the sermon for the feast of the ascension included in
the *Festial* of John Mirk, who wrote at the turn of the fifteenth century in Shropshire
just south of Cheshire.[28] Mirk also cites Bede as his authority for the five causes,
but his more immediate source, and one that he has in common with the author
of the *Stanzaic Life of Christ*, is the *Legenda aurea*. In the *Legenda*, Jacobus de
Voragine, following pseudo-Dionysius, states that as Christ was ascending he was
asked by the superior angels why his garments were red. Jacobus preempts Jesus'
response with his own explanation derived from Bede:

> Here the Lord is said to have had a garment, namely, his body, that was red
> because it was running with blood, since even then, while he was ascending,
> he still bore open scars in his body. Here is what Bede says: 'The Lord kept his
> wounds and will keep them until the Judgment, so that he may build up the faith
> in his resurrection, that he may present his wounds to this Father as he pleads for
> humankind, that the good may see how mercifully they were redeemed and the
> bad may recognize how justly they are damned, and that he may carry with him
> forever the trophies of his victory.'[29]

Jesus alludes to the causes for his bloodiness elaborated by Jacobus de
Voragine, John Mirk, and the anonymous author of the *Stanzaic Life of Christ*
(not to mention Bede) not in the Chester *Ascension* but in the cycle's grand finale,
The Last Judgment. When Jesus re-descends to address the saved and damned

---

[28]   Susan Powell (ed.), *John Mirk's Festial*, EETS 334 (Oxford, 2009), 141.

[29]   'Dominus dicitur habuisse indumentum, id est corpus suum rubrum, id est sanguine
cruentatum, ex eo quod adhuc dum ascenderet in corpore suo cicatrices habebat. Voluit
enim cicatrices in corpore suo seruare, secundum quod dicit Beda, quinque causis. Ait
enim sic: "Cicatrices dominus seruauit et in iudicio seruaturus est ut fidem resurrectionis
astruat, ut pro hominibus supplicando eas patri representet, ut boni quam misericorditer sint
redempti uideant, ut reprobi quam iuste sint dampnati agnsocant, ut perpetue uictorie sue
certum triumphum deferat."' Iacopo da Varazze, *Legenda Aurea*, Giovanni Paolo Maggioni
(ed.), 2 vols (Tavarnuzze, 1998), 1.486. The English translation is Jacobus de Voragine, *The
Golden Legend*, William Granger Ryan (trans.), 2 vols (Princeton, 1993), 1.294. See also
Bede, *In Lucae Evangelium Expositio*, 6.24 (*PL* 92, cols 630–31). I am grateful to Susan
Powell for her assistance in reconstructing the transmission of Bede's five causes through
Jacobus to Mirk.

representatives of humanity assembled before him in that play, he announces that his blood 'freshe-houlden tell nowe I would should be' (24.386).[30] He then enumerates the causes for preserving his blood over so great a period of time, namely, as an offering to the father in exchange for his mercy on those deserving of punishment; as a reminder to those responsible for his death of the depravity of their actions; as a comfort to those who have performed good works – note the echo of the passage in the Ascension pageant to which Christopher Goodman objected – and as a cause of sorrow for the wicked. Jesus concludes this litany with an invitation to those awaiting judgment as well as to the audience to gaze upon the blood and to reflect on its saving power:

> Behould nowe, all men! Looke on mee
> and see my blood freshe owt flee
> that I bleede on roode-tree
> for your salvatyon. (24.425–8)

In a final spectacular gesture, Jesus, according to a stage direction in the manuscripts, 'shall send forth blood out of his side [emittet sanguinem de latere eius]' (24.428+ SD). Even at the last judgment Christ's blood continues to flow as a reminder that the work of salvation did not cease at the crucifixion.

The figure of a bloodied Christ the judge appearing in the last of the Chester pageants and evocative of his blood-drenched counterpart in the *Ascension* represents, moreover, a departure from mainstream late-medieval thinking about Christ's physical nature at the judgment. As Lumiansky and Mills observe in their commentary on the Chester *Judgment* Thomas Aquinas addresses the topic of Christ's appearance at the judgment and especially the status of his human body in Q90a2 of the Supplement to the *Summa Theologiae*. The *Summa* makes it clear that Christ will appear with his humanity fully glorified, and that while his body then will be identical in substance to his body at the time of the crucifixion, it will nevertheless be glorified in form. No evidence of Christ's ability to suffer at the time of his death will be discernible on this perfected flesh; rather, all such marks of his past weakness will be displaced onto external symbols. Aquinas stresses that '[t]he sign of the cross will appear at the judgment, to denote not a present but a past weakness: so as to show how justly those were condemned who scorned so great mercy, especially those who persecuted Christ unjustly'.[31] To the extent that the scars from his wounds will still be visible, they 'will not be

---

[30]   Lumiansky and Mills's base-text gives 'fleshe-houlden' here, but I have emended the text in accord with four of the extant witnesses.

[31]   'Dicendum quod signum crucis apparebit in iudicio, non ad indicium tunc existentis infirmitatis, sed praeteritae: ut per hoc iustior eorum condemnatio appareat qui tantam misericordiam neglexerunt, et eorum praecipue qui Christum iniuste persecuti sunt.' Thomas Aquinas, *Summa Theologiae*, De Rubeis et al. (eds), 4 vols (Turin, 1948–50), 4.1027. The English translation is St. Thomas Aquinas, *Summa Theologiae*, Fathers of the English Dominican Province (trans.), 3 vols (New York, 1947–48), 3.2947.

due to weakness, but will indicate the exceeding power whereby Christ overcame His enemies by His Passion and infirmity'.[32] Aquinas sticks closely here to Peter Lombard's *Sententiae*, which in Book IV, distinction 48, likewise emphasizes that Christ's appearance at the judgment will be in the form of his glorified humanity.[33] In his approach to soteriology through blood, then, the Chester dramatist offers an alternative to other currents in Catholic thought, one that prefers vernacular and Latin literary sources (albeit with their ultimate debt to Bede) to scholastic theology. By eclectically and ecstatically combining disparate yet complementary sources, he not only emphasizes the special saving power of blood but also delineates a salvific timeline that unites the passion and the last judgment in the ascension through the image of fresh streaming blood that exists outside of and ultimately subsumes human history. In her study of blood theology in the late middle ages, Caroline Walker Bynum observes:

> Blood is no mere synecdoche for Christ or incarnation. It works objectively; something happens in the moment of its spilling. Blood changes the history of humankind and reorders the ontological and moral economy of the universe; and it does this by coming out of a dead body in living drops – drops that in some way change or consecrate those for whom and on whom they fall.[34]

Blood in the Chester plays is precisely such a complex symbol. It stands outside of human time, Christ's flesh continuing to bleed until and even during the last judgment, just as fresh as it was on Good Friday. Blood redirects the course of history by subverting the claims of the devil and offering the prospect of redemption where none ought to be possible. Blood is an oblation to the father, a reminder to the wicked, a surprise to the angels. Blood is intimately bound up in the Chester playwright's complex soteriology, where it becomes a multiply signifying and even occasionally ambiguous sign, and it is precisely its multiplicity, ambiguity, polysemy, ahistoricity, and even affectivity that the literal-minded Christopher

---

[32]   '[N]on pertinebunt ad aliquam infirmitatem, sed erunt indicia maximae virtutis qua Christus per passionis infirmitatem de hostibus triumphavit.'

[33]   Peter Lombard, *Sententiae*, IV.48 (*PL* 192, col. 956). See also Philipp W. Rosemann, *Peter Lombard* (Oxford, 2004), 187. It is perhaps worth noting here that the Late Banns describe an ascension that in its representation of Christ's body is closer to Thomas Aquinas and Peter Lombard than to the extant scripts:

> Then se that you Taylors with carage decente
> the storye of the Assention formallye doe frame,
> wherebye *that gloriose bodye* in clowdes moste ardente
> is taken upp to the heavens with perpetuall fame. (161–4)

Lumiansky and Mills, *The Chester Mystery Cycle: Essays and Documents*, 292.

[34]   Bynum, *Wonderful Blood*, 192, although Bynum also argues here against the point that I am making with respect to the Chester cycle that blood 'accomplishes the work of salvation ... not by being born of Mary or by ascending into heaven, but by being shed and sprinkled' (191–2).

Goodman, puritan, co-translator of the Geneva Bible, and polemicist, eschewed in beating his hasty retreat to the comforts of *sola fide*.

Blood, indeed, is a capacious symbol that can accommodate a wide range of interpretations even beyond those imagined by the playwright. Whatever the Chester author's intentions in developing a blood soteriology independent of scriptural and liturgical authority as well as dramatic tradition by drawing on alternative sources like the *Stanzaic Life of Christ*, it is difficult to imagine that in 1572 plays about a martyr, which the blood-sodden Christ of the Chester cycle from the passion sequence through the last judgment most surely is, did not evoke memories of England's bloody fortunes under the Tudor monarchs or fears that the settlement might not suffice to stem the tide of religious violence that mingled the blood of many an English citizen with Christ's own. The Henrician persecutions of the mid-1530s witnessed the deaths of nearly four dozen Catholic dissenters including, famously, Thomas More.[35] In the four years from 1555 until 1558, Mary's regime condemned some 284 protestants, among them fifty-six women, to death by burning.[36] And while the greatest number of Elizabeth's victims would not meet their ends until the 1580s, the queen's excommunication in 1570 had already prompted several executions by the time Christopher Goodman had undertaken his campaign against the plays.[37] By the 1570s, blood in the Chester plays had transcended its origins in the affective aesthetics of the later middle ages and assumed far greater urgency as a symbol of the tumult that coloured England's religious and political landscape. While the tendency to identify all early English biblical drama with the celebration of the Feast of Corpus Christi has rightly gone out of fashion, the Chester cycle can justifiably be called England's '*cruor Christi* play', a spectacle that foregrounded the claims, theological and political, made by blood in an age of martyrdom.

---

[35] Sarah Covington, *The Trail of Martyrdom: Persecution and Resistance in Sixteenth-Century England* (Notre Dame, 2003), 11.

[36] Eamon Duffy, *Fires of Faith: Catholic England under Mary Tudor* (New Haven, 2009), 79.

[37] Covington, *Trail of Martyrdom*, 12. It is perhaps worth emphasizing that while Mary's purges were accomplished primarily by means of bloodless burnings, Catholic martyrs under Henry and Elizabeth were subject to drawing and quartering, disemboweling, and other more sanguinary forms of execution. Catholic dissidents under Henry explicitly identified the blood of contemporary martyrs with that shed by Christ. See Brad S. Gregory, *Salvation at Stake: Christian Martyrdom in Early Modern Europe* (Cambridge, 1999), 122–3.

Chapter 6
Affective Piety:
A 'Method' for Medieval Actors
in the Chester Cycle

Margaret Rogerson

By the late middle ages the process of meditation now known as 'affective piety' was an established part of Christian devotional practice. It was in great favour with the English laity, and clerics such as Nicholas Love, prior of Mount Grace Charterhouse, promoted it energetically. Love's *Mirror of the Blessed Life of Jesus Christ*, a translation of the mid fourteenth-century Franciscan text *Meditationes Vitae Christi*, provided a vernacular manual for lay practitioners that became 'the most popular of all books in fifteenth-century England'.[1] Anne Bartlett and Thomas Bestul remind us that 'works of popular piety' like Love's *Mirror* 'far outnumbered the ... dream visions, lyrics, and narrative poetry' of the fourteenth and fifteenth centuries,[2] indicating their potential influence on contemporary literature as well as their currency in the context of lay spirituality.[3] In the same period, religious theatre, normally 'read' through live performance was, as Jody Enders suggests, 'probably the most popular and available literary form of its day'.[4]

This essay focuses on the devotional aspect of medieval drama to link the popular practice of affective piety with the popular theatre of Chester's mystery play cycle, demonstrating how affective piety's central technique of imaginative meditation constitutes a possible avenue for preparing for a role that was open to actors in pre-Reformation Chester. Meditation through 'devout imagination' as recommended by Love allowed the practitioner to transcend mundane real-time-and-place, to cross into a virtual present-in-the-past and to engage with biblical

---

[1]   Clarissa W. Atkinson, *Mystic and Pilgrim: The Book and the World of Margery Kempe* (Ithaca, 1983), 152.

[2]   Anne Clark Bartlett and Thomas H. Bestul (eds), *Cultures of Piety: Medieval English Devotional Literature in Translation* (Ithaca, 1999), 1.

[3]   Michael G. Sargent argues that Love's *Mirror* influenced the writing of the N-Town Plays, 'Mystical Writings and Dramatic Texts in Late Medieval England', *Religion and Literature* 37.2 (2005): 77–98.

[4]   Jody Enders, *Murder by Accident: Medieval Theater, Modern Media, Critical Intentions* (Chicago, 2009), xvi.

events as they happened.[5] In their private devotions, individuals could focus on the humanity of Christ or on the joys and sorrows of the Virgin; alternatively they could, as Bartlett and Bestul put it, 'identify (or choose not to identify) with a variety of subject positions: handmaid, son or daughter to the Virgin, apostle, bride of Christ, Christian knight, and even covert critic of the institutional Church'.[6] To this list we should add the villains of medieval theatre such as Herod, Annas, Caiaphas, or the soldiers of the Crucifixion, for, as Kathryn Smith suggests in her discussion of the late medieval 'lay engagement with devotional and meditational practices', adopting the subject positions of Christ's tormentors was widely encouraged.[7]

In Chester, as Philip Butterworth points out, individual actors retained for the pageants that made up the cycle received a 'parcel', a written copy of their part rather than the whole play-text of their particular pageant,[8] and from this parcel they were expected to memorize their lines in private, perhaps with the help of a reader, before being tested for accuracy at rehearsal. I argue below that private memorization from the 'parcel' could focus the performer emotionally and imaginatively on their role in a manner analogous to the practice of affective piety and that this constitutes a 'method' for medieval actors.

The possibility of 'identification' raised by Bartlett and Bestul resonates with the process of taking on a theatrical role as it is broadly understood in modern terms; as Dennis Jerz states, the practice of affective piety allowed entry 'into the suffering of the martyr or other holy figure with a psychological totality that we today would probably describe as a very extreme form of method acting'.[9] Given the proviso that what I am suggesting here are general rather than absolute points of contact, we can indeed link the affective piety of actors in Chester in the period of the cycle's initial flowering and modern approaches to acting associated with the foundational work on 'method' by Constantin Stanislavski. Although the received wisdom among theatre scholars, based largely on V.A. Kolve's warnings against Stanislavski in the 1960s,[10] is that 'there was nothing like modern impersonative acting in the medieval theatre' and that to impose its 'techniques' on an actor in a modern performance of medieval plays 'can create

---

[5]   Richard Beadle argues that 'devout imagination' in the *Mirror* is 'a technical term', '"Devoute ymaginacioun" and the Dramatic Sense in Love's *Mirror* and the N-Town Plays', in Shoichi Oguro, Richard Beadle, and Michael G. Sargent (eds), *Nicholas Love at Waseda* (Cambridge, 1997), 9.

[6]   Bartlett and Bestul, *Cultures of Piety*, 7–8.

[7]   Kathryn A. Smith, *Art, Identity and Devotion in Fourteenth-Century England: Three Women and their Books of Hours* (London, 2003), 152, see, especially, Chapter 3.

[8]   Philip Butterworth, 'Parts and Parcels: Cueing Conventions for the English Medieval Player', *METh* 30 (2008), 102.

[9]   Dennis G. Jerz, 'Religious, Artistic, Economic, and Political Aspects of the York Corpus Christi Plays', *(Re)Soundings* 1.2 (1997), <http://marauder.millersville.edu/~resound/vol1iss2/psim/yorkintro.html> (accessed 2 September 2010).

[10]   V.A. Kolve, *The Play Called Corpus Christi* (Stanford, 1966), 24.

unnecessary and unproductive difficulties',[11] a case can be made for some parallels between affective piety as a medieval theatrical 'method' and elements of the 'method' detailed by Stanislavski in *An Actor Prepares* (1936). To distance the performance practices of the middle ages completely from modern philosophical and methodological approaches to theatre is, perhaps, a form of cultural cringe stemming from post-Reformation attitudes to religious drama that blocks us unnecessarily from re-envisioning medieval acting as fully as we might.

Bartlett and Bestul label affective piety as 'flamboyant' in its 'emphasis on self-examination, the inner emotions, and the cultivation of an interior life', with 'its dominant expressions … notable for heightened degrees of emotionalism'.[12] In the course of my discussion, Margery Kempe, a native of Lynn rather than Chester, but the most flamboyant and emotional of all medieval English practitioners of affective piety on record, stands as a model for contemporary actors, even though she appears on stage only metaphorically in the pages of her *Book*. Margery seems to have had no existence outside her fiction,[13] yet despite this and for all her apparent outlandishness, recent commentary endorses her as falling 'within recognized boundaries of lay and female piety',[14] making her an appropriate touchstone in the current context.

The Book of Margery Kempe survives in a single manuscript that, coincidentally, belonged to Love's Mount Grace Charterhouse, where resident monks annotated it approvingly in the fifteenth and sixteenth centuries, reading it as 'a document concerned with various "trewths," … about divine love, human love expressed through tears, and the effects of divine revelation in the world', and sometimes being so moved as to emulate Margery's 'mystical practice of falling down and crying loudly'.[15] Following scholars such as Nanda Hopenwasser, who applauds her as a 'master performance artist', managing to 'maintain contact with the present while living both a mythic and a reconstructed historical past, melding all three into an active theatre of the mind',[16] Margery Kempe can be interpreted through the metaphor of the theatre.

---

[11] Lesley Wade Soule, 'Performing the Mysteries: Demystification, Story-telling and Over-acting like the Devil', *European Medieval Drama* 1 (1997), 221.

[12] Bartlett and Bestul, *Cultures of Piety*, 2.

[13] See, for example, Sarah Rees Jones '"*A peler of Holy Cherch*": Margery Kempe and the Bishops', in Jocelyn Wogan-Browne, Rosalynn Voaden, Arlyn Diamond, Ann Hutchinson, Carol M. Meale, and Lesley Johnson (eds), *Medieval Women: Texts and Contexts in Late Medieval Britain, Essays for Felicity Riddy* (Turnhout, 2000), 378–9.

[14] Kathleen Kamerick, *Popular Piety and Art in the Late Middle Ages* (New York, 2002), 139.

[15] Karma Lochrie, *Margery Kempe and Translations of the Flesh* (Philadelphia, 1991), 208, 210. Lochrie, ibid, 8, notes that the *Book* was available to lay readers in the form of extracts printed by Wynkyn de Worde (1501) and Henry Pepwell (1521).

[16] Nanda Hopenwasser, 'A Performance Artist and Her Performance Text: Margery Kempe on Tour', in Mary A. Suydam and Joanna E. Ziegler (eds), *Performance and Transformation: New Approaches to Late Medieval Spirituality* (Houndmills, 1999), 97, 102.

Similar connections have been made previously by other scholars, two of whom, Peter Cockett from McMaster University and Carolyn Coulson-Grigsby from Shenandoah University, were involved in the 2010 conference on the Chester Cycle in Toronto as directors of plays in the pre-Reformation cycle staged in conjunction with it.[17] Cockett, a professional actor and director, has pointed to 'striking comparisons between the process of (modern) acting' and affective piety in the context of his experience directing Toronto's *Poculi Ludique Societas* production of the Digby *Mary Magdalene* play in 2003.[18] He highlights the physicality of Margery Kempe's imaginative encounters with Christ's passion, concluding that 'the comparison between (her) physical and emotional identification and the practice of (his) own craft is obvious and unavoidable'.[19] Cockett invokes the work of one of Stanislavski's followers, Polish director Jerzy Grotowski, who 'wanted a theatre that moved beyond the representation of everyday reality, or mere naturalness' and achieved 'the psychic or spiritual penetration of actor and audience';[20] this kind of actor/audience 'penetration' was made possible in the biblical theatre of medieval Chester through a shared culture of affective piety.

Like Cockett, Coulson-Grigsby is a trained actor as well as a medieval scholar, whose published work on Margery Kempe describes her in terms that can be applied to the medieval performer: 'an active participant' in 'the holy narrative', 'using speech' to establish the right to be there.[21] Coulson-Grigsby stresses that in her meditational practice 'Margery does not claim to have lost her sense of identity; in fact she actively holds onto her "self" in the text', not losing herself even when she displaces Mary Magdalene as handmaid to the virgin at

---

See also Claire Sponsler, 'Drama and Piety: Margery Kempe', in John H. Arnold and Katherine J. Lewis (eds), *A Companion to* The Book of Margery Kempe (Cambridge, 2004), 129–43.

[17]   Peter Cockett directed *The Last Judgment* and Carolyn Coulson-Grigsby, *Octavian / The Nativity*. Artemis Preeshl from Loyola University, New Orleans, who directed *The Ascension* for the Toronto production, used devotional activities during rehearsals, which 'incorporated the Ignatian method of prayer' and began with 'viewing, or imagining, the action in the readings and Gospels of the day', 'Students Participate in Medieval Play in Toronto and at Loyola', <http://www.loyno.edu/news/story/2010/5/17/2126> (accessed 2 September 2010). The actors improvised on the basis of the readings and the 'devotional prayer method opened the students to a compassionate interpretation of medieval theater' (private correspondence with Artemis Preeshl, to whom I am most grateful for her generous communication). The success of this production provides limited support for the argument expressed in this essay.

[18]   Peter Cockett, 'The Actor's Carnal Eye: A Contemporary Staging of the Digby *Mary Magdalene*', *Baylor Journal of Theatre and Performance* 3.2 (2006), 67.

[19]   Ibid, 71.

[20]   Ibid, 71, 73.

[21]   Carolyn Coulson, 'Mysticism, Meditation, and Identification in *The Book of Margery Kempe*', *Essays in Medieval Studies* 12 (1995): 69–79.

the passion.[22] This observation parallels my argument for a partial connection between Stanislavski's advice to 'modern' actors and medieval affective piety. Margery Kempe would have understood the Russian director's instruction to his actors: 'Never lose yourself on the stage. Always act in your own person, as an artist. You can never get away from yourself.'[23]

'Margery Kempe' infiltrated the biblical narrative of her *Book* by installing herself as an additional player, just as non-biblical characters, like the 'Good Gossips' in the Chester *Noah's Flood*, or Salome and Tebell, the midwives of *The Nativity*, or the 'Ale-wife' of *The Harrowing of Hell* infiltrated the dramatic narrative, eliding the distance between biblical time-past and the medieval present. But while Margery does not take on the roles of biblical characters, she does speak for them in the course of the *Book*, which R.N. Swanson describes as being 'rather like a play in which historical figures make cameo appearances'; her voice as narrator remains 'dominant' to the extent that when Christ speaks, he does so only through her reporting of his words.[24] We can see Margery in theatrical terms as playwright, director, and actor of all the parts, her own and those of others, by ventriloquism.

Another medieval 'actor' who remains conscious of his 'self' during performance features in a sermon *exemplum* where playing the central role in a crucifixion play is used as a metaphor for *imitatio Christi*,[25] one of the major objectives of affective piety: the world is a stage where everyone must play the part of Christ.[26] The *exemplum* is recorded in three manuscripts, attesting to its own popularity and to the familiarity of biblical plays to sermon audiences. The actor playing Christ complains of his physical discomfort and expresses a sense of humiliation:

> Ego *eram* Christus crucifixus … esuriebam, sciciebam, et nemo michi dabat.
> [I *was* Christ and have been crucified … I was hungry, I was thirsty, and nobody was offering (anything) to me.] (my translation, my emphasis)[27]

---

[22]   Ibid, n.p. in online version.

[23]   Elizabeth R. Hapgood (trans.), *Constantin Stanislavski: An Actor Prepares* (London, 1937, rpt 2008), 177.

[24]   R.N. Swanson, 'Will the Real Margery Kempe Please Stand Up!' in Diana Wood (ed.), *Women and Religion in Medieval England* (Oxford, 2003), 142, 145.

[25]   Jesse Njus has argued for the *imitatio* of Elisabeth of Spalbeek, a late thirteenth-century 'trance performer' from the diocese of Liège in the Low Countries, as a possible influence on medieval acting, 'What Did It Mean to Act in the Middle Ages?': Elisabeth of Spalbeek and *Imitatio Christi*', *Theatre Journal* 63 (2011): 1–21. See also Carolyn Muessig, 'Performance of the Passion: the enactment of devotion in the later Middle Ages', in Elina Gertsman (ed.), *Visualizing Medieval Performance: Perspectives, Histories, Contexts* (Aldershot, 2008), 129–42.

[26]   For the text of the *exemplum* and discussion see Siegfried Wenzel, '*Somer Game* and Sermon References to a Corpus Christi Play', *Modern Philology* 86.3 (1989): 274–83.

[27]   Ibid, 278.

Neither the actor nor the author(s) of the *exemplum* have any difficulty with the notion of identification with Christ on stage: 'ego eram Christus'. The problem for the actor is that he is caught up in the literal as well as the metaphorical performance and does not want to play Christ again, even though his fellow actors assure him that he has done well. He has to be persuaded on the metaphorical level that his moment of glory will come when the 'play' is over, when life has been lived in imitation of Christ and he can reap the heavenly rewards. Outside the metaphor, however, the actor remains aware of himself as distinct from the role he is playing; like Margery Kempe he has not 'lost' himself on the stage.

Little is known with any certainty about those who performed in Chester's biblical plays before their demise in the late sixteenth century, but the antiquarian *Rogers Breviary* of 1608–09 would seem to have the last word on the subject; certainly this breviary offers the most extensive commentary available on medieval English theatrical process, albeit a late contemporary one. Yet the manner in which the Rogers, Robert, and his son David, present the actors and the plays that they ostensibly seek to valorize exhibits symptoms of the cultural cringe already mentioned above. Their pronouncements, therefore, should be approached with caution. As protestants the Rogers had a conflict of interest in their commitment to the pre-Reformation plays; this may have affected the tenor of their commentary, particularly in the 'Conclusion' to the Banns of the 1608–09 breviary, which is glossed: 'he wisheth men not to take the sighte of the playe only but to conceaue of the matter so as it mighte be profitable and not offenciue'.[28] The tone here is patronizing and edgy; the audience, we are told, must look beneath the surface and resist the urge to take offence. The 'Conclusion' itself asks that the traditional presenters of the Chester plays be accepted for what they are, simply 'Craftes men and meane men', 'common and contrye players', who lack the 'cunninge' and 'fine wittes' of contemporary theatre practitioners and tell the biblical story without any aspirations to 'fame or treasure'.[29] Mindful of post-Reformation attitudes to the appearance of holy figures on the stage, it suggests that the use of 'face gilte' avoided the problem by obliterating the actor, though this was not necessarily a conscious move; it dwells on the props and machinery that would be used knowingly to this end in the sophisticated seventeenth-century theatre:

> ffor then shoulde all those persones that as godes doe playe
> In Clowdes come downe with voyce and not be seene
> ffor noe man can proportion that godhead I saye
> To the shape of man face nose and eyne
> But sethence the face gilte doth disfigure the man yat deme
> A Clowdye coueringe of a man a Voyce onlye to heare
> And not god in shape or person to appeare.[30]

---

[28]   Elizabeth Baldwin, Lawrence M. Clopper, and David Mills (eds), *REED: Cheshire including Chester*, 2 vols (Toronto, 2007), 1.340.

[29]   Ibid.

[30]   Ibid.

Meg Twycross and Sarah Carpenter note that the actor postulated by the Rogers is not seen as 'representing or pretending to *be* God' but is merely a 'voice in the golden face speaking God's words'.[31] The suggestion that the medieval actor might have been aware that he was neither 'representing or pretending to *be* God' would add weight to anti-Stanislavskian sentiment among modern scholars, but as Twycross and Carpenter comment further, the 1608–09 Banns 'suggest a *religious* uncertainty' that 'does not appear to have operated in medieval performances'.[32] Although the 'Conclusion' may have been written in the late sixteenth century to ward off protestant objections when the Chester establishment still regarded performance as a possibility, it remains questionable as to whether it derives from earlier documents used by the Rogers or is their own invention, one that shows wisdom in hindsight.

The Rogers' characterizing of pre-Reformation actors as a variation on Shakespeare's 'rude mechanicals' of *A Midsummer Night's Dream* can be offset by other documentation. The editors of the Records of Early English Drama volumes for Cheshire conclude that those actors from medieval Chester that 'can be identified were not professionals, but freemen and members of the guilds', although not all were members of the guild responsible for the play in which they performed.[33] As guildsmen they had a special commitment to the performances traditionally supported by their community. Further, the financial records kept by the guilds indicate that even though they were not professionals, the players expected payment for their services, with at least some of them experiencing difficulties extracting what was due to them from the guilds concerned.[34] There are two recorded cases of niggardly conduct towards these amateur actors, one in 1447–48, when Thomas Butler, a baker who had played a devil in his guild's play was demanding the 2s 6d owed to him, and another in 1487–88, when a weaver, John Jankynson, sued for the 8d he had earned playing a devil in the Cooks' play.[35] Whether this reluctance to pay up suggests that these particular local guildsmen failed to satisfy in the execution of their demonic roles must remain a matter for conjecture, but to counteract any hint of a negative appraisal of Chester's performers in general, we can look to the case of Thomas Marser, an actor so much sought after by the Bowyers for their play of *The Trial and Flagellation* that they spent 2d on him 'to get him to pleay' in 1575.[36] Although it might be an exaggeration to claim 'celebrity' status for Marser in the sense that it can be

---

[31]   Meg Twycross and Sarah Carpenter, *Masks and Masking in Medieval and Early Tudor England* (Aldershot, 2002), 195.

[32]   Ibid, 196.

[33]   Baldwin, Clopper, and Mills, *REED: Cheshire*, 1.xxxv; 2.1000, n. 62.

[34]   Ibid, 1.xxxiii. For payments to actors see, for example, ibid, 1.92.

[35]   Ibid, 1.52, 62. The Bakers's play was *The Last Supper* and the Cooks presented *The Harrowing of Hell*.

[36]   Ibid, 1.xxxv, ccvii, n. 19, 163.

afforded to professional London actors of the 1590s,[37] like Edward Alleyn or Richard Burbage, Marser was clearly prized in Chester for his theatrical prowess.

The actors were, for the most part, treated well by the Chester guilds, who provided them with refreshments at rehearsals and throughout the performance itself, paying particularly lavish sums for food and drink at what is termed a 'general rehearsal'.[38] Pamela King suggests that general rehearsals in York and Coventry may have been 'social occasion(s)' with the 'guild supper' associated with them attended by guild members and possibly even members of the 'general public'.[39] The Chester actors may also have enjoyed supper at their 'general rehearsal' as they were guildsmen themselves, many of them members of the guild hosting the meal. This speaks to community theatre of a particular kind; the actors were not merely players, they were conterminous with the guilds and the wider local community to which they belonged. The dividing line between actors and audience was a differently nuanced one from those operating in later theatre as medieval actors and audience were mutually engaged in the cycle as a devotional undertaking.

The *Rogers Breviary* of 1608–09 quoted above states that the players did not seek 'fame or treasure', but William Newhall's proclamation of 1531 indicates that the audience could certainly derive considerable 'treasure' from it. This proclamation records that Bishop Clement granted 1,000 days of 'pardon' for attending the plays peaceably and 'with gode devocion', with a further forty days from the bishop of Chester; alternatively, anyone who did not come with the correct devotional frame of mind and whose conduct marred the performance risked a papal curse, imprisonment, and a fine.[40] The proclamation of York's comparable cycle of biblical plays offered no indulgences for good behaviour and threatened those who disturbed the peace only with imprisonment and the impounding of any weapons they were carrying;[41] the emphasis in Chester, however, was on spiritual punishment through the papal curse, just as the emphasis on the reward for appropriate conduct was also spiritual.

Indulgences for playgoers in the Newhall proclamation certainly underline what David Mills has termed 'a devotional function' of a theatre that 'served both the church and the city',[42] a function that is stressed throughout the

---

[37] See S.P. Cerasano, 'Edward Alleyn, the New Model Actor, and the Rise of the Celebrity in the 1590s', *Medieval and Renaissance Drama in England* 18 (2005): 47–58.

[38] Baldwin, Clopper, and Mills, *REED: Cheshire*, 1.xli. For drink for the players at rehearsals see ibid, 1.166; for the general rehearsal, see ibid, 1.92, 107, 126, 167.

[39] Pamela King, 'Confraternities and Civic Ceremonial: the Siena *Palio*', in Margaret Rogerson (ed.), *The York Mystery Plays: Performance in the City* (Woodbridge, Suffolk, 2011), 185, 186.

[40] Baldwin, Clopper, and Mills, *REED: Cheshire*, 1.72.

[41] Alexandra F. Johnston and Margaret Rogerson (eds), *REED: York*, 2 vols (Toronto, 1979), 1.24.

[42] David Mills, *Recycling the Cycle: The City of Chester and Its Whitsun Plays* (Toronto, 1998), 114.

Chester records. The preamble to the Banns of 1539–40 lauds the plays as a means of promoting the faith and urging the 'myndes of the comen peple to gud deuocion'.[43] 'Devotion' is also attributed to an alleged author of the plays, 'Rondoll Higden a monke in the Abby of Chester', who wrote them 'in great devotion … and discretion', giving the common people 'ye storie of ye bible, yat ye simple in their owne language might undestand'.[44] This statement is from an antiquarian copy of a mayoral list for 1269–70 and, like many antiquarian accounts of the plays, claims their author as a closet protestant.[45] The *Rogers Breviary* of c. 1637 states that Higden 'had noe euill Intension, but secrett deuotion', a motive also attached in this document to the 'Cittizens that did acte and practize the same to their gret coste'.[46] Although 'acte and practize' may refer to the guilds at large rather than specifically to the actors, these antiquarian testimonials, supporting the evidence of the Newhall proclamation, suggest a play that was written as an act of devotion, required devotional attendance on the part of the audience, and was a pious duty of those who saw to the continuation of the tradition within a community imbued with the precepts of affective piety.

Drama scholars invoke affective piety repeatedly in relation to medieval play-texts and their original audiences. Clifford Davidson claimed in 1975 that the York Realist did not want simply to tell the 'audience "*about*" the Passion' but 'to draw them into "direct acquaintance with" a re-enactment' so that 'no viewer could … remain coolly unemotional'.[47] In the same year Thomas Jambeck argued strongly for the operation of 'human culpability' as an affective, devotional response by the playgoers witnessing a performance of the Towneley *Crucifixion* as they were identified with 'those *tortores* who historically crucified Jesus'.[48] Meg Twycross, reflecting on her staging of the York *Resurrection* pageant in 1977, observed that the 'aim' of the playwright was 'that of popular affective piety', that 'the Maries are the figures from the meditations made visible', and that Mary Magdalene 'leads the audience through the stages of affective meditation';[49] and Theodore Lerud in 2008 stressed that mystery plays 'were viewed as devotional aids',[50] a sentiment echoed

---

[43] Baldwin, Clopper, and Mills, *REED: Cheshire*, 1.81. The Banns reiterate that those who came 'with good deuocion merelye' were 'hertely welcome', ibid, 1.86.

[44] Ibid, 1.44.

[45] See also the *Rogers' Breviary* of c. 1619, where the author is said to have written 'in a holy deuotion, that the simple mighte vnderstand the scripture, which in those times was hid from them', ibid, 1.441.

[46] Ibid, 2.580.

[47] Clifford Davidson, 'The Realism of the York Realist and the York Passion', *Speculum* 50.2 (1975), 274–5.

[48] Thomas J. Jambeck, 'The Dramatic Implications of Anselmian Affective Piety in the Towneley Play of the Crucifixion', *Annuale Mediaevale* 16 (1975), 122.

[49] Meg Twycross, 'Playing "The Resurrection"', in P.L. Heyworth (ed.), *Medieval Studies for J.A.W. Bennett* (Oxford, 1981), 284, 295.

[50] Theodore K. Lerud, *Memory, Images, and the English Corpus Christi Drama* (New York, 2008), 57.

in 2009 by Tony Corbett, who described the plays as 'devotional in intention, part of the wave of devotional aids that swept fourteenth- and fifteenth-century England'.[51] Other scholars have suggested that several of the surviving dramatic manuscripts of the period, N-Town, Towneley, and the *Burial and Resurrection of Christ* functioned partly as meditational texts for individual readers.[52] Meditation, as noted above in the case of Margery Kempe, allows you to build the sets, make the costumes, direct the action, and 'play' all the characters in your head, performing an imaginative transference to the present-in-the-past. If the devotional activity of affective piety is so much associated with medieval religious drama as detailed in the discussion so far, we can surely extend it to our understanding of the actor.

Margery Kempe is well known for the starring roles she allots to herself in her imagined passion plays, where she sheds profuse tears and hangs on Christ's garments on the Road to Calvary. In her affective practice, vivid memories of the passion are often unleashed to her by sermons and processions, although sometimes less formal occurrences, such as the sight of a child in a mother's arms or of an animal being beaten, can have the same spectacular effect and result in public outbursts of hysterical weeping. She is present-in-the-past, remembering what she has not witnessed or experienced, in a manner reminiscent of Stanislavski's advice to his actors on 'emotion memory':

> emotion memory can bring back feelings you have already experienced ... some
> people ... are able not only to remember ... things they have seen and heard in
> real life, but they can also do the same with unseen and unheard things in their
> own imagination.[53]

This imaginative 'remembering' was urged in Love's fifteenth-century *Mirror* as practitioners of affective piety looked inwardly in their minds into the 'mirror' of Christ's life. Inward looking allowed them to pass through the mirror into another dimension, where they found themselves in a remembered holy land that they may never have visited in the literal sense, but where they could interact personally with the inhabitants of the biblical past. Scripture and apocryphal writings provided some

---

[51]   Tony Corbett, *The Laity, the Church and the Mystery Plays: A Drama of Belonging* (Dublin, 2009), 80.

[52]   Douglas Sugano and Victor I. Sherb suggest that the N-Town manuscript had 'devotional import for the owner or compiler', *The N-Town Plays* (Kalamazoo MI, 2007), 8. Peter Happé describes the Towneley manuscript as 'devotional rather than theatrical', *The Towneley Cycle: Unity and Diversity* (Cardiff, 2007), 23. Donald C. Baker claims that the plays of the *Burial and Resurrection of Christ* 'begin ... as a narrative aid to meditation', 'When Is a Text a Play? Reflections upon What Certain Late Medieval Dramatic Texts Can Tell Us', Marianne G. Briscoe and John C. Coldewey (eds), *Contexts for Early English Drama* (Bloomington IN, 1989), 36. See further the association of medieval devotional reading with the notion of performance articulated by Jessica Brantley, *Reading in the Wilderness: Private Devotion and Public Performance in Late Medieval England* (Chicago, 2007).

[53]   Hapgood, *Stanislavski: An Actor Prepares*, 168–9.

inspiration for these excursions, but often there was little to go on. In the case of Christ's 'lost years' between the age of twelve, when he met with the doctors in the temple, and the beginning of his ministry at around thirty years of age there was nothing at all. At this point, Love's 'devout imaginer' was directed to supply a drama of everyday life. He or she could see an elderly Joseph practicing his craft of carpentry, Mary attending to her 'distafe & nelde' and other household chores, and Christ himself, a model of humility and helpfulness, assisting them, doing whatever lowly tasks came his way, including setting the table and making the beds.[54] Affective piety, then, required something analogous to the 'emotion memory' Stanislavski required of his actors: bringing back 'feelings' they had 'already experienced' and 'remember[ing] ... unseen and unheard things in their own imagination'.

'Emotion memory' was a skill that Margery Kempe had refined to the point of excellence; furthermore, she was versatile in the range of emotional states she could adopt, assuming humility as readily as she did hysteria. Her temperate mode as handmaid to the extended holy family in Chapter 6 of her *Book*,[55] described by Sarah Beckwith as 'a seamless rendition of the meditations enjoined by Nicholas Love' in his *Mirror*,[56] is a particular case in point. Here she gives herself to meditation, asking Christ for a topic for her devotions: she hears his reply 'in her mind' that she should focus her thoughts on his mother. As she recounts the affective experience Margery takes centre-stage. She sees the pregnant St Anne and moves through the mirror in her own character to join the household of the holy family. She is first handmaiden to St Anne and is present at the birth of Mary; then nurse to Mary throughout her childhood; and finally servant to Mary and Joseph, a position that takes her to the house of Elizabeth for the birth of St John and then on to Bethlehem, where she secures lodgings, food, swaddling clothes for the infant Christ, and bedding for Mary. She sees the adoration of the three kings and goes with Mary and Joseph to Egypt, again organizing their lodgings on the way. She is an unnamed 'character', a servant, within the imagined play but she is still Margery Kempe, domestic, efficient, a humble but excellent manager. She is also an excellent observer and as she hears the members of the holy family speak she repeats their words for her reading audience. Could this be a technique used by the medieval actor reading over the lines provided in the 'parcel' (or learning them from dictation by another person) and responding to them affectively as a 'devotional aid' to secure memories of the biblical past and an emotional engagement with the role? Could the actor's cultural understanding of affective piety assist with imagining the faces and costumes of biblical characters, imagining their actions, imagining (and learning) their words, and then repeating them through live performance on the stage?

---

[54] Michael G. Sargent (ed.), *Nicholas Love's* Mirror of the Blessed Life of Jesus Christ (New York, 1992), 63.

[55] Barry Windeatt (ed.) *The Book of Margery Kempe* (Harlow, Essex, 2000), 75–8.

[56] Sarah Beckwith, 'Margery Kempe's *Imitatio*', in Lynn Staley (ed. and trans.), *The Book of Margery Kempe* (New York, 2001), 285.

Two of the roles in the Chester *Annunciation and Nativity* take the performers from doubt and confusion to joyful acceptance of the virgin birth as they learn their part, that of Mary in the opening section of *The Annunciation* (ll. 5–112) and of Salome, the doubting midwife of *The Nativity* (ll. 489–563), whose antics were listed for condemnation by protestant activist Christopher Goodman in 1571–72.[57] A focus on the actor's 'parcel' in isolation from the rest of the text reveals how this material might have triggered affective responses in the player in the process of memorizing the lines:[58]

[*Mary's 'parcel' (cues in italics)*]		
Gabriell. *and the fruite of thy bodye.*		4
Maria. Ah, lord that syttes high in see,		
that wondrouslye now mervayles mee –		
a simple mayden of my degree		
bee greete this gratiously.		
Gabriell. *had never non before.*		24
Maria. How may this bee, thow beast so bright?		
In synne know I noe worldly wight.		
Gabriell. *impossible is.*		40
Maria. Now syth that God will yt soe bee,		
and such grace hath sent to mee,		
blessed evermore bee hee;		
to please him I am payde.		
Loe, Godes chosen meekelye here –		
and lorde God, prince of powere,		
leeve that yt fall in suche manere		
this word that thow hast sayde.		
Elizabeth, nece, God thee see.		
Elizabeth. *fulfilled and done shalbee.*		64
Maria gaudiens incipiet canticum 'Magnificat' etc. [59]		

For Mary, the first cue from Gabriel is familiar from the liturgy and from the 'Hail Mary'. The actor could use this knowledge to begin a meditation on the virgin and to imagine her wonder at the angelic greeting. In the process of memorizing the lines, repeating them till they were word-perfect, the actor could have used the

---

[57]   Baldwin, Clopper, and Mills, *REED: Cheshire*, 1.147.

[58]   My mock-up of the 'parcels' follows the practice of including the name of the speaker of the cue seen in the late sixteenth-century *Processus Satanae*, W.W. Greg (ed.), *Malone Society Collections: III* (Oxford, 1931). Butterworth, 'Parts and Parcels', 100, and Simon Palfrey and Tiffany Stern, *Shakespeare in Parts* (Oxford, 2007), 19, consider the naming of the cue-giver significant. Palfrey and Stern state that it is 'symptomatic of intimate staging … in which eye contact with the relevant person is a possibility' and that 'knowing the name of the speaker gave vital additional "help" to the uncertain performer', an important factor because the actors were 'strictly amateur'.

[59]   All quotations from the play are from R.M. Lumiansky and David Mills (eds), *The Chester Mystery Cycle*, EETS SS 3 (1974).

techniques recommended for the practice of affective piety, imagining that they were present with Mary as she spoke in the biblical past, and repeating the words for her, as Margery Kempe repeated the words of Christ on so many occasions in her *Book*. Mary's amazement is continued in her next speech (ll. 25–6) following the cue at line 24, 'had never non before', and is resolved after the cue from Gabriel at line 40, 'impossible is', when Mary accepts her destiny with gratitude, praise, and humility and greets Elizabeth (ll. 41–9). The change in emotional state, from wonder to joy, is clearly delineated in the role and the very isolation enforced by the medieval mode of line memorization focuses the actor on Mary's feelings with greater intensity. Mary's final cue in this section of the play is from Elizabeth, 'fulfilled and done shalbee' (l. 64), and her response presents the well-known *Magnificat*, the Canticle of Mary, normally sung at Vespers as 'a congregational piece'.[60] The actor sings some or all of the *Magnificat* in accordance with the stage direction after line 64, and in lines 65–112 translates, paraphrases, and clarifies the Latin, playing both Mary and an expositor figure, simultaneously remaining in the 'self' of the medieval worshipper and repeating the words allotted to the Virgin in the formal but familiar manner.

Margery Kempe's imaginative training in affective piety might easily have prepared her for the role of Elizabeth or Mary, but what about the not quite so virtuous characters? Stanislavski has something to say about this as an issue to be encountered by the modern performer:

> [the actor] may not have in his nature either the villainy of one character or the nobility of another. But the seed of those qualities will be there, because we have in us the elements of all human characteristics, good and bad.[61]

We can see a willing embrace of 'villainy' operating in the medieval practice of affective piety, which did not always focus on virtuous figures. By meditating on the enmity of the Jewish leaders or on the cruelty of the torturers or soldiers at the passion, for example, the 'devout imaginer' was performing the pious act of placing her/himself in alignment with those figures because of shared human frailties. Similarly, as Jonathan Hughes has commented, the mystery play audience (in this case in York) is 'made to realize that in the course of their daily work they crucify Christ when they show spiritual blindness, indifference, cruelty and lack of charity'.[62] Could this not also be true of performers as they memorized their lines, learning them as an act of devotion and going through the motions of imaginative evocation of memories of the biblical narrative customary in the practice of affective piety? Could those who took the roles of Christ's tormentors feel guilty and contrite as they prepared to perform? Might this be more than an

---

[60]   Richard Rastall, *The Heaven Singing: Music in Early English Religious Drama I* (Cambridge, 1996), 333.

[61]   Hapgood, *Stanislavski: An Actor Prepares*, 178.

[62]   Jonathan Hughes, *Pastors and Visionaries: Religion and Secular Life in Late Medieval Yorkshire* (Woodbridge, Suffolk, 1988), 290.

exercise in memorizing a set of lines to be reiterated as an exercise in oratory or elocution? Could it be an exercise in empathetic internalization involving emotional engagement with the character being portrayed?

Salome, the doubting midwife in the Chester *Nativity*, provides a case study of a character that begins her role as somewhat less than perfect. Looking again only at the 'parcel' with the cue lines and speeches that are to be delivered in response to the cues, the range of emotions and the steps of affective meditation that the actor is called upon to go through become clear. This role has a dual aspect, being both a 'biblical/apocryphal' character cynical enough to doubt Mary's virginity and a local Chester midwife of the late sixteenth century, who might be tempted to share those doubts in the medieval present, a clear role-model for the audience. She begins as Chester resident, proud of her expertise in response to the cue at line 488 'are not in *this cyttye*' (my emphasis).[63] Her lines then take her through the meditational mirror of affective piety towards the biblical past as she commands Joseph to 'leade us awaye' (l. 489). Her fellow-midwife Tebell is amazed by the pain-free virgin birth but clearly accepts the truth of what she has seen, while Salome responds with scornful disbelief at the cue from Tebell 'soe wiste I never none' (l. 532). Salome's own lines lead to the action of testing Mary's virginity and her impudent hands wither as punishment, causing her to express abject horror at the vengeance that has come down on her: 'Alas, that I came here tonight / to suffer such anoye' (ll. 546–7). Only the angel's intervention brings Salome to a proper understanding of the biblical events. The angelic cue 'and mende them, leeve thow mee' (l. 555), which is delivered as much to the audience to convince them of God's ability 'to bringe mankinde owt of dangere' (l. 554) as to Salome, prompts her transformation from sinful doubt to virtuous belief and she asks the Christ-child for mercy in the name of his mother's love, acknowledging both the virgin mother and the saviour of humanity. These stages of development across a range of emotions are brought into sharp relief when the 'parcel' is read, in the medieval fashion, in isolation from the rest of the play.

Affective piety encouraged its practitioners to exercise their 'devout imagination' in contemplating the biblical past from what Bartlett and Bestul have termed 'a variety of subject positions', and my contention here is that the 'parcels' for the actors in the Chester cycle could be regarded as templates for such subject positions. The nature of the conventions for the initial steps in preparation for their roles channelled the performers into concentrating on the virtues and shortcomings of their own individual roles and the range of emotions evident in their individual speeches. Butterworth has rightly pointed out that learning lines in isolation before rehearsal 'could be considered a weakness by modern theatrical criteria', and it is certainly possible that medieval actors may not have come together to present 'the kinds of interrelated action and relationships demanded

---

[63]   See discussion of Chester midwifery in Denise Ryan, 'Playing the Midwife's Part in the English Nativity Plays', *Review of English Studies* 54 (2003): 435–48.

by later naturalistic conventions'.[64] But this is not to say that they were without a 'method' to follow in their preparations and that there was no room to come to an emotional understanding of their roles. The practice of affective piety, shared by audience and actors, provided such a method, which in turn has some connections with Stanislavski's advice to his players. Far from being irredeemably estranged from them both culturally and philosophically, the medieval actor can stand alongside modern theatre practitioners because of a capacity to prepare for public performance using techniques advocated for private devotions. We cannot expect that all the actors in medieval Chester approached their roles with the same level of devotion or the same level of experience with the principles of affective piety, or that the end result was the same quality of performance from one actor to another or from one pageant to another on the day of the play. Indeed, we should accept that the quality of their performances would have diverged considerably in terms of expertise and polish and that this range would have been tolerated within the community that fostered the plays and the amateur actors who presented them.

Stanislavski has this to say about the 'modern' actor:

> [he] creates not only the life of his times but that of the past and future as well. That is why he needs to observe, to conjecture, to experience, to be carried away with emotion … if he has to interpret the past, the future, or an imaginary epoch, he has either to reconstruct or to recreate something out of his imagination – a complicated process.[65]

Medieval actors, given their cultural awareness of the practices of affective piety might not have agreed that this was so very 'complicated', but they would certainly have known what was meant by the need to 'recreate something' from the 'imagination' and that to create 'the life of [their] times' as well as of that of the 'past and future' they needed, like Margery Kempe, 'to be carried away with emotion'.

64   Butterworth, 'Parts and Parcels', 106, 113.
65   Hapgood, *Stanislavski: An Actor Prepares*, 192.

PART 3
Elizabethan Religion(s)

Fig. Pt. 3 Christ separates the faithful from the damned in McMaster University's production of *The Last Judgment*.

Chapter 7

The Chester Cycle and Early Elizabethan Religion

Paul Whitfield White

With its sympathetically portrayed 'redeemed' pope and advocacy of purgatory, auricular confession, and the invocation of saints, the extant play of Chester's *The Last Judgment* is arguably the most heretical and politically subversive drama of the entire Elizabethan era. I say 'Elizabethan era' because, thanks to the correspondence of Christopher Goodman, we now have confirmation that a version of *The Last Judgment* was staged at Whitsun, 1572, just two years after Pope Pius V issued a bull of excommunication against the queen. Pius's bull prompted a series of punitive laws threatening the death sentence on those English subjects who promoted the bull or refused to take the oath of allegiance to the English crown. But was the 1572 Whitsun performance of *The Last Judgment* based on the extant manuscripts' version in which the saved pope explicitly advocates papal supremacy? This is one of a host of questions that the Chester cycle as a whole raises about the relationship between religion and civic biblical drama in early Elizabethan Chester.

That relationship is the focus of this chapter. Religion and the Elizabethan Whitsun Cycle at Chester has been a topic of sustained critical interest since the 1980s when Lawrence Clopper, David Mills, and others began examining reformist elements in the Late Banns and select pageants, concluding that the cycle was, in many respects, compatible with mainstream Elizabethan religious culture.[1] Mills has written several recent articles arguing that protestant theology left a significant imprint on the cycle.[2] This approach has been both supported and challenged in the past few years. In their separate reception-oriented studies, Richard K. Emmerson and Heather Hill Vásquez acknowledge some protestant revision of the cycle, but they observe a multiplicity of responses at a time when confessional identities of the

---

[1] Lawrence M. Clopper, 'Lay and Clerical Impact on Civic Religious Drama and Ceremony, in Marianne G. Briscoe and John C. Coldewey (eds), *Contexts for Early English Drama* (Bloomington, 1989), 102–36; see also his *Drama, Play, and Game: English Festive Culture in the Medieval and Early Modern Period* (Chicago, 2001); R.M. Lumiansky and David Mills (eds), *The Chester Mystery Cycle: Essays and Documents* (Chapel Hill, 1983).

[2] David Mills, 'Chester's Covenant Theology', *Leeds Studies in English* 32 (2001), 400; and 'Some Theological Issues in Chester Plays', in David N. Klausner and Karen Sawyer Marsalek (eds), *'Bring furth the pagants': Essays in Early English Drama Presented to Alexandra F. Johnston* (Toronto, 2007), 212–29.

audience varied widely from papist to puritan.[3] Sally-Beth Maclean and Alexandra Johnston maintain that the Chester cycle is deeply conservative, if not outright Catholic, with Johnston's Goodman-influenced script of the 1572 production, used in 'Chester 2010', the boldest statement of this position to date.[4] Theresa Coletti, on the other hand, finds it challenging to see any consistent ideological stance in the Whitsun plays, given so much uncertainty surrounding the script used in any of the Elizabethan performances (or pre-Elizabethan for that matter).[5] Here, Coletti draws out the implications of Lumiansky and Mills's exhaustive textual analysis of the extant play manuscripts – five of which are complete, leading them in 1988 to hypothesize that 'the Regenall included more approved segments within individual plays than were presented in any particular performance and that a selection among segments was made for each performance. Further, the form of the Regenall clearly changed on a number of occasions'.[6] In fact, the scenario was even more complicated: some characters, speeches, and scenes identified in the Late Banns and in Goodman's letters are different from those in the extant texts, and Goodman insists that the sponsoring guilds in performance repeatedly ignored revisions officially sanctioned in the 'Regenall'.

In the discussion that follows, I would like to suggest that, while we may never know the specifics about any of the Whitsun productions staged at Chester under Elizabeth I, we can be confident that their general contents followed the version of the plays in the extant complete manuscripts, at the very least for the production of 1572. We know this in large part from the evidence provided by Goodman's letters, particularly the 'List of Absurdities' attached to the letter of 1572 addressed to Archbishop Edmund Grindal.[7] This list, part eyewitness account of the 1572 production and part commentary on 'the Regenal' at that time, confirms that the Elizabethan cycle was a highly controversial production endorsing a wide range of religious customs at odds with the official teachings of the English church. What the ensuing analysis provides, and what is missing from current scholarship, is an examination of religion on the ground in early Elizabethan Chester. Such an

---

[3]   Richard K. Emmerson, 'Contextualizing Performance: The Reception of the Chester *Antichrist*', *Journal of Medieval and Early Modern Studies* 29 (1999): 89–119; Heather Hill-Vásquez, *Sacred Players: The Politics of Response in the Middle English Religious Drama* (Washington, 2007), 17–50.

[4]   Sally-Beth MacLean, 'Marian Devotion in Post-Reformation Chester: Implications of the Smiths' "Purification" Play', in Tom Scott and Pat Starkey (eds), *The Middle Ages in the North-West*, (Oxford, 1995), 237–55; Alexandra F. Johnston, 'And how the state will beare with it, I knowe not', *Medieval English Theatre* 30 (2008), 3–5.

[5]   Theresa Coletti, 'The Chester Cycle in Sixteenth-Century Religious Culture', *Journal of Medieval and Early Modern Studies* 37 (2007): 531–47; see also Theresa Coletti and Gail McMurray Gibson, 'The Tudor Origins of Medieval Drama', in Kent Cartwright (ed.), *A Companion to Tudor Literature* (Oxford, 2010), 228–45.

[6]   Lumiansky and Mills, *Essays and Documents*, 186.

[7]   For the 'List of Absurdities', see Elizabeth Baldwin, David Mills, and Lawrence M. Clopper (eds), *REED: Cheshire including Chester*, 2 vols (Toronto, 2007), 1.147–8.

analysis, I believe, will help explain how this extraordinary entertainment not only survived Elizabeth's protestant accession but received local political sponsorship and community-wide support for almost two decades into the queen's reign, and in doing so, defied the crown's own ecclesiastical commission which ordered its suppression in 1572 and 1575. It seems to me more than coincidental, for example, that the five mayors who sanctioned the Whitsun plays under Elizabeth were either documented as 'unfavourable' in advancing official church teaching or were suspected of ties to the local Catholic community (more on this below). I contend nevertheless that while the cycle, as a whole, invokes a bygone, perhaps even pre-Reformation, religious sensibility, individual pageants appealed to a broad cross-section of the Cestrian community. If *The Purification* and *Last Judgment* engaged conservatives, the hymn singing and sermonizing featured in *Noah* and *Abraham* pleased mainstream 'prayer book' protestants, while the spectacular theatrics and storytelling of *The Harrowing of Hell* exhibited the 'popular religion' of Cestrians of no fixed confessional affiliation. Finally, I will show that while the Elizabethan Chester cycle projects early Elizabethan religious interests and values, it is no less true to say that the cycle helped shape those interests and values as well. Christopher Goodman's complaint that local 'papists' found in the pageants a forum in which to meet and organize suggests that the experience of rehearsing and performing helped religious conservatives reaffirm and nurture their faith. At the same time, opposition to the cycle gave Goodman and his puritan followers a cause to rally around and a form of 'otherness' against which to define their own individual and collective identity as 'the godly'.

Religion in Early Elizabethan Chester

Several recent developments in the historiography of Elizabethan religion are particularly relevant to the current discussion. First of all, scholars today see far greater continuity with the medieval past in late sixteenth-century religion than previously assumed. Second, that continuity is most manifest in 'popular religion', a collection of disparate, often contradictory, beliefs, practices, and feelings experienced by the masses of English subjects. Third, scholars have expanded the parameters for what constitutes and shapes the religious, to encompass a range of social customs and forms – parish sports, music, the visual arts, and, of course, drama, and they are much more open to exploring regional variations and conditions. Finally, while denominational labels (puritan, prayer book protestant, church papist, Catholic, Anglican, etc.) are useful tools for exploring religious identity and experience, current scholarship is much more attuned to the rhetoricity of such terms, the extent to which their meanings vary according to their users, change over time, and serve partisan purposes (now as well as then).[8]

---

8   See Coletti, 'Chester Cycle', 531–47; Peter Marshall, *Reformation England 1480–1642* (London, 2003), 143–5; Tessa Watt, *Cheap Print and Popular Piety, 1550–1640* (Cambridge, 1991); Christopher Marsh, *Popular Religion in Sixteenth-Century*

Chester's early history with the Reformation is complicated. Unlike English seaports to the south and east which did much business with the protestant Low Countries and Germany, Chester did its overseas trade mainly with Ireland and with that most Catholic of western European nations, Spain.[9] And yet as one of a handful of communities chosen by Henry VIII for a new Cathedral foundation in 1541, the town served as the diocesan seat of Bishop John Bird, a champion of Henry's and Edward VI's reforms before surrendering his bishopric at the accession of Mary I. The Cathedral school probably educated two of the most influential English reformers of the sixteenth century, Christopher Goodman and William Whittingham, who co-edited the Geneva Bible. The mayoralty of Henry Gee (1540) and the town's many economic connections with staunchly protestant Manchester across the border in Lancashire assured an early reception to religious change, but following the accession of Queen Elizabeth, a confluence of factors ensured that the pace of reform would be slow.

Protestantism was officially restored in England within six months of Elizabeth I's accession to the throne in November 1558. The Act of Supremacy established the queen as supreme governor of the church, thereby discrediting (once again) papal authority over the Church of England, and the Act of Uniformity reinstated a protestant order of worship via *The Book of Common Prayer*. The Elizabethan prayer book of 1559 followed the more advanced Edwardian edition of 1552, with two main exceptions: it revoked a polemical clause denouncing the papacy in the litany, and it returned to the wording of the eucharistic liturgy of the 1549 prayer book which allowed for an interpretation of the real presence. The popular success of the prayer book from the outset of the queen's reign has been insufficiently recognized; these concessions account for many Catholics staying within the church during those early years, and its encouragement of congregational psalm- and hymn-singing left its mark on the music of the Whitsun plays, most notably in *Noah's Flood* with its distinctly protestant metrical version of 'Save me, O God' (Psalm 69).[10]

The Elizabethan religious settlement, however, was very unevenly enforced in Chester and surrounding Cheshire. While the majority of clergy took the oath of allegiance to royal supremacy in 1559, the administration of Chester diocese remained under the control of Marian officials until 1562 when the queen finally appointed her former chaplain, William Downham, as the reign's first

---

England: Holding Their Peace (New York, 1998); Beatrice Groves, *Texts and Traditions: Religion in Shakespeare 1592–1604* (Oxford, 2007); Phebe Jensen, *Religion and Revelry in Shakespeare's Festive World* (Cambridge, 2008); Robert Barrett, *Against All England: Regional Identity and Cheshire Writing, 1195–1656* (Notre Dame, 2009). I discuss religion and drama relations in Chester and other provincial communities in *Drama and Religion in English Provincial Society 1485–1660* (Cambridge, 2008).

[9]   D.M. Woodward, *The Trade of Elizabethan Chester* (Hull, 1970).

[10]   Richard Rastall, 'Music in the Cycle', in Lumiansky and Mills, *Essays and Documents*, 157–8. The version was from the psalter of Sternhold and Hopkins, and it may not have been added to *Noah* until Elizabeth's reign (see 158).

protestant bishop. Downham was criticized by the crown and fellow bishops as a lax and inept administrator, particularly towards the end of his twelve-year term (he died in 1574). And yet he faced monumental challenges as the administrator of one of the largest and poorest dioceses in England, which included solidly Catholic Lancashire in its northern half. In the early years of Elizabeth's reign especially, the Church of England faced a drastic shortage of qualified protestant clergy. Christopher Haig asserts that between 1562 and 1569 Bishop Downham 'ordained 176 men, in an attempt to fill vacancies; none were graduates, and fifty-six were ordained despite apparent inadequacies'.[11] Very few of these Cestrian pastors can be described beyond their names. The advowson for the rectory of Holy Trinity was vested in the highly conservative Stanley family, the earls of Derby, who appointed Thomas Tadgyll in 1552. Tadgyll apparently survived into Elizabeth's reign when the rector was accused of reading the prayer book 'quietly and quickly' at services 'to make them sound like the Latin Mass'.[12] John Nixe succeeded him in 1565 as rector. By 1578 the parson was John Blaken who had a reputation for popery. The ecclesiastical visitors in 1578 reported that he 'useth more circumstances at the bidding of fastine daies and holidaies than nedith, after the popishe maner, consuming the tyme unprofitablie'.[13] Not surprisingly, Holy Trinity sheltered many recusants during the first half of Elizabeth's reign.

For better or worse, Downham is significantly responsible for the relaxed conditions under which reformers and conservatives could live out their faith in Chester during the 1560s and early 1570s. Right under his nose in Chester itself, John Murren, a former chaplain of Marian Bishop Bonner, was openly distributing a Catholic pamphlet libelling the queen and denigrating the protestant religion in the early 1560s, and only when an ecclesiastical commissioner across the border in Wales noticed it was Murren's case reported to the privy council.[14] Even during the last years of his term in the early 1570s, Downham tolerated violations of the uniformity act, particularly among conservatives. A case in point is that the churchwardens of three of Chester's main parishes, Holy Trinity, St Bridget's and St John's, failed to record or issue fines for recusancy among their parishioners, as required, in the early 1570s.[15] This bureaucratic lapse may have been mere neglect on the part of the wardens, but probably indicates that religious conservatism remained strong among the lay leadership, since recusancy was usually religiously motivated. Often overlooked is that Bishop Downham was under the thumb of Edward Stanley, third earl of Derby, who was head of

---

[11] Christopher Haigh, *English Reformations: Religion, Politics, and Society under the Tudors* (Oxford, 1993), 249.

[12] Chester Record Office, EDA 12/2, folio 1v; cited in Haigh, *English Reformations*, 248.

[13] K.R. Wark, *Elizabethan Recusancy in Cheshire* (Manchester, 1971), 18; for John Nixe, see George Ormerod, *History of the County Palatine and City of Chester*, 2nd edn, 3 vols (London, 1882), 1.331.

[14] The matter is discussed in Haigh, *English Reformations*, 255.

[15] Wark, *Elizabethan Recusancy*, 16.

the ecclesiastical commission for Cheshire and Lancashire. Downham had worked closely with Stanley, especially in the summer of 1568, to address the recusancy problem in Lancashire, and in choosing between Derby and Edmund Grindal, the archbishop of York threw his lot in with the queen's cousin and the most powerful magnate in the north. A letter by Christopher Goodman strongly suggests that Derby effectively blocked the attempt of Grindal to stop the Whitsun plays in 1572.[16]

The Cathedral Church of Christ and the Blessed Virgin Mary figured significantly in the sponsorship and production of the Whitsun plays under Elizabeth. Cathedrals were something of an anomaly in Reformation England. The queen allowed them to practice a highly traditional and ornate form of worship, with many vestments not permitted for use in parish churches; not surprisingly, therefore, they attracted religiously conservative clergy, even if, as intellectual centres, some recruited university graduates of advanced protestant views (and Chester was no exception, as we shall see). Importantly for the Whitsun entertainments, they were local centres of choral music, with a regimen of Latin sacred works, based mainly on pre-Reformation Roman service books, to function as part of the liturgy.[17] As Richard Rastall has shown, some 'nineteen identifiable items', including 'antiphons, antiphonal mass-chants, a responsory, a responsory verse, canticles, hymns, and the apostles' creed' are featured in the Chester cycle, and since such Latin sacred music was unavailable in the parish churches, the drama's producers depended on the cathedral's skilled and experienced musicians to arrange and perform these works.[18] I will return to this topic when discussing the Smiths' staging of *The Purification*. The cathedral contributed to the community and the cycle in other ways. It was a central part of urban religious culture, with regularly scheduled divinity lectures to which the public was invited and civic services on Sundays involving the procession of the mayor, aldermen, and council.[19] The proclamation of the Whitsun plays, another civic ceremony, was probably delivered either inside the cathedral or at the Abbey Gate on Whitsun Sunday, the day prior to the Whitsun week performances. The Abbey Gate was the setting of the first station, and in 1572 the cathedral authorities arranged for a 'mansion' to be built over it. Cathedral staff also paid for a barrel of beer for the players that same year. Along with the town, the dean and chapter therefore contributed significantly to the success of the Whitsun entertainments, even if, with Robert Barrett, we need to recognize that the area allotted to the Whitsun cycle at the cathedral's entrance

---

[16]   See Goodman's letter to the earl of Huntington, dated 10 May 1572, in Baldwin, Clopper, and Mills, *REED: Cheshire*, 1.143.

[17]   Diarmaid MacCulloch, *The Later Reformation in England 1547–1603* (Basingstoke, 1990), 119–20; Stanford E. Lehmberg, *The Reformation of Cathedrals: Cathedrals in English Society, 1485–1603* (Princeton, 1988), 116, 178–80.

[18]   Richard Rastall, 'Music in the Cycle', 154.

[19]   R.V.H. Burne, *Chester Cathedral, from its founding by Henry VIII to the accession of Queen Victoria* (London, 1958), 58; Mills, *Recycling the Cycle: The City of Chester and Its Whitsun Plays* (Toronto, 1998), 28.

was, like other urban spaces, a site of conflict as well as cooperation between civic and ecclesiastical authorities, 'and audiences outside the Abbey Gate would potentially be cognizant of both'.[20] It was no coincidence that towns in England which continued to stage mystery cycles well into Elizabeth's reign were cathedral towns – York, Coventry, Norwich, as well as Chester.

If Chester's religious leadership and institutions account for the slow pace of reform and the climate of tolerance in the 1560s and 1570s, its civic leadership included influential religious conservatives, and even some prosecuted Catholics, throughout Elizabeth's reign. Among them were the mayors who initiated, authorized, and sponsored the five productions of the Whitsun plays under Elizabeth. To date, however, no attempt has been made to ascertain the religious stance of Chester's early Elizabethan mayors, with the exception of those in office during the last two productions, John Hanky (1572) and John Savage (1575). Of the fourteen individuals who served as mayor between 1558 and 1575, ten are documented in 1564 as justices of the peace or aldermen who are either 'favorable' or 'not favorable' to the crown's protestant religion, according to a report Bishop Downham submitted to the privy council that year.[21] Of those ten, six are viewed as favourable and four not favourable. Interestingly, Downham's report and other evidence indicate that three of Chester's first four Elizabethan mayors were committed protestants. Laurence Smith (1558), a goldsmith whom Downham regarded as a 'justice favorable' in 1564 and a three-time mayor (again in 1563 and 1570), was appointed by the privy council as a commissioner in 1553 (along with Bishop Bird) to take an inventory of confiscated ornaments and vestments from Chester's parish churches.[22] His successor, Henry Hardware, who was the son-in-law of Chester's first protestant mayor, Henry Gee, left an explicitly protestant will.[23] This Hardware, who has been confused with his son, Henry Hardware II

---

[20] Barrett, *Against All England*, 70; see also Lumiansky and Mills, *Essays and Documents*, 187.

[21] Printed in Mary Bateson (ed.), 'A Collection of Original Letters from the Bishops to the Privy Council, 1564', in *Camden Miscellany* (Westminster, 1895), 9.73–8.

[22] Rupert H. Morris, *Chester in the Plantagenet and Tudor Reigns* (Chester, 1894), 150; J.H.E. Bennett (ed.), *The Rolls of the Freemen of the City of Chester, Part 1, 1392–1700* (London, 1906), 42.

[23] Robert Tittler has corrected the mistake made by Clopper and others of conflating Henry Hardware I with Henry Hardware II, the latter of whom introduced harsh puritan reforms in 1599, but he then goes on to say that 'in the absence of any surviving will, we have no particular indication of any puritan sentiment on his [i.e., Henry I's] part'. And yet Henry I's will *does* survive, and it is unmistakably protestant: 'I com[m]end my soule unto the hande of the Almightie and ev[er]lastinge God the Father the Sonne and the Holie Goste three p[er]sons and one God assuredlie beleavinge that through the merite of Jesus Christ verye God and verye man my full and onlye savioure and by whome I am assured by Gode holie spirit that the justice of God for my synnes ys satisfied and that at the lasted aye I shall have a ioyfull resurrec[i]on and [blank] of my bodye and soule and so eternallie as one of Gode electe to lyve and raigne in heaven.' G.J. Piccope (ed.), *Lancashire and Cheshire Wills*

(mayor in 1599), successfully resolved the legal dispute with the privy council over the 1572 and 1575 Whitsun plays during his second term (1575–76). The fourth mayor, William Cowper, was the sheriff of Chester who mounted a brash but failed attempt to rescue Cheshire's only protestant martyr, George Marsh, from burning at the stake at Spital Boughton just outside the town in April 1555, after which he fled to Wales where he remained in hiding until Elizabeth's accession.[24] If Downham's 1564 report is accurate, the next four mayors were alternately conservative and pro-reform: Randle Bamvill ('not favorable'), Laurence Smith (in his second term, 'favorable'), Richard Poole ('not favorable'), and Thomas Green ('favorable').

Perhaps the most significant conclusion to emerge from reviewing the religious stance of Chester's early Elizabethan mayors is that all of those in office during years when the Whitson Cycle was staged were either suspected as religious conservatives by church leaders or had ties to the local recusant community. The first Elizabethan mayor to sponsor the cycle (in 1561), William Aldersey, was the head of a mercantile clan unrivaled in wealth in the town during the queen's reign, and Cestrians owed him a great debt of gratitude in 1560 when, in a three-month trip to London at town expense, he negotiated a significant reduction in duties owed to the crown for imported goods.[25] This William Aldersey is not to be mistaken with his nephew of the same name, the antiquarian mayor of 1595 and 1614. 'Unfavorable' in Downham's report, the elder William died on 12 October, 1577, which has led K.R. Wark to identify him with the Catholic William Aldersey of St Bridget's parish, a linen-draper who was sick in 1577 when he was listed as a recusant in the diocesan report of that year and presented as an absentee and non-communicant at the Metropolitan Visitation of 1578.[26] Whether this is indeed the same person, Aldersey's wife, formerly Margaret Barnes of Cremshaw, Lancashire, was certainly a committed Catholic. Margaret appeared before the High Commission for concealing an image and using a Latin primer in 1562 and was prosecuted repeatedly thereafter as a recusant.[27] There were numerous other Alderseys prosecuted for recusancy in Chester during Elizabeth's reign, including William and Margaret's son, Fulke. It is a testimony to Chester's tolerance for

---

and Inventories from the Ecclesiastical Court, Chester, Volume 54 (Chester, 1861), 25. Robert Tittler, *Townspeople and Nation: English Urban Experiences 1540–1640* (Stanford, 2001), 143. See also Bennett, *Rolls of the Freemen*, 25. On the first Henry Hardware, see also Jenny Kermode, 'New Brooms in Early Tudor Chester?' in John C. Appleby and Paul Dalton (eds), *Government, Religion and Society in Northern England 1000–1700*, (Thrupp, Gloucestershire, 1997), 44–58, 153.

[24]   Morris, *Chester*, 71–2.

[25]   Woodward, *Trade of Elizabethan Chester*, 76–8.

[26]   Wark, *Elizabethan Recusancy*, 139.

[27]   She confessed that she sold the image to a Spaniard, plausible considering that her husband did much of his import/export business with the Spanish. See Wark, *Elizabethan Recusancy*, 6, 139; and Ormerod, *History of the Palatinate*, 2.740.

religious conservatives throughout the period that Fulke, who was elected mayor in 1594, and others with close ties to Elizabethan Catholicism gained high office.[28] The Whitsun cycle was staged in back-to-back years in 1567 and 1568. The mayors were William Sneyd (or Snede) (1567) and Richard Dutton (1568). Sneyd, who appears to have been a lawyer, is another conservative, according to the 1564 report, which does not mention Dutton.[29] A William Sneyd, possibly his father or grandfather, sponsored the Chester cycle as mayor in the year of William Newhall's Proclamation, 1531, and served again in the office in 1543.[30] Little is known specifically about Richard Dutton, a draper, who also was mayor in 1573, but he appears repeatedly in local records as a patron of various entertainments. His family, moreover, had inherited the privilege of licensing in the minstrels' court (minstrels, incidentally, are prominently featured in the Draper's *Fall of Man*).[31] With its county seat in the mid-Cheshire town of Dutton, the family had long been involved in Chester politics and owned property in the town, but many of the Duttons during Elizabeth's reign were in and out of trouble as suspected Catholics, including Richard's brother or cousin, John Dutton of Dutton, who was a Downham 'unfavorable' of 1564 and a recusant for a time.[32] The last two mayors in office when the Whitsun plays were produced, Hanky and Savage, are better known today due to their legal entanglement with the crown over authorizing the plays. Both men earned a place on Downham's list for favouring reform, yet a report to the earl of Leicester indicated that the Savages 'all had sons abroad in 1580 and so perhaps did not sympathize with royal policy'.[33] Hanky, according to Christopher Goodman in 1572, joined 'himself with such persons as be thought of corrupt affection in religion' when he organized the Whitsun plays in that same year.[34] He hosted a masque in his house in the early 1580s, and he may be the 'Hanky' whose home was used for rehearsals in 1567 for the Painters' *Shepherds*, among the most religiously conservative of the pageants in the cycle.[35]

---

[28] See Appendix 1 in Wark, *Elizabethan Recusancy*. For more interesting details on the Alderseys, including the quarrelsome Fulke, see Beck, *Tudor Cheshire*, 10, 14–16, 93; and Woodward, *Trade of Elizabethan Chester*, 106–9. Richard Bird, who became sheriff in 1580, attended masses with his wife in 1585; the Masseys of Chester, a prominent family with aldermen and sheriffs as members, were Catholic; the wife and daughter of Richard Glasier, the Elizabethan Vice-Chamberlain of Chester, were Catholic. See under their names in Wark, *Elizabethan Recusancy*, Appendix I.

[29] Bateson, 'Collection', 73.

[30] See Bennett, *Rolls of the Freemen*, 18, 24, and 39. The Elizabethan mayor was a knight (39).

[31] Mills, *Recycling the Cycle*, 36, 82, 85; Bennett, *Rolls of the Freemen*, 28.

[32] Wark, *Elizabethan Recusancy*, 179.

[33] Mills, *Recycling the Cycle*, 149.

[34] Baldwin, Clopper, and Mills, *REED: Cheshire*, 1.142.

[35] Ibid, 1.122. Hanky appears at this time with fellow alderman, William Bird, who is in the company of our John Hanky at the masque in 1582 (see ibid, 197–8). Mills observes that the John Hanky who made Downham's 'favorable' list in 1564 was a merchant, whereas

In assessing all this evidence about the mayors, my sense is that while there clearly is a mix of protestant and Catholic lay leadership in early Elizabethan Chester, the mayors who were behind the plays tended to be religious traditionalists. It strongly suggests that the main impetus for the Whitsun plays' continued success under Elizabeth came from the religiously conservative side of the town's lay leadership.

Scholars tend to see the period between 1568 and 1572 as a critical phase in solidifying protestantism as the national religion in England. Mary Queen of Scots arrived in 1568 to embolden committed Catholics, but it was the rebellion in the north in 1569 and the queen's excommunication the following year which shocked the crown and parliament into enforcing the oath of supremacy and prosecuting Catholics.[36] Pressures brought about by the excommunication may have accelerated the formation of identities. By 1572, we find evidence of a fairly wide spectrum of religious belief in Chester. On the far right were committed Catholics, who can be identified as recusants through their interrogation and prosecution by the clerical and civic authorities, as evidenced in mayor's book presentments, and in records of various ecclesiastical visitations and commissions during the 1560s and 1570s. Recusants refused to attend church on the grounds of Catholic conscience and were prosecuted for it, since Elizabeth's Act of Uniformity required everyone to attend church or face a financial penalty. K.R. Wark identifies some eighty individuals who were convicted or strongly suspected as Catholic recusants in the parishes of Chester to 1603. Recusants are often difficult to distinguish from 'church papists', a pejorative term in reference to Catholics who outwardly conformed. The cycle-authorizing mayors just discussed likely fall into this category. So also does Edward, the third earl of Derby, the senior politician of the entire region, whose court was reported to be 'a nest of spies'.[37]

The puritan presence, at the opposite end of the spectrum, arrived with Christopher Goodman's return to the area, possibly as early as the spring of 1567 when he hosted the Scottish reformer John Knox at his home in Alforde, a parish south of Chester where he became vicar.[38] Goodman's appointment to the

---

the mayor of 1572 was an innkeeper (Mills, *Recycling the Cycle*, 147). A 'Richard Hankey', perhaps a relative of Hanky's, is listed in the Smiths' accounts for 1553 (ibid, 96).

[36]   Norman Jones, *Birth of the Elizabethan Nation: England in the 1560s* (Oxford, 1993), 80–81. Some scholars have questioned the immediate impact of the excommunication and the rising in the north that prompted Pius IV to publish it. See references in Marshall, *Reformation England*, 173–4.

[37]   Wark, *Elizabethan Recusancy*, 138–73.

[38]   See Jane Dawson and Lionel K.J. Glassey, 'Some Unpublished Letters from John Knox to Christopher Goodman', *Scottish Historical Review* 84.2, no. 218 (2005), 177–8. Previously, Joan Beck and The Victoria County History's report on religion in early modern Chester, updated in 2003, dated Goodman's return to 1584. See 'Early Modern Chester 1550–1762: Religion, 1550–1642', in Christopher Piers Lewis and Alan Thacker (eds), *A History of the County of Chester: Volume 5 Part 1*, 109–12; Beck, *Tudor Cheshire* (Chester, 1969), 94. *REED: Cheshire* dates his arrival as 1568.

ecclesiastical commission of Chester diocese occurred that same year.[39] This would put the controversial reformer in the town during a period in which four Whitsun performances took place – 1567, 1568, 1572, and 1575. Two prebendaries in residence at the Cathedral in 1572, John Lane and John Nutter, were of puritanical conviction. Lane, a co-signer of the letters Goodman sent to the council of the north, preached regular sermons to the public of Chester. He reportedly refused to take communion, apparently because the cathedral wafers imprinted with signs were offered in place of plain bread, what puritans preferred.[40] Lane was rector of Aldford prior to 1580, possibly succeeding Goodman when he was deprived and called before the ecclesiastical commission in London in 1572.[41] Little is known of Goodman's other letter co-signer, Robert Rogerson. Mills has proposed that Rogerson is Robert Rogers, the antiquarian linked to the famous breviary, since a court document of 1590 refers to 'Robert*us* Rogers al*ias* Rogerson'.[42]

How much of a popular following did Goodman have? He talks of 'my brethren & fellow ministers of this city' who supported his opposition to the Whitsun plays.[43] A mayor's book entry for 1574/75 reports that 'some precise Cittizins' were behind the efforts to stop the plays in 1572.[44] Several mayors may well have been sympathetic to Goodman's interests, including the aforementioned Henry Hardware I. Jenny Kermode has traced what she sees as a line of protestants among elite families in Cheshire, identifying the Gee-Hardware line as the most prominent. We hear in the mayors' lists of the 'many who were opposed to the plays', but religion, let alone puritanism, was not necessarily the cause of the opposition. Since Christopher Haig's work in the 1980s and 1990s, scholars generally suspect that puritans remained a minority, perhaps even a small minority in Chester, through much of Elizabeth's reign. Haig says that parishioners were scared of their preaching on intellectual topics and resented their attacks on popular festivity. He famously sees anti-clericalism as not the cause of the Reformation but a result of it.[45]

What about those Cestrians that do not fit into either the Catholic/conservative category on the right or the puritans on the left? Perhaps many people had no serious engagement with religion at all, like William Bullein's fictitious character Medicus

---

[39]   See Wark, *Elizabethan Recusancy*, 9.

[40]   Ibid, 56.

[41]   Recorded in Ormerod, *History of the County Palatine*, 2.760.

[42]   Mills, *Recycling the Cycle*, 147.

[43]   Letter to the Archbishop of York, 4 June 1572, in Baldwin, Clopper, and Mills, *REED: Cheshire*, 1.145.

[44]   Ibid, 162.

[45]   Christopher Haigh, 'Anticlericalism and the English Reformation', in Christopher Haigh (ed.), *Reformation Revised* (Cambridge, 1987); see also Marshall, *Reformation England*, 148.

who is a *nulla fidian*.[46] Certainly contemporary commentators, notably puritans, saw things that way, but recent studies have shown that, whatever their religious convictions, most Elizabethans did make an effort to attend church regularly.[47] Nick Alldridge, for example, has done a study of Chester parishes, maintaining through a complicated methodology that Chester churches between 1563 and 1578 had a rate of attendance between 60 and 83 per cent, with St Michael's Church showing the highest rate at 83 per cent in 1578.[48] That's an average most protestant and Catholic clergy today would be quite happy with. What, then, can we say about those Cestrians 'in the middle' for whom religion was important? This question, for England as a whole, has generated considerable interest in the past twenty years and it is possibly the one common feature of scholarship critics call post-revisionist. Tessa Watt, Christopher Marsh, Peter Marshall, Beatrice Groves, and others have cast their net much wider than earlier historians to examine the religious lives of the masses. What they have concluded is that popular religion was often at odds with orthodox religion; it shows considerable accommodation of traditional preoccupations, it has significant visual and auditory dimensions (in other words, images and music feature prominently), it incorporates much of what doctrinal protestants would consider superstition (belief in spells and portents, etc.), and it has little interest in abstract doctrine, other than beliefs about divine providence. Tessa Watt in particular turns on its head the theory that popular protestantism eschewed the visual.[49]

Catholic and Conservative Elements in the Chester Cycle

Given this picture of Chester's early Elizabethan religious topography, how did the cycle engage it? The 1572 production of the Whitsun cycle offers our best chance at exploring this question, for reasons discussed earlier. What emerges from Goodman's correspondence in conjunction with a re-evaluation of the extant

---

[46]   William Bullein, *A Dialogue ... Against the Fever Pestilence* (1573); cited in Jones, *Birth of the Elizabethan Nation*, 30.

[47]   On puritan commentary about the disbelieving populace, see Marshall, *Reformation England*, 155–6; Jones, *Birth of the Elizabethan Nation*, 19, 30–31.

[48]   Nicholas Alldridge, 'Loyalty and Identity in Chester Parishes, 1540–1640'. In S.J. Wright (ed.), *Parish, Church and People: Local Studies in Lay Religion 1350–1750* (London, 1988).

[49]   Watt, *Cheap Print and Popular Piety*, 178–216. Watt observes that even if protestant writers downplayed the significance of images, religious images were all around them. Even in churches where the walls were whitewashed, stained-glass windows full of traditional religious iconography and pictorial representations of the bible remained in most instances. She also observes that public meeting-places such as inns, taverns, and alehouses, as well as private residences, featured wall paintings, referring to literally thousands of such meeting-places across Elizabethan England. So much for the Walter Ong theory that protestantism was the religion of the word, she concludes.

texts as evidence of the Whitsun performance that year is that in 1572 the cycle was a mixture of highly conservative, some explicitly Roman Catholic, pageants with others which make some effort to accommodate more mainstream popular religious sentiment, though I find no evidence of major changes along orthodox protestant lines.

As Sally-Beth MacLean has shown, the Smiths' *Purification*, when examined in conjunction with their drama-related accounts and the documentation of religious conservatives in early Elizabethan Chester, offers several important revelations.[50] *The Purification* presents Mary as queen of heaven – the boy actor fitted with a crown in 1561 and 1568;[51] it also features an apocryphal account of Simeon's doubt concerning Mary's virginity favoured in medieval Catholic accounts of this biblical episode. A cope and a tunicle hired from the cathedral were probably worn by Simeon, who appears as a bishop in medieval paintings of the purification.[52]

The Purification shows remarkable cooperation between the Smiths' guild and religiously conservative members of the cathedral's musical staff. The surviving expense accounts of the guild between 1554 and 1575 (the only period of extant records) show that the Smiths hired Sir Randle Barnes, a minor canon of the cathedral, to procure singers in 1561, and Sir John Genson, the precentor, in 1567 for the same purpose. For 1561 they also hired '5 boyes for singing' and a singing-man of the foundation, Thomas Ellam. As Rastall observes, large numbers of singers were hired for the 1568 and 1572 Whitsun performances.[53] Among the most remarkable revelations concern Robert White, a composer of considerable accomplishment and fame during Elizabeth's reign. In both 1567 and 1568 White was paid the extraordinary sum of four shillings 'for singinge', and it would appear that he sung the canticle, 'Nunc Dimittis', assigned to Simeon in *The Purification*.[54] Not much is known about White's appointment as 'magister choristarum' of Chester Cathedral. In the year he arrived there, 1567, three extra singing-men, identified as 'Conductis externis', received fees, one of whom was the Reverend Roger Benet, vicar of St Oswald's, among other clergy from neighbouring parishes. This increase of staff may have been due to White's energy and influence, but either way it shows an instance of the interaction between the cathedral and the local clergy.[55] Significantly most of White's extant compositions are in Latin, and he wrote two votive antiphons in honour of the Virgin Mary. In London, moreover, he moved in a circle of Catholic musicians, which included

---

[50]   Sally-Beth MacLean, 'Marian Devotion', 237–55.

[51]   Baldwin, Clopper, and Mills, *REED: Cheshire*, 1.106 and 118.

[52]   See MacLean, 'Marian Devotion', 242–3.

[53]   Rastall, 'Music in the Cycle', 134–7.

[54]   See Rastall, 'Music in the Cycle', 241–2. For more details on White's life and his time at Chester, see Frederick Hudson, 'Robert White and his Contemporaries: Early Elizabethan Music and Drama', in Georg Knepler (ed.), *Festschrift für Ernst Hermann Meyer* (Leipzig, 1973), 163–87.

[55]   See Hudson, 'Robert White', 167.

Sebastian Westcote and William Byrd. If he were not a Catholic himself, he certainly was very traditional in his religious interests.[56]

No less significantly, four known recusants in Chester were involved in one or more of the Elizabethan productions of *The Purification*. They are John Shaw and Robert Jones who, like many recusants, purchased vestments and ornaments from their parish church, Holy Trinity; and Richard Ledsham and Richard Smith, who also appear in the drama records of the Smiths' guild for the purification pageant. The most notable of these was the lawyer Shaw, who loaned 'a doctor's gowne & a hode for our eldest doctor' to the Smiths in 1574–75.[57] Shaw, along with several other parishioners of Holy Trinity, was 'suspected of popery and mainteyne their errors openly in talk' by the visitation of the diocese of Chester authorized by the archbishop of York during the two-year vacancy of the bishop's office following Downham's death in November 1577.[58] The historians of Elizabethan Catholicism have generally overlooked the staging of *The Purification* in considering the debate over the role of Catholic survivalism in the history of the Catholic community in late sixteenth-century England. The evidence here counters the views of John Bossy that Catholic survivalism was inconsequential in the formation of the later Catholic community, and that the missionaries arriving in the wake of the queen's 1570 excommunication account for the remarkable vitality of the small Catholic community in early modern England.[59]

Quite possibly the 1572 rendition of *The Purification* offered a toned-down version of the Virgin – the crown does not appear in the Smiths' accounts for 1572. And we should keep in mind that the purification was a red-letter feast day in the Anglican calendar celebrated as in the Roman church on February 2, and the Elizabethan *Book of Common Prayer* continued to refer to Christ's mother as the Blessed Virgin Mary, allowing for the scene's modification to comply with Church of England teachings.

This cannot be said of the final pageant in the cycle, the Weavers' *Last Judgment*. This pageant has undergone absolutely no revision whatsoever along protestant lines. Catholicism is not removable from *The Last Judgment*. The first 200 lines of the pageant are set on the outskirts of purgatory, where the 'Redeemed' pope, emperor, king, and queen, newly purged of their sins, face their final judgment before Christ, imploring entrance to paradise. The play appears to have been written or revised late in the reign of Henry VIII or possibly

---

[56]   I have looked at White's will and have found nothing that clearly indicates he was a Catholic, which surprised me because the *Catholic Encyclopedia* has a substantial piece on him as a faithful Romanist.

[57]   Baldwin, Clopper, and Mills, *REED: Cheshire*, 1.168.

[58]   Wark, *Elizabethan Recusancy*, 17, 163.

[59]   See discussion of the debate over the role of survivalism in the development of the late Elizabethan Catholic community in Marshall, *Reformation England*, 176–8; and Haigh, *English Reformations*, 259–60. John Bossy's influential book is *The English Catholic Community, 1580–1870* (Oxford, 1976).

during Queen Mary's reign, since the script makes unmistakable references to the plundering of the religious houses and dwells repeatedly on royal lechery.[60] Purgatory was reluctantly approved by Henry VIII's Six Articles Act of 1539, but the whole infrastructure behind Catholic rites for the dead was gutted in 1547 with the Chantries Act, passed by Edward VI, which banned chantries, seized their assets, and outlawed all rites associated with purgatory, notably masses said for the deceased.[61] When discussing purgatory in early Elizabethan England, Peter Marshall says that 'The death of purgatory was a slow and lingering business' and adds that related customs continued well into Elizabeth's reign.[62] In 1571, intercessory prayers, bell ringing at funerals, praying before crosses on gravesites, were so much of a problem in York diocese that Archbishop Grindal inveighed against all of these customs in his new injunctions introduced that year. In Tilston, 5 miles south of Chester, as late as 1578 one 'Rafe Leche useth praier for the deade and willeth the people to praie for them and saie a paternoster and *De profundis* for the dead when the people do rest with the dead corps'.[63] At Holy Trinity in Chester, the parish clerk Randall Griffeth was repeatedly rebuked because he 'ringeth mo peales at the funeralles of the dead than is decent'.[64] Christopher Goodman and his peers were outraged by the affirmation of purgatory in the Weavers' pageant, but my own sense is that its representation in *The Last Judgment* would not have been deeply offensive to most Cestrian playgoers.

The depiction of a sympathetically treated 'redeemed' pope is another matter entirely. Most provocatively, in all the manuscript versions, the pope remarks that 'They [sic] highest office under thee / on earth thou puttest me in' (55–6). In the stanza that follows, the redeemed pope explains what he means when he refers to occupying the 'highest office' on earth:

> Thou grantest me, lord, through thy grace,
> Peters power and his place.
> Yett was I blent. Alas, alas,
> I dyd not thyne assent.
> But my fleshlye will that wicked was,
> the which raysed nowe thou hasse,
> I forthered, lord, before thy face
> shall take his judgment. (57–64)

---

[60]   See *The Last Judgment*, where the 'Damned King' regrets having 'reaved' (i.e., plundered) 'Relygion' and engaged in lechery (255–7); adding that 'To reave and robbe relygion, / that was all my devotyon' (321–2). Line references to the Chester cycle here and throughout this essay are to Lumiansky and Mills (eds), *The Chester Mystery Cycle*, 2 vols, Early English Text Society, 1.440 (57–64).

[61]   Haigh, *English Reformations*, 171–2; Marshall, *Beliefs and the Dead in Reformation England*, 94–5.

[62]   Marshall, *Beliefs and the Dead in Reformation England*, 124.

[63]   Ibid, 127.

[64]   Ibid, 163.

There can be no more explicit affirmation of the legitimacy of the papal office than this. *The Last Judgment* features a hierarchy of earthly leadership, which places the Roman pontiff on top as 'highest' of the world's officers, followed by emperor, king, and queen. Today it is difficult to fully appreciate the potential explosiveness of this play, as it survives in a text dating less than two years after Pope Pius's bull of 1570 excommunicated the queen, absolving her subjects from their allegiance, cursing those who obeyed her, and declaring her to be deposed. There was no other contemporary play *like* Chester's *The Last Judgment*. None of the other great mystery play cycles features a pope. And in the only English-language play of the period which does, Bale's *King Johan*, the pope as Usurped Power offers a startling exercise in contrast: the holy father wanders onto the stage in a 'light' gown, tells a few obscene jokes, and invites his cohorts in vice to sing a merry song. This carnivalesque send-up was meant to be funny, but it was not amusing to one Henry Totehill who was questioned by the authorities following a performance of the play in 1538, when he complained that the pope's treatment was 'petie and nawghtely done'.[65] Might not the Elizabethan authorities have been equally sensitive to any publicly uttered affirmation of papal supremacy in a play featuring the pope vested in full pontificals on stage? After all, just for affixing the pope's bull to the gate of the bishop of London's palace shortly after the excommunication was announced, John Felton was hanged to death in a public execution.[66] For this important question, we will never have a definitive answer.

What is particularly interesting is that Christopher Goodman's 'List of Absurdities' makes no reference to either the saved or damned pope on stage. His objections to *The Last Judgment* are limited to 'Purgatory affirmed, preaching of merits of man. The divell speaking in Latin, & setteth forth invocation of Saints'.[67] How could player popes on stage have missed his attention, especially given his abhorrence of Catholic vestments? Perhaps he just overlooked the popes in the text, or perhaps the speech prefixes to the characters were missing in the mayor's copy of the cycle. Lumiansky and Mills have an intriguing gloss to the stanza which features the dialogue on the papal office. They note that George Bellin's second complete cycle manuscript, BL Harley 2013, omits the entire 8 lines of the stanza. They comment: 'R's omission may be a scribal error, but seems more probably deliberate, censoring the lines which make explicit the identification of the "highest office under thee" (55) with the papacy. Missing these lines, the speaker could stand as representative of the clergy without Catholic implications.'[68] My own view is that a bishop, a casting change that

[65]   I discuss the matter in *Theatre and Reformation: Protestantism, Patronage, and Playing in Tudor England* (Cambridge, 1993), 29.

[66]   For Felton's execution and the aftermath of the excommunication, see David Starkey, *Elizabeth: The Struggle for the Throne* (London, 2000), 320.

[67]   Baldwin, Clopper, and Mills, *REED: Cheshire*, 1.148.

[68]   Lumiansky and Mills, *Chester Mystery Cycle*, 2.355–6.

would have in an instant defanged the play of its most inflammatory feature, substituted for the pope. Even without the pope, *The Last Judgment* is a pretty conservative play, and if performed in 1572, must have been approved by the Weavers' guild.

The Coming of Antichrist and the Eucharist

In the extant manuscripts' version of play 18, *The Resurrection*, Christ delivers an extraordinary speech – his lines are delivered in a stanzaic form unique to the cycle – in which he expounds on the eucharist.[69] Faith, or 'beleeffe', he states, is necessary for the experience of communion to be effectual:

> And that bread that I you give,
> your wicked life to amend,
> becomes my fleshe through your beleeffe
> and doth release your synfull band. (174–7)

This meaning, however, was not the version used in 1572 according to Christopher Goodman. The 1572 script's unrevised version read: 'And therto a full ryche messe, in bred myn one bodie, & that bred I you gyve, your wyked lyffe to amend, becomen is my fleshe, through wordes 5 betwyxt the prestes handes.'[70] Christ states that during the mass the bread becomes the body of Christ through the miracle of transubstantiation, which occurs when the priest consecrates the host by holding it up with both hands between his thumb and forefinger and pronounces the five words, 'Hoc est enim Corpus Meum' ['For this is my body'].

Christ's words on the eucharist in *The Resurrection* are controversial, but they are only words in a speech. Far more sensational, if no less entertaining, is the climactic moment in play twenty-three, *The Coming of Antichrist*, when Elijah produces a eucharistic wafer, blesses it with the sign of the cross, resulting in a blaze of light, which exposes the fraud of the two men supposedly raised from the dead by Antichrist. The print of the cross on the wafer, combined with the intense light, terrifies the first dead man. This moment in *The Coming of Antichrist* constitutes a conflation of the transubstantiation of Christ with the transfiguration of Jesus as it appears in all three synoptic gospels.[71] The conflation had a long history, perhaps originating outside of orthodoxy. According to Charles Caspers, the abundant literature of miraculous occurrences produced in the high and late middle ages offers instances in which miraculous hosts suddenly appear with intense

---

[69]   For the stylistic shift here, see ibid, 2.283; and Mills, 'Some Theological Issues', 222–3.

[70]   Baldwin, Clopper, and Mills, *REED: Cheshire*, 1.148.

[71]   I am indebted for this discussion of the conflation of transubstantiation and transfiguration to Purdue Ph.D. student, Philip Schaust.

light, precisely as Christ did at the transfiguration.[72] And this is what occurs in *The Coming of Antichrist*, as well as in a wall painting of the transfiguration in Chester Cathedral.[73] Significantly, we cannot gloss this staged miracle in protestant terms. The miracle is a Catholic moment, and no amount of explaining by an expositor (as in the Old Testament pageants) can contain its heterodoxy in 1572 Chester. The moment either has to be depicted or cut completely. Goodman, however, has the episode taking place in 1572, at least in the mayor's copy of the script he may have examined. Was this pageant dropped in the performance of 1575? Mills says it was; Richard Emmerson argues that the case of Andrew Taylor, the dyer who was jailed for non-payment of dues, demonstrates that *The Coming of Antichrist* was staged in 1575.[74]

Genevan Protestantism in *Abraham* and Other Pageants?

What about on the other side of the religious divide, the puritans? What do the cycle texts and the commotion surrounding its 1572 performance tell us about their presence in 1572 Chester and how their history in the town at this time intersected with the Whitsun plays? Goodman opposed the plays on the grounds of their popery, but he also mentions in his letters the waste of public funds and misspent labour, the violation of the rights of those citizens who are coerced into contributing money to their guilds, and the breaking of the peace.[75] They are not mentioned in his notes or elsewhere directly, but Goodman must have been especially disturbed by the numerous clerical vestments featured in the Whitsun plays. At least a third of the pageants feature roles for actors wearing copes, albs, and other controversial dress, and the streets of Chester in Whitsun play years must have displayed more clerical dress than had been seen since monastic times.[76]

---

[72]   Charles Caspers, 'Wandering between Transubstantiation and Transfiguration: Images of the Prophet Elijah in Western Christianity', in Marcel Poorthuis and Joshua Schwartz (eds), *Saints and Role Models in Judaism and Christianity* (Leiden, 2004), 335–54.

[73]   Sally-Beth MacLean, *Chester Art: A Subject List of Extant and Lost Art including Items Relevant to Early Drama*. EDAM Reference Series 3 (Kalamazoo, 1982), 35.

[74]   Mills's argument, developed in 'Some Theological Issues', 217–18, is controversial, but it should not be taken lightly. See also Emmerson, 'Contextualizing Performance', 89–119. Clopper, in *Drama, Play and Game*, 286–93, sees no major cuts for 1575.

[75]   Baldwin, Clopper, and Mills, *REED: Cheshire*, 1.144–6.

[76]   Dawson and Glassey, 'Some Unpublished Letters', 193; the editors date the letter in question to late May or early June 1567 (192). In light of this, John Knox, in a letter to Goodman in late May 1567 remarks: 'At the last in your garden at Aldford you & I walking alone, you said that you durst not so to do [wear popish vestments], lest god wold forsake youe: because, said youe, I have knowen of late dyvers persons excellently well learnyd of right & zealouse judgement very profitable to the Church of god as well in doctrine as by good example of living, but syns they have received thes kinds of clothing they are become cold & of no value in comparison to that they have been.'

In correspondence with John Knox, Goodman expressed the notion that the habitual wearing of Catholic clothing turns one 'cold' to the gospel, as if the clothing itself had that kind of effect.

David Mills finds Calvinist thinking and sentiment in several of the Chester cycle pageants. He argues for 'a recurrent strain of covenant theology' in the cycle, citing parallels between select passages drawn mainly from *Noah's Flood*, *Abraham and Isaac*, and *Balaack and Balaam*.[77] Despite some interesting parallels, I remain unconvinced that the source is protestant theology, as he maintains. The concept of divine promise and its signs can be traced directly to the bible itself where, in the story of Noah treated in Genesis 6 through 9, the word 'covenant' (or the Latin equivalent) appears some fourteen times.[78] I believe Mills and Clopper are right, however, in discerning a reformed protestant voice in the Late Banns, and I am not among those scholars who view the Late Banns' gesturing towards protestantism as a cynical ploy to appease reformed censors. As Clopper observes, the Late Banns repeatedly defend the representation of scripture on the stage and justify the occasional embellishment of biblical speeches and events.[79] The cycle, indeed, contributes to the emerging protestant debate in England over the propriety of staging the bible, already discernible in the defensively written prologue to Calvinist Lewis Wager's interlude, *The Life and Repentance of Mary Magdalene* (published in 1566).

Protestantism is most palpably evident in pageant four, *Abraham and Isaac*, according to both Mills and Clopper. Clopper argues that the Melchizedech segment of *Abraham and Isaac* is a late Henrician development to praise the new protestant king as supreme head of the church.[80] This is unlikely. Melchizedech, who offers Abraham gifts of bread and wine, is in the pageant because he features significantly in the Sarum rite's liturgy of the mass as a prototype of the eucharistic offering, and given the Late Banns' warning to the Barbers and Wax-Chandlers to 'Suffer yow not in enye poynte the storye [of Melchizedech's offering] to decaye', probably the pre-Reformation version followed the cycle's main theological source, *The Stanzaic Life of Christ*, in supporting the Catholic mass.[81] The expositor somewhat defensively emphasizes memory rather than sacrifice in the scene's 'signification' of the eucharist, and this emphasis certainly sounds doctrinally protestant. The very paralleling of the bread and wine offered by Melchizedech

---

[77]   Mills, 'Chester's Covenant Theology', 400. Mills develops this line of thinking further in 'Some Theological Issues', 212–29.

[78]   On the other hand, the word 'covenant' appears in the cycle only once, at line 108 of pageant one. Protestant covenant theology in dramatic form is illustrated by John Bale's interlude, *God's Promises*, which figures nowhere in Mills's discussion.

[79]   Clopper, *Drama, Play and Game*, 290–91.

[80]   Ibid, 185.

[81]   'The Late Banns', line 84, in Lumiansky and Mills, *The Chester Mystery Cycle*, 288. David Mills acknowledges the debt to *The Stanzaic Life*; he cites the relevant passage from the medieval work in 'Some Theological Issues', 224.

with the lord's supper was highly controversial in protestant Europe and major reformers condemned it as a 'popish' misreading of the biblical account. Both Luther and Calvin in their commentaries on Genesis see Melchizedech's provision of wine and bread as simply illustrating hospitality toward Abraham, with Calvin adding that St Paul in the Book of Hebrews 'says not a word concerning bread and wine' in his detailed comparison of Christ to the Old Testament priest-king.[82] My guess is that the revisions in *Abraham* which focus on the expositor were introduced possibly as late as Edward's reign, when tensions over the eucharist were at their highest in England, in order to police the meanings associated with Melchizedech, who, as Marcel Poorthuis argues, had long been associated with the real presence.[83] They may have been the work of either a lay guild member or a non-university-trained chaplain, in either case an individual with reformed sympathies. My sense is that this same hand is present in the expositor's speeches in play five on Moses and Balaam, and in revised passages on the eucharist in the Bakers' *Last Supper* and the Skinners' *Resurrection*. I also agree with Mills that the doctor's prophecies drawn from 'The Holy Scripture' in the Vintners' play eight have a strong protestant colouring, reminiscent of those dramatized in Bale's prophet's play, *God's Promises*. Where I part company with Mills, however, is in his assertion that these revisions are the work of a theological expert.[84]

Popular Religion in *The Harrowing of Hell* and Other Pageants

In the final part of my discussion, I return to what I think the cycle's main appeal was for most Cestrians, at least in religious terms. Early Elizabethan Cestrians had ceased to be Catholic, but I do believe that a good part of their religious sensibility drew on many features we tend to associate with the old church: the importance of the visual in religious devotion, a deep-rooted fascination with the miraculous, a love of sacred music as an expression of praise for the divine, and a privileging of biblical story over doctrine. As observed earlier, scholars have identified all of these features as the popular piety of ordinary people in early modern England. This popular religion I find illustrated in the Cooks' play, *The Harrowing of Hell*. The story of Christ's descent into hell was kept alive in the popular imagination by wall paintings in churches and public meeting places and in such texts as *The Gospel of Nicodemus* and *Piers Plowman*, both of which went through multiple

---

[82]   See Calvin, *Commentaries on the First Book of Moses, Called Genesis*, John King (trans.), 1843; rpt Grand Rapids MI, 1981; Martin Luther, *Luther's Works: Volume 2: Lectures on Genesis Chapters 6–14*, Jaroslav Pelikan and Daniel E. Poellot (eds) (St. Louis, 1960), 384–5.

[83]   Marcel Poorthius, 'Enoch and Melchizedek in Judaism and Christianity: A Study in Intermediaries', in Marcel Poorthius and Joshua Schwartz (eds), *Saints and Role Models in Judaism and Christianity* (Boston, 2004), 118–19.

[84]   Mills, 'Some Theological Issues', 225.

editions in sixteenth-century England, right down to the end of Elizabeth's reign.[85] All the reformers had to acknowledge the truth of Christ's descent to the dead after the crucifixion, because it was in the apostles' creed. Elizabethan churchmen were divided over the harrowing of hell, with Calvinists inclined to dismiss it as fictional, but parishioners recited the apostles' creed each Sunday from the *Book of Common Prayer*, and the harrowing was explicitly affirmed in the Elizabethan Book of Homilies. Clearly what appealed to the Elizabethans were the ludic and pictorial dimensions of the harrowing. After the crucifixion, Christ as warrior enters limbo, 'defeats Satan, and rescues the souls of the dead from the gated prisonhouse of hell'.[86] Following the fifteenth-century *Stanzaic Life of Christ*, the action is spectacular: Christ arrives at the gates of hell amidst triumphant shouts and rolling thunder, Satan and the diablerie are stunned and confused by his sudden appearance; demanding entry, the gates fall with a tremendous crash and Christ binds the devil and frees the saints, who process out of hell singing 'Te Deum laudamus', a popular hymn prescribed in *The Book of Common Prayer* ~~Canticle~~ for matins. The music here is an important devotional element of the pageant, as it is in *Noah's Flood*, where Psalm 69, 'Save me, O God', draws on a popular piece of congregational singing, again drawn from the *Book of Common Prayer*. The redeemed thief on the cross joins the process from paradise, the actor arduously carrying a cross on his back, a piece of spectacle that Goodman found offensive. The pageant combines sensational entertainment with the kind of spiritual celebration found in such devotional works as John Foxe's pamphlet on Christ's harrowing, *Christ Jesus Triumphant* (1579), which features a woodcut of Christ 'rising out of the tomb, trampling on death and carrying a victor's palm'.[87] A puritan, Alexander Hume, mocked this woodcut in a 1590s debate on the harrowing of hell.[88] Goodman and most puritans hated this sort of spectacle, but most Cestrian playgoers probably found the pageant not the least bit offensive. The comical sequence with the alewife that ends most manuscript versions of the pageant adds a final touch of carnivalesque humor. Again, popular religion welcomed mixing revelry with sacred narrative. Popular religion accommodated such contradictions, and the concluding episode, in its topicality, would have presumably generated a sense of solidarity, since everyone was in on the joke.

---

[85] While no public art on the harrowing survives in Chester (see index to MacLean, *Chester Art*), wall paintings and stained glass on the subject surviving elsewhere in English churches illustrate its continuing popularity, according to Beatrice Groves, *Texts and Traditions*, 136–7. Among the sources she cites are C.E. Keyser, *A List of Buildings in Great Britain and Ireland having Mural and other Painted Decorations of Dates Prior to the Latter Part of the Sixteenth Century*, 3rd edn (London, 1883); Clifford Davidson and Jennifer Alexander, *Early Art of Coventry* (Kalamazoo, 1985); and Thomas Habington, *A Survey of Worcestershire by Thomas Habington*, John Amphlett (ed.) (Oxford, 1893).

[86] Groves, *Texts and Traditions*, 135.

[87] Cited in ibid, 136.

[88] Ibid, 137.

Conclusions

Especially in the wake of the queen's excommunication in 1570, pageants such as *The Purification*, *The Coming of Antichrist*, and *The Last Judgment* struck protestant leaders as radically papist, *anti*-protestant, and perhaps even treasonous. It is therefore no surprise that local puritans called on national authorities to shut the Chester Whitsun plays down. But I am doubtful that the average Cestrian playgoer viewed these plays and the cycle in general as deeply offensive. In 1575 the city council voted thirty-five to eleven to revive the Whitsun plays, and that seems as good indication as any of the favourable/unfavourable ratio within the community three years earlier. My guess is that the spectacular theatrics of *The Coming of Antichrist* would have overshadowed any serious offense given by the staging of a Roman Catholic host. And as I have argued, the elimination of the saved pope from *The Last Judgment* likely blunted the pageant's polemical edge in 1572. In 1575, *The Coming of Antichrist* appears to have been reformed to comment on 'whoe be Antechristes the worlde rownde aboute', although, as Mills suggests, both antichrist plays and the Weaver's pageant may have been dropped from the midsummer performance that year.

Another conclusion is that the Catholic recusants and fellow travellers who are documented as participants in the 1572 *Purification*, and almost certainly controlled the production of *The Last Judgment*, clearly used the plays, as Goodman claims, to assemble and organize religious conservatives and to reassert their faith ('giveth great comfort to the rebellious papist').[89] Such 'assembling and conference' included, of course, the two or three major rehearsals used to prepare the pageants for production.[90] Having said that, one should also be open to the possibility that with some spectators the pageants may have engendered doubt rather than faith. *The Coming of Antichrist* features as its hero an actor who impersonates Christ in a story where false images masquerade as truth. Some Elizabethan playgoers, however, who already disbelieved in the sacred host that the pageant highlights as the centre of Christian faith, may have possibly questioned protestantism's own exclusive claims to religious truth. The last year of the cycle, 1575, was only a decade or so away from the great religious tragedies of Marlowe, Shakespeare, and Webster, wherein, arguably, the representation of religion on stage raised as many questions about the Christian faith as it answered.

---

[89]   Baldwin, Clopper, and Mills, *REED: Cheshire*, 1.143–4.

[90]   Surviving cycle accounts published by REED suggest this. See Tiffany Stern, *Rehearsal from Shakespeare to Sheridan* (Oxford, 2000), 26–34.

Chapter 8
'Erazed in the booke'?:
Periodization and the Material Text
of the Chester Banns

Kurt A. Schreyer

Christopher Goodman begins his 10 May 1572 letter to the earl of Huntingdon with a brief historical sketch of the Chester mystery plays: 'certain plays were devised by a monk about 200 years past in the depth of ignorance, & by the Pope then authorized to be set forth, & by that authority placed in the city of Chester to the intent to retain that place in assured ignorance & superstition according to the Popish policy. against which plays all preachers & godly men since the time of the blessed light of the gospell have inveyed and impugned'. Goodman's religious views obligate him to divide Chester history, not simply into ancient and modern or past and present periods, but rather Catholic and protestant epochs, a 'past time of monkish ignorance' and a 'godly present time of the blessed light of the gospel'.[1] This history is, of course, hardly neutral; it is ideologically driven and has as its goal the destruction of the Chester cycle. Not until the enlightenment project of the eighteenth century and Hegel's world history in the following century would a decisive historical break between the middle ages and the Renaissance, with the Reformation as the pivotal epochal moment, be assumed as a matter of course.[2] Goodman's letter, therefore, asks us to consider how late sixteenth- and early seventeenth-century Cestrians viewed their city's past, particularly their theatrical history.

Such a consideration might seem irrelevant given current trends in early English drama studies. Nearly fifty years have passed since O.B. Hardison overturned E.K. Chambers's teleological model of dramatic history, the secularization thesis that drove a wedge between the 'Renaissance' stage and its 'medieval' antecedents. Recent scholarship, on the other hand, seems to have reached a consensus in its search for continuities rather than disjunctions between the professional London companies, especially Shakespeare's, and the earlier drama and culture of the sixteenth century.

---

[1] Goodman's letter is quoted from Elizabeth Baldwin, Lawrence M. Clopper, and David Mills (eds), *Records of Early English Drama: Cheshire including Chester* (Toronto, 2007), 1.143.

[2] See Margreta de Grazia, 'World Pictures, Modern Periods, and the Early Stage', in John D. Cox and David Scott Kastan (eds), *A New History of Early English Drama* (New York, 1997), 17–21.

'Aesthetic and cultural models that once opposed a primitive medieval drama to the mature achievements of Elizabethan theater have now', as Theresa Coletti explains, 'been all but abandoned, as has the teleological narrative that posited English drama's sixteenth-century progress toward formal complexity and secular mimesis'.[3] There are many reasons why the abandonment of strict periodization is now well underway. The treasure trove of archival material brought to light by the Records of Early English Drama (REED) project housed at the University of Toronto has, as David Matthews and Gordon McMullan have noted in their collection *Reading the Medieval in Early Modern England* (itself a significant contribution to 'cross-period engagement') encouraged early English drama specialists to traverse the customary medieval-Renaissance divide.[4] Having recognized, moreover, that what is often labelled as 'medieval' drama survives in sixteenth-century manuscripts, many scholars of the 'middle ages' feel quite at home in the latter decades of their traditional disciplinary field. Renaissance studies have followed the lead of Stephen Greenblatt in exploring the carryover of medieval culture onto the stages of the professional London playhouses. Helen Cooper, Michael O'Connell, and John D. Cox have contributed important work demonstrating how elements of traditional dramaturgy enjoyed a long stage career.[5] Scholarship on the Queen's Men and on the practices of touring has blurred distinctions between the drama of London and the provinces, and in the process helped us to rethink critical categories and distinctions. Journals such as *Early Theatre* and the *Journal of Medieval and Early Modern Studies* encourage further disciplinary cross-fertilization, as do academic associations like the Medieval and Renaissance Drama Society.

But our eagerness to elide the once sacrosanct medieval-Renaissance divide must not overlook the fact that centuries before E.K. Chambers's 1903 *The Mediaeval Stage* accounted for the growth and evolution of the Renaissance stage at the expense of earlier dramatic forms, pre-Reformation English drama was, if not ignored, often decried. Goodman was not alone in his desire 'for the repressing of Papacy, & advancing of godliness' through the suppression of drama.[6] In his 1607 sermon, the protestant preacher William Crashaw offered a genealogy of the English stage in which medieval mysteries, the popish progeny of ancient heathen theatre, were seen as direct conduits of the ungodly errors put on display in London's public playhouses: 'The vngodly Playes and Enterludes so rife in this

---

[3]   Coletti, 'The Chester Cycle in Sixteenth-Century Religious Culture', *Journal of Medieval and Early Modern Studies* 37.3 (Fall 2007), 531.

[4]   The phrase is borrowed from Matthews and McMullan, *Reading the Medieval in Early Modern England* (Cambridge, 2007), 5. As their collection recognizes and represents, the push against 'period parochialism' extends beyond early theater studies.

[5]   See Cooper, *Shakespeare and the Medieval World* (London, 2010); O'Connell, *The Idolatrous Eye: Iconoclasm and Theater in Early-Modern England* (New York, 2000) as well as his 'Vital Cultural Practices: Shakespeare and the Mysteries', *Journal of Medieval and Early Modern Studies* 29 (1999): 149–68; Cox, *The Devil and the Sacred in English Drama, 1350–1642* (Cambridge, 2000).

[6]   Baldwin, Clopper, and Mills, *REED: Cheshire*, 1.144.

nation; what are they but *a Bastard of Babylon*, a daughter of error and confusion, a hellish deuice ... deliuered to the *Heathen*, from them to the *Papists*, and from them to vs?'[7] Reminding King James that the primitive church had condemned plays, Crashaw called for the destruction of this 'tower of Babel' as part of a larger programme of religious reformation. As Cathy Shrank reminds us, we ought to view reformist narratives with considerable suspicion whether, as in the case of John Bale that she considers, they promote novelty and chronological difference or, as with Crashaw, they insist on historical continuity.[8] Yet defenders of the early public theatres were also skittish about early English religious drama. Thomas Heywood's 1612 *Apology for Actors* responded to anti-theatricalists like Crashaw by simply ignoring religious drama altogether. Holding up pagans (not the church) as the bearers of 'antiquity and dignity' to English theatre, he wrote: 'Thus our Antiquity haue we brought from the *Grecians* in the time of *Hercules*, from the *Macedonians* in the age of *Alexander*, from the Romans long before Iulius Caesar.'[9] Embracing theatre's pagan origins, Heywood is careful to exclude popish forms of drama: 'I omit the shewes and ceremonies euen in these times generally vsed amongst the Catholikes, in which by the Churchmen & most religious, diuerse pageants, as of the Natiuity, Passion, and Ascension, with other Historicall places of the Bible, are at diuerse times & seasons of the year vsually celebrated.'[10] While both Crashaw and Heywood abhor mystery drama and agree that the London playhouses revive antiquity in some way, their conflicting accounts raise questions about the place of pre-Reformation plays in the history of early English drama. According to Crashaw, the theatre persists in a continuous history of corruption and heathen degeneracy. In Heywood's narrative, on the other hand, commercial theatre has disclaimed a dark ages of Catholic drama in order to recuperate respectable pagan virtues. Neither opponents of the professional London acting companies nor their supporters, it would seem, had much use for mystery plays. And yet, given that both Crashaw's sermon and Heywood's *Apology* were composed decades after the suppression of the mysteries, this powerful dramatic form was apparently not easily forgotten.

Considering the theatrical genealogies offered by Goodman, Crashaw, and Heywood, the current scholarly push for historical continuity in early English drama seems less straightforward than it first appears. However artificial and arbitrary period divisions are, they seem likewise ineluctable, and while this essay cannot claim to solve this dilemma, it does suggest that a historical perspective may be beneficial. I will therefore interrogate the traditional medieval-Renaissance

---

[7]   William Crashaw, 'The sermon preached at the Crosse' (London, 1607), STC (2nd edn) 6028, Z1r.

[8]   Cathy Shrank, 'John Bale and reconfiguring the "medieval" in Reformation England' in David Matthew and Gordon McMullan (eds), *Reading the Medieval in Early Modern England*, 179–92.

[9]   Thomas Heywood, *Apology for Actors* (London, 1612), STC (2nd edn) 13309, G2v-G3r.

[10]   Ibid, E4r.

divide and address current efforts to elide it altogether by suggesting that we look to the surviving texts of the Chester Banns for their perspective on pre- and post-Reformation drama. The 1619 *Breviary of Chester History* calls the Banns 'the breeife of the whole playes', for this proclamation not only advertised the upcoming performance of the plays and encouraged audience attendance, but also promoted the contributions of the various guilds.[11] Divided into poetic stanzas, the Banns announce which guilds will present each pageant, draw attention to significant events in each performance, and highlight noteworthy pieces of craftsmanship such as carriages, props, or costumes. The Banns also articulate what I believe to be a productive alternative account of sixteenth-century theatrical history from those outlined above, a narrative that seeks to preserve synchronic contact with past theatrical objects and practices even as the Banns themselves record and perform diachronic historical change.

Of Custome Olde

Two versions of the Banns survive: the first (often called 'Early' or 'Catholic') survives to us only in Harley MS 2150 and was, according to Lawrence Clopper, originally composed for Corpus Christi play performances between 1505 and 1521, then revised by a scribe between 1521 and 1532, when the plays were moved to Whitsun and expanded. They were most likely transcribed into their present form around 1540. Clopper maintains that a scribe copied them onto folios 85v to 88v of Harley 2150 sometime in the late sixteenth century (c. 1570), but the story of their emendation does not end there by any means. During the period 1630–68, long after any Chester audiences had seen their famous mysteries performed, Chester antiquarian Randle Holme II collated the Early Banns with other sixteenth-century civic records by adding previously omitted lines and explicitly marking passages which had been 'erazed' in the authorized post-Reformation version of the Banns (the 'Late Banns') during the previous century.[12] Perhaps most significant, and certainly most striking, are his marginalia. Holme drew black vertical lines to the left of lines 156 through 163 of the Banns with a horizontal line above line 156 (Figure 8.1). Holme also marked lines 164 through 171 with a vertical line in the left-hand margin, with a horizontal line drawn beneath line 171. Holme labelled both of these boxed-in passages as 'erazed in the booke', presumably referring to the city's official 'White Book of the Pentice'. These passages describe liturgical and Marian elements of the cycle similar to those that outraged protestant

---

[11]   Quoted from Baldwin, Clopper, and Mills, *REED: Cheshire*, 1.332. The *Breviary* was written by Robert Rogers, archdeacon of the Cathedral of St. Werburgh in the late 1500s (he died in 1595), and completed by his son David, who produced five copies of four versions of the Breviary between 1609 and about 1637 (see p. cxcvi of the same volume).

[12]   Lawrence M. Clopper, 'The History and Development of the Chester Cycle', *Modern Philology* 75 (1978), 231. R.M. Lumiansky and David Mills, *The Chester Mystery Cycle: Essays and Documents* (Chapel Hill, 1983), 273.

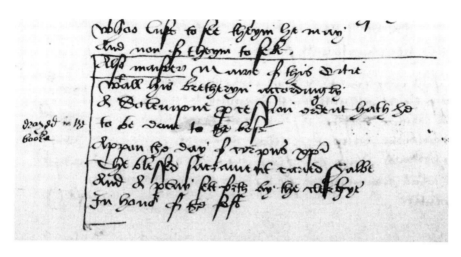

Fig. 8.1   British Library MS Harley 2150, fol. 88^r detail. © British Library
Board.

clergyman Christopher Goodman. The bold lines that box in these passages call
the reader's attention to the censored material, and in doing so invite us to consider
Holme's purpose in drawing them, particularly in light of the fact that they appear
to be unique: no other material that he copied into the Harley 2150 manuscript
is similarly delimited. These border lines may simply reflect Holme's assiduous
record keeping; they carefully delineate which passages had been erased in order
to make the Banns conform to the suppression of the feast of Corpus Christi and
Marian devotion. But I want to go further and suggest that they hinge upon the
very same historical periodization that is also at work in Goodman's letter of
10 May 1572. To see the historiographical work Holme's marginalia performs, we
must first turn to the later version of the Chester Banns.

Surprisingly, the Late Banns – the late sixteenth-century (frequently labeled
'post-Reformation' or 'protestant') proclamation composed and revised several
times between 1548 and 1572 – do not hide the fact that these plays were, in
Goodman's words, 'devised by a monk about 200 years past in the depth of
ignorance' but in fact share his periodized view of Chester history.[13] Unlike the

---

[13]   Four versions of the Late Banns survive; when I use the term 'Late Banns' I
refer primarily to the version that survives in Rogers's 1609 *Breviary* in the Chester City
Archives (Baldwin, Clopper, and Mills, *REED: Cheshire*, 1.332–40) which includes the
'conclusion' and, given what Clopper calls its 'apologetic' tone, is probably a later revision.
On the approximate date of 1572, see Clopper, 'The History and Development of the
Chester Cycle', 236–41. On the vagaries of these manuscripts, see Lumiansky and Mills,
The Chester Mystery Cycle: Essays and Documents, 272–7.

outspoken preacher, however, the Late Banns consider the historical distance of the mystery plays to be their saving virtue, preserving and protecting them from contemporary critics like Goodman. To defuse this hostility, the Late Banns present the plays as relics of a bygone age:

> we moste humblye praye
> Not to compare this matter or storye
> With the age or tyme wherein we presentlye staye
> But to the tyme of Ignorance whearein we doe straye
> And then dare I compare yat this lande throughout
> None had the like. nor the like durste set out
> …
> If noe matter or shewe. thereof enye thinge speciall
> Doe not please but mislycke ye moste of the trayne
> Goe backe againe to the firste tyme I saye
> Then shall yow finde the fine witte at this daye aboundinge
> At yat day & yat age, had uerye smale beinge[14]

The Late Banns divide the history of the Chester mysteries into periods for a strategic purpose. Carefully deploying the categories of 'old' and 'new', the Late Banns avoid responsibility for any lingering superstition by reminding the audience that the plays were written in the remote 'tyme of Ignorance'. Elsewhere, they encourage the belief that the cycle was established by the city's first mayor, Sir John Arneway, and written by Ranulf Higden, 'Moncke of Chester Abbaye', though they know quite well that many of the pageants were written and added in Tudor times.[15] The decision to antiquate the city's mystery cycle is peculiar. Whatever the virtues of age-old customs and traditions, they raise the spectre of the old religion in a climate of increasing protestant suspicion. What is at stake in the Late Banns' historicization is the very survival of the plays and Chester's unique civic identity, which, as Sheila Christie argues in this volume, was deeply rooted in its Roman heritage. Note the thinly veiled pride which views Chester as an exceptional city even in its darker days: 'dare I compare yat this lande throughout / None had the like. nor the like durste set out'. Perhaps this sense of civic identity explains why the Banns do not entirely conform to later more extreme protestant views but seek instead to preserve vast amounts of 'Auntient' material for modern performance.[16] The Banns, for example, urge that the traditional appearance of the devil be preserved:

---

[14]   Baldwin, Clopper, and Mills, *REED: Cheshire*, 1.334.

[15]   Ibid, 332. For the argument that 'the cycle as we know it was largely an invention of Tudor times', see Clopper, 'The History and Development of the Chester Cycle'.

[16]   Compare Meg Twycross and Sarah Carpenter who write, 'The new Banns comment extensively on the plays, showing a rather defensively apologetic attitude towards their "old-fashioned" drama', in *Masks and Masking in Medieval and Early Tudor England* (Burlington VT, 2002), 194.

And nexte to this yow the Butchers of this Cittie
The storye of Sathan yat woulde Criste needes tempte
Set out as accustomablie vsed have ye
The Deuell in his ffeathers all Rugged and rente[17]

This description is quite literal: the Chester REED documents tell us that shredded rags of canvas were used to make 'dye menes Covtes' for the *Harrowing of Hell*.[18] Making even the smallest details of time-honored stage properties, like the demons' costumes, present once more is part of the attraction, and therefore of the advertising, of this production. The Late Banns excuse disagreeable topics and stage practices by depicting the plays as the products of a bygone age of ignorance that is divided from the 'age or tyme wherein we presentlye staye'. In doing so, they ingeniously co-opt Goodman's historical periodization and turn it on its head: they shove the cycle plays into the popish past not to destroy but to protect them.

Though protective of past customs, the Late Banns are quite aware of tenuous present circumstances and are forced to drastically reinterpret the theological and dramatic significance of certain stage properties and practices. A passage unique to the Late Banns admonishes the audience concerning the embodied representation of the godhead and was perhaps written with Goodman and his fellow preachers in mind:

Of one thinge warne you now I shall
That not possible it is those matters to be contryued
In such sorte and cunninge, & by suche players of price
As at this daye good players & fine wittes. coulde deuise
ffor then shoulde all those persones that as godes doe playe
In Clowdes come downe with voyce and not be seene,
ffor noe man can proportion that Godhead I saye
To the shape of man face. nose and eyne
But sethence the face gilte doth disfigure the man yat deme
A Clowdye coueringe of the man. a Voyce onlye to heare
And not god in shape or person to appeare[19]

In order to defend the players from the charge of idolatry, the Banns admonish the audience to excuse the embodied representation of God. If you see a player in a gilt mask playing God, then imagine it's a cloud or that you only hear a voice, the

---

[17]   Baldwin, Clopper, and Mills, *REED: Cheshire*, 1.337.

[18]   Ibid, 261. See also Meg Twycross, 'The Chester Cycle Wardrobe', in David Mills (ed.), *Staging the Chester Cycle* (Leeds, 1985), 121.

[19]   Baldwin, Clopper, and Mills, *REED: Cheshire*, 1.340. I read the beginning of this passage as: 'Since it's impossible even for our talented, present-day actors to devise an alternative means of staging, I must caution you that you will see God impersonated by an actor in a gilt mask.' Compare Twycross and Carpenter, *Masks and Masking*, 195. Also see Mills, *The Chester Mystery Cycle: A New Edition with Modernised Spelling* (East Lansing MI, 1992), 12.

Banns prescribe. Consequently, a gilt mask that had previously made God visible, could now be supposed to render him invisible, merely audible.[20]

What is so surprising is not that the Late Banns give a note of warning, but to whom that word of caution is spoken: they admonish the audience to adjust its thinking. There is never any question that dubious pre-Reformation material will be resurrected and staged. The Late Banns are not, as we might expect on such an incendiary religious issue, bowing to Goodman's accusations, but in fact urging tolerance of traditional (read 'Catholic') stagecraft.[21] Human flesh will continue to be gilded, deified if you will, as before. Yet if fault is to be found with this stage practice then, according to the Late Banns, it lies with the audience, not the players, for misinterpreting what is being performed. As with previous subject matter, historical precedent is underscored so as to assuage any discomfort:

> That not possible it is those matters to be contryued
> In such sorte and cunninge, & by suche players of price
> As at this daye good players & fine wittes. coulde deuise.[22]

In other words, even contemporary craftsmen-actors cannot develop an effective alternative to staging Christ without somehow incarnating him, and therefore they must adopt the traditional technique of painted masks. These matters were the product of a rude, bygone age, the Late Banns admit, and yet, as there is no present alternative, the audience must appreciate their historicity and excuse them.

A Siege Wall of Ink

But what about those vertical black lines Randle Holme added in the margins of the Early Banns? As a palimpsestic record of Chester theatrical history, Harley 2150 reflects not one moment in time but many, and I would now like to propose that what the Late Banns accomplish rhetorically, the material text of the Early Banns accomplishes graphically. Just as the Late Banns attempt to preserve the sixteenth-century Chester cycle as 'auntient' history dating to the city's founding, the ink on folios 88 recto and verso marks particular dramatic material as past, superseded, and indeed 'erased in the booke'.[23] The Late Banns co-opt the biased historical periodization of protestants like Christopher Goodman in an effort to ensure the

---

[20]   See Twycross and Carpenter's discussion of 'disfigure' in this Banns passage in *Masks and Masking*, 194–5. As their explanation demonstrates, the Banns' curious precaution touches many scenes of the cycle production and underscores how volatile the mystery plays could be in post-Reformation England.

[21]   Compare Twycross and Carpenter, *Masks and Masking*, 195, 196.

[22]   Baldwin, Clopper, and Mills, *REED: Cheshire*, 1.340.

[23]   My subsequent discussion of the materiality of the Chester Banns is indebted to Jonathan Gil Harris's work on Renaissance theories of matter and 'palimpsested time' in *Untimely Matter in the Time of Shakespeare* (Philadelphia, 2009).

cycle's continued performance. Perhaps Holme's annotation of 'erazed' material similarly preempts an iconoclastic practice of erasure in order to retain rather than obliterate the textual record of past Catholic devotion and practice. We will probably never know the reasons for Randle Holme's collation and emendation of this censored text. Perhaps he carefully recorded the textual permutations of the Banns in response to the ideological upheavals occurring in his own time. Active in his antiquarian pursuits from the 1630s into the 1660s, including the bitter siege years of 1644–45, perhaps he feared iconoclastic outbursts as a result of the civil war. Julie Spraggon has studied numerous instances of iconoclasm performed by parliamentarian armies, and while she acknowledges that much of the destruction may have been the result of the wreckage and looting common to all wars, she contends that these men often saw their army as a godly agent of anti-papist reformation. As Canterbury Cathedral was being ransacked, for example, one fervent soldier played a parliamentary song on the organ and sang of his willingness 'to fall in battle to maintain / God's worship' and to 'extirpate Papacy'.[24] Altar rails, organs, sacred images, service books, and vestments obviously met their violent disapprobation, but in their zeal to eradicate popery in all of its forms, soldiers also targeted books and parish records for destruction. As Spraggon explains, 'the suspicion of the written records of the church can be seen at Peterborough, where the soldiers believed the records they destroyed to be papal bulls. Similarly, at Ashover and Derbyshire, soldiers burnt an old parish register because it was written in Latin, and they believed it, therefore, to be 'full of popery and treason'.[25] They might have viewed the manuscripts of the Chester cycle in a similar light as Christopher Goodman in the previous century. Goodman represented the texts of 'the old Popish plays of Chester', full of manifold 'absurdities' which he felt obliged to catalogue in a letter to the Archbishop of York, as threats to queen and commonweal.[26] Holme's antiquarian collections might therefore bear witness to his ideological undertakings. Defiant acts of recusancy (perhaps civically rather than doctrinally motivated), they aimed both to restore what had been iconoclastically 'erazed' by the predecessors of the Roundheads nearly a century before and, perhaps, to anticipate further acts of erasure. As scholars have noted, Holme was a zealous scribe 'who in many cases reproduced the same spellings, abbreviations, contractions, and the like of his manuscript source'.[27] Whatever his motives or intentions, Holme does not merely resurrect the 'Early' or 'Catholic' version of the Banns, but collates it with the censored, post-Reformation copy that was available

---

[24]   Spraggon, *Puritan Iconoclasm during the English Civil War* (London, 2003), 202.

[25]   Ibid, 209.

[26]   For Goodman's account of 'absurdities' in 'the old Popish plays of Chester' see Baldwin, Clopper, and Mills, *REED: Cheshire*, 1.146–8; for the perceived 'peril' and 'danger to Her Majesty' etc., see 144 of the same volume.

[27]   Even when Holme made minor variations in spelling and the like, REED editors believe we can be confident in the accuracy of the large quantity of records that he was responsible for transmitting (Baldwin, Clopper, and Mills, *REED: Cheshire*, 1.cxcvi).

to him. As a result, the horizontal and vertical lines he has drawn between accepted and erased passages have a double effect: they preserve the act of censorship but also cordon off and seemingly protect forbidden areas. Antiquarian recuperation therefore blurs strict temporal distinctions of 'present' and 'past' even as it records the effects of historical (and ideological) change.

In his theory of the ruin in *The Origin of German Tragic Drama* (1928), Walter Benjamin explores the manner in which past objects, particularly the stage properties of *Trauerspiel*, may persist in the present precisely as superseded remnants.[28] 'Rather than signaling the advent of another epoch's renewal', Benjamin's ruin, writes Julia Lupton, 'itself constitutes a kind of rebirth, a rebirth as ruin – namely, the survival of a work beyond the period of its cultural currency'.[29] In the wake of Henrician and Edwardian reforms, the Chester plays were losing their cultural currency. For this reason, the Banns text was updated, and it begged the pardon of its now post-Reformation audience for the vestiges of popish ignorance. Yet in doing so the Late Banns give their matter a rebirth, a rebirth as 'accustomed' cultural artefacts of the city's 'ancient' past. They revive the mysteries but prevent them from being swept away in the current tide of Reformation by anchoring them in the city's ancient past, 'that age' which seems so remote from 'the age or tyme wherein we presently staye', that time loathed by Goodman because it is buried in 'the depth of ignorance' and 'Popish policy'. In a similar fashion, Chester antiquarian Randle Holme did not simply recopy the Early Banns with the previously excised material restored to its original place, but transposed the Early Banns with the forbidden material set apart as superseded matter. We might say that Holme, like Benjamin's historical materialist, resurrects shards of Chester's Catholic past that have been 'sundered from official [protestant] history and now presents the possibility of doing and imagining things differently'.[30] His ink forms a siege wall to protect an oppressed, beleaguered Catholic past from present protestant assault.

---

[28]   Yet coalescing sixteenth-century narratives and seventeenth-century textual practices with twentieth-century theory risks losing sight of the virtue of the Banns, namely their temporal proximity to both the mysteries and the professional London playhouses. The Banns, unlike Benjamin, narrate a history of early English drama free from any consideration of Burkhardt's *Kulturgeschichte* and Hegel's dialectics. So, while I wish to hold up Benjamin's ruin as an illustrative point of comparison, overstating the relevance of his work may unwittingly lead us to dwell upon, rather than to work around, the language of vestiges, precursors, and leftovers – and, perhaps, to a tacit recapitulation of Chambers's secularization thesis (itself derived from a Hegelian scholastic tradition).

[29]   Julia Reinhard Lupton, *Afterlives of the Saints: Hagiography, Typology, and Renaissance Literature* (Stanford, 1996), 28.

[30]   Harris, *Untimely Matter*, 94.

Synchronic Diachrony

To the ecclesiastical opponents of the mysteries and to their proponents as well, the annual pageants in Chester and elsewhere were, as Michael O'Connell explains, still vital enough in the late sixteenth century to expend tremendous legal and political energy. 'The question', O'Connell adds, 'lies in what sense they remained'.[31] The Late Banns can help contemporary scholars answer that question. They demonstrate that late sixteenth-century audiences could and did look back across the Reformation divide to the mystery plays, not merely to condemn them like Goodman and Crashaw, and not to overlook them like Heywood. For, though they speak again and again 'of Custome olde', they express an unmistakable sense of the present vitality and material efficacy of the cycle even in the beleaguered days of the late sixteenth century. The Banns urge the guilds to 'be bolde' and to 'weathelye' and 'Lustelye' bring forth their traditional costumes and pageants regardless of how 'costelye' they are. We have noted the Banns' eager desire to see devils 'accustomablie' staged in their ragged costumes as well as their earnest defence of traditional gilt masks for Deus and Jesus. Other examples of the Banns' enthusiasm for stage properties, time-honoured and otherwise, abound: the star of the nativity, the 'bludshede' of the crucifixion, Noah's ark 'in all poyntes ... prepared', Balaam's talking ass, Melchizedek's bread and wine, the Tanners' 'Apparell comlye'. The Mercers are directed to 'tryme up your Cariage as custome euer was' and the Shoemakers' conventional 'Ierusalem carriage' is requested. Other materials and technologies are implicit in the Banns' description. In order to satisfy their wish to see 'yat gloriose bodye in Clowdes moste ardente / Is taken vppto the heauens', the Tailors' pageant must include a hoist mechanism to achieve the spectacle of Christ's ascension. In order to 'shew ... forthe howe Antechriste shoulde rise', the Shearmen and Clothiers must outfit their wagon with a sepulcher.[32] Thus eager for the 'lyuelye' and 'comlye' use of 'accustomed' stage properties and practices despite the protests of antitheatricalists, this fascinating late sixteenth-century proclamation urges us to explore the afterlives of mystery play techniques and technologies on the professional London stage.

Taking Richard Emmerson's suggestion, then, the goal for scholars of early English drama is 'to discover the similar as well as the dissimilar and to highlight continuities as well as discontinuities'. He argues for a 'synchronic analysis of drama during this period'. Emmerson is by no means calling for a synchronous view that reduces sixteenth-century theatrical experience into a homogenous whole, but rather a methodology that juxtaposes concurrent theatrical traditions previously separated by disciplinary and period divisions. Synchronic study is therefore as much concerned with complexity and range as it is with temporal overlap. Borrowing an example from the Chester mystery cycle as an illustration, Emmerson writes: 'Synchronic analysis ... would ask how the meaning of a play

---

[31]   O'Connell, 'Vital Cultural Practices', 152–3.
[32]   Baldwin, Clopper, and Mills, *REED: Cheshire*, 1.332–40.

about Antichrist staged over seven decades changes over time as the essence of the apocalyptic figure is polemicized, and suggest how the play would be received differently in pre-Reformation Chester, during the Henrician Reformation, and finally under Elizabeth.'[33] Like Emmerson I am eager to overcome the 'rigid periodization that has 'frozen dramatic forms into prescribed time frames associated with their origins'; the Chester Banns, however, caution us not to take our desire for a synchronous 'theatrical era' too far, thus replacing one form of periodization with another.[34] They recognize – indeed their own material existence has come about as a result of – an unmistakable historical difference between the 'then' of the old faith plays and the 'now' in which the Whitsun plays are under assault. As we've seen, the Late Banns manipulate, and often exaggerate, that temporal difference to their advantage. Yet, even though the Late Banns locate the Whitsun plays in a remote and ignorant time, their diachronic narrative is not reducible to our modern notion of a medieval-Renaissance divide. Rather than freezing 'dramatic forms into prescribed time frames associated with their origins', the Banns' diachrony creates the possibility of preserving past objects and practices in the present, creates the possibility, paradoxically enough, of synchrony.

Conclusion

This synchrony within (and resulting from) diachrony is significant for two reasons. First, it avoids the construction of an artificial and inflexible period boundary that divorces pre- and post-Reformation dramatic forms. Second, it recognizes historical change and difference but avoids the pitfalls of E.K. Chambers's biological narrative of the growth and evolution of early English drama. 'If I may venture to define for myself the formula of my work', he writes in the preface to *The Mediaeval Stage*, 'I would say that it endeavours to state and explain the pre-existing conditions which, by the latter half of the sixteenth century, made the great Shakespearean stage possible'.[35] From the outset, then, the project of his *Mediaeval Stage* is mere pretext: what truly matters are the flourishing 'palmy days' of Shakespeare and his contemporaries.[36] So while the study of Shakespeare cannot proceed without first grasping medieval origins, it is equally the case for Chambers that Shakespeare justifies the study of early English drama. The Banns, on the other hand, offer a historical account of the mysteries that is free from Shakespeare's monolithic presence. They view, moreover, sixteenth-century theatrical objects,

---

[33]   Richard K. Emmerson, 'Dramatic History: On the Diachronic and Synchronic in the Study of Early English Drama', *Journal of Medieval and Early Modern Studies* 35.1 (Winter 2005), 56.

[34]   My cautionary note is aimed at my own present study, and I do not mean to imply that Emmerson's careful essay is deficient in this regard; his aim, as quoted above, is to uncover 'the similar as well as the dissimilar and to highlight continuities as well as discontinuities'.

[35]   Chambers, *The Mediaeval Stage* (London, 1903), 1.v-vi.

[36]   Chambers, *The Elizabethan Stage* (London, 1923), 1.307.

not the Renaissance author, as the source of dramatic inspiration and audience entertainment.[37] True, the Banns attribute the Chester pageants to the famous author of the *Polychronicon*, but they have no desire to see the pageants staged as Higden originally intended. To the contrary, they willingly impose modern interpretations upon traditional stage practices in order to avoid controversy. Literary meaning is jettisoned to guarantee the object's literal stage presence. The Banns invoke Higden for the same reason they invoke Mayor Arneway and repeatedly underscore the authority of ancient custom: to preserve the familiar sights, sounds, and spectacles of the pageant wagons, props, and costumes. Palpable objects not transcendent subjects, and Shakespeare least of all, shape the historical narrative of the Chester Banns. Far from being dead, superseded precursors, as Chambers would have it, the material elements of the mystery plays are the great attractions that the Banns implore audiences to come and see. Their stated goal is to have the guilds resurrect these treasures of Chester theatre history. Material craft thus precedes the author's pen. If Hegelian histories (like that of Chambers) strain arduously toward the *telos* of freedom for the individual subject, then the Banns, it would seem, narrate a history in which material objects are set free, not by breaking away from the past, but by becoming synecdochically tied to it.

In their rhetorical and graphic historiography, the Chester Banns engage in calculated acts of periodization, but if they erect a temporal divide, it is a curious partition that creates the possibility of temporal proximity as well as distance. Gilt masks are (must be) new precisely because they are covered, and therefore protected by, the patina of past custom. Holme's ink acts as an open box or reliquary that contains yet exhibits dangerously idolatrous theatrical customs from England's Catholic past. If the late sixteenth-century apologies of the Late Banns and the seventeenth-century marginalia in the Early Banns manuscript tell us anything, therefore, it is that despite the emendation and eventual suppression of the mysteries, this dramatic material was not entirely superseded. It had by no means lost its old Catholic signification and therefore belonged to a 'past time of monkish ignorance'. And yet for many people these plays could not so easily be banished to a previous age. Certainly for Goodman they were not bygone but a present 'perill or danger to … the common weal'.[38] If Shakespeare and his professional colleagues had not forgotten the mysteries, they may, like Heywood, have ignored them. But it is possible that, like the Banns, they viewed them as sources of 'lyuelye' and 'comlye' inspiration and entertainment.

---

[37]   I am indebted for this phrase regarding the agency of past objects to Gil Harris, *Untimely Matter*, 25.

[38]   Baldwin, Clopper, and Mills, *REED: Cheshire*, 1.144.

PART 4
Space and Place in Chester

Fig. Pt. 4   A troupe of Purdue University actors attempt to squeeze their wagon through an archway at the University of Toronto campus for their production of *The Fall of Man*.

Chapter 9
When in Rome:
Shifting Conceptions of the Chester Cycle's Roman References in Pre- and Post-Reformation England

Sheila Christie

Rome in the middle ages was a complex signifier. According to twelfth-century Cestrian author Lucian, Rome was more than just a city; it was *Urbs*, the quintessential city against which all other urban settlements could be measured.[1] As a symbol, Rome could signify imperial might – a cultural heritage of military strength and secular administration – as well as Roman Catholicism and the authority of the pope. Medieval writers could evoke either or both of these associations, making Rome a highly flexible and constantly shifting metaphor, capable of carrying both positive and negative connotations depending on the context and the author's purpose.[2] Roman characters, including those found in English cycle drama, reveal local conceptions of Rome as signifier which in turn reflect and shape aspects of local identity. Whereas many plays portray Romans negatively, Chester's cycle casts them as ideal authority figures, rational men (and women) who recognize and respect divinity and are capable of enforcing peace through military order. These positive connotations are in keeping with medieval Chester's awareness of and pride in its own Roman heritage, an identification found in other Cestrian writing. Ironically, after the Reformation these same connotations would become potentially damning in the eyes of anti-Catholic critics, such as Christopher Goodman. An intertextual consideration of Rome's signification in medieval and early modern Chester demonstrates that the Chester cycle proved resistant to post-Reformation adaptation not – or not only – on account of local religious conservatism, but also because the cycle's Roman characters reflected the city's secular heritage and identity.

Unlike the York cycle and the texts in the Towneley and N-town compilations, Chester presents a largely positive depiction of Roman characters. While Towneley's

---

[1]   John Doran, 'Authority and Care: The Significance of Rome in Twelfth-Century Chester', in Éamonn Ó Carragáin and Carol Neuman De Vegvar (eds), *Roma Felix: Formation and Reflections of Medieval Rome* (Aldershot, 2007), 321.

[2]   See Suzanne M. Yeager, '*The Siege of Jerusalem* and Biblical Exegesis: Writing about Romans in Fourteenth-Century England', *The Chaucer Review* 39.1 (2004), 70–102.

emperor Octavian is a fulminating tyrant and York's Pilate is ultimately in collusion with Christ's tormentors, Chester's versions of these characters are rational and just. An explanation for this positive Cestrian interpretation of Roman characters appears in other locally written texts which reflect upon medieval Chester's sense of origin and civic identity, in particular the works of three Benedictine monks: Lucian, Ranulph Higden, and Henry Bradshaw. All three writers discuss Rome and consider Rome's relationship to Chester, and their texts reveal a great deal about the status of Rome in the local cultural imaginary.[3]

Lucian and Higden both wrote prior to the development of the cycle, Lucian in the late twelfth century and Higden in the mid thirteenth century, whereas our first record of a cycle play in Chester dates from 1421.[4] Lucian's text, *De Laude Cestrie* [*On the Glory of Chester*], is an allegorical interpretation of the local architectural geography written, in part, to reinforce the authority of his abbey, St. Werburgh's.[5] Discussing Lucian's Roman references, John Doran states that Lucian gives Rome 'an overwhelmingly positive gloss' despite 'writing at a time of unparalleled English hostility to the Roman curia'.[6] Even as he develops this 'positive gloss', Lucian makes use of tension between culturally dominant critiques of Rome and his generally positive view to heighten his praise of Chester. In his interpretation of St. Peter's church in Chester, Lucian contrasts negative contemporary stereotypes of unruly Romans with images of Chester as a peaceful and restful society. Eliding the local church with the person of St. Peter, Lucian asserts that in Rome, Peter 'is found in the law courts, here in dens of sanctuary. There he is usually harassed, here he is at leisure. There the hustle of a rabble, here the solace of calm. There a nation makes a din, here very few seek him. There he is famed for handling lawsuits, here he is carefree. There indeed is the tumult of

---

[3]   Pamela M. King calls for a consideration of 'particular intertextualities born of the available reading materials in the respective locations of composition' in 'Playing Pentecost in York and Chester: Transformations and Texts', *Medieval English Theatre* 29 (2009): 60–74. The term 'cultural imaginary' overlaps with intertextuality, but is intended to reflect the narratives which circulate in popular culture and which are informed by and can be glimpsed in material texts. The term has its origins with Lacan and has been adapted by scholars working in cultural studies.

[4]   Elizabeth Baldwin, Lawrence M. Clopper, and David Mills (eds), *REED: Cheshire, including Chester* (Toronto, 2007), 1.47–8.

[5]   Doran, 'Authority and Care', 325–31. There is no complete edition of Lucian's text, but partial editions include M.V. Taylor (ed.), 'Extracts from the MS. Liber Luciani De laude Cestrie Written about the Year 1195 and Now in the Bodleian Library, Oxford', *The Record Society of Lancashire and Cheshire* 64 (1912): 1–78; and Mark Faulkner (ed.), 'De Laude Cestrie – Lucian', *Mapping Medieval Chester*, <http://www.medievalchester. ac.uk/texts/scholarly/Lucian.html>. My discussion of Lucian's text is informed by Faulkner's edition, his notes on the manuscript (personal correspondence), and Doran's 'Authority and Care'. For further discussion of Lucian, see Faulkner's contribution to this volume.

[6]   Doran, 'Authority and Care', 307.

business, here tranquillity of leisure'.[7] Even as he privileges Chester as a place of tranquility, Lucian praises Rome as the centre of legal deliberation and order, establishing a symbiosis whereby the legal elements of Rome are the cause of the peaceful elements of Chester. This symbiosis serves Lucian's purpose, building up the pontifical authority that protected his abbey, while simultaneously asserting Chester's preeminence. Rome retains its status as an ideal, but one which, for Lucian, Chester nonetheless exceeds.

Since Lucian's text exists only in a single manuscript, delivered to its patron upon completion, it was likely limited in its readership and circulation. While it may reflect local thinking on Rome, it would not necessarily contribute to a generally circulating conception of Rome and Rome's relationship to Chester. Higden's *Polychronicon*, on the other hand, was an extraordinarily popular text. Higden's attempt to rationalize disparate sources and compile a coherent history of the world, the *Polychronicon* remains extant in over one hundred copies, and later writers often added to it.[8] Aspects of classical Rome feature significantly in the first five of Higden's seven volumes. It was a subject 'on which he bestowed much care', and this central feature of his universal history makes especially relevant his discussions of the relationship between Rome and Chester.[9] That he makes an effort to connect the topic which occupies his central attention to the place in which he lives and writes suggests that this connection is in and of itself important. Speaking of Chester, Higden writes, 'cujus fundator ignoratur. Nam intuenti fundamenta lapidum enormium videtur potius Romano seu giganteo labore, quam Britannico sudore fundata extitisse'.[10] In asserting that Chester's stone foundations must be the work of either Romans or giants, Higden unabashedly reveals his admiration for the Romans, comparing their skills to the mythical giants' unmatchable might. That which seems beyond the scope of ordinary people, the Britons, is attributable to the extra-ordinary Romans. Higden's nostalgic wonder grants Chester a Roman inheritance, even as he admits that the city's founders are unknown. Although Higden fails to identify a specific founder, he states that Chester was a base of Roman operations under both Julius and Claudius Caesar, and he draws attention to material remains which, implicitly and explicitly, demonstrate a Roman presence. He writes of 'viae subterraneae, lapideo opera mirabiliter testudinatae, insculpti lapides pergrandes antiquorum nomina praeferentes', marvelous subterranean

---

[7]   Faulkner, 'De Laude Cestrie', Excerpt 21.

[8]   John Taylor, *The Universal Chronicle of Ranulf Higden* (Oxford, 1966), 152–8, 111–33.

[9]   Ibid, 41.

[10]   Churchill Babington and Joseph Rawson Lumby (eds), *Polychronicon Ranulphi Higden Monachi Cestrensis; Together with the English Translations of John Trevisa and of an Unknown Writer of the Fifteenth Century*, 9 vols (London, 1865–86), 2.78. All quotations from Higden and Trevisa are from this edition. Trevisa's translation is reasonably close: 'Þe foundour of þis cite is vnknowe, for who þat seeþ þe foundementis of þe grete stones wold raþer wene þat it were Romayns work, oþer work of geauntes, þan work i-made by settynge of Bretouns' (2.79).

vaults and stonework with ancient inscriptions, a description which recalls
Higden's earlier association of the Romans with Chester's stone foundations.
More directly, he also notes the presence of Roman coins: 'Numismata quoque,
Julii Caesaris aliorumque illustrium inscriptione insignita'.[11] While his actual
evidence is scant, Higden asserts a significant Roman influence on Chester's early
development, grounding the city's thirteenth-century glory in its Roman past. The
attention both Lucian and Higden pay to Rome reflects a local interest in and
awareness of Chester's Roman heritage.

The third writer to mention the Cestrian-Roman connection demonstrates the
continuing currency of this idea in the early sixteenth century even as he attempts
to deny it. Bradshaw's *Life of St Werburghe* is a hagiography that celebrates the
abbey's patron saint and her relationship to the city. In the midst of a discussion
of the city's origins, Bradshaw explicitly rejects Higden's implied Roman origin
story, privileging a British one instead:

> Ranulphus in his cronicle yet doth expresse
> The cite of Chestre edified for to be
> By the noble romans prudence and richesse
> Whan a legion of knyghtes was sende to the cite,
> Rather than by the wysdome of the Britons or policie;
> Obiectyng clere agaynst the britons fundacion,
> Whiche auctour resteth in his owne opinion.[12]

Bradshaw's need to identify the Roman origin story with Higden and refute it
as mere opinion testifies to the story's currency. As Catherine Clarke notes,
'Bradshaw ... mis-reads Higden at this point, in order to emphasise his own claims
for the British origins of the city', and indeed, Bradshaw argues that the city's
founder was 'Kynge Leil, a briton sure and valiaunt'.[13] Bradshaw acknowledges
the Roman expeditions involving Chester under Julius and Claudius Caesar (st. 54),
but gives priority to Leil, who, according to Geoffrey of Monmouth, was a
descendant of Brutus and a pre-Roman historical figure.[14] As such, Bradshaw's
rejection of Chester's Roman foundation serves a nationalistic agenda, but it
also relates to his agenda with respect to local politics. Both Clarke and Robert

---

[11]   Ibid, 2.80. Trevisa's translation is looser here: 'In þis cite beeþ weies vnder erþe,
wiþ vawtes of stoonwerk wonderliche i-wrouʒt, þre chambers works, greet stones i-graued
wiþ olde men names þere ynne. Þere is also Iulius Cesar his money wonderliche in stones
i-graued and oþere noble mennes also wiþ þe writynge aboute' (2.81).

[12]   Catherine Clarke (ed.), 'Life of St. Werburge – Henry Bradshaw', *Mapping Medieval
Chester*, <http://www.medievalchester.ac.uk/texts/scholarly/bradshaw.html>, stanza 56, lines
386–92. All Bradshaw quotations are taken from this edition.

[13]   Ibid, n. 56 and l. 383.

[14]   Geoffrey of Monmouth, *History of the Kings of Britain*, Aaron Thompson (trans.),
J.A. Giles (rev.) (Cambridge Ontario, 1999), 27, see especially Book 2, Chapter 9, <http://
www.yorku.ca/inpar/geoffrey_thompson.pdf>.

Barrett see Bradshaw as writing to strengthen the abbey's position with respect to jurisdictional conflicts between the abbey and Chester's secular civic franchise.[15] If, by the time Bradshaw wrote his *Life*, the Chester cycle reflected an established and positive civic association with Rome (for reasons I will suggest below), then his bias in the abbey's favour would lead him to reject that civic association in favour of an origin story which privileged a native founder, giving his abbey and patron saint stronger ties to local history. Bradshaw's depiction of Romans as late arrivals to the city serves his desire to represent Chester's civic authorities as the interlopers who presume to usurp the honour and authority due to the 'true' founders and their inheritors.

Ultimately, Bradshaw reveals the continuing currency of an association between the city and Rome, one he draws on elsewhere in his writing. In stanza 69, while discussing the survival of the abbey during the Anglo-Saxon subjection of the Britons, Bradshaw compares the stability of the abbey to 'the faith of Peter neuer fayled at Rome'. Similarly, when lamenting a fire which threatened to destroy Chester, Bradshaw compares the local disaster to the destruction of Troy and to the great fire of Rome (st. 233). Even though Bradshaw is careful to deny the primacy of Rome in Cestrian identity, he continues to see Rome as the natural point of comparison for the city.

The Chester cycle draws upon the cultural imaginary as represented in these three Benedictine texts, a local cultural narrative which positions Chester as successor to both a material and moral Roman heritage. In the cycle, Rome serves as a double for Chester, wherein the actions of Roman characters reflect and promote a positive image of secular authority. The first and most significant of the Roman characters is Octavian, emperor at the time of Christ's birth and the instigator of the census which Luke 2:1 identifies as Mary and Joseph's motivation for the journey to Bethlehem. When he first appears in pageant six, Octavian seems like a stock tyrant:

> I, preeved prince most of powere,
> under heaven highest am I here;
> fayrest foode to fight in fere,
> noe freake my face may flee.
> All this world, withowten were –
> kinge, prynce, baron, batchlere –
> I may destroy in great danger
> through vertue of my degree. (6.185–92)[16]

---

[15]   Catherine Clarke, 'Henry Bradshaw, Life of St Werburge', *Mapping Medieval Chester*, <http://www.medievalchester.ac.uk/texts/introbradshaw.html>; Robert W. Barrett, Jr, *Against All England: Regional Identity and Cheshire Writing, 1195–1656* (Notre Dame, 2009), 47–51.

[16]   R.M. Lumiansky and David Mills (eds), *The Chester Mystery Cycle*, 2 vols, EETS SS 3, 9 (London, 1974, rpt 1986). In-text citations for pageants refer to the first volume of this edition by pageant and line number, while citations for editorial material refer to the second volume by volume and page number in the notes.

Octavian speaks in highly alliterative verse, a feature which often characterizes the entrance of tyrants, and he begins by boasting, threatening retribution, and asserting his uncontested power, actions which implicitly challenge God's authority.[17] Faced with these verbal and gestural cues, a medieval Christian audience would be prepared to classify Octavian as an enemy of Christ, but the text resists this oversimplified categorization. Octavian is cast as tyrant inasmuch as he is a pagan ruler, but despite his religious handicap, he is still a good ruler, one who has expanded the empire, ended war, and brought about peace (6.237–8). His decision to 'send about and see / how many heades I have' so that 'All the world shall written bee' (6.243–5) reveals him to be a savvy administrator, using a census as a means of maintaining his effective rule. Admittedly, that census is also an opportunity for taxation. In the following scene, Joseph articulates the common man's frustration with arbitrary taxation rates when he asks, 'shall poore as well as rych paye?' (6.414). The extensive scene with Octavian prior to Joseph's complaint nonetheless demonstrates an admiration for Roman martial and administrative efficacy that modifies the negative signals which open the scene.

This element of positive characterization increases when Octavian's senators offer to honour him 'as God' (6.300, 306) and he refuses, politely but firmly, stressing that he is only 'flesh, blood, and bonne … borne of a woman' (6.321–2). He shows awareness of his own limitations when he defines godhead as that which 'hath noe begininge / ne never shall have endinge' and states 'none of this have I' (6.330–32). Even as he denies the senators' request, he diplomatically offers to seek a second opinion from the prophetess Sybil, again asserting that he will 'take noe more one mee / then I am well worthye' (6.343–4). When Sybil predicts Christ's birth he does not react angrily, as Herod will in pageant eight, but instead asks when Christ will be born. Later in the pageant, when Sibyl points out the signs of Christ's birth, Octavian responds with appropriate devotion, enacting an entirely ahistorical conversion as he offers incense to the image of the Christ child, identifies himself as Christ's 'subject' (673), and encourages his senators to worship Christ 'with full heart all that you can' (688). In this way, the Octavian episode introduces Rome as a symbol of not only secular ideals but also of spiritual potential. Octavian's initially negative characteristics are connected to his uninformed paganism which he corrects as soon as he is faced with signs of the true faith.

The story of Octavian and the Sibylline prophecy is not unique to the Chester cycle – it circulated widely in texts such as the *Golden Legend*, and locally in the

---

[17]   Garrett Epp, 'Passion, Pomp, and Parody: Alliteration in the York Plays', *Medieval English Theatre* 11 (1992), 157. Epp discusses the association of alliteration with tyrants and notes that levels of alliteration are relative. The Chester *Nativity* opens with the angel Gabriel's alliterative speech, but by the time Octavian enters, alliteration in the dialogue is incidental, giving his opening lines a more disruptive feel.

Polychronicon and the *Stanzaic Life of Christ* – but it was rare for English drama.[18] Of the other extant cycle plays and compilations, only Towneley features Octavian, and there the emperor is an unredeemable tyrant who swears 'by mahowne' (9.9) and flies into a rage when he hears of Christ's birth.[19] As R.M. Lumiansky and David Mills note in their edition of the Chester cycle, Chester's Roman emperor 'follows the more favourable picture of Octavian'; as well, 'The reasons for deification' that his senators present 'constitute a picture of the ideal ruler'.[20] The cycle's fascination with all things Roman is further advanced in the Expositor's two speeches from the same pageant. The first describes at length Rome's magical Temple of Peace which collapsed at Christ's birth, while the second reaffirms Octavian's vision and describes the foundation of the Santa Maria in Aracoeli, a church commemorating the vision. These two passages echo admiration for imperial Rome, and celebrate its transformation into the Christian seat of power.

Unlike Octavian, Pilate is necessarily a central character in Christ's story, and he is, as Lumiansky and Mills note, 'not usually presented in a favourable light'.[21] Non-dramatic texts, including the *Golden Legend* and Higden's *Polychronichon*, assign Pilate a sordid past of fratricide and political corruption.[22] Most dramatic texts present Pilate as either easily pressured or in outright collusion with Christ's Jewish adversaries. In the York cycle, Pilate welcomes Christ's prosecutors as 'my prelates' (30.271).[23] Although he initially resists the Jewish priests' insistence that he put Christ to death, he ultimately accepts their claim that Christ has committed treason by calling himself a king (33.328–35) despite his earlier rejection of hearsay testimony. Towneley's Pilate echoes the non-dramatic texts in presenting a thoroughly corrupt character who celebrates his own 'sotelty, / Ffalshed, gyll, and trechery' (22.10–11) and worships 'mahowne' (22.3, 39). Chester's Pilate, however, 'emerges more creditably' in both 'his close attention to [Christ's] words and repeated efforts to save him'.[24] Like Jesus in his initial trial before the Pharisees, Pilate uses the word 'justefye' (16.50, 156), a word with positive legal connotations, and other aspects of his language and behaviour associate him with good justice. Pilate states three times that he can 'fynd no cause' to punish Christ (16.143–4, 215, 291–2), the third time following an extended discussion with

---

[18]   Jacobus de Voragine, *The Golden Legend: Readings on the Saints*, 2 vols, William Granger Ryan (trans.) (Princeton, 1993), 1.40–41; Babington and Lumby, *Polychronicon Ranulphi Higden*, 4.298–300; Frances A. Foster (ed.), *A Stanzaic Life of Christ*, EETS OS 166 (London, 1926), ll. 593–644.

[19]   Martin Stevens and A.C. Cawley (eds), *The Towneley Plays*, 2 vols, EETS SS 13–14 (Oxford, 1994). All citations for Towneley plays refer to this edition by play and line number.

[20]   Lumiansky and Mills, *Chester Mystery Cycle*, 2.84–5 and 2.87.

[21]   Ibid, 2.229.

[22]   *The Golden Legend*, 213–14; *Polychronicon*, 4.316–20; *Stanzaic Life*, ll. 6433–544.

[23]   Richard Beadle (ed.), *The York Plays* (London, 1982). All citations for the York cycle refer to this edition by pageant and line number.

[24]   Lumiansky and Mills, *Chester Mystery Cycle*, 2.229.

Christ on the nature of truth and authority. Pilate also offers to replace Christ with Barabas twice, as opposed to the single scriptural offer. In the conventional act of washing his hands to distance himself from the crowd's judgment, Pilate explicitly laments shedding 'this rightwise manns blood' (16.242), and when Pilate delivers Christ to the Jews for crucifixion, he regrets that 'save him I ney maye' (16.369). As representative of Roman law, Pilate is at least able to see the truth, even though he is unable to prevent its perversion.

The final element of the Chester cycle which reinforces an overall positive depiction of Roman authority is in the passion itself. Despite the Pharisees' acknowledgment that Jewish law forbids them from taking 'lyth ne lymme' (16.249), the same four Jewish tormentors are responsible for the buffeting, scourging, and crucifixion. Scripturally, the crucifixion should be carried out by Roman soldiers, but all of the cycle plays and compilations blur this distinction, with York assigning the action to several soldiers (Miles) from the start of the passion sequence, and the others attributing the entire action to the Jews. In Chester, however, the continued presence of the Jewish tormentors not only emphasizes, as Lumiansky and Mills suggest, 'the Jews' essential responsibility for Christ's death', but also distances the remaining Roman characters from the negative act.[25] Aside from Pilate, the only explicitly Roman characters at the crucifixion are the centurion, who recognizes Christ's divinity at the moment of his death, and Longeus, the blind soldier who drives a spear into Christ's side and is miraculously healed by his blood. Both characters are conventional witnesses, and like Octavian, can be admired for their ability to recognize Christ's divinity despite their pagan origins.[26] On a stage otherwise cleared of Roman culpability, the centurion and Longeus reinforce the positive Roman identity throughout the cycle as a whole.

In the Chester cycle, then, Romans stand for good governance, justice, and moral authority. Moreover, the text repeatedly enacts conversions and transformations which make admirable Roman qualities available to a Christian audience. Lucian's, Higden's, and Bradshaw's relatively contemporary texts suggest that Cestrians saw themselves as inheritors of Roman authority, with the result that these positive qualities reflect the very characteristics that Cestrians believed their city embodied.[27] As long as Rome remained a flexible metaphor, the cycle could both reflect and shape a conception of Chester as an alternative Rome, one which fulfilled the best administrative and moral qualities of the ancient empire. In the Reformation, however, the metaphor of Rome became

---

[25]   Ibid, 2.241.

[26]   Peter W. Travis, *Dramatic Design in the Chester Cycle* (Chicago, 1982), 188–9.

[27]   Chester was not the only city to conceive of itself as Rome's successor; see William Hammer, 'The Concept of the New or Second Rome in the Middle Ages', *Speculum* 19.1 (1944): 50–62. Hammer focuses on continental cities that explicitly claimed the title *Roma nova* or *Roma secunda*, but he demonstrates the popularity of claiming the authority of Roman identity.

more politically charged and increasingly fixed. Protestant hegemonic discourse identified the pope as the antichrist, and Rome as Babylon, the corrupt prostitute of Revelations.[28] Particularly in the years following the initial break with Rome and after Queen Mary's attempt to reassert Catholicism, Rome represented the Catholic threat to English protestantism.

Even in Chester, a city known for Catholic recusancy, this shift in signification would have had major implications for a cycle which tied positive Roman characteristics to local identity.[29] Revising these references would be difficult without entirely altering the text. Indeed, in Chester's *Resurrection* pageant, revisions which attempt to bring the text in line with post-Reformation theology also undermine positive Roman associations. While there are echoes of the rational and diplomatic Pilate of the earlier pageants, Pilate in *The Resurrection* largely fulfils the negative stereotypes familiar in other dramatic texts. As in York, Chester's *Resurrection* Pilate treats Annas and Caiaphas as equals, identifying himself as 'a trewe Jewe' and asking them to confer 'amonge us three' (18.46).[30] When the soldiers report that Christ has risen, Pilate initially responds tyrannically, threatening and insulting the soldiers. His final lines, however, reassert a Pilate who 'appeals to the loyalty of the soldiers to keep the matter quiet until a full enquiry can be held' and who 'is not thereby involved in a conspiracy with the Jews to conceal the truth indefinitely'.[31] Significantly, Pilate's tyrannical outbursts do not match the standard eight-line, Chester stanza with its aaabaaab or aaabcccb rhyme scheme. Like the risen Christ's speech, which is 'willfully obscure' on points of controversial theology, Pilate's uncharacteristic speech predominantly features an abab rhyme scheme.[32] Although the two sections differ in metre and stanza length, they both appear to represent changes from earlier versions of the pageant. While it is impossible to date these revisions securely, or even to link them together,

---

[28] For the shifting conception of Antichrist in the Tudor period, see Richard K. Emmerson, 'Contextualizing Performance: The Reception of the Chester *Antichrist*', *Journal of Medieval and Early Modern Studies* 29.1 (1999): 89–119. For the English association of Rome and Babylon during the Reformation, see John N. King, 'The Roman Babylon', in *English Reformation Literature: The Tudor Origins of the Protestant Tradition* (Princeton, 1982), 371–87. For anti-Roman rhetoric more generally, see Stefanie Ruck, 'Patriotic Tendencies in Pamphleteering during the Reigns of Henry VIII and Edward VI', in Herbert Grabes (ed.), *Writing the Early Modern English Nation: The Transformation of National Identity in Sixteenth- and Seventeenth-Century England* (Atlanta, 2001), 1–45.

[29] Emmerson, 'Contextualizing Performance', suggests that Cestrians were aware that scriptural metaphors were 'vehemently contested' (105), despite their reputation for religious conservatism (105–9).

[30] David Mills compares Pilate's behaviour in York and Chester in '"I Know My Place": Some Thoughts on Status and Station in the English Mystery Plays', *Medieval English Theatre* 27 (2005): 5–15, although he does not discuss the Pilate of Chester's *Resurrection*.

[31] Lumiansky and Mills, *Chester Mystery Cycle*, 2.286.

[32] Ibid, 2.282.

Rome's increasingly post-Reformation negative connotations provide a clear motivation for changing Pilate's character. Since the local council only approved the final production of the Chester cycle 'with such reformacion as master maior with his advice shall think meet & convenient', perhaps the new version of Pilate represents an attempt to appeal to popular, anti-Catholic sentiment.[33]

Regardless of when Pilate's lines were revised, his changed character also helps to disguise the repeated conversion formula developed in the earlier Roman episodes. Pilate's soldiers are initially boastful, claiming that, should Christ rise, they will 'beate him adowne' (18.145), but they are quick to witness his divinity once the resurrection has occurred. The second soldier laments that 'in a wicked tyme we / nayled him on the roode-tree' (18.222–3), and the third acknowledges Christ as 'Goddes Sonne verey' (18.227). Unlike the soldiers of York and Towneley, who contemplate lying to Pilate, Chester's soldiers report Christ's resurrection openly, identifying their words as 'sooth' (18.242) and swearing by their honour as knights (18.258). While the stage directions suggest the soldiers are bribed into silence, as they are in other resurrection pageants, the text makes no mention of the bribe, allowing for the possibility that this action, too, is a consequence of revision. In their own words, and the actions implied by their dialogue, they are introduced as loyal, if misguided, pagans who experience conversion when faced with Christ's divinity. This echo of an earlier formula suggests that the disjunctions within the pageant and in relation to other pageants in the cycle are the result of uneven attempts at revision.

Ultimately, as Christopher Goodman's 1572 complaints suggest, protestant revisions were unsatisfactory for all involved. Writing to the archbishop of York, Goodman states, 'albeit divers have gone about the correction of the same at sundry times & mended divers things, yet hath it not been done by such as are by authority allowed, nor the same their corrections viewed & approved according to order, nor yet so played for the most part as they have been corrected'.[34] In his list of 'absurdities', Goodman singles out *The Resurrection* as one pageant not played as corrected (noting references to transubstantiation not in the extant manuscripts), and he also takes detailed exception to the Octavian sequences in *The Nativity*. He complains that the treatment of Sybil is superstitious, and he objects to the Expositor's discussion of the magical Roman temple and to Octavian's vision, among other 'feigned miracles'.[35] In addition to his consistent rejection of miracles, Goodman makes note of a reference to 'Frier Bartholomew' and records that Octavian 'sensed the starr', in all cases highlighting elements which suggest Catholic practices. In his concern for protestant orthodoxy, however, he misses the local cultural significance of Roman characters, and the importance of their conversion. While the unperformed revisions and the retention of 'absurdities' may

---

[33]   Baldwin, Clopper, and Mills, *REED: Cheshire*, 1.160.

[34]   Ibid, 1.146.

[35]   Ibid, 1.147.

well relate to conflicts over religious belief, they may also reflect an entrenched local identity with which Cestrians were reluctant to part.

Chester's Roman heritage was one element of civic identity reflected in the cycle, and the Roman characters represented Cestrian ideals of authority. Goodman's focus on religious controversy kept him from acknowledging the local cultural context and recognizing the challenges of dismantling a text central to local conceptions of identity. For him, the text's positive Roman associations could only confirm the cycle's papist origins, but in rejecting the cycle, he also rejected the city's stories of its own unique origins. Although Goodman, and many subsequent critics, saw the Chester cycle primarily in terms of religious thought and controversy, we must recognize that the performers and spectators of the cycle could also see it on other levels, especially as a cultural text which engaged their local concerns and identities.

Chapter 10
Exegesis in the City:
The Chester Plays and
Earlier Chester Writing

Mark Faulkner

Reverend lordes and ladyes all
that at this tyme here assembled be,
by this message understande you shall
that sometymes there was mayor of this cittie
Sir John Arnewaye, knighte, whoe moste worthelye
contented himselfe to sett out in playe
the devise of one Rondall, moncke of Chester Abbaye.

This moncke – not moncke-lyke in Scriptures, well seene,
in stories traveled with the best sorte –
in pageantes sett forthe apparante to all eyne,
interminglinge therewithe onely to make sporte
some thinges not warranted by anye wrytte
which glad the hartes – he woulde men to take hit. (1–13)[1]

The Late Banns begin their announcement of a performance of the Chester Whitsun plays by looking backwards to the plays' legendary origins, attributing the first production to John Arneway (1268–78), supposed first mayor of the city, and Ranulph Higden, monk of St Werburgh's Abbey (d. 1364) and a prolific author of works theological, grammatical, and historical.[2] Higden is implausibly depicted as a putative proto-protestant martyr, translating the bible into 'a common Englishe tonge' (22) despite the threat of 'burninge, hangeinge, or cuttinge of heade' (25). This 'moncke – not moncke-lyke in Scriptures' (8), this 'moncke – and noe

---

[1] I cite the Late Banns from R.M. Lumiansky and David Mills (eds), *The Chester Mystery Cycle: Essays and Documents* (Chapel Hill, 1983), 272–310. I would like to thank Catherine Clarke and Alexandra da Costa for their comments on a draft of this article. All references to the Chester plays are to R.M. Lumiansky and David Mills (eds), *The Chester Mystery Cycle*, EETS SS 3 and 9 (London, 1974–86).

[2] For Higden's oeuvre, see Richard Sharpe, *A Handlist of the Latin Writers of Great Britain and Ireland Before 1540*, Publications of the Journal of Medieval Latin 1 (Turnhout, 1997), 453–4.

moncke' (24), is central to the Late Banns' attempt to 'to preserve a wholesome, and spiritually profitable, form of recreation still in the process of reformation'.[3]

The Late Banns must date from the plays' revival during the reign of Elizabeth I, when they were performed in 1561, 1567, 1568, 1572, and 1575.[4] Performing the plays became more and more contentious during these two decades,[5] with the puritan clergyman Christopher Goodman compiling his famous list of 'absurdities' in 1572 and the plays rescheduled in 1575 from the liturgically freighted Whitsun to the safe secular time of Midsummer.[6] If Clopper is correct that the Late Banns were read before the mayor and council in 1572, then they may have been instrumental in ensuring the survival of the cycle.[7] Their masterful if wholly mendacious rhetoric was particularly suited to this act of persuasion. The Late Banns skilfully mediate not only between pre- and post-Reformation religious sensibilities, praising Higden's brave translation of scripture while censuring certain aspects of the content and vocabulary as belonging 'to the tyme of ignorance' (39), but also between the civic and religious authorities. Though the Benedictine Abbey of St Werburgh had been dissolved on 20 January 1540, it was reconstituted as a cathedral on 26 July 1541; several of the former monks obtained new positions in the diocesan hierarchy.[8] By depicting the initial performance of the plays as a joint initiative between the mayoralty and the monastery, the Late Banns solicit the cathedral's involvement in the post-Reformation plays.[9]

The figure of Higden enables the Late Banns to navigate the fraught spiritual and jurisdictional geographies of post-Reformation Chester. Taking their lead, this essay uses another Chester (or perhaps Cheshire) monk and author, Lucian, to explore how the Chester plays negotiate the changing spiritual economy of the sixteenth century. Lucian's mammoth late twelfth-century urban encomium, *De laude Cestrie*, uses Chester's topography to teach, compel, and beseech his Cestrian audience to understand, appreciate, and praise God's generosity in

---

[3]   Paul Whitfield White, 'Reforming Mysteries' End: A New Look at Protestant Intervention in English Provincial Drama', *Journal of Medieval and Early Modern Studies* 29 (1999), 135.

[4]   For a more elaborate account of their composition, see Lawrence M. Clopper, 'The History and Development of the Chester Cycle', *Modern Philology* 75 (1978), 235–40.

[5]   See, in particular, Richard K. Emmerson, 'Contextualizing Performance: The Reception of the Chester *Antichrist*', *Journal of Medieval and Early Modern Studies* 29 (1999).

[6]   For the 'absurdities', see Elizabeth Baldwin, Lawrence M. Clopper, and David Mills (eds), *REED: Cheshire including Chester*, 2 vols, (Toronto, 2007), 1.147–8. On the rescheduling of the plays to midsummer, see also Heather S. Mitchell-Buck's article in this volume.

[7]   Clopper, 'The History and Development of the Chester Cycle', 240.

[8]   R.V.H. Burne, *Chester Cathedral: from its founding by Henry VIII to the accession of Queen Victoria* (London, 1958), 1–5.

[9]   In 1572, the clergy built a 'mansyon' over the abbey gates, and gave beer to the players: Baldwin, Clopper, and Mills, *REED: Cheshire*, 1.137.

creating the city – as Deus himself says at the very opening of the cycle, 'all the likeinge in this lordshipp / be laude to my laudacion' (1.48–9).

My essay accordingly compares *De laude Cestrie* and the Chester cycle as urban texts that use exegesis to educate and edify. It examines the Chester plays' use of urban space, before turning to the role of the expositor, and his likely significance in performances from the 1560s and 1570s. I begin with an account of Lucian's text, since it will be unfamiliar to many readers.

Lucian's *De laude Cestrie*

The text which Lucian called *De laude Cestrie* [*On the Glory of Chester*] is just over 82,000 words long.[10] It is a massive testament to Lucian's faith that 'nothing on earth is done without a voice cause',[11] that, to a trained observer, urban topography and local history can reveal the very nature of God.

The text proper begins with some reflections on the value of studying place and history. Lucian then describes how he was inspired to write by an unnamed canon of St John's. This canon inspired him to consider the etymology of Chester (*Cestria*), which Lucian explains derives from *cis tria* ('threefold'), relating the name to the merits of Chester's bishop, archdeacon, and clergy; to its lords, citizens, and monks; and to the supplies which come from Ireland, Wales, and England. Lucian describes Chester's location, natural resources, trading partners, and street plan in vivid detail, encouraging its citizens to notice how generously God has provided for the city. Lucian's description culminates by encouraging anyone standing in the marketplace to look east to St John's Cathedral, west to St Peter's, north to the Benedictine monastery of St Werburgh, and south to St Michael's.

Lucian proceeds by expounding the spiritual significance of the dedication of each church. He begins with St John's, explaining that John the Baptist should be honoured because of his close relationship with Christ, his virginity, and martyrdom. Lucian then imagines John introducing the historical St Peter. Lucian's ensuing discussion of St Peter's church includes a lengthy comparison of Chester and Rome which emphasizes that Peter (and thus the pope) is a most fitting guardian for Chester. Lucian turns from the eastern and western churches, St John's and St Peter's, to the northern and southern churches, St Werburgh's and St Michael's, by recounting the story of the widow of Sarephta collecting sticks,[12] which was traditionally taken to refer to the beams which formed the cross on which Christ was crucified. With a neat transition – 'comodet itaque nobis hec duo ligna, ut tradamus unum precursori Domini atque ipsius portario, alterum uero committamus

---

[10]   I cite from my own partial edition and translation, Mapping Medieval Chester Project, <http://www.medievalchester.ac.uk>, accessed 25 August 2010, by excerpt number. I cite from the single extant manuscript, Oxford, Bodleian Library, Bodley 672, whenever the passage is not included in my edition.

[11]   Job 5:6. All biblical quotations are taken from the Douay Rheims version.

[12]   3 Kings 17:8–24.

Virgini et Arcangelo'[13] – Lucian moves to discuss St Werburgh's. St Werburgh is admirable first and foremost because she was a virgin. Lucian argues that virgins are fertile in spiritual works, emphasizing Werburgh's willingness to intercede with God on behalf of Cestrians, manifest in the vigilance of the monks of the monastery dedicated to St Werburgh. Finally, Lucian turns to St Michael's, meditating on St Michael's status as an archangel and the nature of angels' heavenly home. He discourses on the creation of the angels and their nine orders, suggesting that, since Michael overthrew Satan, he is readily able to defend Chester.

Lucian next turns to the various houses in Chester dedicated to Mary, beginning with some general reflections on the Virgin. Focusing specifically on the nunnery, Lucian compares the nuns to Amazons, identifying the spiritual weapons wielded by the nuns. He then recapitulates his argument, adding a few further things (*pauca que restant*), once again thanking his patron and defending his work against those who might carp.

The final two-fifths of Lucian's text are devoted to the proper organization of the church. His comments are never explicitly related to Chester, but they apply implicitly. He begins by comparing priests to monks, and argues that bishops owe a duty of care to monks. He then looks within the abbey, at the duties of the abbot, the prior, and the sub-prior. Eventually Lucian fittingly turns his attention to the final things, briefly describing purgatory, hell and heaven, and then the day of judgment. His emphasis on the rewards due to Mary, Michael, and John the Baptist neatly closes the text.

We know nothing about Lucian except what we can infer from *De laude Cestrie*. The text implies that he was a monk, and scholars have usually assumed he was a monk of St Werburgh's. There is, however, no positive evidence in favour of this conjecture and some which might tell against it.[14] He may, in fact, have been a Cistercian monk from Combermere, an abbey 25 miles south-west of Chester.[15] The text is datable between 1195 and 1200 on the evidence of the manuscript, which appears to be autograph, and contains an Easter table which begins in 1195 and added annals describing events from 1199 and 1200. The work has never been printed in full, but a partial edition and translation is now available as part of the Mapping Medieval Chester website and I am working on a full edition.[16]

---

[13]   *De laude Cestrie*, excerpt 22: 'and so he [God] provides us these two pieces of wood so that we can give one to the precursor of God and to his gatekeeper and so that we can give the other to the Virgin and the Archangel'.

[14]   For example, 'ideo miramur Cestrenses monacos' (*De laude*, fol. 60r); 'da eis gustum' (fol. 61v). Had Lucian been a monk of St Werburgh's, he is unlikely to have written the former sentence, and would probably have written 'da nobis gustum' instead of 'da eis gustum'.

[15]   I raise this possibility in Mark Faulkner, 'The Spatial Hermeneutics of Lucian's *De laude Cestrie*', in Catherine A.M. Clarke (ed.), *Mapping the Medieval City: Space, Place and Identity in Chester c. 1200–1500* (Cardiff, 2011), 93.

[16]   This supersedes M.V. Taylor, *Extracts from the MS. Liber Luciani De laude Cestrie written about the year 1195 and now in the Bodleian Library, Oxford*, Record Society of Lancashire and Cheshire 64 (Chester, 1912). Two short passages (corresponding to

De laude Cestrie seems to have had an extremely limited circulation, and the surviving manuscript, conceivably a presentation copy, is perhaps the only copy ever to have existed. It is therefore extremely unlikely it was known to anyone involved with the Chester plays during Elizabeth's reign. Not even the local antiquarian Robert Rogers (d. 1595) seems to have been familiar with the text.[17] Nonetheless, it is a self-consciously monastic work which seeks by expounding Chester's urban topography to nourish the piety of the city's inhabitants, and, as such, is an excellent comparison for the Chester cycle as conceived by the post-Reformation Banns.[18]

The Chester Plays and Chester Space

The fundamental premise of *De laude Cestrie* is that, though mortal life is mud, lowland, and prison compared to the exalted existence of the elect in heaven, the physical topography of Chester can, when interpreted through the lens of the bible, reveal God's nature and divine plan.[19] The Chester cycle shares with Lucian the confidence that the city can be the locus of spiritual learning.

I have described Lucian's 'spatial hermeneutics' in more detail elsewhere, but I will give one or two examples here of the way in which he reads urban space.[20] The first passage concerns the crossroads at the centre of the city, which was also the location of the marketplace in the twelfth century:[21]

---

excerpts 27, 'in una comes caput ciuium … lucere in terris uitam angelorum', and 28, 'iustissime igitur atque pulcherrime … ad eterni regis gloriam officiosissime salutare' on the Mapping Medieval Chester website) are edited and translated in Baldwin, Clopper, and Mills, *REED: Cheshire*, 2.35–6, 2.922–3, 2.94. The explanatory notes on these passages are questionable: *miraculum* means 'marvel' and has nothing to do with 'unruly or disruptive games'. Likewise, *preliatur* refers to spiritual struggle against temptation, not 'dancing or some kind of spring festival in a churchyard'.

[17]   David Mills, *Recycling the Cycle: The City of Chester and Its Whitsun Plays*, Studies in Early English Drama 4 (Toronto, 1998), 53.

[18]   For further discussion of *De laude*'s aims, see Catherine A.M. Clarke, *Literary Landscapes and the Idea of England, 700–1400* (Cambridge, 2006), 98–105; John Doran, 'Authority and Care: The Significance of Rome in Twelfth-century Chester', in Éamonn Ó Carragáin and Carol Neuman de Vegvar (eds), *Roma Felix: Formation and Reflections of Medieval Rome* (Aldershot, 2007); Robert W. Barrett, Jr, *Against All England: Regional Identity and Cheshire Writing* (Notre Dame, 2009), 29–43, as well as the materials on the Mapping Medieval Chester website.

[19]   See my 'Lucian's *De laude Cestrie*: introduction', Mapping Medieval Chester Project, <http://www.medievalchester.ac.uk>, accessed 25 August 2010.

[20]   Faulkner, 'Spatial Hermeneutics'.

[21]   *De laude Cestrie*, excerpt 9: 'Chester also has two perfectly straight streets intersecting like the blessed cross, which form four roads, culminating at the four gates, mystically revealing that the grace of the Great King dwells in the very city, who, through the four evangelists, showed the twin law of the old and new testaments to be completed

Habet eciam plateas duas equilineas et excellentes in modum benedicte crucis, per transuersum sibi obuias et se transeuntes, que deinceps fiant quattuor ex duabus, capita sua consummantes in quattuor portis, mistice ostendens atque magnifice, magni Regis inhabitantem graciam se habere, qui legem geminam noui ac ueteris testamenti per misterium sancte crucis impletam ostendit, in quattuor euangelistis …. Hoc simul intuendum quam congrue in medio urbis, parili positione cunctorum, forum uoluit esse uenalium rerum, ubi, mercium copia complacente precipue uictualium, notus ueniat uel ignotus, precium porrigens, referens alimentum. Nimirum ad exemplum panis eterni de celo uenientis, qui natus secundum prophetas *in medio orbis et umbilico terre*, omnibus mundi nationibus pari propinquitate uoluit apparere. Illud precipue prudens aliquis gaudenter attendat, quod Deus omnipotens paterna bonitate prospexit, et ad salutem ciuium, altius et eminentius ordinauit.

Lucian exploits spatial and numerical patterns here: the crossroads is cross-shaped, the two streets that intersect to form it are the two testaments, and the four roads that lead from it are the four gospels. All function as a reminder of Christ's incarnation. The position of the marketplace likewise reflects the historical circumstances of incarnation. Christ, the 'eternal bread which came from heaven', was, as it was prophesied, born 'in the centre of the earth'.[22] To the prophets, 'the centre of the earth' denoted Jerusalem, but to Lucian it applies to the relative position of the marketplace within the city. Chester becomes a microcosm of the world as Lucian equates the historical moment of Christ's birth in Jerusalem with contemporary life in Chester. As God has it at the opening of the Tanners' play, 'hit is, yt was, it shalbe thus' (1.4).

In my second example, Lucian advocates a tropological interpretation of the three roads that lead east from Chester:[23]

---

through the mystery of the holy cross […]. It is also worth understanding how fitting it is that, all things being equal, a marketplace for the selling of things should be placed in the middle of the city, where, with an abundance of merchandise, particularly food available, a native or a foreigner may come to buy provisions. Doubtlessly, as with the eternal bread which came from heaven which, according to the prophets, was formed in *the centre of the earth*, God wanted to supply all nations of the world equally. Let everyone wise observe this joyfully because almighty God provided for us with paternal goodness, and arranged fully and nobly for the prosperity of the citizens.'

[22]   See Psalm 73:12, Ezekiel 5:5, John 6:59.

[23]   *De laude Cestrie*, excerpt 25: 'the inhabitant of Chester should notice, leaving the East Gate, how three roads are presented to him and how they and their names prove to be beautiful subjects for consideration; indeed, not only beautiful, but also congenial. For if he walks a little way directly out of the city, a place immediately appears in front which they call the village of Christ; if he turns to the right, another place appears which they call the Old Ford; if however he turns to the left, he has come to the place which they rightly call the Valley of Demons, since it is a hiding place for robbers.

We may use this to show that everything happens as a consequence of a moral reason since he finds Christ to be the true east, who goes straightly; he who strays to the right in defiance of scripture will show himself to have strayed at the Day of Judgement; he who

Intendat Cestriae habitator, exeunti portam orientalem, qualiter ei trinus uiarum trames aperitur et pulcra super locorum uocabulis, que se offerunt, consideracio inuenitur; nec solum pulcra, set etiam iocunda. Nam progressus paululum a ciuitate si directus incedit, statim a fronte uenientem locus excipit, quem nominant Villam Christi; si uero flectit ad dexteram alter locus, quem uocant incole, Veterem Vadum; si autem uertitur ad sinistram, uenitur ad locum, quem de latibulis insidiantium, recte dicunt Vallem Demonum.

Vt autem nos ex manifesta re utamur morali racione consequenter omnia occurrunt, quia Christum inuenit uerum orientem, qui recte tendit; qui declinat in dexteram contra scripturam prohibentem deuiasse ad ultimum se probabit; qui flectit in leuam, lesionem uitare non poterit. Errores autem contrarios hinc inde sic accipiamus, ut errantium dextera uideatur esse superba iusticia, leua autem segnis morum custodia et in qualibet harum deuius, a dextris mordeatur a draconibus, a sinistris spolietur a latronibus, ut experimento tactus in reliquum rectus discat incedere et pro sua salute deuia declinare. Legitur enim, *inter uicia contraria, medius limes uirtus est* [cp. Horace, *Epistulae* 1. 18. 9]. Et noster Iohannes: *dirigite uiam Domini, rectas facite inquit semitas Dei nostri* [Luke 3:4], quia, qui ambulat simpliciter, ambulat confidenter. Et sepe felicius ac melius ualefacit humanis rebus simplex et innocens uita quam uersutus sensus et alta sapientia. Nam qui, per confidentiam meriti uel contumatiam sullimis ingenii, regiam inter errores medios uiam relinquit, superbos anfractus in gaudium non transmittit, qui ad dextram uel leuam temere declinauit. Vnde colligitur nichil utilius, nichil melius, quam in progressu uiarum uelut in porta urbium recte incedere ac recte uiuere, quia per linearum ductum itineris ad lucem tenditur orientis.

Lucian's wordplay on the names of three villages to the east of Chester – Christleton, Aldford, and Hoole Heath – enables him to interpret the traveller's option on leaving the East Gate as a moral choice between laxity, sternness, and the middle way and thus to provide a powerful warning to anyone contemplating straying from the way of the Lord. For Lucian, then, city space is a constant source of edification for the observant inhabitant. The Chester cycle contains far fewer

---

turns to the left, will not be able to avoid injury. We should admit two sources of error, in that to the right is excessive sternness and to the left is the lax preservation of morals and harmed whatever way he deviates, to the right bitten by dragons, to the left robbed by thieves, the righteous man learns by practice to go straight ahead in the future and, for his health, to avoid detours. It is read, indeed, that *between two evils the middle path is virtue* [cp. Horace, *Epistulae* 1. 18. 9]. And John says in the scriptures *make straight the way of the Lord, make straight his paths* [Luke 3:4], because he who walks innocently, walks confidently. And often a life led simply and innocently will end more happily than one led in accordance with cunning and ambitious intelligence. For he who through an obstinate belief in his exalted understanding abandons the royal highway for the uncertainties either side, straying to the left or the right, does not tread these proud diversions in joy. From this nothing more useful is learnt than to advance straight through streets and the gates of cities and to live rightly because one comes to the true east through a journey travelled straight.'

references to specific features of Cestrian topography, but likewise asserts the possibility for spiritual learning in the city.

While recent work has explored the ways in which the Chester plays gained meaning when performed in particular locations around the city, references to city life in the texts themselves have not been the subject of particular critical focus, in part because the urban topography features so seldom in the plays.[24] Discovering how prominently Chester locations featured in the scripts used in the performances of the 1560s and 1570s is not easy. The most thorough textual witnesses to the Chester cycle are all more than twenty years later than the final performance, and no witness presents a text fully compatible with any of the surviving contemporary accounts of the plays. I therefore reluctantly rely on H, the manuscript taken by Lumiansky and Mills as the base text for their Early English Text Society edition.

Precise references to specifically Cestrian space are rare. Octavian promises Preco 'the highest horse besydes Boughton' (6.279) as a reward for his assistance in coordinating the census, probably a sarcastic reference to the gallows which stood in the eastern suburb of the city. The shepherds feast on local delicacies including 'butter that bought was in Blacon' (7.115), a village 2 miles north-west of Chester, and 'ale of Halton' (7.117), 10 miles north-east of Chester. Before Jesus raises Lazarus in the Glovers' play, he says:

> For worldes light I am verey,
> and whoesoe followeth me, sooth to saye,
> hee may goe no Chester waye,
> for light in him is dight. (13.353–6)

While H's 'thester' is almost certainly the original reading for l. 355, 'Chester' is an intriguing error,[25] that betrays no great love for the city and accords with the negative image of urban life elsewhere in the cycle, most forcibly expressed through the damned alewife at the end of the Cooks' *Harrowing of Hell*.[26] She confesses she was 'sometyme ... a taverner, / a gentle gossippe and a tapster' (17.285–6), before stating:

> Tavernes, tapsters of this cittye
> shalbe promoted here with mee
> for breakinge statutes of this contrye,
> hurtinge the commonwealth. (17.301–4)

---

[24]   One exception is Mills, *Recycling the Cycle*, 173–8. For the former approach, see, for example, Barrett, *Against All England*, 59–95.

[25]   See John 11:9–10. Confusion of *t* and *c* is explicable palaeographically.

[26]   On the character of the alewife, see R.M. Lumiansky, 'Comedy and Theme in the Chester *Harrowing of Hell*', *Tulane Studies in English* 10 (1960); Mary Wack, 'Women, Work, and Plays in an English Medieval Town', in Susan Frye and Karen Robertson (eds), *Maids and Mistresses, Cousins and Queens: Women's Alliances in Early Modern England* (Oxford, 1999).

The deictic 'this cittye' can only refer to Chester, where Mayor Henry Gee had legislated against tapsters in 1541.[27] Thus, as Mary Wack has argued, the play 'works as an ideological justification of the restrictive legislation barring them from their customary trade'.[28] The play's association of urban life with drinking, loose talk, deceit, and hangovers also finds expression in the third pageant, where Noah's wife remains stubbornly attached to the town and her gossips and refuses to board the ark (3.200). The alewife's ongoing popularity (the mayor specially demanded her presence at the midsummer festival of 1614)[29] may suggest Cestrians were also somewhat proud of their reputation for bad behaviour.

These particular plays encourage a ready equation between urban life and sin, which problematizes the willingness of the cycle to redesignate Cestrian space as biblical space. In the Wrights' *Nativity*, the pageant wagon is Rome at one moment (6.275), Bethlehem the next (6.456, 473). In the Corvisers' *Christ and the Money-lenders*, it becomes Jerusalem to stage what is perhaps the archetypal city entry. Some plays also co-opted the streets surrounding the pageant wagon into the performance space. In the Cappers' play, Balaack tells Balaam to observe 'Godes people all in feare. / Cittye, castle and ryvere' (5.273–4). According to the stage directions, Balaam then turns south, north, and finally east (5.279 SD, 303 SD, 319 SD), on each occasion refusing to curse the people. Looking north, he even comments on the 'fayre wonninge' (5.304) and concludes that 'God made all this, / his folke to lyve in joye and blys' (5.309). In the Skinners' *Resurrection*, Peter and John leave the stage looking for Jesus, 'hic per aliam viam ille per alteram' (18.420 SD). The willingness of the cycle to co-opt the city as performance space shares Lucian's confidence that the city can be the site of spiritual learning, despite its degeneracy.

The plays therefore engage with Cestrian space in several ways. First, the pageant wagon and surrounding streets are redesignated as historical time and space: one day the Israel that Balaack insists Balaam curses; the next, the Jerusalem that welcomes Christ. The inevitable use of deictic language like 'here' and 'this' makes this almost an automatic consequence of staging biblical drama. The plays differ from Lucian's *De laude Cestrie*, where Cestrian topography retains its autonomy, but is interpreted through a biblical lens. When the plays do make their rare use of local colour – Blacon butter, Hatton ale, the gallows at Broughton, the peccadillos of the city's tapsters – they domesticate biblical time and space, asserting that it is commensurate with contemporary time, space, and mores. Yet while the Chester plays happily redesignate Chester as Israel, they never attempt to read Cestrian space in light of this equation; Balaam's 'halles, chambers … valles, woodes, grasse growinge, / fayre yordes, and eke ryvere' (5.305–7) remain convenient abstractions rather than genuine features of Chester's topography. Though they do so in different ways, both Lucian's *De laude Cestrie* and the

---

[27]   Rupert H. Morris, *Chester in the Plantagenet and Tudor Reigns* (Chester, 1894), 425.

[28]   Wack, 'Women, Work, and Plays', 42.

[29]   David Mills, 'Who are Our Customers? The Audience for Chester's Plays', *Medieval English Theatre* 20 (1998), 114.

Chester cycle connect the contemporary city with biblical time and space, a necessity of their shared use of traditional exegetical methods. Lucian's use of these sophisticated methods in a Latin text written for a coterie audience of literate Cestrians ran no risks, but its employment in the cycle ran counter to the intellectual conservatism of royally-authorized protestant exegesis in the 1570s, and earned the plays criticism from the puritan Goodman.

Lucian and the Expositor

As the extensive quotations in the previous section made clear, much of *De laude Cestrie* is devoted to exegesis. It is therefore natural to compare Lucian with the expository character who appears in five of the Chester plays.[30] Stage directions refer to him as either an expositor or a doctor. His duties include explaining the allegorical significance of old testament stories like *Abraham and Isaac*, interpreting signs and prophecies, and summarizing intervening action which would be too lengthy to present dramatically. The manuscripts give no indication how he should be costumed, but – given his role in the plays – he may have worn some kind of clerical dress, as most of the pageants chose to present him in the May 2010 Toronto performance.

In this section, I explore the expositor's role in the plays, suggesting that the cycle acknowledges some doubt about the validity of biblical exegesis. Nonetheless, the expositor's exegesis in the plays, particularly the Barbers' play of *Abraham and Isaac*, is considerably more intellectually adventurous than the simple typological equations and moral lessons drawn from the story in official Elizabethan texts like the Bishops' Bible and *The Sermons or Homilies* … . A passage from Lucian's *De laude Cestrie* serves to open the discussion.

Lucian's implied readership is a narrow elite, the literate inhabitants of Chester, though the text hints that he hoped his ideas would circulate more widely in the city through the preaching and pastoral efforts of his readers.[31] His exegetical methods are illustrated by the following passage:[32]

---

[30]   In general, see David Mills, 'Brought to Book: Chester's Expositor and his Kin', in Philip Butterworth (ed.), *The Narrator, the Expositor and the Prompter in European Medieval Theatre*, Medieval Texts and Cultures of Northern Europe 17 (Turnhout, 2007).

[31]   The literate inhabitant is addressed in *De laude Cestrie*, extract 19: 'may the learned inhabitant observe the voice of the Lord' (*prudenter aduertat saltem literatus habitator Domini uocem*). In extract 24, Lucian explains 'I have judged these four gates worth depicting, o city of Chester, so that what the reader has in books, the inhabitant may hold in his gaze and memory' ['haec de quattuor portis tuis pingenda credidi ciuitas Cestria, ut quod habet lector in litera, teneat habitator in oculis et memoria']. The subjunctive *teneat* suggests that Lucian expects the inhabitant to learn from the reader.

[32]   *De laude Cestrie*, extract 25: 'Therefore let my reader carefully notice how this lady, our Virgin of virgins, whom, in accordance with the facts, we said has two churches within the walls dedicated to her, was happy to establish a third outside the walls near the church of John,

Itaque lector meus attendat, qualiter ipsa domina nostra uirginum Virgo, quam, sicut res docent, duas habere memorie sue basilicas diximus infra muros urbis, terciam sibi constitui placuit extra muros, uicinam ecclesiae Iohannis Domini precursoris, pulcro ueraciter ordine, gestorum plenissima racione. Nempe apud Nazareth Galilee, olim saluata ab archangelo, cum concepisset de spiritu sancto plena gaudiorum, propter salutem orbis terrarum, *exurgens cum festinacione abiit in montana* [Luke 1:39] *et intrauit domum Zacharie et salutauit Elisabeth* [Luke 1:40] cognatum suam. Nimirum ex celesti nuncio et comuni gaudio omnium conditorum suaue nimis ac sublime editura colloquium, pariter et seni ac prouecte mulieri ipsa expedicior et liberior, facilior et fecundior, quamuis altior et eminentior tamen uirgo iuuencula, prebitura pietatis obsequium, iam in suo portans utero filium, qui postea lauit pedes apostolorum.

Iustissime igitur atque pulcherrime apud nostram Cestriam, pro sua matre matri Domini quasi refundens uicem suae in Christo familie, inspirauit Iohannes Baptista consuetudinem, ut festis temporibus atque dominicis diebus, coris incedentibus et uocibus dulcissimis resonantibus, gloriosae uirginis ac Domini genitricis ecclesiam deuotissime satagant uisitare et consuetis officiis pro more uenerabilis cleri, ad Eterni Regis gloriam officiosissime salutare. Veraciter tanquam diceret Baptista clarissimus sibi ministrantibus rebus simul et racionibus: 'Quia tria uidentur in temporibus, semel, sepe, ac semper, per humilitatem et iusticiam contendere satagamus, et reddamus regine celi officii et gratie fecundissimum fenus, ut crescentibus comodis, quia semel in terris dignata est meam matrem salutare, nos ei sepe curemus dignissimas laudes salutando refundere, quatinus eius gloriosis precibus mereamur in celis, semper et aeternaliter himnos nostros cum angelis sociare.'

---

precursor of the Lord, a truly beautiful location with great historical significance. Certainly at Nazareth in Galilee, having been greeted by the Archangel Gabriel when full of joy concerning the holy spirit and the salvation of the entire world *Mary went into the hill country with haste* [Luke 1:39] *and she entered into the house of Zachary, and saluted Elizabeth* [Luke 1:40], her kinswoman. Evidently she had a most sweet and sublime conversation with the pregnant woman because of the heavenly messenger and the common joy of all creation, though compared to the aged woman she was more unencumbered and free, more fecund and fertile, and though a young virgin, higher and more eminent, who would behave with pious obedience carrying in her womb her son who later washed the feet of the apostles.

Therefore, thanking Christ for the fortune of his family like his mother thanking the mother of the Lord, John the Baptist very properly and beautifully established a custom in Chester, by which on holy days and Sundays, with choirs proceeding and their very sweet voices resounding they visit the church of the glorious Virgin and mother of the Lord with great devotion and with the formalities typical of that venerable clergy most dutifully visit them to the glory of the eternal king. It is as if the most illustrious Baptist had spoken to those attending to him in both word and deed: "We must try to act with meekness and justness because this may be seen three times in history: once, often and always. We should pay back the queen of heaven with most fruitful kindness and goodwill when, with increasing benefit, we undertake to lavish most fitting praise on her by visiting, since she once on earth deigned to greet my mother, so that we may earn her glorious prayers in heaven to always and eternally share our hymns with angels."' I have modified the text and the translation slightly.

This passage describes a weekly liturgical procession from St John's Cathedral to the church of St Mary on the Hill, which has been considered the precursor of the later Corpus Christ procession.[33] Lucian begins by directing his reader to this detail of local ceremonial (*lector meus attendat*), asserting its importance lies in its 'great historical significance'. For Lucian, the procession is a type of Mary's visit to John's mother when newly pregnant with Jesus, but, by insisting John the Baptist himself instituted the procession in Chester, he vivifies and historicizes the typological interpretation. Such divine coincidences (which Lucian elsewhere calls 'a sacred offering and a charming mystery [which] comfort men's spirits and encourages contemplation')[34] are a mainstay of *De laude Cestrie*. Lucian ventriloquizes John to assert the significance of Mary's visit 'once, often and always', explaining his meaning in a marginal note: 'once, often, always: the first in mountainous Judea, the second in Chester, the third in eternity'.[35] The events are thus important historically to Mary and Elizabeth (in mountainous Judea), tropologically to the canons of St John's and people of Chester (who 'should pay pay back the queen of heaven with most fruitful kindness and goodwill'), and anagogically (present-day ceremonial will permit us to 'eternally share our hymns with angels'). Lucian's interpretation of the procession collapses time (past, present, and future) and space (Judea, Chester, heaven), just as the plays must in their attempt to stage the whole span of Christian history in three days on Chester's streets. For both, typology, tropology, and anagogy are essential tools. Unlike Lucian, the Chester plays show some anxiety about their use.

The expositor, who most often wields these tools in the cycle, is polite, learned, and somewhat pompous.[36] He addresses his audience as 'lordinges' (4.113, 193, 460, etc.), devotes himself to instructing the 'unlearned' (4.113), and is careful not to outstay his welcome (5.45–8). He is a caring pastor who prays for his listeners (4.476–83), but, particularly in the Clothworkers' play of *The Prophets of Antichrist*, a pastor who insists on his hieratic status. He understands the prophecies; the audience must 'beleeve … fullye withouten weene' his interpretations (22.37). Several features of the plays conspire to reduce his authority. In the Cappers' play of *Moses* and *Balaack and Balaam*, the Doctor's final words are those of a theatrical impresario:

> Prayenge you all, both east and west
> where that yee goe, to speake the best.
> The byrth of Christe, feare and honest,
> here shall yee see; and fare yee well. (5.452–5)

---

[33] Baldwin, Clopper, and Mills, *REED: Cheshire*, 2.994.

[34] 'Sollempne munus, suaue misterium [quod] confortat animos et pascit intuitum': *De laude Cestrie*, excerpt 9.

[35] 'Semel, sepe, semper: unum montanis Iudee, alterum Cestrie, tercium in eternitate'. I have emended my translation from the website.

[36] He does not have a monopoly on their use: the three kings explain the significance of the frankincense, myrrh, and gold themselves (9.88–95, 96–103, 104–11), while Christ is allowed to expound the meaning of John 11:9–10 (13.349–56).

These words could be seen as a tongue-in-cheek prophecy of the next day's performance of Christ's nativity, a less-than-serious counterpart to the procession of prophets that closes the play in MS H, and they align the otherwise humourless expositor with Goobett-on-the-Greene who announces the Barbers' play of *Abraham and Isaac* (4.1–16).[37] More damaging to the expositor's integrity is the Doctor who appears in the Vintners' play of *The Three Kings*. This doctor, described by Herod as 'my clarke' (8.232), represents 'the chief priests and the scribes of the people',[38] who are summoned by Herod to predict where Jesus had been born. The doctor acknowledges the instability of his position in his opening speech:

> Nay, my lord, bee ye bould;
> I trowe noe prophetes before would
> write anythinge your hart to could
> or your right to denye.
> But syth your grace at this tyme would
> that I the prophets declare should,
> of Christes comminge as they have tould,
> the trueth to certyfie,
> I beseech your ryall majestee
> with patience of your benignitie
> the trueth to here, and pardone mee
> there sayenges to declare. (8.245–56)

Some exegetes, the doctor implies, would bend the truth to placate a tyrant's ear, a supposition confirmed when a doctor later appears among Antichrist's retinue (23.420, 432–9). When the doctor does interpret the prophecies forthrightly in accordance with tradition, Herod responds by breaking his sword, blaspheming, and tearing up the doctor's books (8.350–51). The doctor's words and the action of the play cast material doubt on the validity of exegesis in the cycle.

Several of these hints were developed during the performance of the plays in Toronto in May 2010. The expositor was almost invariably dressed in priestly or academic dress and often carried a book.[39] In the University of Toledo's production of the Butchers' *The Woman Taken in Adultery*, the book was an outsized copy of the *Glossa ordinaria*, which the expositor held open and gestured towards as she spoke. Herod's violence towards the doctor and her books was vividly depicted in the University of Waterloo's *Three Kings*. While the University of Saskatchewan

---

[37] This observation invalidates the suggestion that Goobett's name serves to prevent possible identification with the expositor: Richard Axton, *European Drama of the Early Middle Ages* (London, 1974), 185.

[38] Mt 2:4.

[39] Many of the expositors were female. I do not know the purpose of these casting decisions.

offered a static (and perhaps authentic) interpretation of *The Prophets of Antichrist*,[40] two plays memorably portrayed tensions in the characterization of the expositor. In Ryerson University's *Abraham and Isaac* and *Moses and the Law*,[41] God, who otherwise faced the audience, turned his back when the expositor addressed the audience, before the expositor reciprocated by looking irritated when God spoke. In Shenandoah University's *Nativity*, the expositor's fellow cast members decided to drag him off stage as his list of 'other myracles ... that befell that ilke daye / that Jesus Christ was borne' (6.568, 570–71) threatened to continue without end. We cannot say whether such anticlericalism was a part of the performances in the 1560s and 1570s, but there are hints in the text that the expositor was a problematic character.

The expositor lives up to this billing by employing a much wider variety of exegetical methodologies than are found in royally-authorized exegesis from the 1570s. Neither mainstream protestants nor puritans like Goodman found the practice of exegesis in itself objectionable, though Goodman disagreed with many of the expositor's specific interpretations. The simplest method utilized by the expositor is historical narrative, which he uses, for example, in his proleptic summary of the carving of the new tablets of the law (5.41–64). Even narrative, however, is to some degree interpretive, as is evident from Goodman's objection that 'the Ark [is] called a Shrine' in this speech (5.61). The expositor extends this method when interpreting prophecies, which is his role in the procession of prophets uniquely preserved in MS H's version of *Balaack and Balaam* and in *The Prophets of Antichrist*.[42] To interpret the messianic prophecies of the former, the expositor shows how the New Testament fulfills the Old Testament, even suggesting that some prophecies are too simple to need explanation (App 1B.205–6, 369–71). This allegorical model also underlies the doctor's attempts to connect Christ's temptation in the wilderness with Adam's temptation in paradise, a self-acknowledged borrowing from Gregory's *Homilia in evangelia* (12.169–216). By contrast, the expositor adopts an anagogical method in interpreting the apocalyptic prophecies of *The Prophets of Antichrist*, reading – for example – the 'little horn' of Daniel 7:8 as 'Antechriste' (22.161), an interpretation he shared with Bullinger, Luther, and Oecolampadius (who further explained that this Antichrist was the pope), but not Calvin, who believed that all Daniel's prophecies had been fulfilled before Christ's birth or shortly thereafter.[43] This anagogical method could also lead to Goodman's disfavour, and 'the exposition of Malachy's prophecy concerning Enoch and Elias approving a religious life' and 'the exposition of Iohn's revelation

---

[40]   Mills imagines him speaking in front of a silent tableau: Mills, 'Brought to Book', 316.

[41]   Alexandra Johnston's 2010 text joined 4.289–475 with 5.1–96.

[42]   On this genre, see Robert A. Brawer, 'The Form and Function of the Prophetic Procession in the Middle English Cycle Play', *Annuale Medievale* 13 (1972).

[43]   Richard A. Muller, 'The Hermeneutic of Promise and Fulfillment in Calvin's Exegesis of the Old Testament Prophecies of the Kingdom', in David C. Steinmetz (ed.), *The Bible in the Sixteenth Century* (Durham NC, 1990), 71.

that Enoch and Elias are in paradise in the flesh' appear on his list of 'absurdities'. The expositor also makes limited use of tropological interpretation in the plays, most memorably when he explains that the miraculous withering and healing of the midwife Salome's hands as she tries to test Mary's virginity shows 'that unbeleefe is a fowle sinne' (6.721).

We can gain some sense of the significance of the expositor's explanatory endeavours by comparing his interventions in the Barbers' play of *Abraham* with licensed sixteenth-century exegesis of these episodes. No other English cycle narrates the story of Melchizedek and the covenant and circumcision.[44] The expositor interprets the bread and wine Melchizedek gives to Abraham as a type of the eucharist (4.113–43), circumcision as a type of baptism (4.194–208), and Abraham's willingness to sacrifice Isaac as a prefiguration of the incarnation (4.460–75). Neither the Geneva Bible (1560), nor the Bishops' Bible (1568), nor *The Sermons or Homilies appointed to be read in Churches* (enlarged version, 1571) explicitly offer a sacramental interpretation of these episodes, instead offering the well-worn typological equation of Isaac and Christ, first expounded by Paul in his Letter to the Romans, and a simple, moral gloss.[45] The Bishops' Bible explicitly denies a sacramental interpretation of Abraham's meeting with Melchizedek, explaining he offered the bread and wine 'for to refreshe Abram and his soldiers, and not make any oblation'.[46] The *Sermons* offer Abraham as an exemplum of faith, and his victory over the five kings as evidence that 'GOD doth oftentimes prosper iust and lawfull enemies'.[47] For the compilers of the Geneva Bible, circumcision was a sign 'to shewe that all that is begotten of man is corrupt and must be mortified', and Abraham's example showed 'the onley way to ouercome all tentations is to rest vpon Gods prouidence'.[48]

---

[44]   For further discussion, see Yumi Dohi, 'Melchisedech in Late Medieval Religious Drama', *Early Drama, Art and Music Review* 16 (1994), rpt in Clifford Davidson (ed.), *The Dramatic Tradition of the Middle Ages*, AMS Studies in the Middle Ages 26 (New York, 2005).

[45]   Geneva's paraphrase of Genesis 22 baldly states 'Izhák is a figure of Christ' (sig. c. iv), but this is not developed in the notes. *The Sermons* imply that Abraham's faith was bolstered by his confidence that God 'was able by his omnipotent power to rayse [Isaac] from death', a detail that seems to propose the same equation: Mary Ellen Rickey and Thomas B. Stroup, *Certaine Sermons or Homilies Appointed to be Read in Churches in the Time of Queen Elizabeth I (1547–1571): a facsimile reproduction of the edition of 1623* (Gainesville FL, 1968), 24.

[46]   *The Holy Byble, conteyning the Olde and Nevve Testament wherevnto is ioyned the whole seruice, vsed in the Church of England* (London, 1577), 7v.

[47]   Rickey and Stroup, *Certaine Sermons*, 24, 301. In general, see Luc Borot, 'The Bible and Protestant Inculturation in the *Homilies* of the Church of England', in Richard Griffiths (ed.), *The Bible in the Renaissance: Essays on Biblical Commentary and Translation in The Fifteenth and Sixteenth Centuries*, St Andrews Studies in Reformation History (Aldershot, 2001).

[48]   Lloyd E. Berry, *The Geneva Bible: A Facsimile of the 1560 Edition* (Madison, 1969), sig. b. iii (r), c. i(v).

The practice of allegorical exegesis in the sixteenth century cannot be labelled 'protestant', 'Catholic', or with any sectarian tag. For all its emphasis on reform and rupture, sixteenth-century exegesis still relied on late medieval methods.[49] Expository figures, like Bale's Prolocutor, appeared in protestant drama. Different protestant factions also held variant attitudes towards exegetical theory and practice: one of the bishops' major objections to the Geneva Bible was the 'divers prejudicial notes'.[50] Yet the predominant reliance of authorized protestant exegesis on a simple, moral interpretation of the Abraham and Isaac episode, combined with the puritan Goodman's persistent objections to the expositor's ideas, confirm the ambiguity regarding the practice of exegesis ingrained in the plays, and suggest the cycle's debt to medieval and therefore Catholic exegetical practice was one reason they were problematic to stage in the 1570s.

The Chester Plays and Mapping Medieval Chester

Inspired by the fictitious account of the Whitsun plays' origins offered in the Late Banns, this article has explored the intersections between the exegetical practices of Lucian's *De laude Cestrie* and the Chester plays. In this concluding section, I want to use the resources developed by the Mapping Medieval Chester project to suggest some further lines of enquiry regarding the cycle's status as a Cestrian text.

The Mapping Medieval Chester project, which ran for one academic year (2008–09), was a collaboration between an urban geographer, three medieval literature specialists, and several experts in digital humanities, funded by the UK's Arts and Humanities Research Council. It produced a website (<http://www.medievalchester. ac.uk>) containing a variety of resources, including partial editions of Lucian's *De laude Cestrie*, Henry Bradshaw's *Life of St Werburghe*, a series of Welsh and Latin poems relating to Chester, and new static and interactive maps of the medieval city. The project's objective was to explore the relationship between literary and geographical mappings and it is accordingly possible to move dynamically between the texts and the interactive map. The website's indices of people and places reconstruct the cultural framework which medieval Cestrian writers shared.

The Chester cycle was excluded on the grounds of its length and complex textual history, as well as our lack of expertise. In retrospect, I think this was a wise decision, since the plays contain very few specific references to Cestrian topography, and neither generic references like Balaam's 'halles' and 'chambers' (5.305) nor deictic references to the temporary position of pageant wagons could readily be mapped

---

[49]   David C. Steinmetz, 'Calvin and the Patristic Exegesis of Paul', in Steinmetz, *The Bible in the Sixteenth Century*; Richard A. Muller, 'Biblical Interpretation in the Era of the Reformation: The View from the Middle Ages', in Richard A. Muller and John L. Thompson (eds), *Biblical Interpretation in the Era of the Reformation: Essays Presented to David C. Steinmetz in Honor of his Sixtieth Birthday* (Grand Rapids MI, 1996).

[50]   David Daniell, *The Bible in English: its history and influence* (New Haven CT, 2003), 341.

according to our methodologies. The website is nonetheless an invaluable resource for contextualizing the plays and assessing the extent to which they partake in a distinctively Cestrian literary tradition, the existence of which is posited by both Mapping Medieval Chester and Robert W. Barrett, Jr.'s recent *Against All England*.[51]

This essay has shown the similarities between Lucian's twelfth-century *De laude Cestrie* and the Chester cycle, but the other texts edited on the website provide equally fertile material for investigation. Writing about *The Shepherds Play*, with its stereotypical depiction of the Welsh pastors Hannekynn, Harvy, and Tudd eating leeks (7.156) and practising magic (7.19–20), David Mills suggests 'the shepherds are amusing incomers and their presence in Chester serves to define the civic community negatively as "non-Welsh". But they are presented affectionately, not as foolish country folk'.[52] The texts edited on the website evince a complex relationship between the Welsh and Chester. Poems like Tudor Penllyn's *I Reinallt ap Gruffudd o 'r Twr* [*To Rheinallt ap Gruffudd ap Bleddyn of the Tower*], a bloodthirsty encomium to an attack on the men of Chester at Mold in 1464, and Guto'r Glyn's *I Wiliam Herbart* [*To William Herbert*] indicate fifteenth-century Welsh hostility to Chester. At the same time, Welsh pilgrims frequently visited St John's Cathedral and its relic of the true cross, as Maredudd ap Rhys's *I'r Groes o Gaer* [*Poem to the Cross at Chester*] records. The ambivalence of Chester's attitude to the Welsh is evident from Henry Bradshaw's *Life of St Werburghe*, where Bradshaw emphasizes the role of the British in founding and converting Chester, before explaining that from the time of King Alfred they 'euer to the saxons ha[d] inwarde hate'.[53] These complex local attitudes problematize understanding the characterization of the Welsh shepherds as simply 'amusing'.

Welsh poems like Lewys Glyn Cothi's 'Dychan i Ŵyr o Gaer' ['Satire on the Men of Chester'], which opens by petitioning Rheinallt fab Gruffydd fab Bleddyn to slaughter fifty Cestrians in revenge for the theft of Lewys's possessions, show just how fraught ethnic tensions between the English and the Welsh could be. With its slurs on Chester's untrustworthy mayor and licentious, bisexual monks, this poem depicts a very different city hierarchy to the Late Banns with their reverent description of the Chester cycle as a pious collaboration between Higden and Arneway. Bradshaw, like Higden a Benedictine monk of St Werburgh's, fails to mention the mayor once, and is unhesitating in his insistence that the city's elites owe their first loyalty to St Werburgh and her monastery. Lucian, with his second threefold interpretation of *Cestria* as 'the honesty of her nobles, the faith of her citizens, the religion of her monks', shares the Late Banns' affirmation of the value of collaboration between Chester's civic and religious institutions. This similarity and the others detailed in this paper confirm the Chester plays' status as a Chester text.

---

[51]   See n. 18 above.

[52]   Mills, *Recycling the Cycle*, 177.

[53]   Henry Bradshaw, *Life of St Werburghe*, ed. Catherine A.M. Clarke, Mapping Medieval Chester Project, <http://www.medievalchester.ac.uk>, accessed 27 August 2010, 2.687.

Chapter 11
Maintaining the Realm:
City, Commonwealth, and Crown in Chester's Midsummer Plays

Heather S. Mitchell-Buck

Despite the best efforts of Christopher Goodman, Chester undertook one more large-scale production of biblical drama following the 1572 performance. On 30 May 1575, Mayor John Savage of Chester met with the city's common council in order to determine 'whether the accostomed plaes called the whitson plaes shalbe sett furth & plaied at midesummer next or not'. The vote was thirty-three to twelve in favour of performance.[1] Despite the approval of more than two-thirds of the city's primary governing body, however, this final performance was significantly different from that of previous years: only some of the plays were presented, and the performance date was shifted from Whitsun week to the secular Midsummer festival. The controversy surrounding this final performance draws attention to the vexed state of the English Church in the 1570s. The move from Whitsun to Midsummer (24 June) suggests that Pentecost, a feast that celebrates the church as a unified community and commemorates a time when those with seemingly insurmountable differences were able to understand one another,[2] was no longer thought to be an appropriate context for the plays. For the English church, particularly in the northwest, was anything but unified in 1575.

Although scholars have generally assumed that the relocation of the plays to Midsummer was the work of those inclined towards protestantism, I contend that the shift represents the resolution of Chester's leading citizens – largely traditionalist in their religious sympathies – to keep the plays alive under the auspices of the city, and signals their determination to resist the national protestant understandings of community to which they had increasingly been required to subscribe. As Peter Lake, Paul White, and others have shown, religious identities

---

[1]   The vote is recorded in the city's Assembly Files (Cheshire Record Office, ZAF, f. 25). For a transcription, see Lawrence M. Clopper (ed.), *REED: Chester* (Toronto, 1979), 103–4. For discussion of the circumstances surrounding the final performance, see R.M. Lumiansky and David Mills (eds), *The Chester Mystery Cycle: Essays and Documents* (Chapel Hill, 1983), 192–4.

[2]   At the first pentecost as described in Acts 2, Peter and the apostles were given the gift of speaking in the tongues of many nations by the holy spirit, allowing them to preach to and baptize those with whom they previously had no common ground.

at this time were shifting and changing along a wide spectrum from recusant to puritan, and the labels of 'protestant' and 'Roman Catholic' tend to suggest a binary that did not, in fact, exist.[3] Yet apparent Catholic beliefs and practices persisted in Chester well past the 1575 performance, even though documented recusancy was by no means as widespread as in neighbouring Lancashire. The privy council reprimanded Chester's Bishop Downham in 1568 and again in 1575 for failing to actively suppress recusancy amongst his flock, not only in Lancashire but also in West Cheshire.[4] Clerics who had refused to subscribe to the oath of supremacy were permitted to continue serving in their parishes, and those who did gradually replace them were largely indifferent and uneducated – in protestant doctrine or anything else.[5] Even though the majority of Cestrians outwardly conformed to the new church, protestant fervour was still a rare thing among the city's gentry and leading citizens in 1575.[6] Given Chester's historical desire to manage its local affairs in its own way,[7] attempts to suppress performances of the Whitsun plays must have been seen as yet another of the crown's efforts to interfere in the running of their city.

For those involved in the common council meeting on 30 May and the performances that followed, the most pressing attack on the plays was the official 'inhibition' sent by the archbishop of York to prevent the cycle in 1572. The explanation provided in the city's records for ignoring the archbishop's order

---

[3]   See Peter Lake, 'Religious Identities in Shakespeare's England', in David Scott Kastan (ed.), *A Companion to Shakespeare* (Oxford, 1999), 57–84, and Peter Lake and Michael Questier, 'Introduction', in Peter Lake and Michael Questier (eds), *Conformity and Orthodoxy in the English Church c. 1560–1660* (Woodbridge, 2000), ix–xx, as well as Paul Whitfield White's essay in this volume.

[4]   B.E. Harris (ed.), *A History of the County of Chester*, 3 vols, *The Victoria History of the Counties of England* (Oxford, 1980), 3.20. See also Richard K. Emmerson, 'Contextualizing Performance: The Reception of the Chester *Antichrist*', *Journal of Medieval and Early Modern Studies* 29.1 (1999), 108.

[5]   Christopher Haigh, *Reformation and Resistance in Tudor Lancashire* (London, 1975), 239.

[6]   Harris, *A History of the County of Chester* 3.89 notes that 42 out of 66 lay justices were largely unfavourable to the settlement as of 1564. C.P. Lewis and A.T. Thacker (eds), *A History of the County of Chester*, vol. 5, part 1, *The Victoria History of the Counties of England* (Suffolk, 2003), 109–10 note that even in the 1570s, Chester had few prominent protestant laymen, and that Chester's primary overseas trade 'was not with ports where protestantism was entrenched', preventing protestant doctrine from entering into Chester's culture via that route. While relatively few Cestrians were accused of recusancy, it seems unlikely that many would have undergone a radical change of heart without a strong clerical hand to guide them.

[7]   According to Harris, *A History of the County of Chester*, 2.5, 'Chester stood apart, in the minds of contemporaries, from England'. Although the term 'palatinate' was unofficial until the 1290s, Chester nonetheless seems to have had the privileges, if not the title, from shortly after the conquest. The county owed no taxes or military service to the crown, and was not within the purview of royal justices. For additional discussion, see the introduction to Robert W. Barrett, Jr, *Against All England: Regional Identity and Cheshire Writing, 1195–1656* (Notre Dame, 2009).

is that his missive 'came too late',[8] in spite of Goodman's assertion that the letters did reach Chester's bishop and mayor.[9] Three years later, the Cestrian council could no longer rely upon pretence and evasion, for Mayor Savage found himself summoned by Elizabeth's privy council in November 1575 to explain why the city had, once again, defied the archbishop's injunction. In response to a letter from Savage, which states that 'it hathe bene enformed to the prevey Counsell that I caused the plays laste at Chester to be sett forwarde onely of my sellf which your selues do know the contrary ... that they ... were sett forwarde as well by the counsell of the Citie as for the comen welth of the same',[10] the Cestrian council prepared and sent a 'certificate' to Elizabeth's advisors to refute the charges.[11] This certificate rehearses the accusations brought against Savage by the archbishop and the earl of Huntingdon, lord president of the North, in the following terms:

> it is reported that he ... did then of his owne power and auctorite in the saide tyme he was maior, *to the great abuse of the same office, unleafullie* and by indirect and synistre ways and meanes cause and procure to be plaide within the same citie certen pagions or plays, comonlie there called Witteson Playes, *for the satisfying of his owne singuler will, luste, and pleasure* to the great coste and charges, losse and harme of the citizens and inhabitaunts of the saide citie ... and not by the orderly assente of his then bretherne, the aldermen and the Comen Counsell ... *nor to and for the wealth, benefite, and comoditie of the same citie* acordinge to his dutie.[12] (My emphasis)

The document appropriates a familiar vocabulary of tyranny from the writings of Aquinas, Fortescue, and others: the unlawful rule of a singular will, the satisfaction of personal lusts and pleasures, and the abuse of office, all of which run contrary to the common good and benefit of the realm.[13] Such language seems excessive relative

---

[8]   Clopper, *REED: Chester*, 97.

[9]   David Mills, *Recycling the Cycle: The City of Chester and its Whitsun Plays* (Toronto, 1998), 147.

[10]   Corporation Lease Book (Cheshire Record Office ZCHB/3) f. 28. See also Clopper, *REED: Chester*, 112; Lumiansky and Mills, *Essays and Documents*, 221. The case seems to have been brought against Savage with some urgency, as he exhorts them to send their testimony 'with as muche convenient speede as is possible'.

[11]   Assembly Books (Cheshire Record Office ZAB/1) f. 162v. See also Clopper, *REED: Chester*, 113.

[12]   Lumiansky and Mills, *Essays and Documents*, 223–4. Their text as quoted is compiled from the Corporation Lease Book and Harley 2173.

[13]   Ptolemy of Lucca and St. Thomas Aquinas, *De Regimine Principum*, ed. James M. Blythe (Philadelphia, 1997), 63–5 describes a king as 'one who governs the multitude of one city or province for the common good', but a tyrant as 'one who brings about an unjust government by seeking individual profit from the government, and not the good of the multitude subject to that rector'. John Fortescue, *On the Laws and Governance of England*, Shelley Lockwood (ed.) (Cambridge, 1997), 85, characterizes a tyrant as one who 'would not have [his realm] governed by any other rule or law, but by his own will'.

to the performance of plays in a provincial market town when the accused has served out his term as mayor and is no longer in office.[14] We cannot know for certain whether this vocabulary accurately reflects the accusations made against Savage. Although Chester had appeared frequently on the privy council's agenda in recent years, in matters as private as the 'peticion of William Benson, a poore soldiour … clayminge a debt of one William Clogge in the county',[15] and as public as 'divers controversies, debates, and strifes betwene the officers of her Majesties Coourte of thexchequer … and the Mayor and certen Aldermen of that citee, touching the jurisdiction of the said Coourte and pretended exemption of the citie from the same',[16] no discussions of Chester's plays are preserved in the privy council's records from the 1570s[17] or in their recent communications with Cestrian officials. Nor does this language appear in the inhibition sent by Archbishop Grindal in 1572.

The general scope of the certificate, which places the cycle in a political context, does accord with the city's view of their plays even if the specific accusations of tyranny remain surprising. Civic officials had long felt their plays to be an important contribution to the 'comen welth' of their city and, not so long ago, that opinion had been shared by the crown. Newhall's 1531 proclamation, for example, reminded spectators 'in the kyngez name' that Chester would not tolerate any disturbance of the plays as they were presented 'not only for the Augmentation & incres of the holy & Catholick faith … but also for the commenwelth & prosperitie of this Citie'.[18] In the minds of the Chester common council, the language of commonwealth and benefit to the city would thus have seemed appropriate to the situation. The Cestrian council, I suggest, chose to exaggerate the accusations against Savage, to put words in the mouths of Elizabeth's councillors, in order to emphasize the plays' civic importance. By staging a classic 'straw man' argument, the common council asserted its desire to preserve a local understanding of 'wealth, benefite, and comoditie',

---

[14]   While tyrants have, of course, done much more extravagant things to gratify their own pleasures, a mayor, serving a one-year term, is unlikely to have exerted such influence, even in a town like Chester with a fairly entrenched oligarchical structure. The office of mayor was not a glamorous and highly sought office by this time; a 1550 law, prompted by the reluctance of citizens to hold the office because of its attendant financial obligations, required a £100 fine of anyone who refused the office (Cheshire West and Chester Council, 'History of the Mayorality', Cheshire West and Chester, <http://www.cheshirewestandchester.gov. uk/visiting/heritage/chester_history_and_heritage/ mayors_of _chester.aspx>). Emmerson would perhaps disagree with this assessment; 'Contextualizing Performance', 91, describes Savage as 'a powerful man unlikely to have tolerated much opposition'.

[15]   *Acts of the Privy Council of England* n.s. vol. 8 (London, 1894), 347. This item of business, conducted on 25 February 1574, took the form of a letter to Mayor John Savage, in which he was urged to settle the matter.

[16]   Ibid, 223.

[17]   While the Council's surviving records are certainly detailed, their thoroughness is impossible to ascertain; the absence of this matter does not mean that Savage and the Chester plays were not an item of business.

[18]   From William Newhall's 1531 Proclamation, in Clopper, *REED: Chester*, 27.

rather than the crown's newer notion of 'commonwealth' that consisted not of one's most immediate neighbours but rather of the whole nation and its church.

If the common council's intent were indeed to emphasize the plays' civic importance, Archbishop Grindal's 1572 inhibition may have inspired the wording of the certificate. The letter stresses Grindal's power 'in the Queen's Majesty's name by vertue of her Highnesses Commission for causes Ecclesiasticall within the province of York' and uses strong verbs throughout – will, require, charge, command – that are intended to put the Cestrians in their place. He states that the plays are not to be performed again until they have been 'perused corrected & reformed by such learned men as by us shall be thereunto appointed', and then only after 'signification of our ... allowance be given to you in writing under the hands of us or other our Associates'. Grindal also emphasizes that, should the Cestrians fail to abide by his order, they 'will an-swer the contrary at your perills'.[19] Cestrians convinced of the plays' significance may well have perceived Grindal's efforts to prevent the performance – particularly when expressed in a letter that seems less interested in God's word than in self-aggrandizement – as tyrannical and as adequate justification for the extreme language used in the certificate.

Although I am convinced that the language of tyranny and common good originated with Chester's refutations of the charges against Savage, the ambiguity and uncertainty of the situation provide an undeniable reflection of the political and religious state of affairs in Chester at the time. Unlike their neighbours in Lancashire, most traditionalists in Chester seem to have kept their heads down, outwardly conforming while secretly adhering to the old ways.[20] The resulting incongruence between behaviour and belief made it impossible for Cestrians to differentiate between faithful conviction and political expediency. The appeal of the stage at such a time, in such a climate, can be easily understood. Dramatic performances provided a public space in which to explore the fascination with pretence (or to use a more contemporary term, 'feyning') that must have accompanied Elizabeth's policies. Those who felt themselves to be 'feyning' in their everyday lives by appearing faithful to the tenets of a church in which they did not believe would surely have been drawn to the plays as a venue where 'feyning' was not only socially acceptable, but actually endorsed (at least locally) as a contribution to the common good of the city. Yet the 'feyning' in Chester's plays takes place on many levels, and audiences may have been surprised to find that the figure of King Herod the Great is, perhaps, the greatest 'feyner' of all.

The role of Herod has long been recognized as one notable for its excesses – of language, of gesture, of costume.[21] Hamlet's famous reference to actors who

---

[19]   For the text of the letter, see Mills, *Recycling the Cycle*, 147.

[20]   For a helpful discussion, see K.R. Wark, *Elizabethan Recusancy in Cheshire, Remains Historical and Literary Connected with the Palatine Counties of Lancaster and Chester*, vol. 19, third series (Manchester, 1971), 12–20.

[21]   Herod on the early English stage is often discussed as a conflation of two figures who bookend the life of Christ: Herod the Great, who ruled Judea around the time of Jesus'

'out-Herod Herod' has ensured that the tradition of overacting associated with the role remains familiar even today. These excesses, however, are in large part what made Herod both an audience favourite and one of the most easily recognizable personae of the medieval stage. In Coventry, the records of the Smiths' guild indicate that up to 20 shillings could be spent per year to maintain Herod's costume and necessary props;[22] however, expenditure alone did not ensure Herod's success. The Smiths' guild understood that the actor playing Herod deserved a hefty salary; in 1478, for example, he was paid four shillings – more than double the amount paid to the actor playing Jesus in the same pageant.[23] The Coventry actor, like any other player taking on this exceptional role, was certainly expected to earn his four shillings with a boisterous and energetic performance. Jonathan Gil Harris has referred to Herod's 'hyperbolic' performance style as 'acting up'; this terminology is useful because it connotes not only the immoderation of the character, but also the 'socially transgressive behaviour' of a fifteenth- or sixteenth-century artisanal actor playing at being a middle eastern despot.[24] Herod's 'acting up' seems to have become the key feature of the pageants in which he appeared, even overtaking the lavish costuming and props by which he was originally recognized. While Chester's Early Banns (c. 1505–21) refer to Herod as 'proude in paulle', the Late Banns (c. 1548–61)[25] focus instead on 'how Herode did rage'.[26] The shift suggests that the way in which Herod was performed (indicated here by his overwhelming rage), rather than the character's leading signifiers (his 'proude', or costly and luxurious, apparel), had become the primary interest for his audience. If the Banns

---

birth, and Herod Antipas, his son, who is known primarily for his association with the trials leading up to Jesus' crucifixion.

[22]   R.W. Ingram (ed.), *Records of Early English Drama: Coventry* (Toronto, 1981), 71, lists detailed expenses for Herod's costume in 1489: 'Item, paid for a gowen to Arrode, vij s iiij d; paid for peynttyng and stenyng theroff, vj s iiij d; item, paid for Arrodes garment peynttyng that he went a prossassyon in, xx d; item, paid for mendyng off Arrodes gouen to a taillour, viij d; item, paid for mendyng off hattes, cappus, and Arreddes creste, with other smale geyr belongyng, iij s.' Costume expenses recorded for other years range from 4d up to 2s 3d.

[23]   Ibid, 61. Records for the 1478 pageant indicate payments of 20d to Jesus and 4s to Herod. Similar payments are recorded in 1477 (Herod 3s 4d, Jesus 22d 'for gloves & all'), 1489 (Herod 3s 4d, God 2s), and 1490 (Herod 3s 4d, God 2s). Whether the 1478 Herod was a particularly fine actor, or whether we can attribute his higher pay that year to another cause is subject for speculation elsewhere.

[24]   Jonathan Gil Harris, '"Look not big, nor stamp, nor stare": Acting Up in *The Taming of the Shrew* and the Coventry Herod Plays', *Comparative Drama* 34.4 (2000–01), 366–7.

[25]   Dating of the initial writings of Early and Late Banns according to Lawrence M. Clopper, 'The History and Development of the Chester Cycle', *Modern Philology* 75.3 (1978): 219–46. Clopper suggests that the Early Banns were revised in the 1520s to 1530s, when the performance of the plays was shifted to Whitsun, and that the Late Banns were further revised prior to 1572. For a full edition of both Banns, see Lumiansky and Mills, *Essays and Documents*, 278–95.

[26]   Lumiansky and Mills, *Essays and Documents*, 280, l. 59 and 290, l. 112.

were only able to highlight one 'selling point' of each pageant, it would doubtless have been the feature most likely to draw a crowd. Chester's Herod, however, is a far more nuanced figure – and a far better 'feyner' – than these descriptions from the Banns, or the melancholy Dane, might lead us to expect.

Unlike the Towneley Magnus Herodes, whose ranting and empty threats seem to know no bounds, Chester's Herod chooses his words with care. When he does indulge in rhetorical fireworks, Herod's anger never causes him to stumble over his words. If anything, his lines suggest quite the opposite:

> I kinge of kinges, non soe keene;
> I soveraigne syre, as well is seene;
> I tyrant that maye both take and teene
> castell, towre, and towne!
> I weld this world withouten weene;
> I beate all those unbuxone binne;
> I drive the devills all bydeene
> deepe in hell adowne.
> For I am kinge of all mankynde;
> I byd, I beate, I loose, I bynde;
> I maister the moone. Take this in mynd –
> that I am most of might.
> I am the greatest above degree
> that is, or was, or ever shalbe;
> the sonne yt dare not shine on me
> and I byd him goe downe. (8.169–84)[27]

Initially, the grandiose claims made here seem similar to those of other grasping stage tyrants. The Towneley Herod, for example, boasts that 'all erthly thyng bowes to my hand'.[28] Regardless of these similarities, the Chester Herod ultimately thinks bigger thoughts. His claims to master the moon, the sun, and even the 'devills ... deep in helle' indicate his desire to appropriate the authority that rightfully belongs to God alone.[29] Yet even as we are struck by the wildly improper content of his assertions, we must also notice the beauty of their form. As David Mills has convincingly argued, the hyperbole of this speech is at odds with its well-crafted sentences and carefully controlled rhetorical structure.[30]

---

[27] All citations of the Chester Plays are from R.M. Lumiansky and David Mills, *The Chester Mystery Cycle*, EETS SS 3, 9 (London, 1974) and will be given parenthetically by pageant and line number.

[28] Martin Stevens and A.C. Cawley, *The Towneley Plays*, EETS SS 13–14 (Oxford, 1994), 14.11.

[29] For further discussion of this point, see Peter W. Travis, *Dramatic Design in the Chester Cycle* (Chicago, 1982), 133.

[30] David Mills, 'Some Possible Implications of Herod's Speech', *Neuphilologische Mitteilungen* 74 (1973),133, concisely details the artistry of this passage, noting that '*I* is repeated six times in initial stressed position; the details are presented in two cumulative

The longer Herod speaks, the more we are struck by the repetitions and patterns in his words. Thus the increasingly heretical claims he makes are inevitably associated with the artistry used to express them. The play seems to purposefully draw our attention to the nature of his speech as carefully crafted rhetoric, as *performance*.

The stage directions that appear alongside this speech further emphasize the importance of seeing Herod as a performer. The marginal words 'Staffe', 'Sword', 'Cast up', etc., specify some of Herod's movements, as well as his props and costumes, even suggesting that he changes his 'gowne' at one point.[31] Although stage directions are rare in the surviving manuscripts of early English drama, all of the extant texts of the Chester cycle include them in this scene,[32] indicating that they are not just suggestions for appropriate actions, or a record of an actor's choices in a particular performance, but an integral component of the pageant.[33] The Chester playwright wants Herod's performance to engage our active attention in a way that precludes all possibility of what a modern audience would call 'suspension of disbelief'. We are meant to see Herod as a speaker of lines, dependent on props, costumes, and stage business, because the tyrant is meant to be interpreted as a 'feyner', a performer, an imitator: someone *playing at* the role of king.

In this way, Chester's Herod participates in an understanding of tyranny best articulated in Trevisa's translation of *The Governance of Kings and Princes*. Trevisa defines a tyrant as a ruler who can do no more than 'fayneþ to do þe same' as a 'verrey kyng'.[34] Although it might seem preferable to live under the rule of

---

three line sequences to give a climactic effect … and the climax is further emphasized by the use of enjambment … accompanied by the continuation of *t*-alliteration … and of *d*-alliteration …; a further progression is provided by the movement from the voiceless *k-s-t* alliteration … to the voiced *w-b-d* alliteration'.

[31]   MSS Harley 2124 and Bodley 175 give this direction alongside Herod's lines 'But now you may both here and see / that I reconed up my rialte' (8.209–10). The directions in Harley 2124 are in Latin; thus Herod in this MS sports a 'toga' – not an easy on-stage costume change!

[32]   Though there are some variations in the placement, these stage directions do not seem to have been omitted from the various MSS, suggesting they appear in the Exemplar and/or Pre-Exemplar posited in Lumiansky and Mills, *Essays and Documents*, 1–86. For placement, see *The Chester Mystery Cycle: A Facsimile of MS Bodley 175* (Leeds, 1973); *The Chester Mystery Cycle: A Reduced Facsimile of Huntington Library MS 2* (Leeds, 1980); and *The Chester Mystery Cycle: A Facsimile of British Library MS Harley 2124* (Leeds, 1984).

[33]   Lumiansky and Mills suggest, in their note to s.d.156 that the stage directions 'perhaps also indicate that the exemplar had served as a practical acting-text, bearing a producer's annotations'. Were such stage directions present in each of the different pageants as they are in this play, this theory would carry greater force. Having stage directions at all is atypical, suggesting that the playwright felt them to be of particular importance in the portrayal of Herod. King Balaack, as featured in play five, is given a few similar stage directions, suggesting the cycle's interest in the metatheatricality of tyrants goes beyond Herod.

[34]   John Trevisa, *The Governance of Kings and Princes*, David C. Fowler, Charles F. Briggs, and Paul G. Remley (eds) (New York, 1997), 3.2.9, 338.

a tyrant who 'fayneþ' to look after the common profit of the realm rather than one who openly seeks the misery and poverty of his subjects,[35] the verb 'fayneþ' is loaded with negative connotations. Though it can be used in a more or less neutral way to describe the production of any form of fiction,[36] to 'feyn' is more commonly to disguise, to forge, to counterfeit, to conceal, to lie.[37] The feigning tyrants described by Trevisa do not truly seek to emulate kingly behaviour. Rather, they seek to deceive their subjects into thinking of them as 'verrey' kings while they are in fact 'besy aboute [their] owne profit'.[38] Chester's Herod does prove himself to be a clever, artful feigner: he mimics the actions of legitimate rulers and tries to fool us, if only for moments at a time, into forgetting what lurks behind his façade.

In one key example from play ten, *The Massacre of the Innocents*, Herod demonstrates the people skills of a cagey CEO as he orders his soldiers to carry out the massacre he has planned. He could certainly have presented his commands in a simple and straightforward fashion, reminding the soldiers that disobedience is likely to incur his wrath, but he chooses not to do so. Herod seems to know his knights well; he is able to coax them into not only doing his bidding but also enjoying their work by emphasizing the virility of the task ahead of them.[39] He stresses that in implementing his orders they will 'lett yt be seene / and you be men of mayne', and dwells on the fact that they are to do their work 'manfully' (10.140–41). When the knights complain that killing 'a shitten-arsed shrowe' (10.157) is beneath their dignity, Herod neither punishes them for disobedience, nor rants about their reluctance, but instead speaks the words he knows will encourage them. His conspiratorial response is 'Nay, nay, it is neither on nor two / that you shall sley, as mott I goo, / but a thousand and yett moo' (10.169–71). Herod calculates his smooth and conversational tone to sound as casual as possible, and the mild

---

[35]   Aristotle suggests this course of action in *Politics* 5.11 to the tyrant who wishes to maintain his power: he should 'act, or at any rate appear to act, in the role of a good player of the part of king'. By showing himself as a 'trustee' or 'guardian' of his realm, rather than a tyrant, his people 'will be people of a better sort', and 'he will himself attain a habit of character, if not wholly disposed to goodness, at any rate half-good' (*Politics*, Ernest Barker [ed. and trans.] [Oxford, 1995], 221, 224).

[36]   *MED*, s.v. feinen (v.) definitions 1, 2a, 5a and b.

[37]   *MED*, s.v. feinen (v.). The majority of definitions for the verb carry a negative connotation, e.g. 2b, 'to trump up … to bring false accusations'; 3b, 'to disguise or conceal (deceit, falsehood)'; 4, 'to adulterate (something)'; 6, 'to dissemble, make false pretenses, play the hypocrite, lie'. Even def. 5a, 'to make a likeness of something', which initially seems to resist imposing a value judgment, includes the sense of 'counterfeit' and 'to forge'.

[38]   Trevisa, *On the Governance of Kings and Princes*, 3.2.9, 338–9.

[39]   See Theresa Coletti, '"Ther Be But Women": Gender Conflict and Gender Identity in the Middle English Innocents Plays', *Mediaevalia* 18 (1995): 245–61 for a discussion of the kinds of masculinity and chivalry to which Herod's soldiers aspire. See also Aquinas, *De Regimine Principum* 1.4, which notes that those living under tyrants become fearful and their idea of masculine virtue degenerates.

oath 'as mott I goo' brings his speech more in line with the colloquial phrasing employed by his soldiers while simultaneously remaining decorously clear of their vulgar, lower-class profanity.

In moments such as these, Chester's Herod reveals himself as a cathectic figure who highlights the flaws of royal policies that emphasize outward conformity at the expense of regional ideals and individual convictions. He is a master of the kind of artful and manipulative 'feyning' of which I believe the authors, actors, and audiences of the Chester cycle were wary. This is a Herod ready, willing, and able to convince those within his power that he has their interests, rather than his own, at heart. If even Herod, the ultimate tyrant, could be imagined as successfully 'feyning' the appearance of a 'verrey king', what might Archbishop Grindal, or even fellow-citizens like Christopher Goodman, be hiding behind an outward commitment to 'the common good'? How could you even begin to determine whether the privy councillors, or Elizabeth herself – who were too distant for most Cestrians to ever encounter face to face – actually practised the commonwealth that they preached? And how was it possible to embrace a new national understanding of community at a time when it was dangerous to express allegiance to the church that had first taught you how to love your neighbour?

Such concerns are at the heart of the scenes in which Chester's Herod decides how to deal with the infant king that has been born within his realm. Unlike his counterparts in Towneley and York, Herod in the Chester cycle does not simply react in rage or become petrified by fear. Before taking any action, he stops to consider his options. He even consults the scriptures for guidance, not only acknowledging their authority but also demonstrating his familiarity with their teachings. Herod intelligently lists the prophets whose writings are relevant to his current dilemma[40] and then calls upon a doctor that is 'cheife ... of clergie' (8.233) to interpret their meaning for him. This scene requires the audience to come to terms with a Herod who at least 'feyns' an interest in aligning his actions with a moral and religious framework.

Although Herod ultimately chooses to disregard both his learned counsellor and the will of God in favour of fulfilling his own wishes, he makes an attempt – albeit a misguided one – to take the common good into consideration:

> Therfore that boye, by God almight,
> shall be slayne soone in your sight,
> and – though it be agaynst the right –
> a thousand for his sake.
> Alas, what purpose had that page
> that is soe yonge and tender of age,

---

[40]   David Staines, 'To Out-Herod Herod: The Development of a Dramatic Character', in C.J. Gianakaris (ed.), *The Drama in the Middle Ages: Comparative and Critical Essays* (New York, 1982), 224 contrasts the Chester Herod's 'great erudition' with the 'unresourceful' tactics of the Towneley Herod, who is unable to think of a book which might be useful in his deliberations.

that would bereave my heritage,
that am so micle of might?
Forsooth that shrewe was wondrouse sage
agaynst me anye warre to wage!
That recked rybauld for all his rage
shall not reve mee of my right. (10.21–32)

This speech, which more closely resembles a Shakespearean soliloquy than a typical medieval tyrant's rant, prevents us from seeing Herod as an agent of pure evil, careless of morality or the consequences of his actions: he knows that his plan is 'agaynst the right'. Herod is the consummate tyrant of the Christian tradition because of the seemingly unredeemable nature of such a choice. Yet the Chester playwright encourages us to imagine the kind of factors that could possibly have motivated that choice. Herod does not seek to defend only his own interests. He describes Jesus not only as an infant but also as a 'wondrous sage', a powerful adversary planning to wage war upon Herod's kingdom for unknown purposes. In a similar moment in play eight, *The Three Kings*, Herod suggests that should he fail to protect his lands from this rival, 'everye man may well say thus, / that I maynteane my realme amysse' (8.386–7). These speeches build upon Matthew 2:3, which describes Herod, 'and all Jerusalem with him', as troubled by the idea of a rival king being born within the realm. Competing kings, after all, are rarely a recipe for peace and prosperity. Though we ought, of course, to reject his methods, we are made to see that Herod's goal is to preserve not only his own power, but also the safety and stability of the realm under his care.

Herod's direct address to the audience further complicates the speech's moral positioning. Like Iago and Richard III after him, Herod invites his audience into his own culpability by sharing his plans before he carries them out, encouraging 'everye man' to think carefully about the boundaries of what a monarch may acceptably do to 'maynteane' a realm. A well-placed second-person pronoun in the reminder of what is about to come in the next scene – that the boys are about to be killed 'in *your* sight' – prevents the audience from escaping a share of the responsibility for what is to take place. We are both purposeful witnesses to, and willing participants in, the actions played out before us. The moment completes Herod's embodiment of the dangers of trusting in surface appearance: not only has he 'feyned' a concern for his subjects' well-being and an interest in the teachings of scripture, but in doing so, he draws in those around him, to make them – at least momentarily – share in the guilt of the unthinkable destruction that is about to take place.

Herod's effective 'feyning' ultimately reveals the vulnerabilities of the spiritual realm when a temporal ruler decides that it falls within his purview. In both York and Towneley, the slaughter of the innocents and the flight into Egypt are separated into two pageants. This separation has the effect of distancing the holy family from the horrific events that take place at Herod's command. Chester, on the other hand, sandwiches the angel's warning between Herod's orders to his soldiers and their execution of them, highlighting that the danger is acutely at hand.[41] The moment has a desperate and hurried feel, due in part to a break in the play's stanza structure. For the past 150 lines, the dialogue between Herod and his soldiers was comprised of long speeches, no character speaking less than a full 8-line stanza at a time. Joseph, however, reacts to the angel's warning in a brief, 4-line speech made up primarily of short one- and two-syllable words:

> A, lord, blessed most thou bee.
> Thyder anone we will flye.
> Have we companye of thee,
> we will hye one our waye. (10.265–8)

The responses of Mary and the angel are spoken in a similar manner, and these short speeches feel rushed and compressed after Herod's and the soldiers' long-winded oaths and protestations. The mood of this short scene is underscored by the active verbs and emphatic modifiers used throughout – aryse, warne, flye, hye, buskes, flytt, hitt – all of which convey a sense of urgency and haste on their own, but when used in phrases such as 'aryse and that anon' or 'Herode buskes him you to deare / as fast as hee maye', the feeling is even more palpable. The holy family has no time to waste, for as soon as the angel leads them away, the soldiers and women appear on the stage and the slaughter begins. Though we know that Jesus will escape, the moment nonetheless stresses that God's son in his human form is as vulnerable as any other subject living under Herod's rule.

And yet, the pageant also emphasizes that God's will must eventually triumph over those who oppose it. Herod ensures his own downfall not *in spite of* the steps taken to preserve his earthly kingdom, but *because of* them. He chooses to trust in his own power rather than accepting the will of God. The dangers of this strategy are made abundantly clear when a demon appears just moments after the slaughter, sent 'to fetch this kinges sowle here present / into hell' (10.442–4). In Chester, as in the N-Town play, Herod the 'feyning' tyrant must pay the price for his lies and deceptions, knowing that Christ the 'verrey kyng' survives to redeem humanity. Although reducing Herod to a theatrical figuration of Elizabeth or any other particular monarch would be simplistic, such an ending may well have provided the 'great comfort' that Goodman feared 'the rebellious papist' might glean from the plays,[42] a sense of reassurance that those who sought to redirect the will of God to their own ends would reap no heavenly reward for doing so.

---

[41]   The N-Town playwright also makes this choice, but the inclusion seems perfunctory at best; the angel's warning and Joseph's response comprise only a stanza apiece – 16 short lines that convey little other than the fact that Jesus will be spared. Mary does not even speak a single word. The Digby *Killing of the Children* also includes this material but the sequence never implies that the holy family is in any real danger: Mary has time to nurse her son while Joseph packs their 'gere', including all of his carpenter's tools, before they depart.

[42]   Elizabeth Baldwin, Lawrence M. Clopper, and David Mills (eds), *Records of Early English Drama: Cheshire including Chester* (Toronto, 2007), 1.143.

Such reassurances did not prevent the Chester common council from making a more immediate attempt to restate what they believed to be the true will of God and the true nature of the commonwealth. In the certificate sent to the privy council in 1575, the Cestrians refute the charges against Mayor Savage by assuring Elizabeth's councillors that the plays were in fact presented

> acordinge to an order concluded and agreed upon for dyvers good and great consideracons redoundinge to the comen wealthe, benefite, and profitte of the saide citie in assemblie there holden, according to the auncyente and lawdable usages and customes there hadd … and with the assente, consente, and agreamente of his saide then bretherne, the aldermen of the saide cities, and of the Comen Counsell of the same.[43]

The authors of the document emphasize that the plays are a central component of their understanding of 'the common good' by the use of synonyms, multiplicities, and lists: they were produced for 'the comen wealthe, benefite, and profitte' of the city, the customs according to which the decision was made to present them are both 'auncyente and lawdable', the order for them was 'concluded and agreed upon', and they all gave their 'assente, consente, and agreamente'. They also note at eight different points (in a not overly lengthy document)[44] that they are a 'Comen Counsell', perhaps to differentiate themselves from the secretive operations of the 'Privy Counsell' to whom they address themselves; they make their testimony 'in the name of the corporation of this citie' and under its 'commen seale'.[45] The Cestrian council here demonstrates that their reliance on the city's 'auncyente and lawdable usages and customes' – of which the plays and other Catholic traditions were certainly understood to be a part – is what prevents any of its leading citizens from satisfying their personal interests at the city's expense. Unlike the changeable policies of a crown both distant and distinct from Chester, such 'auncyente customes' were too familiar, too much a part of the history and fabric of the city to be 'feyned'. These were the 'customes' upon which Cestrians chose to enact the common good in 1575.

Though Mayor Savage seems to have been cleared of the charges made against him,[46] there are no records of the Chester cycle being performed after 1575; whether because of the warnings of the privy council and the archbishop, a growing protestant base among Chester's citizens, dissatisfaction with the abridged and emended form the cycle had now taken, or, as is most likely, a combination of all of these factors, we will never know. There do seem to have been some

---

43   Lumiansky and Mills, *Essays and Documents*, 224.

44   The original text fits onto one side of a folio-sized page in the original MS.

45   Lumiansky and Mills, *Essays and Documents*, 224.

46   Ibid, 193 notes that Savage was still involved in civic government in November 1577, which suggests either that no action was taken against him or that the punishment was minimal. Either way, Chester seems to have welcomed his continued involvement in city affairs.

performances, however, of individual biblical plays, either from the Whitsun cycle or quite similar plays. The mayors' list of 1577 notes that 'the Earle of Darbie and his sonne' were 'entertayned' with a performance of 'the Sheppeardes playe … at the hie Crosse'.[47] Also, more textual evidence of Chester's plays survives than of any other English biblical drama: the city's official and antiquarian records preserve much of the play's history, and five complete texts of the cycle,[48] dating from 1591–1607, up to 32 years after its final performance, provide testimony of continued investment in the plays as an important part of Chester's religious, social, and political life. Even those who were against the very idea of biblical plays – such as David Rogers, whose early seventeenth-century *Breviary* of Chester history is a key source of information on Chester's processional route and wagon stages – have sought to document and describe their production and performance.[49] Despite the crown's concerted efforts to erase the Whitsun plays from Chester's understanding of the 'common good', the city nonetheless found ways in which to preserve their 'auncyente and lawdable' customs for posterity.

---

[47]   Clopper, *REED: Chester*, 124. The same record notes that 'other Trivmphes' were played 'one the Roode Deey', southwest of the city walls. See also 126 for a separate listing of the same event.

[48]   Chester is the only medieval 'cycle' to exist in more than one MS. In addition to the five complete texts, there are also three extant MS that contain plays or fragments thereof. See Lumiansky and Mills, *Essays and Documents*, 3–86 for comparison on the MSS texts as well as discussion of Exemplar MSS that may have pre-existed the extant texts.

[49]   Despite meticulously collecting and recording information about the plays in his historical materials about the city, Rogers nonetheless saw them as 'an abomination of desolation', based on 'a cloud of ignorance' (Lumiansky and Mills, *Essays and Documents*, 260, 266).

Afterword
Origins and Continuities:
F.M. Salter and the Chester Plays

JoAnna Dutka

The 2010 Toronto event marks the first production of the Chester plays as listed and described by Christopher Goodman in 1572. It also marks the 75th anniversary of the first publication of Professor F.M. Salter's research on the plays, 'The Trial & Flagellation of Christ: a New Manuscript', for the Malone Society[1] and the 55th anniversary of the publication of his landmark book *Mediaeval Drama in Chester*,[2] the text of his Alexander Lectures at the University of Toronto. The book represents the distillation of those two decades of Professor Salter's work on the plays, years punctuated by editions of crucial texts and the discovery of new manuscripts. His critical edition of the plays for The Early English Text Society was incomplete at his death, lacking only a general introduction. That his research and its results are not outdated nor have been superseded is most notably attested to by the 2007 REED volume *Cheshire, including Chester* with its many citations from Professor Salter's publications.

Professor Salter's reputation, however, rests on more than just his research on the Chester plays. His interest in the history and practice of English vocabulary and his experience with fifteenth- and sixteenth-century vernacular manuscripts led to his publishing three substantial and influential studies on John Skelton, including Skelton's translation of Diodorus Siculus' *Bibliotheca Historica* and a reassessment of that somewhat neglected poet's significance in the development of the language. Professor Salter firmly established Skelton's position as a

---

[1]   'The Trial & Flagellation of Christ: a New Manuscript,' in W.W. Greg (ed.), *The Trial and Flagellation with Other Studies in the Chester Cycle*, Malone Society Studies (Oxford, 1935), 1–83. Quotations from and references to Professor Salter's published works are indicated as such by footnotes. All others are from letters, papers, and notes held in the F.M. Salter Collection, currently being digitized, in the Archives of the University of Alberta and from personal papers in the possession of Professor Salter's daughter, Dr Elizabeth Salter. Grateful thanks are owed the archivists at the University of Alberta, especially Raymond Frogner, who were extraordinarily helpful, and my deepest gratitude is to Dr Elizabeth Salter for her generosity in sharing time, information, and reminiscences. I owe more thanks to Trinity College, University of Toronto, for the travel grant that enabled me to consult the Salter Collection at the University of Alberta.

[2]   (Toronto and London, 1955).

Fig. A.1   A photograph of Professor F.M. Salter. Courtesy of his daughter, Dr Elizabeth Salter.

humanist and as an extraordinary 'enricher' of the English language through new terms or special senses of words already in use.[3]

For many years Salter also taught a course in creative writing at the University of Alberta that was summed up in the posthumously published book *The Art of Writing*.[4] His ability to recognize and encourage aspiring writers definitively determined the shape of Canadian literature: Sheila Watson is considered the mother of modernist fiction in Canada with her novel *The Double Hook*; W.O. Mitchell created the prairie coming-of-age novel with *Who Has Seen the Wind*; and Rudy Wiebe's *Peace Shall Destroy Many* mapped the immigrant experience and gave it validity as fictional subject. Mitchell said of Salter: 'as a reader of fiction, he possessed a destructive honesty, but also an ear, an eye, and a heart that the writer could depend on'.

His undergraduate Shakespeare course had students sitting on the floor of an over-full classroom despite that potentially 'destructive honesty'. He covered the margins and blank pages of their marked papers in spidery handwriting with comments that ranged from constructive praise for clarity and promising readings, to chastening faint praise: 'there is less here than meets the eye'. Professor Salter, from his election to the Royal Society of Canada in 1942, gave, almost yearly, papers to the membership on various aspects of Shakespeare's plays – these were in the process of being revised and collected into a volume before he took ill.

Professor Salter's academic interests were clearly wide-ranging. In a letter addressed to me some years ago, David Mills remarked: 'I would like to talk with you about [Salter] some time; I am most curious to know what kind of person he was.' To consider the 'kind of person he was' one can track his biography in tandem with his Chester studies –'the kind of scholar he was'. Born in 1895 in Chatham, New Brunswick, he could trace his ancestors to English dissenters who reached Boston in 1623 (not so long after the Mayflower). By 1749, they had settled in Halifax, Nova Scotia, with Malachy Salter representing that city in the legislature. The family moved to New Brunswick early in the nineteenth century, and Professor Salter was often rhapsodical in his memories of Miramichi: 'what I would give for one good deep breath of the spruce. For one long look at that wide river'. He lost both his parents before he reached his early teens and, as a boy, worked ten-hour days in the coal mines of Cape Breton. He was, however, able to enter Dalhousie University, where he received his BA in 1916. World War I, of course, was in progress: he had enlisted, though under-age, but was sent back to university by his elder brother and guardian. Nonetheless, he rejoined the army and served nearly four years in the Canadian Field Artillery in the front-line trenches. As with so many

---

[3]   F.M. Salter and H.L.R. Edwards (eds), *The Bibliotheca Historica of Diodorus Siculus Translated by John Skelton*, 2 vols. Early English Text Society (London, 1956–57); 'John Skelton's Contribution to the English Language', Transactions of the Royal Society of Canada, Third Series, Section II, 39 (1945), 119–217; 'Skelton's *Speculum Principis*', *Speculum* 9 (1934): 253–64.

[4]   H.V. Weekes (ed.) (Toronto, 1971). This work was first printed as *The Way of the Makers*, H.V. Weekes (ed.) (Edmonton, 1967).

others, the experience marked him for life. I think here of a 1957 lecture given at the University of Victoria that was passionate in its references to the horrors of war and the obligation of thinking people to create peace in the present and for the future.

The post-war years were difficult ones, and he held various jobs – in an auto factory, as a salesman, on a newspaper. But, surprisingly, as he put it, he found himself enrolled in graduate studies at the University of Chicago. He was accepted into the Department of English on the recommendation of Archibald MacMechan (the Canadian scholar who is credited with restoring American interest in Melville's works), his undergraduate mentor at Dalhousie. This was his introduction to J.M. Manly, head of the department, and the beginning of ten years that Salter characterized as 'a high privilege'. After receiving his MA in 1922, he taught for two years at the University of Alberta, returning to Chicago in 1924 to begin work on a doctorate and, soon after, to join Manly and Edith Rickert in their great project to edit *The Canterbury Tales*. Salter taught classes in Chaucer's poetry, worked on various paleographical tasks described by Manly as studying 'erasures and corrections in faded and almost illegible writings', and trained Manly's assistants in converting into practical work the editing principles that were the foundation of the project. He left the Chaucer Laboratory in 1928 to work as Manly's research assistant in England on what Manly vaguely called 'a project in medieval drama'. By now, Salter had thoroughly absorbed the rigorous methods of textual criticism that Manly taught and had honed his own remarkable skills in paleography, language, and literary intuition. All these tools enabled him to begin the most fruitful period of his scholarly life, one in which he collaborated with Sir Walter Greg, published manuscript discoveries and analyses, and settled upon the Chester plays as his object of study.

It would be useful here to attempt to situate Salter in the scholarly tradition he was now becoming a part of and, second, to suggest where he departed from it. Manly and Rickert's *Canterbury Tales* project was known as the Chaucer Laboratory; Manly had published a collection of early plays under the title *Specimens of the Pre-Shakespearean Drama* (1897), while Greg's manuscript studies produced *The Calculus of Variants* (1927) – in literary studies, the prevailing ethos was that of scientific discovery. Good science rests upon systematic argument, experiment, evidence, accuracy, intelligibility, verifiable results. Hypotheses and theories are not precluded, of course, and the question is thereby raised: can textual criticism and the study of manuscripts legitimately call itself scientific, acknowledging these same criteria, and as a result achieve the same stature as science in the intellectual world? Greg clearly thought so; Manly firmly believed in the value of his methods; Salter, too, argued from elegant presentation of the results of his statistical investigations of Skelton's vocabulary, his collations and comparisons of variants. As today, humanists then had to justify their research, its intrinsic importance, its validity in a skeptical and often hostile milieu. One needs merely to mention funding – a problem that Manly, too, dealt with in many letters from two points of view: the effects of the Depression and the goals of his own university.

But the scientific mode – the science – of studying early drama was not totally new: it already existed, not based in symbolic logic or mathematical demonstration or verifiable experiments but in palaeontology and biology. The discoveries of these sciences were the background to the overwhelming influence of Sir E.K. Chambers and to his belief in the development of drama. And Salter worked within that tradition as well: drama evolved from its origins (whatever they were), and the pinnacle of that evolution was 'the great Shakespearean stage' (Chambers), or, as Salter puts it in the first sentence of his book, 'the great river of Elizabethan drama'.[5] The higher forms of drama that Chambers envisaged were, however, purely secular; Salter's own research indicated the opposite, and he argued cogently and vigorously for the coexistence of religious and secular plays and for the excellence of the former. He valued Karl Young's *Drama of the Medieval Church* as a basic work, necessary for understanding English religious drama in the middle ages, but unlike Hardin Craig, whom he takes to task in a lengthy, thoughtful, if somewhat severe review of 1957, he could not accept that individual plays necessarily had their beginnings in a liturgical source.[6] Further, development did not necessarily include inevitable progress, he believed, using these plays as his examples. He puts them in their temporal context and without entering the great Shakespeare debate shows how they are neither trivial nor negligible.

Chambers's approach was important in another way as well: his inclusion of what he called 'outside information' – social and economic context – provided the impetus for Salter's most abiding legacy: the application of documentary evidence to textual and literary criticism in order to produce an accurate and comprehensive history of the biblical plays and their performance. This was his central aim: from his earliest reports back to Manly in 1930 he makes it clear that

> a study of the craft guilds and their history would shed light on the physical history of the text as upon the circumstances of production ... . What needs to be done is to gather together and present all the pertinent records ... , taking up play after play for special study. I also think a history might be written in which individual minstrels and players could be followed from town to town ... . Something more might be done in tracing the tours of dramatic companies through the provinces.

And Records of Early English Drama is now accomplishing what Salter envisioned more than a half-century ago.

Salter began his study with the York plays because he believed they were the 'most important of the cycles', but York was abandoned for Chester when he discovered a new manuscript of the Coopers' *The Trial and Flagellation* play. The possibility of using the methods he had learned at Chicago on a group of manuscripts so complex and controversial together with extensive and informative records of production was irresistible. The project won him the first International

---

5   *Mediaeval Drama*, 1.

6   Review of *English Religious Drama of the Middle Ages*, by Hardin Craig. *Journal of English and Germanic Philology* 56 (1957): 253–64.

Research Fellowship at the Huntington Library where he was able to study the 1591 manuscript of the cycle, the manuscript he decided to establish as the base text for his critical edition of the plays.

In this approach, Salter worked alone. No one else was studying or attempting to study the plays as he was proposing to do. Even Manly, sympathetic and supportive as he was, chose to focus his attention and energy on the formidable Chaucer edition. W.W. Greg, however, was not only interested in Salter's work, but also challenged in his own theory of the relationship of Chester play manuscripts by Salter's discovery of the Coopers' play. Sir Walter had been studying the Chester plays as early as 1906, thinking to publish three volumes of early English plays. Though, as he said, 'the scheme never came to anything', he did edit and publish two of the plays from Chester, and his manuscript studies were described in the Sanders Lectures at Cambridge in 1913 and, ultimately, in his analytical and difficult work *The Calculus of Variants* (1927). He was a man of scrupulous integrity, and when Salter submitted to Greg himself the work on the new material, coming to different conclusions on the relationships of the Chester play manuscripts, Sir Walter published the paper in a Malone Society Studies volume (1935)[7] that is remarkable in its presentation: Salter's work was given first place, Greg followed with his rebuttal and with other material that he felt could cast light upon the manuscript relationships. Here was a publication that showed two fine scholars agreeing to disagree in mutual respect.

Research and college teaching in Kansas City, Missouri, followed until 1938, when Salter left for a year's work in England as a Guggenheim Fellow. His next important publication was his study (1939–40) of the Early and Late Banns of the Chester plays. Again, his object was to show through meticulous examination that they could 'yield an epitome of the larger history of the cycle during the last hundred years of its existence'. Again, too, he engaged with Greg's views on manuscript relationships and generously conceded that his own theory was 'distinctly questionable' and that 'the truth may lie between our theories or beyond either of them'.[8] What mattered was to present the textual and contextual evidence and suggest possible conclusions drawn from that evidence.

He returned to Canada, taking up a position at the University of Alberta in 1939, where he remained for the rest of his life. The years of the Second World War and its aftermath severely restricted his work on Chester. University responsibilities (he became head of the department of English) and, as a Flight Lieutenant in the University Air Squadron, teaching navigation to fledgling war pilots fully occupied his time. But he continued to write, almost annually offering to the Royal Society of Canada significant studies of Shakespearean theatre. He was also elected president of the humanities section of the Royal Society. In 1950, he received a British Council award that enabled him to resume his Chester studies, which were recognized by the University of Toronto with an invitation to deliver the

---

7   See n. 1, above.

8   'The Banns of the Chester Plays', *Review of English Studies* 15 (1939), 432, 441, 439.

Alexander Lectures. Their publication followed, as did an honorary doctorate from the University (1955) and election to the Royal Society of Literature in England. Professor Salter's reaction to these honours, so well deserved, is exhibited winningly in the preface to *Mediaeval Drama in Chester*: 'I must express my gratitude for hospitality, overwhelming and heart-warming. But most of all I must thank [Toronto] for giving me an opportunity – and a deadline – to clothe in comely print ideas too long left unrecorded'.[9] Professor Salter died seven years later.

All of Professor Salter's work demonstrated his interest in the contemporary performance of the cycle plays as revealed by production records. This is, in fact, another significant instance of his prescience: his recognition of the importance of the theatricality of the plays. He was never able to see a production of the mystery plays, except with his mind's eye and his imaginative sensitivity. Nevertheless, I am convinced he would have welcomed productions, whether period or modern, because he grasped the plays' performativity and their grounding in actual stage practice (otherwise he would not have spent so much time and effort in demolishing David Rogers's description of the Chester pageant wagons): 'What we should look for in drama is drama ... the same things that we always look for in the theatre: entertainment, beauty, representation of human life, the power to grip and hold an audience, and – above all – meaning or significance or, if I may say so, moral value.'[10]

But what would Professor Salter have made of Christopher Goodman's accusations that the seditious popish plays do not provide moral value but contain dangerous absurdities? He would, first of all, have been excited by such an important piece of evidence in the unknotting of the tangled history of the Chester plays. Goodman's letters, however, also reveal the depth of reforming hostility to the Church of Rome and its instruments, the plays. With that hostility, as Salter puts it, 'a sneaping wind tarnished their finery'[11] and that of religious plays throughout the country. A 'whole community's cooperative enterprise dedicated to brisk business and the glory of God' was at an end,[12] thanks to the efforts of Goodman, that follower and friend of John Knox, puritanly intransigent till his death, and men like him. Personally, Professor Salter would also have recognized the drift of those efforts: his seventeenth-century dissenting forebears on the one hand and on the other and more immediately, his maternal grandfather who, he said, came to Canada from Scotland 'to serve a stern God sternly in some fifty years of Presbyterian ministry'. He even recalled an incident from his childhood, when the congregation splintered over the use of the 'worldly' organ in worship.

Goodman's moral and, perhaps, political fervour helped put down the plays. Professor Salter's work has brought them back firmly into our sight. The Records of Early English Drama project – its aims and accomplishments – would have gratified him, for it provides the documentary evidence that can be studied along

---

[9]   *Mediaeval Drama*, ix.
[10] *Mediaeval Drama*, 84.
[11] *Mediaeval Drama*, 53.
[12] *Mediaeval Drama*, 52.

with extant play texts so as, first, to understand the textual history of each play, not only the whole cycle or group and, second, to illuminate the circumstances of production and performance. In other words, text and theatre, both essential. The discovery of new manuscripts would equally have been welcomed – another version of Rogers's Breviary, another of the Late Banns. He had acknowledged in his seminal article on the Banns that whatever theory of relationship of manuscripts he was putting forth could well change: 'further evidence will no doubt one day make it clear'.[13] Professor Salter's response to such evidence would have been the same as that of Greg in his Malone Society printing of Salter's first important discoveries: magnanimity and generous respect.

When he was at the Huntington, a professor at the University of Southern California, whom he had taught at Chicago, asked him to give a lecture to her class on Chaucer:

> she wants me to give them such a human dose as I gave my Chicago class ... .
> I think I shall not talk about Chaucer, however, but about Mystery Plays – about
> their beauty and their pathos, their perduring appeal in every town and village
> of the old world ... . And I shall produce some of the records I have painfully
> read from old town records in York and Chester and elsewhere, and amuse them
> with payments of sixpence 'ffor gilding the fface of the little god' and with
> inventories, 'Item, a nangel, wants a wing.' And if I do it properly, perhaps some
> will go out and read a few mystery plays, be caught perhaps by the tremendous
> appeal of the most vivid drama in the world, in its medieval dress.

Typically Salter. As one of his colleagues remarked, 'to the end of his life he retained the ability to respond directly, passionately to dramatic literature and literary study', or as he shrewdly and self-knowingly described himself, he was an enthusiast. But balancing enthusiasm (without which, he commented in another context, 'good work cannot be done') was that equally important ability to apply rigorous acuity of mind to the most intricate logical and intellectual problems of manuscripts and their relationships. His three outstanding works, *Mediaeval Drama in Chester*, *The Trial and Flagellation*, and *The Banns of the Chester Plays*, still matter and are still valuable, anything but outdated. It seems fitting that a volume of new essays on the Chester plays should conclude with a reminder that the reconstruction of the history of those plays owes its inception and inspiration to F.M. Salter, whose work has informed Lumiansky and Mills's subsequent studies and their edition of the plays, Larry Clopper's thorough review of the cycle's development, and REED's *Cheshire*.

In Professor Salter's understanding of what the plays attempted and achieve, he humanized them; through his meticulous, exacting, and sustained textual scholarship he provided those who followed him with a model of brilliant intellect. I trust this would have satisfied David Mills as to the sort of person, the sort of scholar, Millett Salter was.

---

[13]   'Banns', 439.

Bibliography

Acts of the Privy Council of England. N.s., vol. 8. London, 1894.

Aers, David and Sarah Beckwith. 'Reform and Cultural Revolution: Introduction'. *Journal of Medieval and Early Modern Studies* 35.1 (2005): 3–11.

Alldridge, Nicholas. 'Loyalty and Identity in Chester Parishes, 1540–1640'. In *Parish, Church and People: Local Studies in Lay Religion 1350–1750*, S.J. Wright (ed.), 85–124. London: Hutchinson, 1988.

An Admonition to the Parliament. Imprinted we know where, and whan, judge you the place and you can [i.e., Hemel Hempstead?]: J.T.J.S. [J. Stroud?], [1572]. STC 10847.

Aquinas, Thomas. *Summa Theologiae*, 3 vols. De Rubeis et al. (eds), and the Fathers of the English Dominican Province (trans.). New York: Domus Editorialis Marietti, 1947–48.

Arber, Edward (ed.), [*Ralph*] *Roister Doister*. English Reprints. London, 1869.

Aristotle. *Politics.* Ernest Barker (ed. and trans.). Oxford: Oxford University Press, 1995.

Ashley, Kathleen M. 'Divine Power in Chester Cycle and Late Medieval Thought'. *Journal of the History of Ideas* 39.3 (1978): 387–404.

Atkinson, Clarissa W. *Mystic and Pilgrim: The* Book *and the World of Margery Kempe.* Ithaca: Cornell University Press, 1983.

Aveling, J.C.H. *Post-Reformation Catholicism in East Yorkshire, 1558–1790.* York: East Yorkshire Local History Society, 1960.

———. *The Catholic Recusants of the West Riding, 1558–1790.* Leeds: Leeds Philosophical and Literary Society, 1963.

———. *Northern Catholics: The Catholic Recusants of the North Riding of Yorkshire, 1558–1790.* London: Chapman, 1966.

———. *Catholic Recusancy in the City of York, 1558–1791.* London: Catholic Record Society, 1971.

Axton, Richard. *European Drama of the Early Middle Ages.* London: Hutchinson, 1974.

Babington, Churchill and Joseph Rawson Lumby (eds). *Polychronicon Ranulphi Higden Monachi Cestrensis; Together with the English Translations of John Trevisa and of an Unknown Writer of the Fifteenth Century*, 9 vols. London: Longman, 1865–86.

Baker, Donald C. 'When Is a Text a Play? Reflections upon What Certain Late Medieval Dramatic Texts Can Tell Us'. In *Contexts for Early English Drama*, Marianne G. Briscoe and John C. Coldewey (eds), 20–40. Bloomington: Indiana University Press, 1989.

Baker, Donald C., John L. Murray, and Louis B. Hall Jr (eds). *The Late Medieval Religious Plays of Bodleian MSS Digby 133 and E Museo 160*. EETS ES 283. Oxford: Oxford University Press, 1982.

Baldwin, Elizabeth, Lawrence M. Clopper, and David Mills (eds). *REED: Cheshire, including Chester*, 2 vols. Toronto: University of Toronto Press, 2007.

Bale, John. *God's Promises, Johan Baptystes Preachynge, the Temptation of our Lord, and Three Laws*. In *The Complete Plays of John Bale*, 2 vols. Peter Happé (ed.). Cambridge: DS Brewer, 1986.

Barish, Jonas. *The Antitheatrical Prejudice*. Berkeley: University of California Press, 1981.

Barnum, Priscilla Heath (ed.). *Dives and Pauper*, 2 vols. EETS 275. Oxford: Oxford University Press, 1994.

Barrett, Robert W., Jr. *Against All England: Regional Identity and Cheshire Writing, 1195–1656*. Notre Dame IN: University of Notre Dame Press, 2009.

Bartlett, Anne Clark and Thomas H. Bestul (eds). *Cultures of Piety: Medieval English Devotional Literature in Translation*. Ithaca: Cornell University Press, 1999.

Bateson, Mary (ed.). 'A Collection of Original Letters from the Bishops to the Privy Council, 1564'. In *Camden Miscellany*, vol. 9, 73–8. Westminster: The Camden Society, 1895.

Beadle, Richard. '"Devoute ymaginacioun" and the Dramatic Sense in Love's *Mirror* and the N-Town Plays'. In *Nicholas Love at Waseda: Proceedings of the International Conference, 20–22 July, 1995*, Shoichi Oguro, Richard Beadle, and Michael G. Sargent (eds), 1–17. Cambridge: DS Brewer, 1997.

——— (ed.). *The York Plays*. London: Edward Arnold, 1982; EETS SS 23 (2009).

Beadle, Richard and Alan Fletcher (eds). *Cambridge Companion to Medieval English Theatre*, 2nd edn. Cambridge: Cambridge University Press, 2008.

Beck, Joan. *Tudor Cheshire*. Chester: The Cheshire Community Council, 1969.

———. 'Early Modern Chester 1550–1762: Religion, 1550–1642'. In *A History of the County of Chester: Volume 5 Part 1*, Christopher Piers Lewis and Alan Thacker (eds), 109–12. Oxford: Oxford University Press for the Institute of Historical Research, 2003.

Beckwith, Sarah. 'Margery Kempe's *Imitatio*'. In *The Book of Margery Kempe*, Lynn Staley (ed. and trans.), 284–7. New York: Norton, 2001.

———. *Signifying God: Social Relation and Symbolic Act in the York Corpus Christi Plays*. Chicago: University of Chicago Press, 2001.

Becon, Thomas. *A newe dialog betwene thangell of God, & the shepherdes in the felde concernynge the natiuite and birthe of Jesus Christ our Lorde & Sauyoure*. STC 1733.5. London, 1547[?].

Bennett, J.H.E. (ed.). *The Rolls of the Freemen of the City of Chester, Part 1, 1392–1700*. London: Printed for the Record Society, 1906.

Berry, Lloyd E. (introd.). *The Geneva Bible: A Facsimile of the 1560 Edition*. Madison: University of Wisconsin Press, 1969.

Bevington, David. *Tudor Drama and Politics*. Cambridge: Harvard University Press, 1968.

Bildhauer, Bettina. *Medieval Blood*. Cardiff: University of Wales Press, 2006.

Boddy, G.W. 'Players of Interludes in North Yorkshire in the Early Seventeenth Century'. *North Yorkshire Record Office Review* 4 (December 1976): 95–130.

The booke of common praier, and administration of the sacramentes. STC 16292. London, 1559.

Borot, Luc. 'The Bible and Protestant Inculturation in the *Homilies* of the Church of England'. In *The Bible in the Renaissance: Essays on Biblical Commentary and Translation in the Fifteenth and Sixteenth Centuries*, Richard Griffiths (ed.), 150–75. Aldershot Hants and Burlington VT: Ashgate, 2001.

Bossy, John. *The English Catholic Community, 1580–1870*. Oxford: Oxford University Press, 1976.

Bowsher, Julian and Pat Miller. *The Rose and the Globe – Playhouses of Shakespeare's Bankside, Southwark*. London: Museum of London Archaeology Service, 2010.

Braekman, W.L. 'Fortune-telling by the Casting of Dice: A Middle English Poem and its Background'. *Studia Neophilologica* 52.1 (1980): 3–29.

Brantley, Jessica. *Reading in the Wilderness: Private Devotion and Public Performance in Late Medieval England*. Chicago: University of Chicago Press, 2007.

Brawer, Robert A. 'The Form and Function of the Prophetic Procession in the Middle English Cycle Play'. *Annuale Medievale* 13 (1972): 88–123.

Burne, R.V.H. *Chester Cathedral: from its founding by Henry VIII to the accession of Queen Victoria*. London: S.P.C.K., 1958.

Bush, Michael. *The Pilgrimage of Grace: A Study of the Rebel Armies of October 1536*. Manchester: Manchester University Press, 1996.

Butterworth, Philip. 'Parts and Parcels: Cueing Conventions for the English Medieval Player'. *Medieval English Theatre* 30 (2008): 99–120.

Bynum, Caroline Walker. *Wonderful Blood: Theology and Practice in Late Medieval Northern Germany and Beyond*. Philadelphia: University of Pennsylvania Press, 2007.

Calvin, Jean. *Calvin's Commentaries: The Epistles of Paul the Apostle to the Romans and to the Thessalonians*. Ross Mackenzie (trans.). Grand Rapids MI: Eerdmans, 1961.

———. *Commentaries on the First Book of Moses, Called Genesis*. John King (trans.). Grand Rapids MI: W.B. Eerdmans Pub. Co., 1981.

Caspers, Charles. 'Wandering between Transubstantiation and Transfiguration: Images of the Prophet Elijah in Western Christianity'. In *Saints and Role Models in Judaism and Christianity*, Marcel Poorthuis and Joshua Schwartz (eds), 335–54. Leiden: Brill, 2004.

Cawley, A.C. (ed.). Appendix I. In *The Wakefield Pageants in the Towneley Cycle*. Manchester: Manchester University Press, 1958.

Cerasano, S.P. 'Edward Alleyn, the New Model Actor, and the Rise of the Celebrity in the 1590s'. *Medieval and Renaissance Drama in England* 18 (2005): 47–58.

Chambers, E.K. *The Mediaeval Stage*, 2 vols. London: Oxford University Press, 1903.

———. *The Elizabethan Stage*, 4 vols. London: Oxford University Press, 1923.

The Chester Mystery Cycle: A Facsimile of British Library MS Harley 2124. Leeds, 1984.

The Chester Mystery Cycle: A Facsimile of MS Bodley 175. Leeds, 1973.

The Chester Mystery Cycle: A Reduced Facsimile of Huntington Library MS 2. Leeds, 1980.

Clarke, Catherine A.M. *Literary Landscapes and the Idea of England, 700–1400*. Cambridge: DS Brewer, 2006.

——— (ed.). 'Life of St. Werburge – Henry Bradshaw'. In *Mapping Medieval Chester*, 2008, <http://www.medievalchester.ac.uk/texts/scholarly/Lucian.html> (3 August 2011).

Clarke, W.K. Lowther and Charles Harris. *Liturgy and Worship: A Companion to the Prayer Books of the Anglican Communion*. London: S.P.C.K., 1932; rpt 1936.

Clopper, Lawrence M. 'The History and Development of the Chester Cycle'. *Modern Philology* 75.3 (1978): 219–46.

——— (ed.). *REED: Chester*. Toronto: University of Toronto Press, 1979.

———. 'Lay and Clerical Impact on Civic Religious Drama and Ceremony'. In *Contexts for Early English Drama*, John C. Coldewey and Marianne Briscoe (eds), 102–36. Bloomington: Indiana University Press, 1989.

———. *Drama, Play, and Game: English Festive Culture in the Medieval and Early Modern Period*. Chicago: University of Chicago Press, 2001.

———. 'Is the *Treatise of Miraclis Pleyinge* a Lollard Tract Against Devotional Drama'. *Viator* 34 (2003): 229–71.

Cockett, Peter. 'The Actor's Carnal Eye: A Contemporary Staging of the Digby *Mary Magdalene*'. *Baylor Journal of Theatre and Performance* 3.2 (2006): 67–83.

Coldewey, John C. 'Some Economic Aspects of the Late Medieval Drama'. In *Contexts for Early English Drama*, John C. Coldewey and Marianne Briscoe (eds), 77–101. Bloomington: Indiana University Press, 1989.

Coletti, Theresa. '"Ther Be But Women": Gender Conflict and Gender Identity in the Middle English Innocents Plays'. *Mediaevalia* 18 (1995): 245–61.

———. 'The Chester Cycle in Sixteenth-Century Religious Culture'. *Journal of Medieval and Early Modern Studies* 37.3 (Fall 2007): 531–47.

Coletti, Theresa and Gail McMurray Gibson. 'The Tudor Origins of Medieval Drama'. In *A Companion to Tudor Literature*, Kent Cartwright (ed.), 228–45. Oxford: John Wiley and Sons, 2010.

Collinson, Patrick. *From Iconoclasm to Iconophobia: The Cultural Impact of the Second English Reformation*. Reading: University of Reading, 1986.

Cooper, Helen. *Shakespeare and the Medieval World*. London: A&C Black Publishers, 2010.

Corbett, Tony. *The Laity, the Church and the Mystery Plays: A Drama of Belonging*. Dublin: Four Courts Press, 2009.

Cotton, Charles. *The Compleat Gamester*. Harvard University Library/Wing c6382 136:12. London, 1674.

Coulson, Carolyn. 'Mysticism, Meditation, and Identification in *The Book of Margery Kempe*'. *Essays in Medieval Studies* 12 (1995): 69–79.

Covington, Sarah. *The Trail of Martyrdom: Persecution and Resistance in Sixteenth-Century England*. Notre Dame IN: University of Notre Dame Press, 2003.

Cox, John D. *The Devil and the Sacred in English Drama, 1350–1642*. Cambridge: Cambridge University Press, 2000.

Craig, Hardin. *English Religious Drama*. Oxford: Clarendon Press, 1955.

Crashaw, William. 'The sermon preached at the Crosse'. STC [2nd edn] 6028. London, 1607.

Crockett, Bryan. *The Play of Paradox: Stage and Sermon in Renaissance England*. Philadelphia: University of Pennsylvania Press, 1995.

da Varazze, Iacopo. *Legenda Aurea*, 2 vols. Giovanni Paolo Maggioni (ed.). Tavarnuzze: Sismel, Galluzzo, 1998.

Daneau, Lambert. *Discourse of Gaming*. In *True and Christian Friendshippe*, Thomas Newton (trans.). British Library, STC [2nd edn]: 6230. London, 1586.

Daniell, David. *The Bible in English: Its History and Influence*. New Haven: Yale University Press, 2003.

Danner, Dan G. 'Christopher Goodman and the English Protestant Tradition of Civil Disobedience'. *Sixteenth Century Journal* 8.3 (1997): 61–73.

Davidson, Clifford. 'The Realism of the York Realist and the York Passion'. *Speculum* 50.2 (1975): 270–83.

———. 'The Anti-Visual Prejudice'. In *Iconoclasm vs. Art and Drama*, Clifford Davidson and Ann Eljenholm Nichols (eds), 33–46. Kalamazoo MI: Medieval Institute Publications, 1989.

———. '"The Devil's Guts": Allegations of Superstition and Fraud in Religious Drama and Art during the Reformation'. In *Iconoclasm vs. Art and Drama*, Clifford Davidson and Ann Eljenholm Nichols (eds), 92–144. Kalamazoo MI: Medieval Institute Publications, 1989.

———. *[A Tretise of Miraclis Pleyinge*. Kalamazoo MI: Medieval Institute Publications, 1993.

———. 'Sacred Blood and the Late Medieval Stage'. In *History, Religion, and Violence: Cultural Contexts for Medieval and Renaissance Drama*. Aldershot Hants and Burlington VT: Ashgate, 2002.

——— (ed.). *The Dramatic Tradition of the Middle Ages*. AMS Studies in the Middle Ages 26. New York: AMS, 2005.

———. 'York Guilds and the Corpus Christi Plays: Unwilling Participants?' *Early Theatre* 9.2 (2006): 11–33.

Davidson, Clifford and Jennifer Alexander. *Early Art of Coventry*. Kalamazoo MI: Medieval Institute Publications, 1985.

Davies, J.G. *He Ascended into Heaven: A Study in the History of Doctrine*. New York: John Gordon Davies, 1958.

Davis, Norman (ed.). *Non-cycle Plays and Fragments*. EETS SS 1. London: Oxford University Press, 1970.

Dawson, Jane and Lionel K.J. Glassey. 'Some Unpublished Letters from John Knox to Christopher Goodman'. *The Scottish Historical Review* 84.2, no. 218 (2005): 166–201.

de Grazia, Margreta. 'World Pictures, Modern Periods, and the Early Stage'. In *A New History of Early English Drama*, John D. Cox and David Scott Kastan (eds), 17–21. New York: Columbia University Press, 1997.

de Voragine, Jacobus. *The Golden Legend: Readings on the Saints*, 2 vols. William Granger Ryan (trans.). Princeton: Princeton University Press, 1993.

Diehl, Huston. *Staging Reform, Reforming the Stage: Protestantism and Popular Theater in Early Modern England*. Ithaca: Cornell University Press, 1997.

Dohi, Yumi. 'Melchisedech in Late Medieval Religious Drama'. *Early Drama, Art and Music Review* 16 (1994): 77–95.

Doran, John. 'Authority and Care: The Significance of Rome in Twelfth-Century Chester'. In *Roma Felix: Formation and Reflections of Medieval Rome*, Éamonn Ó Carragáin and Carol Neuman de Vegvar (eds), 307–32. Aldershot Hants and Burlington VT: Ashgate, 2007.

The Drama of Medieval Europe. Proceedings of the Colloquium held at the University of Leeds 10–13 September 1974. Leeds: University of Leeds Graduate Centre for Medieval Studies, 1975.

Duffy, Eamon. *The Stripping of the Altars: Traditional Religion in England c.1400–c.1580*. New Haven: Yale University Press, 1992; 2nd edn, 2005.

———. *Fires of Faith: Catholic England under Mary Tudor*. New Haven: Yale University Press, 2009.

Dutka, JoAnna. 'The Lost Dramatic Cycle of Norwich and the Grocers' Play of the Fall of Man'. *Review of English Studies* 35.137 (1984): 1–13.

Elizabeth I. *The effect of certaine braunches of the statute made in anno xxxiii Hen. viii*. Queen's College Library, STC [2nd edn]: 8047.4. London, 1570.

Emmerson, Richard K. 'Contextualizing Performance: The Reception of the Chester *Antichrist*'. *Journal of Medieval and Early Modern Studies* 29.1 (Winter 1999): 89–119.

———. 'Dramatic History: On the Diachronic and Synchronic in the Study of Early English Drama'. *Journal of Medieval and Early Modern Studies* 35.1 (2005): 39–66.

Enders, Jody. *Murder by Accident: Medieval Theater, Modern Media, Critical Intentions*. Chicago: University of Chicago Press, 2009.

Epp, Garrett. 'Passion, Pomp, and Parody: Alliteration in the York Plays'. *Medieval English Theatre* 11 (1992): 150–61.

Faulkner, Mark (ed.). 'De Laude Cestrie – Lucian'. In *Mapping Medieval Chester*, 2008, <http://www.medievalchester.ac.uk/texts/scholarly/Lucian.html> (3 August 2011).

———. 'The Spatial Hermeneutics of Lucian's *De laude Cestrie*'. In *Mapping the Medieval City: Space, Place and Identity in Chester c. 1200–1500*, Catherine A.M. Clarke (ed.). Cardiff: University of Wales Press, 2011.

Fortescue, John. *On the Laws and Governance of England*. Shelley Lockwood (ed.). Cambridge: Cambridge University Press, 1997.

Foster, Frances A. (ed.). *A Stanzaic Life of Christ*. EETS OS 166. London: Oxford University Press, 1926.

Foxe, John. *Acts and Monuments*. STC 11222. London, 1563.

Gardiner, Harold. *Mysteries' End: An Investigation of the Last Days of the Medieval Religious Stage*. Yale Studies in English 104. New Haven: Yale University Press, 1946.

Gatton, John Spalding. '"There must be blood": Mutilation and Martyrdom on the Medieval Stage'. In *Violence in Drama*, Themes in Drama 13, James Redmond (ed.), 79–91. Cambridge: Cambridge University Press, 1991.

Geck, John, '"On yestern day, in Feverere, the yere passeth fully": On the Dating and Prosopography of *Mankind*'. *Early Theatre* 12.2 (2009): 33–56.

Gibson, James. '"Interludum Passionis Domini": Parish Drama in Medieval New Romney'. In *English Parish Drama*, Alexandra F. Johnston and Wim Hüsken (eds), 137–48. Atlanta and Amsterdam: Rodopi Press, 1996.

——— (ed.). *REED: Diocese of Canterbury*. Toronto: University of Toronto Press, 2002.

——— (ed.). *REED: Kent*, 3 vols. Toronto: University of Toronto Press, 2002.

Gramatica, Aloisius (ed.). *Bibliorum Sacrorum, Iuxta Vulgatam Clementinam, Nova Editio*. Vatican: Typis Polyglottis Vaticanis, 1913.

Greenblatt, Stephen. *Shakespearean Negotiations: The Circulation of Social Energy in Renaissance England*. Berkeley: University of California Press, 1988.

——— (ed.). *The Norton Shakespeare*, 1st edn. New York: W.W. Norton, 1997.

Greg, W.W. (ed.). *Malone Society Collections III*. Oxford: Oxford University Press, 1931.

Gregory, Brad S. *Salvation at Stake: Christian Martyrdom in Early Modern Europe*. Cambridge: Harvard University Press, 1999.

Groves, Beatrice. *Texts and Traditions: Religion in Shakespeare 1592–1604*. Oxford: Oxford University Press, 2007.

Habington, Thomas. *A Survey of Worcestershire by Thomas Habington*. John Amphlett (ed.). Oxford: J. Parker, 1893.

Haigh, Christopher. *Reformation and Resistance in Tudor Lancashire*. London: Cambridge University Press, 1975.

———. 'Anticlericalism and the English Reformation'. In *Reformation Revised*, Christopher Haigh (ed.), 56–74. Cambridge: Cambridge University Press, 1987.

———. *English Reformations: Religion, Politics, and Society under the Tudors*. Oxford: Clarendon Press, 1993.

Hammer, William. 'The Concept of the New or Second Rome in the Middle Ages'. *Speculum* 19.1 (1944): 50–62.

Hapgood, Elizabeth R. (trans.). *Constantin Stanislavski: An Actor Prepares.* London: Theatre Arts Inc., 1937; rpt London, 2008.

Happé, Peter. *The Towneley Cycle: Unity and Diversity.* Cardiff: University of Wales Press, 2007.

Harris, B.E. (ed.). *A History of the County of Chester*, 3 vols. *The Victoria History of the Counties of England.* Oxford: Oxford University Press, 1980.

Harris, Jonathan Gil. '"Look not big, nor stamp, nor stare": Acting Up in *The Taming of the Shrew* and the Coventry Herod Plays'. *Comparative Drama* 34.4 (2000–01): 365–98.

———. *Untimely Matter in the Time of Shakespeare.* Philadelphia: University of Pennsylvania Press, 2009.

Henry VIII. *The proclamacion made and de[vised by the] kynges hyghnesse our soueraygne lorde and his honorable counsaile.* British Library, STC [2nd edn]: 7771. London, 1528.

Heywood, Thomas. *Apology for Actors.* STC [2nd edn] 13309. London, 1612.

Hill-Vásquez, Heather. *Sacred Players: The Politics of Response in the Middle English Religious Drama.* Washington: CUA Press, 2007.

The Holy Byble, conteyning the Olde and Nevve Testament wherevnto is ioyned the whole seruice, vsed in the Church of England. London, 1577.

Hopenwasser, Nanda. 'A Performance Artist and Her Performance Text: Margery Kempe on Tour'. In *Performance and Transformation: New Approaches to Late Medieval Spirituality*, Mary A. Suydam and Joanna E. Ziegler (eds), 97–131. Houndmills: Palgrave Macmillan, 1999.

Hoyle, R.W. *The Pilgrimage of Grace and the Politics of the 1530s.* Oxford: Oxford University Press, 2001.

Hudson, Frederick. 'Robert White and his Contemporaries: Early Elizabethan Music and Drama'. In *Festschrift für Ernst Hermann Meyer*, Georg Knepler (ed.), 163–87. Leipzig: Deutscher Verlag f. Musik, 1973.

Hughes, Jonathan. *Pastors and Visionaries: Religion and Secular Life in Late Medieval Yorkshire.* Woodbridge, Suffolk: Boydell & Brewer, 1988.

Hunt, Alice. *The Drama of Coronation: Medieval Ceremony in Early Modern England.* Cambridge: Cambridge University Press, 2008.

Ingram, R.W. (ed.). *REED: Coventry.* Toronto: University of Toronto Press, 1981.

Injunctions Giuen by the most reuerende father in Christ, Edmonde … in his Metropolitical visitation to the Prouince of Yorke. STC 10375. London, 1571.

Jackson, Ken and Arthur Marotti. 'The Turn to Religion in Early Modern English Studies'. *Criticism* 46.1 (2004): 167–90.

Jambeck, Thomas J. 'The Dramatic Implications of Anselmian Affective Piety in the Towneley Play of the Crucifixion'. *Annuale Mediaevale* 16 (1975): 110–27.

Jensen, Phebe. *Religion and Revelry in Shakespeare's Festive World.* Cambridge: Cambridge University Press, 2008.

Jerz, Dennis G. 'Religious, Artistic, Economic, and Political Aspects of the York Corpus Christi Christi Plays'. *(Re)Soundings* 1.2 (1997), <http://marauder. millersville.edu/> (2 September 2010).

Johnston, Alexandra F. 'The *York Cycle* and the *Chester Cycle*: What do the Records Tell Us?' In *Proceedings of the Nineteenth Conference on Editorial Problems: Editing Medieval Drama: Special Problems New Directions, Toronto, 1983*, Alexandra F. Johnston (ed.), 18–35. New York: AMS Press, 1987.

———. 'The City as Patron: York'. In *Shakespeare and Theatrical Patronage in Early Modern England*, Suzanne Westfall and Paul Whitfield White (eds), 150–75. Cambridge: Cambridge University Press, 2002.

———. 'Fifteenth Century Yorkshire Drama: an Hypothesis'. In *Music and Medieval Manuscripts*, John Haines and Randal Rosenfeld (eds), 263–79. Aldershot Hants and Burlington VT: Ashgate, 2004.

———. 'Parish Playmaking before the Reformation'. In *The Late Medieval Parish*, Clive Burgess and Eamon Duffy (eds), 325–41. Harlaxton Medieval Studies 14. Donington: Shaun Tyas, 2006.

———. 'An introduction to medieval English theatre'. In *The Cambridge Companion to Medieval English Theatre*, 2nd edn, Richard Beadle and Alan Fletcher (eds), 1–25. Cambridge: Cambridge University Press, 2008.

———. 'And how the state will beare with it I knowe not'. *Medieval English Theatre* 30 (2008): 3–25.

Johnston, Alexandra F. and Margaret Rogerson (eds). *REED: York*, 2 vols. Toronto: University of Toronto Press, 1979.

Johnston, William B. (trans.). *Calvin's Commentaries: The Epistle of Paul the Apostle to the Hebrews and The First and Second Epistles of St. Peter*. Grand Rapids MI: Oliver and Boyd, 1963.

Jones, Norman. *Birth of the Elizabethan Nation: England in the 1560s*. Oxford: Blackwell Publishers, 1993.

Jones, Sarah Rees. '"*A peler of Holy Cherch*": Margery Kempe and the Bishops'. In *Medieval Women: Texts and Contexts in Late Medieval Britain, Essays for Felicity Riddy*, Jocelyn Wogan-Browne, Rosalynn Voaden, Arlyn Diamond, Ann Hutchinson, Carol M. Meale, and Lesley Johnson (eds), 377–91. Turnhout: Brepols, 2000.

Justice, Steven. 'Did the Middle Ages Believe in Their Miracles?' *Representations* 103 (2008): 1–29.

Kamerick, Kathleen. *Popular Piety and Art in the Late Middle Ages: Image Worship and Idolatry in England, 1350–1500s*. New York: Palgrave Macmillan, 2002.

Kendall, Ritchie. *The Drama of Dissent: The Radical Poetics of Nonconformity, 1380–1590*. Chapel Hill: University of North Carolina Press, 1986.

Kermode, Jenny. 'New Brooms in Early Tudor Chester?' In *Government, Religion and Society in Northern England 1000–1700*, John C. Appleby and Paul Dalton (eds), 144–58. Thrupp Gloucestershire: Sutton Pub., 1997.

Kesselring, K.J. *The Northern Rebellion of 1569: Faith, Politics, and Protest in Elizabethan England*. Basingstoke: Palgrave Macmillan, 2007.

Keyser, C.E. *A List of Buildings in Great Britain and Ireland having Mural and other Painted Decorations of Dates Prior to the Latter Part of the Sixteenth Century*, 3rd edn. London: H.M.S.O., 1883.

King, John N. *English Reformation Literature: The Tudor Origins of the Protestant Tradition*. Princeton: Princeton University Press, 1982.

———. *Tudor Royal Iconography: Literature and Art in an Age of Religious Crisis*. Princeton: Princeton University Press, 1989.

King, Pamela. 'Faith, Reason and the Prophets' dialogue in the Coventry Pageant of the Shearmen and Taylors'. In *Drama and Philosophy*, James Redmond (ed.), 37–46. Cambridge: Cambridge University Press, 1990.

———. 'The York and Coventry Mystery Cycles', *REED Newsletter* 22 (1997): 20–25.

———. 'Playing Pentecost in York and Chester: Transformations and Texts'. *Medieval English Theatre* 29 (2009): 60–74.

———. 'Confraternities and Civic Ceremonial: the Siena *Palio*'. In *The York Mystery Plays: Performance in the City*, Margaret Rogerson (ed.), 181–204. Woodbridge Suffolk: York Medieval Press, 2011.

Klausner, David N. 'The Modular Structure of *Wisdom*'. In *'Bring furth the pagants': Essays in Early English Drama Presented to Alexandra F. Johnston*, David N. Klausner and Karen Marsalek (eds), 181–96. Toronto: University of Toronto Press, 2007.

Knapp, Jeffrey. *Shakespeare's Tribe: Church, Nation, and Theatre in Renaissance England*. Chicago: Chicago University Press, 2002.

Kolve, V.A. *The Play Called Corpus Christi*. Stanford: Stanford University Press, 1966.

Lake, Peter. 'Religious Identities in Shakespeare's England'. In *A Companion to Shakespeare*, David Scott Kastan (ed.), 57–84. Oxford: Blackwell, 1999.

Lake, Peter and Michael Questier. 'Introduction'. In *Conformity and Orthodoxy in the English Church, c. 1560–1660*, Peter Lake and Michael Questier (eds), ix–xx. Woodbridge: Boydell Press, 2000.

Lander, S.J. 'The Diocese of Chester'. In *A History of the County of Cheshire*, vol. 3. B.E. Harris (ed.). Oxford: Oxford University Press, 1980.

Laughton, Jane. *Life in a Late Medieval City: Chester 1275–1520*. Oxford: Windgather Press, 2008.

Lehmberg, Stanford E. *The Reformation of Cathedrals: Cathedrals in English Society, 1485–1603*. Princeton: Princeton University Press, 1988.

Lerud, Theodore K. *Memory, Images, and the English Corpus Christi Drama*. New York: Palgrave Macmillan, 2008.

Lewis, C.P. and A.P. Thacker (eds). *A History of the County of Chester: The City of Chester, General History and Topography*, 5 vols. *The Victoria History of the Counties of England*. Suffolk: Boydell and Brewer, 2003.

Lochrie, Karma. *Margery Kempe and Translations of the Flesh*. Philadelphia: University of Pennsylvania Press, 1991.

Lombard, Peter. *Sententiae*. In *Patrologia Latina*, J.P. Migne (ed.), 192. Paris, 1855.

Lumiansky, R.M. 'Comedy and Theme in the Chester *Harrowing of Hell'*. *Tulane Studies in English* 10 (1960): 5–12.

Lumiansky, R.M. and David Mills (eds). *The Chester Mystery Cycle: Essays and Documents*. Chapel Hill: University of North Carolina Press, 1983.

———. *The Chester Mystery Cycle*, 2 vols. EETS SS 3 and 9. London: Oxford University Press, 1974; rpt 1986.

Lupton, Julia Reinhard. *Afterlives of the Saints: Hagiography, Typology, and Renaissance Literature*. Stanford: Stanford University Press, 1996.

Luther, Martin. *Luther's Works: Volume 2: Lectures on Genesis Chapters 6–14*. Jaroslav Pelikan and Daniel E. Poellot (eds). St. Louis: Concordia Publishing House, 1960.

Lydgate, John. *The testament of Iohn Lydgate monke of Berry*. British Library: STC: 1:21. London, 1520.

MacCulloch, Diarmaid. *The Later Reformation in England 1547–1603*. Basingstoke: Macmillan Education, 1990.

———. *Reformation: Europe's House Divided, 1490–1700*. London: Penguin, 2003.

MacLean, Sally-Beth. *Chester Art: A Subject List of Extant and Lost Art including Items Relevant to Early Drama*. EDAM Reference Series 3. Kalamazoo MI: Medieval Institute Publications, 1982.

———. 'Marian Devotion in Post-Reformation Chester: Implications of the Smiths' "Purification" Play'. In *The Middle Ages in the North-West*, Tom Scott and Pat Starkey (eds), 237–55. Oxford: Leopard's Head Press, 1995.

Maltby, Judith. *Prayer Book and People in Elizabethan and Early Stuart Culture*. Cambridge: Cambridge University Press, 1998.

Marsh, Christopher. *Popular Religion in Sixteenth-Century England: Holding Their Peace*. New York: St. Martin's Press, 1998.

Marshall, Peter. *Reformation England 1480–1642*. London: Arnold Pub., 2003.

Matthews, David and Gordon McMullan. 'Introduction'. In *Reading the Medieval in Early Modern England*, David Matthews and Gordon McMullan (eds), 1–17. Cambridge: Cambridge University Press, 2007.

McCarthy, Jeanne. '"The Sanctuarie is become a Plaiers Stage": Chapel Stagings and Tudor "Secular" Drama'. *Medieval and Renaissance Drama in England* 21 (2008): 56–86.

McMillin, Scott and Sally-Beth MacLean. *The Queen's Men and Their Plays*. Cambridge: Cambridge University Press, 1998.

Meredith, Peter (ed.). *The Mary Play from the N-Town Manuscript*. London: Longman, 1987.

——— (ed.). *The Passion Play from the N-Town Manuscript*. London: Longman, 1990.

Mills, David. 'Some Possible Implications of Herod's Speech: Chester Plays VIII 153–204'. *Neuphilologische Mitteilungen* 74 (1973): 131–43.

———. *The Chester Mystery Cycle: A New Edition with Modernised Spelling*. East Lansing MI: Colleagues Press, 1992.

————. *Recycling the Cycle: The City of Chester and Its Whitsun Plays*. Toronto: University of Toronto Press, 1998.

————. 'Who are Our Customers? The Audience for Chester's Plays'. *Medieval English Theatre* 20 (1998): 104–17.

————. 'Chester's Covenant Theology'. *Leeds Studies in English* 32 (2001): 399–412.

————. '"I Know My Place": Some Thoughts on Status and Station in the English Mystery Plays'. *Medieval English Theatre* 27 (2005): 5–15.

————. 'Brought to Book: Chester's Expositor and his Kin'. In *The Narrator, the Expositor and the Prompter in European Medieval Theatre*, Philip Butterworth (ed.), 307–25. Turnhout: Brepols, 2007.

————. 'Some Theological Issues in Chester's Plays'. In *'Bring furth the pagants': Essays in Early English Drama Presented to Alexandra F. Johnston*, David N. Klausner and Karen Sawyer Marsalek (eds), 212–29. Toronto: University of Toronto Press, 2007.

————. 'The Chester Cycle'. In *The Cambridge Companion to Medieval English Theatre*, 2nd edn, Richard Beadle and Alan Fletcher (eds), 125–51. Cambridge: Cambridge University Press, 2008.

Monmouth, Geoffrey. *History of the Kings of Britain*. Aaron Thompson (trans.) and J.A. Giles (rev.). Cambridge, Ontario: In Parentheses Publications, 1999, <http://www.yorku.ca/inpar/geoffrey_thompson.pdf> (3 August 2011).

Montrose, Louis. *The Purpose of Playing: Shakespeare and the Cultural Politics of the Elizabethan Theatre*. Chicago: University of Chicago Press, 1996.

Morris, Rupert H. *Chester in the Plantagenet and Tudor Reigns*. Chester, 1894.

Muessig, Carolyn. 'Performance of the Passion: the enactment of devotion in the later Middle Ages'. In *Visualizing Medieval Performance: Perspectives, Histories, Contexts*, Elina Gertsman (ed.), 129–42. Aldershot Hants and Burlington VT: Ashgate, 2008.

Muller, Richard A. 'The Hermeneutic of Promise and Fulfillment in Calvin's Exegesis of the Old Testament Prophecies of the Kingdom'. In *The Bible in the Sixteenth Century*, David C. Steinmetz (ed.), 68–82. Durham NC: Duke University Press, 1990.

————. 'Biblical Interpretation in the Era of the Reformation: The View From the Middle Ages'. In *Biblical Interpretation in the Era of the Reformation: Essays Presented to David C. Steinmetz in Honor of his Sixtieth Birthday*, Richard A. Muller and John L. Thompson (eds), 3–22. Grand Rapids MI: W.B. Eerdmans, 1996.

Njus, Jesse. 'What Did It Mean to Act in the Middle Ages?: Elisabeth of Spalbeek and *Imitatio Christi*'. *Theatre Journal* 63 (2011): 1–21.

O'Connell, Michael. 'Vital Cultural Practices: Shakespeare and the Mysteries'. *Journal of Medieval and Early Modern Studies* 29 (1999): 149–68.

————. *The Idolatrous Eye: Iconoclasm and Theater in Early-Modern England*. New York: Oxford University Press, 2000.

Ormerod, George. *The History of the County Palatine and City of Chester*, 3 vols, 2nd edn. London: George Routledge and Sons, 1882.

Palfrey, Simon and Tiffany Stern. *Shakespeare in Parts*. Oxford: Oxford University Press, 2007.

Palmer, Barbara. '"Towneley Plays" or "Wakefield Cycle" Revisited'. *Comparative Drama* 22 (1988): 318–48.

———. 'Recycling "The Wakefield Cycle": The Records'. *Research Opportunities in Renaissance Drama* 41 (2002): 88–130.

Piccope, G.J. (ed.). *Lancashire and Cheshire Wills and Inventories from the Ecclesiastical Court, Chester, Volume 54*. Chester: Printed for the Chetham Society, 1861.

Pineas, Rainer. *Tudor and Early Stuart Anti-Catholic Drama*. Nieuwkoop: B. De Graaf, 1972.

Poorthius, Marcel. 'Enoch and Melchizedek in Judaism and Christianity: A Study in Intermediaries'. In *Saints and Role Models in Judaism and Christianity*, Marcel Poorthius and Joshua Schwartz (eds), 97–120. Boston: BRILL, 2004.

Powell, Susan (ed.). *John Mirk's Festial*. EETS 334. Oxford: Oxford University Press, 2009.

Ptolemy of Lucca and Thomas Aquinas. *De Regimine Principum*. James M. Blythe (ed.). Philadelphia: University of Pennsylvania Press, 1997.

Rastall, Richard. 'Music in the Cycle'. In *The Chester Mystery Cycle: Essays and Documents*, R.M. Lumiansky and David Mills (eds), 111–64. Chapel Hill: University of North Carolina Press, 1983.

———. *The Heaven Singing: Music in Early English Religious Drama I*. Cambridge: DS Brewer, 1996.

Reinhard, Wolfgang. 'Reformation, Counter-Reformation, and the Early Modern State: A Reassessment'. *Catholic Historical Review* 75.3 (1989): 383–404.

Rickey, Mary Ellen and Thomas B. Stroup (eds). *Certaine Sermons or Homilies Appointed to be Read in Churches in the Time of Queen Elizabeth I (1547– 1571): a facsimile reproduction of the edition of 1623*. Gainesville FL: Scholars' Facsimiles & Reprints, 1968.

Riggs, David. 'Marlowe's Quarrel with God'. In *Marlowe, History, and Sexuality*, Paul Whitfield White (ed.), 15–37. New York: AMS Press, 1998.

Robertson, J. and D.J. Gordon (eds). 'A Calendar of Dramatic Records in the books of the Livery Companies of London'. In *Malone Society Collections III*, W.W. Greg (ed.). Oxford: Oxford University Press, 1931.

Romany, Frank and Robert Lindsey (eds). *Christopher Marlowe: The Complete Plays*. London: Penguin Books, 2003.

Rosemann, Philipp W. *Peter Lombard*. Oxford: Oxford University Press, 2004.

Ruck, Stefanie. 'Patriotic Tendencies in Pamphleteering during the Reigns of Henry VIII and Edward VI'. In *Writing the Early Modern English Nation: The Transformation of National Identity in Sixteenth- and Seventeenth-Century England*, Herbert Grabes (ed.), 1–45. Atlanta: Rodopi, 2001.

Ryan, Denise. 'Playing the Midwife's Part in the English Nativity Plays'. *Review of English Studies* 54 (2003): 435–48.

Salter, F.M. 'Skelton's *Speculum Principis*'. *Speculum* 9 (1934): 253–64.

———. 'The Trial & Flagellation of Christ: a New Manuscript'. In *The Trial and Flagellation with Other Studies in the Chester Cycle*, W.W. Greg (ed.). Oxford: Malone Society Studies, 1935.

———. 'Review of W.W. Greg's edition of *The Play of Antichrist* from the Chester Cycle'. *Review of English Studies* 13 (1937): 341–54.

———. 'The Banns of the Chester Plays'. *Review of English Studies* 15 (1939): 432–57; 16 (1940): 1–17, 137–48.

———. 'John Skelton's Contribution to the English Language'. *Transactions of the Royal Society of Canada*, Third Series, Section II, 39 (1945): 119–217.

———. *Mediaeval Drama in Chester*. Toronto and London: University of Toronto Press, 1955.

———. Review of *English Religious Drama of the Middle Ages*, by Hardin Craig. *Journal of English and Germanic Philology* 56 (1957): 253–64.

———. *The Way of the Makers*. H.V. Weekes (ed.). Edmonton, 1957; rpt as *The Art of Writing*. H.V. Weekes (ed.). Toronto: Ryerson Press, 1971.

Salter, F.M. and H.L.R. Edwards (eds). *The Bibliotheca Historica of Diodorus Siculus Translated by John Skelton*, 2 vols. London: EETS, 1956; rpt 1957.

Sargent, Michael G. (ed.). *Nicholas Love's* Mirror of the Blessed Life of Jesus Christ. New York: Garland Pub., 1992.

———. 'Mystical Writings and Dramatic Texts in Late Medieval England'. *Religion and Literature* 37.2 (2005): 77–98.

Sharpe, Richard. *A Handlist of the Latin Writers of Great Britain and Ireland Before 1540*. Publications of the Journal of Medieval Latin 1. Turnhout: Brepols, 1997.

Shrank, Cathy. 'John Bale and reconfiguring the "medieval" in Reformation England'. In *Reading the Medieval in Early Modern England*, David Matthew and Gordon McMullan (eds), 179–92. Cambridge: Cambridge University Press, 2007.

Simpson, James. *The Oxford English Literary History: Reform and Cultural Revolution 1350–1547, Volume 2*. Oxford: Oxford University Press, 2002; rpt 2004.

———. *Burning to Read: English Fundamentalism and its Reformation Opponents*. Cambridge MA: Harvard University Press, 2007.

Sinanoglou, Marcus Leah. 'The Christ Child as Sacrifice: A Medieval Tradition and the Corpus Christi Plays'. *Speculum* 48.3 (1973): 491–509.

Smith, Kathryn A. *Art, Identity and Devotion in Fourteenth-Century England: Three Women and their Books of Hours*. London: The British Library, 2003.

Soule, Lesley Wade. 'Performing the Mysteries: Demystification, Story-telling and Over-acting like the Devil'. *European Medieval Drama* 1 (1997): 219–31.

Spector, Stephen (ed.). *The N-Town Play*, 2 vols. EETS. New York: Oxford, 1991.

Sponsler, Claire. 'The Culture of the Spectator: Conformity and Resistance to Medieval Performances'. *Theatre Journal* 44.1 (1992): 15–29.

————. 'Drama and Piety: Margery Kempe'. In *A Companion to* The Book of Margery Kempe, John H. Arnold and Katherine J. Lewis (eds), 129–43. Cambridge: DS Brewer, 2004.

Spraggon, Julie. *Puritan Iconoclasm during the English Civil War*. London: Boydell Press, 2003.

Staines, David. 'To Out-Herod Herod: The Development of a Dramatic Character'. *c.... L...it' In The Drama in the Middle Ages: Comparative and Critical Essays, C.J. Davidson Gianakaris (ed.), 207–31. New York: AMS, 1982.

Starkey, David. *Elizabeth: The Struggle for the Throne*. London: HarperCollins, 2000.

Steinmetz, David C. 'Calvin and the Patristic Exegesis of Paul'. In *The Bible in the Sixteenth Century*, David C. Steinmetz (ed.), 100–118. Durham NC: Duke University Press, 1990.

Stern, Tiffany. *Rehearsal from Shakespeare to Sheridan*. Oxford: Oxford University Press, 2000.

Stevens, Martin and A.C. Cawley (eds). *The Towneley Plays*, 2 vols. EETS SS 13 and 14. New York: Oxford University Press, 1994.

Sugano, Douglas with Victor I. Sherb (eds). *The N-Town Plays*. Kalamazoo MI: Medieval Institute Publications, 2007.

Swanson, R.N. 'Will the Real Margery Kempe Please Stand Up!' In *Women and Religion in Medieval England*, Diana Wood (ed.), 141–65. Oxford: Oxbow, 2003.

Tanner, Norman P., S.J. (ed.). *Decrees of the Ecumenical Councils*, 2 vols. Washington: Sheed & Ward, 1990.

Taylor, Charles. *A Secular Age*. Cambridge: Belknap, 2007.

Taylor, John. *The Universal Chronicle of Ranulf Higden*. Oxford: Clarendon Press, 1966.

Taylor, M.V. (ed.). *Extracts from the MS. Liber Luciani De laude Cestrie Written about the Year 1195 and Now in the Bodleian Library, Oxford*. The Record Society of Lancashire and Cheshire 64 (1912): 1–78.

Thornton, Tim. *Cheshire and the Tudor State 1480–1560*. New York: Woodbridge, Suff, and Rochester, 2000.

Tittler, Robert. *Townspeople and Nation: English Urban Experiences 1540–1640*. Stanford: Stanford University Press, 2001.

Travis, Peter W. *Dramatic Design in the Chester Cycle*. Chicago: University of Chicago Press, 1982.

Trevisa, John. *The Governance of Kings and Princes*. David C. Fowler, Charles F. Briggs, and Paul G. Remley (eds). New York: Garland, 1997.

Twycross, Meg. 'Playing "The Resurrection"'. In *Medieval Studies for J.A.W. Bennett*, P.L. Heyworth (ed.), 273–96. Oxford: Clarendon Press, 1981.

————. 'The Chester Cycle Wardrobe'. In *Staging the Chester Cycle*, David Mills (ed.), 100–123. Leeds: University of Leeds School of English, 1985.

Twycross, Meg and Sarah Carpenter. *Masks and Masking in Medieval and Early Tudor England*. Aldershot Hants and Burlington VT: Ashgate, 2002.

Wack, Mary. 'Women, Work, and Plays in an English Medieval Town'. In *Maids and Mistresses, Cousins and Queens*, Susan Frye and Karen Robertson (eds), 33–51. Oxford: Oxford University Press, 1999.

Wager, Lewis. *Life and Repentance of Mary Magdalene*. In *Reformation Biblical Drama in England*, Paul Whitfield White (ed.), 1–66. New York: Garland, 1992.

Walker, Gilbert. *A Manifest Detection of the Moste Vyle and Detestable Vse of Diceplay*. In *Rogues, Vagabonds, and Sturdy Beggars: A New Gallery of Tudor and Early Stuart Rogue Literature Exposing the Lives, Times, and Cozening Tricks of the Elizabethan Underworld*, Arthur F. Kinney and John Lawrence (eds), 59–84. Amherst: University of Massachusetts Press, 1990.

Walker, Greg. *Plays of Persuasion: Drama and Politics at the Court of Henry VIII*. Cambridge: Cambridge University Press, 1991.

———. *The Politics of Performance in Early Renaissance Drama*. Cambridge: Cambridge University Press, 1998.

Wark, K.R. *Elizabethan Recusancy in Cheshire*. Remains Historical and Literary Connected with the Palatine Counties of Lancaster and Chester, vol. 19, third series. Manchester: Chetham Society, 1971.

Watt, Tessa. *Cheap Print and Popular Piety, 1550–1640*. Cambridge: Cambridge University Press, 1991.

Wenzel, Siegfried. '*Somer Game* and Sermon References to a Corpus Christi Play'. *Modern Philology* 86.3 (1989): 274–83.

White, Paul Whitfield. 'Calvinist and Puritan Attitudes towards the Stage in Renaissance England'. *Explorations in Renaissance Culture* 14 (1988): 41–55.

———. 'Drama in the Church: Church-Playing in Tudor England'. *Medieval and Renaissance Drama in England* 6 (1993): 15–35.

———. *Theatre and Reformation: Protestantism, Patronage, and Playing in Tudor England*. Cambridge: Cambridge University Press, 1993.

———. 'Reforming Mysteries' End: A New Look at Protestant Intervention in English Provincial Drama'. *Journal of Medieval and Early Modern Studies* 29.1 (1999): 121–47.

———. 'The Bible as Play in Reformation England'. In *The Cambridge History of British Theatre, Vol. 1: Origins to 1660*, Jane Milling and Peter Thomson (eds), 87–115. Cambridge: Cambridge University Press, 2004.

———. *Drama and Religion in English Provincial Society, 1485–1660*. Cambridge: Cambridge University Press, 2008.

Wickham, Glynne. *Early English Stages, 1300 to 1660*, 2 vols. London: Routledge, 1963; rpt 1972.

Williams, Arnold. *The Drama of Medieval England*. East Lansing: Michigan State University Press, 1961.

Williamson, Elizabeth. *The Materiality of Religion in Early Modern English Drama*. Aldershot Hants and Burlington VT: Ashgate, 2009.

Windeatt, Barry (ed.). *The Book of Margery Kempe*. Harlow, Essex: DS Brewer, 2000.

Woodes, Nathaniel. *Conflict of Conscience*. STC 25966 and 25966.5. London, 1581.

Woodward, D.M. *The Trade of Elizabethan Chester*. Hull: University of Hull, 1970.

Woolf, Rosemary. *The English Mystery Plays*. London: Routledge and Kegan Paul, 1972.

Yeager, Suzanne M. '*The Siege of Jerusalem* and Biblical Exegesis: Writing about Romans in Fourteenth-Century England'. *The Chaucer Review* 39.1 (2004): 70–102.

Index

Note: Page numbers in **bold type** indicate illustrations.

Abbey Gate 116–17, 162n9
Abraham (character) 129–30, 175
Abraham and Isaac (Chester: Barber
    Surgeons, Leechers, Waxchandlers)
    29, 113, 129–30, 170, 173–5
Abraham and Melchizedek (Chester
    episode) 30–32, 175
Actor Prepares, An 95; *see also* Stanislavski
Acts and Monuments 5, 48n4
Acts, book of 83, 86–7, 87n26, 179n2
Adam (character) 2, 30
Admonition to the Parliament, An 48n6
affective piety 93–107
Alberta, University of 193n1, 195–6, 198
albs (costumes) 128
aldermen 119n28, 119n35
Aldersey, Fulke 118, 119n28
Aldersey, Margaret nee Barnes 118
Aldersey, William of St Bridget 118
Aldersey, William the elder 118
Aldersey, William the younger 118
Aldford, Ches 120–21, 128n76, 167
alewives (character) 76, 97, 131, 168–9
Alexander Lectures 193, 199
Alfred, king 177
Allen, Thomas 19
Alleyn, Edward 100
Ambidexter (character) 9
angels (character) 13, 38, 41, 57, 83–4, 86–7,
    106, 154n17, 190; *see also* Gabriel
Annas (character) 94, 157
Annunciation (Chester episode) 30–31
Annunciation and the Nativity, The (Chester:
    Daubers, Wrights, Slaters, Thatchers,
    Tilers) 3, 29, 31, 96n17, 96–7, 104,
    106, 154n17, 158, 169, 173–4
Antichrist (character) 9, 47, 54, 127,
    143–4, 157n28, 173

Apology for Actors 135
apostles (character) 48, 50, 53–4, 75,
    83, 86
Apostles' Creed 116, 131
Aquinas, Thomas 53, 89, 89n31, 90,
    181, 181n13
Arian doctrine 39
arks (prop) 29–30, 143, 174
Armagh, archbishops of 19
Arneway, Sir John 138, 145, 161, 177
Ascension, feast of 84, 88
Ascension, The (Chester: Tailors) 13–14,
    27, 79–91, 96n17, 143
Ascension, The (N-Town) 87
Ascension, The (Towneley) 86–7
Ascension, The (York) 87
Ashmolean Museum 21
Ashover, Derbs 141
Asquith, Robert 2
Assumption of the Virgin, The (Chester:
    Wives) 2
Athanasian Creed 39
Avarice (character) 7

'Baines note, the' 62–3
Bakers (Chester guild), play of *see*
    Last Supper
Balaack (character) 31, 169, 186n33
Balaack and Balaam (Chester: Cappers,
    Linen-Drapers, Pinners,
    Wiredrawers) 29–30, 129, 169,
    172, 174
Balaam (character) 143, 169
Balaam and Balaack (Prophets) (Chester
    episode) 30–31
Bale, John 5–7, 55–8, 60–61, 63, 126,
    129n78, 130, 135
Baleus Prolocutor (character) 57, 176
Bamvill, Randle 118
Banns 14, 21, 101n43, 133–45, **137**,
    144–5, 184, 200

Early Banns (1539–40) 2–3, 22, 101,
    136, 138n16, 140–42, 145, 184, 198
Late Banns (1608–09) 2–3, 14, 22,
    39, 43, 90n33, 98–9, 111–12, 129,
    136–140, 142–3, 145, 161n1,
    161–2, 165, 176–7, 184, 198, 200
Banns (N-Town) 22
Barbers (Chester guild) 129
    play of *see Abraham and Isaac*
Barnes, Margaret 118
Barnes, Sir Randle 123
Becon, Thomas 56–8, 60–61, 63
Bede 88, 90
Bedford, William 21
Bellin, George 21, 40, 126
Benet, Roger 123
Benjamin, Walter 142, 142n28
Benson, William 182
Betrayal (Chester episode) 33–4
Betrayal of Christ, The see Last Supper
Beza, Theodore 51
Bibliotheca Historica 193
Bird, John, bishop 114, 117
Bird, Richard 119n28
Bird, William 119n35
Bishops' Bible 170, 175
bishops (character) 126–7
Blacon, Ches 168–9
Blaken, John 115
Blessed Trinity, fraternity of 41
Blind Man (Chester episode) 33
blood (prop) 13, 143
blood (symbolism) 79–91
Bodleian Library 19–21
Bodley, Thomas 19
Bonner, Edmund, bishop 4, 115
Book of Common Prayer 48, 114–15,
    124, 131
'Book of Homilies, The' 131
Book of Margery Kempe see Kempe,
    Margery
Bowyers (Chester guild) *see Trial and
    Flagellation of Christ*
Bradshaw, Henry *see Life of St Werburghe*
bread or wafers (prop) 54, 127, 143, 175
*Breviary of Chester History see Rogers'
    Breviaries*
Brewers (Chester guild) 21

Bridgwater, earls of 20
British Council 98
British Library 20–21
Broughton ('Boughton'), Ches 168–9
Brussels 8
Brutus 152
Bucer, Martin 50, 50n14
Bullein, William 121–2
Bullinger 174
Bunbury, Ches 20
Burbage, Richard 100
Burial and Resurrection of Christ, The
    (play) 102
Butchers (Chester guild) 139
Butler, Thomas 99
Byrd, William 124

Caiaphas (character) 74, 94, 157
Cain and Abel (Chester episode) 30–31
Calvin, John 48n3, 51, 80, 82n11, 130, 174
Cambises 9
Cambises (character) 9
Cambridge University 198
Canadian Field Artillery 195
'Candilmas-day pageant' *see Purification
    of the Virgin Mary*
Canterbury Cathedral 141
Canterbury, Kent 62, 62n47
Canterbury Tales, The 196, 198, 200
'Canticle of Mary' *see Magnificat, The*
canvas (props) 139
Cape Breton 195
Cappers (Chester guild), play of *see
    Balaack and Balaam*
carriages *see* pageant wagons
centurions (character) 156
Chadderton, William 4
Chambers, E.K. 133–4, 142n28,
    144–5, 197
Chantries Act 125
Chatham, New Brunswick 195
Chaucer, Geoffrey 196, 198, 200
Chaucer Laboratory, The 196, 198
Cheshire, county of 20–21, 75, 77, 88, 114,
    116, 120, 125
Chester, bishops of 4, 21, 100, 114, 117,
    124, 163; *see also* Downham,
    William

Chester Cathedral 21, 114, 116–17, 121, 123, 128, 136n11, 162; *see also* St Werburgh's Abbey
Chester, city of
  aldermen 119n28, 119n35
  guilds 21, 79–91, 99, 100, 136; *see also individual guilds by name or play titles*
    Barbers 129
    Brewers 21
    Butchers 139
    Clothworkers 143
    Coopers 21
    Glaziers 3
    Mercers 143
    Painters 3
    Shearmen 143
    Shoemakers 143
    Tailors 143
    Tanners 143
    Wax-Chandlers 129
  mayors 4, 25–6, 75–6, 113–14, 117–19, 119n30, 119n35, 120, 121, 138, 145, 161–2, 169, 179, 181–2, 182n15, 183, 191
  Minstrels' Court 119
  sheriffs 118, 119n28
  vice-chamberlains 119n28
Chester cycle 5, 8, 14, 25, 180; *see also* Banns; costumes; properties and scenery
  audience pardons/indulgences 100
  audience punishment 100
  conjectural division 27–32
  manuscript survival 12, 14, 19–22, 24, 26, 28, 31, 35, 40, 66, 79n3, 112, 122–3, 126–7, 141
  modern production (Toronto, 2010) 12, **17**, 25, 27–35, **45**, 72–4, 80n5, 96, 109, 112, **147**, 170, 173, 193
  music 114, 116, 123
  parcels (play-text parts) 94, 103–4, 106
  performance route 15
  playing time 38
  plays of; *see also Abraham and Isaac*; *Annunciation and the Nativity*; *Ascension*; *Balaack and Balaam*; *Coming of the Antichrist*; *Crucifixion, or The Passion of Christ*; *Fall of Lucifer*; *Harrowing of Hell*; *Last Judgment*; *Last Supper*; *Noah's Flood*; *Purification of the Virgin Mary*; *Resurrection*; *Shepherds*; *Temptation of Christ*; *Three Kings*; *Trial and Flagellation of Christ*
    Assumption of the Virgin, The (Wives) 2
    Christ and the Money-lenders (Corvisers) 169
    Christ's Appearance Before the Doctors (Cutlers, Furbishers, Pewterers, Smiths) 28, 32
    Fall of Man, The (Drapers) 119; modern production (2010) **147**
    Massacre of the Innocents (Goldsmiths, Masons) 32, 34, 187
    Moses and the Law (Cappers, Linen-Drapers, Pinners, Wiredrawers) 29–30, 172, 174
    Offering of the Three Kings, The (Mercers, Spicers) 32, 34
    Pentecost, The (Fishmongers, Fleshmongers) 3, 28, 75
    Prophets of Antichrist, The (Clothworkers, Shearmen) 172, 174
    Raising of Lazarus, The (Glovers) 168
    'Trinity' play 41
    Woman Taken in Adultery, The (Butchers) 33, 173
  Reginall, the ('original') 79n3, 112
  rehearsals 100, 106, 119, 132
  stage directions 42–3
  teaching of 32
  Whitsun (1572) staging 12, 20, 25–35, 47, 51, 111–14, 116–23, 128, 132, 136, 144, 161–2, 179–80, 184n25
Chester, diocese of 4–5, 114, 121, 124
Chicago, University of 196–7, 200
Christ among the Doctors (Chester episode) 3, 33
Christ and the Money-Lenders (Chester: Corvisers) 169
Christ (character) 27, 59, 97–8, **109**, 124, 127, 131–2, 143, 157, 172n36

Christ Jesus Triumphant 131
Christian Custance (character) 7
Christleton, Ches 167
Christmas 5
Christ's Appearance Before the Doctors
  (Chester: Cutlers, Furbishers,
  Pewterers, Smiths) 28, 32
Claudius Caesar 151–2
Clement, Bishop 100
Clogge, William 182
Clothworkers (Chester guild) 143
  play of *see Prophets of Antichrist*
cloud effects (scenery/prop) 39n6, 83, 98,
  139, 143
coats (costume) 139, 143
Cockett, Peter (director) 96, 96n17
Combermere, Ches 164
Coming of the Antichrist, The (Chester:
  Dyers, Bellfounders, Hewsters) 20,
  41, 54, 127–8, 132
Compassion, daughter of God (character) 7
compleat gamester, The 66n5, 67
Conflict of Conscience 61
Cooks (Chester guild), play of *see*
  Harrowing of Hell
Coopers (Chester guild) 21
  play of *see Trial and Flagellation*
  of Christ
Cop, Michael 50
copes (costumes) 123, 128
Corpus Christi, feast of 3, 56, 76, 91,
  136–7, 172
'Corpus Christi' (play) 49n8
Corvisers (Chester guild), plays of
  Christ and the Money-lenders 169
  lost segment 48
costumes 10, 58, 136
  albs 128
  coats 139, 143
  copes 123, 128
  crowns 123–4
  gowns 124, 184n22, 186
  hoods 124
  tunicles 123
  vestments 128–9
Cotton, Charles 66n5, 67
Cotton, Robert Bruce 20
Coulson-Grigsby, Carolyn (director) 96
Council of the North 2, 4, 77, 121

lord presidents 4, 25, 79, 181
Council of Trent 80n6
Coventry, city of 19, 117, 184
Coventry pageants 1n2, 4–5, 25, 100, 184
  for Hock Tuesday 1
  Purification of Christ and the
  Doctors, The 19
Cowper, family 21
Cowper, William 118
Craig, Hardin 23, 197
Crashaw, William 134–5, 143
Creation (of Lucifer, of Man) (Chester
  episode) 30–31
'Creation' (play), St Laurence, church of,
  Reading, Berks 22
'Creed, The' (York pageant) 2
Cremshaw, Lancs 118
Criplyng, Robert 2
Cromwell, Thomas 55
Croo, Robert 1
crosses (prop) 33, 77, 131
Crow, Robert 19
crowns (costume) 123–4
Crucifixion (Chester episode) 33–4
Crucifixion, The, or The Passion of Christ
  (Chester: Ironmongers, Ropers) 5,
  19, 21, 32, 65–77
Crucifixion, The (Towneley) 101
Crucifixion, The (York) 70n13
Cruelty (character) 10
cruor Christi see blood

Dalhousie University 195–6
Daneau, Lambert 66n5, 75–6
De Honestis Ludis 50n14
De Laude Cestrie 15, 150–51, 156,
  162–72, 176–7
De Regimine Principum 181n13, 187n39
Denial of Peter (Chester episode) 34
Derby ('Darbie'), earls of 115–16, 120, 192
Derbyshire, county of 141
devils/demons (character) 99, 138–9, 143
Devonshire, dukes of 20–21
Dialogue ... Against the Fever
  Pestilence, A 122n46
dice games (staged) 13, 65–77
Digby, plays
  Killing of the Children 190n41
  Mary Magdalene 96

Digby, Sir Kenelm 19
Discipline (character) 8
Discourse of Gaming 66n5, 75–6
Dissimulation (character) 11
Dives and Pauper 75
doctors (character) *see* expositors
Doubting Thomas (York) 19
dove (prop/character?) 56n29
Downham, William, bishop 2, 4–5,
    114–19, 124, 180–81
Drapers (Chester guild), play of
    Fall of Man 119
    modern production (2010) **147**
Dublin, Ireland 20
Dutton, Ches 119
Dutton, John 119
Dutton, Richard 119
Dyers (Chester guild), play of *see Coming*
    of the Antichrist

Early Banns (1539–40) *see under* Banns
East Gate 166n23, 167
ecclesiastical commissions 4, 26, 113,
    115–16, 120–21, 183
Edward I, king of England 5
Edward VI, king of England 56, 114,
    125, 130
Egerton, family 20–21
Egerton, John, earl of Bridgwater 20
Egerton, John, Esq. 20
Egton, Yorks NR 5n21
Elijah (Elias) (character) 47, 54, 127, 175
Elisabeth of Spalbeek 97n25
Elizabeth (character) 104–5
Elizabeth I, queen of England 5–6, 8, 76,
    79n1, 91n37, 111, 113–15, 188
Ellam, Thomas 123
emotion memory 102–3
emperors (character) 124, 126; *see*
    also Octavian
Enoch (character) 47, 54, 175
Entry (Chester episode) 33–4
Eve (character) 2
Everyman 9, 23
Exchequer, Court of 182
Expositor (character) 9, **17**, 54, 105,
    128–30, 155, 158, 163, 170–76

Faith (character) 59
Fall of Lucifer (Chester episode) 30–31
Fall of Lucifer, The (Chester: Barkers,
    Tanners) 12, 29, 34, 38–43, 166
Fall of Man (Chester: Drapers) 119
    modern production (2010) **147**
Fall of Man (Chester episode) 30–31
Fall of Man, The (Norwich play) 1–2
Farel, William 50
Felton, John 126
Festial 88
First Jew (character) 66, 68, 70, 72n17,
    73–4, 76; *see also* Jews
fishermen (character) 53
Flagellation (Chester episode) 33–4
Fortescue, John 181, 181n13
'Fortune-Telling by the Casting of Dice'
    (game-poem) 67
Fourth Angel (character) 30; *see*
    also angels
Fourth Jew (character) 66, 67n9, 68–70,
    72–3, 75; *see also* Jews
Fourth Soldier (character) 73; *see*
    also soldiers
Foxe, John 5, 48n4, 131
Fraud (character) 11
Friar Bartholomew (character) 129, 158
Fulwell, Ulpian 8–9

Gabriel (character) 62, 104–5, 154n17
Gee, Henry 75–6, 114, 117, 169
Geneva 48n3, 50–51, 79n1
Geneva Bible 91, 114, 175
Genson, Sir John 123
Geoffrey of Monmouth 152
Gerontus (character) 11
Glasier, Richard 119n28
Glaziers (Chester guild) 3
    play of *see Shepherds*
Gloria 68
'Gloria in excelsis' (song) 3, 57
Glossa ordinaria 173
Gloucester Hall, Oxford 19
Glovers (Chester guild), play of
    Raising of Lazarus 168
God (character) 12–13, 38–9, 41–3,
    139–40, 143, 174

Godly Queen Hester 11
God's Law (character) 59
God's Promises (play) 55–8, 129n78, 130
Golden Legend, The (*Legenda aurea*) 47,
    88, 154–5
Goobett-on-the-Greene (character) 173
Good Gossips (character)
Goodman, Christopher 4, 8, 10–15, 22,
    25–7, 28, 30–35, 37, 47–51, 55,
    62–3, 79–81, 84, 89–91, 104,
    111–14, 116, 119–22, 125, 127–9,
    131, 133–43, 145, 149, 158–9, 162,
    174, 179, 188, 190, 193, 199
    letters 3–4, 11, 25–6, 35, 79, 112, 116,
      121, 128–9, 133, 137, 141, 181–3
    'list of absurdities' 3, 22, 25–9, 31–2,
      35, 47, 62, 79, 79n3, 112, 126, 141,
      158, 162, 174–5
Gospel of Nicodemus, The 130
Gosson, Stephen 50, 62n47
Governance of Kings and
    Princes, The 186–7
gowns (costume) 124, 184n22, 186
Green, Thomas 118
Greg, Sir Walter (W.W.) 196, 198, 200
Gregorie, Edward 20
Gregory, pope 174
Griffeth, Randall 125
Grindal, Edmund, archbishop 3–4, 26, 37,
    49, 62, 79, 112, 116, 125, 141, 158,
    180–83, 188, 191
Grotowski, Jerzy 96
'Group Manuscripts, The' 66–7, 69, 71–2;
    see also manuscript survival *under*
    Chester cycle
Guggenheim Fellow 198
Guto'r Glyn *I Wiliam Herbart* [*To William
    Herbert*] 177

halls 19, 76
Hamlet 23–4
Hamlet (character) 24, 183–4
Hankey, Richard 120n35
Hanky, John 117, 119
Hannekynn (character) 177
Hardware, Henry the elder 117, 121
Hardware, Henry the younger 117–18
Harley, Robert, earl of Oxford 20

Harrowing of Hell, The (Chester: Cooks)
    32, 33–4, 76, 97, 99, 113, 130,
    139, 168
Harvy (character) 177
Hastings, Henry, earl of Huntingdon 25–6,
    79, 133, 181
Hatton ('Halton'), Ches 168–9
Hegge, Robert 19
Henry VIII, king of England 75–6, 91n37,
    114, 124–5
Herber, Richard 21
Herod (character) 15, 32, 94, 154, 173,
    183–90, 186n33
Hester (character) 7
Hewyk, Robert, of Leeds 24
Heywood, Thomas 135, 143, 145
Higden, Ranulph (Ranulf), monk 15, 101,
    133, 137–8, 145, 150–52, 155–6,
    161–2, 177
High Cross 192
Hock Tuesday (Coventry pageant) 1
hoist mechanism (prop) 143
Holme, family 21
Holme, Randle 14, 21, 136–7, 140–42, 145
Holy Trinity, church of 115, 124–5
Holy Trinity, feast of 41
Homilia in evangelia 174
Honour (character) 9
hoods (costume) 124
Hoole Heath, Ches 167
Hospitality (character) 11
How Superior Powers Ought To Be
    Obeyd 79n1
Hume, Alexander 131
Huntingdon, earls of 25–6, 79, 133, 181
Huntington, Henry E. 21
Huntington Library 20–21, 198, 200
Hutton, Matthew 2, 49n8
Hypocrisy (character) 10

'In and In' (game) 67
Infideltie (character) 59
International Research Fellowship 197–8
Ireland 19, 25, 55–6, 114, 131, 163
Isaias, book of 83–4, 87

Jack Juggler 7
Jankynson, John 99

'Jerusalem carriage' 143
Jesus (character) 13, 46, 56n29, 48, 54, 58,
    80–81, 83–6, 89, 140, 143, 168–9,
    184; *see also* Christ
Jesus Christus (character) 58
Jews (character) 66–8, 73–5, 77, 105,
    156; *see also* First, Second, Third,
    Fourth Jew
Johan the Baptystes Preachynge (play)
    55–6, 56n29, 58
Johanes Baptista (character) 58
John the Baptist (character) 56n29, 58
Johnston, Alexandra J. (play-text adapter)
    72–3, 112
Jones, Robert 124
Joseph (character) 29–30, 62–3, 106,
    154, 190
Joseph's Troubles (Chester episode) 30–31
Judas to High Priests (Chester episode) 33–4
Judgment, The (York) 24
Julius Caesar 151–2
Justice, daughter of God (character) 7
Justification (character) 59
Justus Noah (character) 56

Kansas City, Missouri 198
Katherine of Aragon, queen of England 7
Kemble, John 21
Kempe, Margery 13, 95–8, 102–3, 105, 107
Kent, county of 22, 24, 62, 62n47
Killing of the Children (Digby) 190n41
King Johan (play) 5–6, 58n31, 126
King John (character) 6
kings (character) 124, 125n60, 126
Knowledge of Sinne (character) 59
Knox, John 25, 80, 120, 129, 199

Lady Lucre (character) 11
Lancashire, county of 114–16, 118, 180, 183
Lane, John 121
Laneham, Robert 1
Last Judgment, The (Chester: Weavers) 34,
    38, 82n11, 88–9, 96n17, 111, 113,
    124–7, 132
    modern performance **109**
Last Supper, The (Chester: Bakers, Millers)
    2–3, 27, 33, 47–9, 99, 130
Last Supper (Chester episode) 33–4

Late Banns (1608–09) *see under* Banns
Lazarus (character) 168
Lazarus (Chester episode) 33
Leche, Rafe 125
Ledsham, Richard 124
Legenda aurea see Golden Legend
Leicester, earls of 119
Leicester's Men 11
Leil, king 152
Lewys Glyn Cothi, 'Dychan i Ŵyr o Gaer'
    ['Satire on the Men of Chester'] 177
*Life and Repentance of Mary Magdalene,
    The* 58–9, 129
Life of St Werburghe 152–3, 156, 176–7
Light of the Gospel (character) 10
Like Will to Like 8
linen cloth (prop) 48
Lombard, Peter 90
London 100, 118, 121, 123
    playhouses 50, 60, 60n35, 134–5,
        142n28, 143
    professional companies 133, 135
London, bishops of 4, 115, 126
*Longer Thou Livest, The More Fool Thou
    Art, The* 8
Longeus (character) 156
lord presidents *see under* Council of
    the North
Love (character) 59
Love, Nicholas 93, 95, 102, 103
Loyola University 96n17
Lucian 15, 149–52, 156, 162–72, 176–7;
    see also De Laude Cestrie
Lucifer (character) 9
Luke, Gospel of 82–3, 86
Luther, Martin 27, 48n3, 130, 174
Lydgate, John 65n2
Lynn, Norfolk 95

MacMechan, Archibald 196
magic camels 32
Magnificat, The 104–5
Manchester, Lancs 114
Manchester manuscript 22n12
Manifest Detection of Diceplay 66n5,
    67, 76
Mankind 23
Manly, J.M. 196–8

manuscript survival 95, 102; *see also*
 'Group Manuscripts' *and*
 manuscript survival *under*
 Chester cycle
Mapping Medieval Chester Project 165,
 176–7
Maredudd ap Rhys *I'r Groes o Gaer*
 [*Poem to the Cross at Chester*] 177
Marlowe, Christopher 62–3, 62n47, 132
Marser, Thomas 99–100
Marsh, George 118
martyrs and martyrdom 80, 91, 91n37, 94,
 118, 161
Mary (character) 47, 104–6, 123, 190
Mary I, queen of England 5–8, 79n1,
 91n37, 114, 125, 157
Mary Magdalene (character) 7, 53, 59,
 59n33, 101
Mary Magdalene (Digby) 96
Mary Play (N-Town) 22, 35
Mary, Queen of Scots 120
masks, gilt (costume) 139–40, 143, 145
masques 23, 119
Massacre of the Innocents, The 32, 34, 187
Massey, family 119n28
Matthias (character) 87n26
McMaster University 96, **109**
Medicus (character) 121
Meditationes Vitae Christi 93
Melchizedeck (character) 129–30, 143, 175
Mercatore (character) 11
Mercers (Chester guild) 143
 play of *Offering of the Three
  Kings* 32, 34
Mercers (York guild) 24
Messenger (*Nuntius*) (character) 29
method acting 94–5, 107
Middleton Massey, Richard 21
Midsummer 162, 179
Midsummer Night's Dream, A 99
midwives (character) 3, 14, 29, 47, 97,
 104, 106
Mights (character) 23
Miller, James 21, 66, 71–3
minstrels 30, 119, 197; *see also* music
 and musicians
Minstrel's Court 119
Miramichi, New Brunswick 195
Mirk, John 82n11, 88

Mirror of the Blessed Life of Christ 93,
 102–3
Mold, Wales 177
More, Thomas 91
Moros (character) 8
Moses (character) 56, 62
Moses and the Law (Chester: Cappers,
 Linen-Drapers, Pinners,
 Wiredrawers) 29–30, 172, 174
Moses and the Law (Chester episode)
 30–31
Mount Grace Charterhouse 93, 95
Murren, John, bishop 4, 115
music and musicians 24, 30, 84, 114, 116,
 122–3, 130–31; *see also* minstrels

National Library of Wales 20
Nativity (Chester episode) 30–31
*Nativity, The see Annunciation and
 the Nativity*
Nemesis (character) 7
New Brunswick 195
New Custom 8–11
New Custom (character) 10
New Romney, Kent 22, 24, 62n47
*newe dialog betwene thangell of God, &
 the shepherds in the felde, A* 56
Newhall, William, his proclamation 100,
 119, 182
Nichol Newfangle (character) 9
Nixe, John 115
Noah (character) 143
Noah (Chester episode) 30–31
Noah's Flood (Chester: Waterleaders/
 Drawers) 97, 113–14, 129, 131, 169
Noah's wife (character) 169
Norwich, city of 1–2, 117
'Novem-cinq' (game) 67n8
N-Town compilation
 manuscript 19–20, 22, 86, 102
 plays of 1, 22–3, 35, 39, 41, 149, 190
  Ascension 87
  Mary Play 22, 35
  Passion Play 22, 35
  Trial of Mary and Joseph, The 35
  Woman Taken in Adultery, The 35
'Nunc Dimittis' (canticle) 123
Nuntius see Messenger
Nutter, John 121

Octavian (character) 15, 29, 74, 150,
   153–4, 156, 158, 168
Octavian and Sybil (Chester episode) 29, 31
Oecolampadius 174
Offering of the Three Kings, The (Chester:
   Mercers, Spicers) 32, 34
*On the Laws and Governance of
   England* 181n13
Ouse Bridge, York 2
Oxford 21
Oxford, earls of 20
Oxford University 19

pageant wagons 15, 42, 54, 71, 76, 136,
   143, 145, **147**, 169, 176, 192, 199
Painters (Chester guild) 3
   play of *see Shepherds*
parcels (play-text parts) 94, 103–4, 106
*Passion of Christ, The see The Crucifixion
   or The Passion of Christ*
Passion Play (N-Town) 22, 35
'Passion, The' (New Romney) 22,
   24–5, 62n47
Pater Coelestis (character) 56, 58
Paul (character) 53
Pauper (character) 75
Peace, daughter of God (character) 7
Peniarth manuscript 22n12
Pentecost, feast of 75, 179–80
Pentecost, The (Chester: Fishmongers,
   Fleshmongers) 3, 28, 75
Perverse Doctrine (character) 10
Peter (character) 53, 75, 169
Peterborough, Camb 141
Pharisees (character) 33, 156
Philip II, king of Spain 6
Piers Plowman 130
Pilate (character) 15, 67–9, 73–4, 77,
   150, 155–8
Pilgrims (Towneley) 53
Pius V 111, 126
Pius VI 120n36
Play of the Dice (Towneley) 65n2,
   66–71, 73–4, 77
players (character) 23–4
Poculi Ludique Societas (PLS) 96
Polonius (character) 23
Polychronicon 145, 151, 155–6
Poole, Richard 118

popes (character) 124–7
Preeshl, Artemis (director) 96n17
Presentation in the Temple, The (Chester
   episode) 3
Preston, Thomas 9
Primus Angelus (character) 83; *see also*
   angels; Gabriel
Privy Council 4–5, 115, 117–18, 180–82,
   188, 191
Processus Satanae 104n58
Prolocutor (character) 57, 176
Prologue (character) 10, 57–9
Promise of Isaac (Chester episode) 30–31
properties and scenery 38, 136; *see also*
   cloud effects; bread or wafers;
   pageant wagons; wine
   arks 29–30, 143, 174
   blood 13, 143
   canvas 139
   crosses 33, 77, 131
   dove (?) 56n29
   halls 76
   hoist mechanism 143
   linen cloth 48
   sepulchers 143
   staff 186
   'stage furniture' 10, 42–3
   star of nativity 143
   swords 186
   tables 48
   talking ass 143
prophets (character) 54, 173
Prophets (Chester episode) 31
Prophets of Antichrist, The (Chester:
   Clothworkers, Shearmen)
   172, 174
Prymer in Englyshe, A 65n2
Prynne, William 49–50
Purdue University **147**
Purification (Chester episode) 33
Purification of Christ and the Doctors, The
   (Coventry) 19
Purification of the Virgin Mary, The
   (Chester: Cutlers, Furbishers,
   Pewterers, Smiths) 3, 28, 32, 113,
   116, 123–4, 132

queen (character) 7, 124, 126
Queen's Men 11, 60, 134

Raising of Lazarus (Chester: Glovers) 168
Ralph Roister Doister 6n25, 7
Reading, Berks 22
Records of Early English Drama (REED)
    22, 60, 134, 197, 199–200
Reginall, the ('original') 79n3, 112
Repentance (character) 59
'Report of the Council of the North on
    Abuses in Cheshire' 77
Respublica 5–7
Respublica (character) 7
Resurrection, The (Chester: Girdlers,
    Hatmakers, Pointers, Skinners,
    Tanners) 3, 22n12, 34, 127, 130,
    157–8, 169
Resurrection, The (Towneley) 53
Resurrection, The (York) 101
Rickert, Edith 196
Rogers' Breviaries 98–101, 121, 136,
    136n11, 192, 199–200
Rogers, David 98–9, 136n11, 192,
    199–200
Rogers, Robert 98–9, 121, 136n11, 165
Rogerson, Robert 121
Rome 15, 74, 149–59
Rows, the, 76
Royal Society of Canada 195, 198
Royal Society of Literature 199
'rude mechanicals' 99
Ryerson University 174

Sacrifice of Isaac (Chester episode) 30–31
St Bridget, parish of 115, 118
St John, cathedral church of 115, 163,
    172, 177
St Laurence, church of, Reading, Berks 22
St Mary, guild of 41
St Mary on the Hill, church of 172
St Michael, parish of 122, 163–4
St Michael, person of 164
St Oswald, parish of 123–4
St Peter, church of 150, 163
St Peter, person of 150, 163
St Werburgh's Abbey 101, 138, 150–51,
    153, 161–4; *see also* Chester
    Cathedral
saints (character) 131
Salome (character) 14, 29, 97, 104, 106, 175

Salter, Frederick Millet (F.M.) 15,
    193–200, **194**
Salter, Malachy 195
Sanders Lectures 198
Sarephta, widow of 163
Saskatchewan, University of 173–4
Satan (character) 46, 58, 131
Satan Tentator (character) 56
Savage, John 25–6, 117, 119, 179, 181,
    181n10, 182, 182n15, 183, 191
'Save Me, O God' (psalm) 114, 131
Scotland 25, 199
Second Jew (character) 66, 68–73, 76; *see
    also* Jews
Second Shepherd's Play (Towneley) 57
Selden, John 20
senators (character) 154–5
Sententiae 90, 90n33
sepulchers (prop) 143
sermon exemplum 97–8
'Sermon preached at the Crosse, The'
    135, 135n7
Sermons or Homilies 170, 175
Severity (character) 9
Shakespeare, William 23, 99, 132–3, 144–5
Shaw, John 124
Shearmen and Clothiers (Chester guild) 143
Shenandoah University 96, 174
shepherds (character) 3, 56–7, 68, 177
Shepherds, The (Chester episode) 30–31
Shepherds, The (Chester: Embroiderers,
    Glaziers, Painters) 3, 29–32, 34,
    119, 177, 192
sheriffs 118, 119n28
Shoemakers (Chester guild) 143
Shropshire, county of 88
Sick Man's Salve, The 56
Simeon (character) 28, 54, 123
Simon the Apostle (character) 3, 28
Simon the Leper (Chester episode) 33–4
Simon the Pharisee (character) 59
Simony (character) 11
Simpson, Christopher, his company 5n21
Sincere Doctrine (character) 10
Sincerity (character) 11
Sisamnes (character) 9
Six Articles Act 125
Skelton, John 193, 196

Skinner (Chester guild), play of
　　Resurrection 130, 169
Smith, Laurence 117–18
Smith, Richard 124
Smiths (Chester guild) 3
　　Purification 112, 116, 123–4, 132
Smiths (Coventry guild) 184
Sneyd (Snede), William 119
Sneyd (Snede), William the elder 119
Society of Antiquaries 20
soldiers (character) 72–3, 105, 156–8,
　　187–8, 190
songs and singing 56n29, 113
Spital Boughton, Ches 118
staff (prop) 186
stages *see* pageant wagons
Stanislavski, Constantin 94–7, 99, 102–3,
　　105, 107
Stanley, Edward, earl of Derby 116, 120
Stanley, family 115
Stanzaic Life of Christ 82n11, 87–8, 91,
　　129, 131, 155
star of nativity (prop) 143
Sternhold and Hopkins Psalter 114n10
Stubbes, Philip 50
Summa Theologiae 89, 89n31, 90
Susanna (character) 7
swords (prop) 186
Sybil (character) 29, 154, 158

tables (prop) 48
Tadgyll, Thomas 115
Tailors (Chester guild) 143
　　play of *see Ascension*
talking ass (prop) 143
Tanners (Chester guild) 143
　　plays of *see Fall of Lucifer*;
　　Resurrection
Taylor, Andrew 128
'Te Deum Laudamus' (hymn) 131
Tebell (character) 29, 97, 106
Temptation of Christ (Chester episode) 33
Temptation of Christ, The (Chester:
　　Butchers) 33
　　modern performance (2010) **17**, **45**
Temptation of our Lord, The (play) 55–6,
　　56n29, 58
Tertius Angelus (character) 84
Testament of John Lydgate 65n2

thieves (character) 131
Third Jew (character) 66, 67n9, 69–72;
　　see also Jews
Third Soldier (character) 72–3; *see
　　also* soldiers
Thomas of India (Towneley) 53
Three Kings, The (Chester: Merchants and
　　Vintners) 28, 32, 130, 173, 189
Three Ladies of London, The 8, 11
Three Laws 58n31
*Three Lords and Three Ladies of London,
　　The* 11
thrones (prop) 42–3
Tilston, Ches 125
Toledo, University of **17**, **45**, 173
tormentors and persecutors
　　(character) 150, 155–6; *see
　　also* torturers
Toronto, University of 198; *see also*
　　Records of Early English Drama
　　modern production (2010) of Chester
　　cycle at 12, **17**, 25, 27–35, **45**,
　　72–4, 80n5, 96, **109**, 112, **147**, 170,
　　173, 193
torturers (character) 13, 68–71, 105
Totehill, Henry 126
Towneley compilation 1n2, 5, 21–3, 24n27,
　　38, 40, 42, 65, 102, 149, 155, 158,
　　185, 188–9
　　plays of
　　　Ascension 86–7
　　　Crucifixion 101
　　　Pilgrims 53
　　　Play of the Dice 65n2, 66–71,
　　　　73–4, 77
　　　Resurrection, The 53
　　　Second Shepherd's Play 57
　　　Thomas of India 53
Towneley, family 5, 35
Trauerspiel 142
Treatise of Miraclis Playing 49–50
Trent, Council of 80
Trevisa, John 151n10, 152n11, 186–7
Trial and Flagellation of Christ, The
　　(Chester: Bowyers, Coopers,
　　Fletchers, Turners, Stringers) 19,
　　21, 22n12, 32–3, 70, 99, 197–8
Trial before Annas and Caiaphas (Chester
　　episode) 34

Trial of Mary and Joseph, The
     (N-Town) 35
Trials (Chester episode) 33–4
Trinity College, Dublin 19–20
Trinity, figure of 39–41
'Trinity' (Chester play) 41
Troy 153
Truth, daughter of God (character) 7
Tudd (character) 177
Tudor Penllyn *I Reinallt ap Gruffudd o'r*
     Twr [*To Rheinallt ap Gruffudd ap*
     Bleddyn of the Tower] 177
tunicles (costume) 123

Udall, Nicholas 6–7
Ussher, Henry 19
Usury (character) 11

vestments (costumes) 128–9
Vice (character) 9
vice-chamberlains 119n28
Victoria, University of 196
'View of Popish Abuses yet Remaining in
     the English Churche, A' 48
Vintners (Chester guild), play of *see*
     Three Kings
Virtuous Living (character) 9
Visit of the Magi to Herod (Chester
     episode) 28
Voragine, Jacobus de 88, 88n29

wafers (prop) *see* bread or wafers
Wager, Lewis 58–60, 129
Wager, William 8–9
wagons *see* pageant wagons
Wakefield, Yorkshire WR 49n8
Walker, Gilbert 66n5, 67, 76
Wax-chandlers (Chester guild) 129
     play of *see Abraham and Isaac*

Weavers (Chester guild), play of *see*
     The Last Judgment
Weavers (Coventry guild) 19
Webster, John 132
Westcote, Sebastian 124
'White Book of the Pentice' 136
White, Robert 123–4
Whitsuntide *see* Whitsun (1572) staging
     under Chester cycle
Whittingham, William 114
Widow England (character) 6–7
Wilson, Robert 8, 11
wine (prop) 129–30, 143, 175
Wisdom 23–4
Wives (Chester guild) 2
Woman Taken in Adultery (Chester
     episode) 33
Woman Taken in Adultery, The (Chester:
     Butchers) 33, 173
Woman Taken in Adultery, The (N-Town) 35
Woodes, Nathaniel 61

York, archbishops of 2–4, 26, 37, 49, 62,
     79, 112, 116, 124–5, 141, 158,
     180–83, 188, 191
York, city of 2, 23–4, 117
York cycle 1–2, 5, 22–4, 38–9, 42, 100,
     105, 149, 156, 158, 188–9, 197
  plays of
     Ascension 87
     Crucifixion, The 70n13
     Doubting Thomas 19
     Judgement 24
     Resurrection 101
York, deans of 2, 49n8
York Realist 101
Yorkshire NR 5n21
Yorkshire WR 49n8
Young, Karl 197